THE WHITI

THE
WHITE RAJAHS

A HISTORY OF SARAWAK
FROM 1841 TO 1946

BY

STEVEN RUNCIMAN

CAMBRIDGE

AT THE UNIVERSITY PRESS

1960

CAMBRIDGE UNIVERSITY PRESS
Cambridge, New York, Melbourne, Madrid, Cape Town, Singapore,
São Paulo, Delhi, Dubai, Tokyo

Cambridge University Press
The Edinburgh Building, Cambridge CB2 8RU, UK

Published in the United States of America by Cambridge University Press, New York

www.cambridge.org
Information on this title: www.cambridge.org/9780521128995

First published 1960
This digitally printed version 2009

A catalogue record for this publication is available from the British Library

ISBN 978-0-521-06168-1 Hardback
ISBN 978-0-521-12899-5 Paperback

CONTENTS

v

LIST OF ILLUSTRATIONS

PLATES

MAPS

PREFACE

This book was undertaken on the suggestion of the Government of Sarawak, to whose kindness and consideration I am deeply indebted. Owing to its generosity I have been enabled to make three separate visits to the country and to travel about it at leisure. I have been given free access to all the papers and documents in its archives, which I have been able to study under the most agreeable conditions. At the same time, I have been encouraged to tell the story in my own way. This is not an official history. The views that I express in it are my own and are based on an objective attempt to interpret the available evidence. I only hope that my findings will be considered to be fair and will not cause hurt or disappointment in any quarter. Part of this work concerns modern times. Many of the actors are still living or have only recently died. It is difficult at so close a perspective to see clearly what really happened and why it was done. An historian dealing with characters long dead may legitimately assign motives, speculate on rumours and even indulge in a little scandal-mongering. It is neither courteous nor helpful nor wise for him to do so when he is dealing with the fringes of the present. The time has not yet come when, for instance, a full and definitive history of the cession of Sarawak to the British Crown can be written.

For quite other reasons the whole history of Sarawak under its White Rajahs is not easy to write. The raw material is at times abundant, but at other times full of gaps. It would be easy to compile an anthology of travellers' tales; for a number of naturalists, ethnologists and travellers for travel's sake have visited Sarawak and written of their experiences books that often give vivid accounts of the country and the lives of its inhabitants. Their works form the greater part of the literature that concerns Sarawak; and they are useful in providing a background. But few of the writers wished or were in a position to tell of the progress of the country. They can only illuminate certain districts at certain times. Much in the sequence of events remains obscure. The only fully documented aspect of Sarawak history is its relations with Great Britain, for which the British official records are complete and indispensable.

For the career and personality of the First Rajah the evidence is plentiful. He wrote prolifically himself and was not at all averse to having his letters and journals published. He was a prominent and picturesque figure in his time; summaries of his career appear in almost every account of the more adventurous Victorian worthies. Within twenty-one years of his death two serious biographies of him had appeared. The first, by Miss Gertrude Jacob, was adulatory; but it was conscientiously compiled; and though she never knew him herself she knew many of his relatives and friends and had access to a number of personal documents. The second, by his friend Spencer St John, who had worked for many years with him, is rather more critical in its admiration and provides a first-hand account of the more important years of his life. With their help and with the help of the letters and journals published in turn by his friends Keppel, Mundy and Templer, and his more recently discovered correspondence with the future Baroness Burdett-Coutts, it is possible to trace his life fairly completely; and further gaps can be filled from the papers kept in his nephew Brooke Brooke's family, which have been ably used by Miss Emily Hahn in her recent biography. But there is practically no evidence of what happened in Sarawak when he was not present there. Most of the relevant documents of the early years perished during the Chinese rebellion of 1857. Very few of the documents of his later reign have survived the rigours of the climate, unsystematic storing, and the Japanese occupation during the last war. These documents can never have been numerous. The Rajah's government was highly personal, and his European staff was small. Most of the business of government was done by personal contact; and records were thought to be unnecessary. Were it not that Charles Brooke, the Second Rajah, wrote two volumes on his life as a district officer, we would have had no direct information about life up-country during those years.

In many ways we are worse off when it comes to the reign of Rajah Charles. He lacked his uncle's liking for publicity. Apart from that account of his earlier life he never burst into print, except to air his views on certain political problems. No life of him has been written. His wife in her books treats him with a somewhat detached mixture of admiration and exasperation—he felt the same about her—his daughter in-law, the Ranee Sylvia, in her books treats him with a frank dislike, which he seems to have reciprocated. His history and the history of his reign must be derived almost exclusively from three sources: his letter-book, which survives in the Sarawak archives, containing manuscript copies of almost every letter that he wrote between 1880 and 1916; the

Sarawak Gazette, a semi-official periodical which appeared sometimes fortnightly, sometimes monthly, from 1870 up till the Japanese occupation in 1942 (and again after 1946); and the *History of Sarawak* written by S. Baring-Gould and C. A. Bampfylde. This is in effect an official history; indeed Rajah Charles paid for its publication in 1909. Baring-Gould's part in it was merely to write up material given to him; but Bampfylde had been for many years an important officer in the Sarawak service. He had access to all the documents that existed, and he himself took part in many of the events of the Second Rajah's reign. The tone of the book is necessarily uncritical, but it is indispensable as a collection of reliable facts. The Sarawak archives also contain several of the Second Rajah's Order Books, containing an extraordinarily mixed number of edicts, regulations, directives and personal instructions; there are also a few Confidential Reports. For this period, also, there have survived several manuscript volumes of reports from the out-stations. They are, however, somewhat unrewarding, consisting mainly of records of petty civil and criminal cases and the judgments given on them. They serve to illustrate the type of task that befell a district officer, but little more. The government was still paternal. Anything of importance was referred, often by word of mouth, to the Rajah or his representative, and was seldom recorded. Decisions made when the Rajah toured the districts or when his officers visited him in Kuching were not always recorded. The minutes of the State Councils contain the more important political decisions. But much is missing.

It is not much better when we come to the reign of the Third Rajah. The system of government was fundamentally the same; and though more bodies came into being which kept records, much perished during the last war. Only the legal records appear to be complete. I have depended largely on the *Sarawak Gazette* for those years; and, happily, there are many men and women still living who knew Sarawak in those days and are ready to talk of them.

In addition to the Second Rajah's letter-book, various personal letters survive in the Sarawak archives. I have also been fortunate in having been allowed to see a number of private letters of relevance. I am particularly grateful to Mr David Fiennes, who lent me a series of letters written by his father when he was acting as tutor to the Second Rajah's sons.

Above all, I am indebted to members of the Brooke family, in particular the Tuan Muda (Captain Bertram Brooke), his son Anthony, the former

Rajah Muda, and his daughter, Lady Halsey. They have generously put all their papers at my disposal, to make what use of them I please, and have supplied me with a vast amount of personal information. Without their disinterested help I should have been quite unable to write this book.

My thanks are also due to many past members of the Sarawak Government service. Mr A. B. Ward, who joined the service in 1899, and Mr R. G. Aikman, former Chief Secretary, have been particularly kind. Mr D. C. White, now Her Majesty's Commissioner in Brunei, has given me much information as well as much hospitality. Many present members of the Sarawak Government, Malay, Chinese and Dyak as well as British, have kindly added to my knowledge. To them and to such eminent citizens of Kuching as Dr Marjoribanks, who have told me stories of the past, I am very grateful. I should have been able to do little without the unfailing kindness, encouragement and hospitality of Sir Anthony Abell, Governor of Sarawak at the time of my visits, and without the help of two successive Chief Secretaries, the late Mr Hugh Ellis and the late Mr John Barcroft. Radio Sarawak, under its Director, Mr Peter Ratcliffe, has been continuously helpful, as has the Kuching office of the British Council. I owe perhaps my greatest debts of gratitude to Mr Philip Jones, at that time Director of the Information Office, and his staff for the ungrudging trouble that they took on my behalf, as well as for lavish hospitality, and to the staff of the Kuching Museum and its distinguished head, Mr Tom Harrisson, without whose good will and readiness to impart his vast knowledge no one could venture to approach any subject concerning Sarawak. To all of them and to the many other friends who have supplied me with documentation or personal information I am profoundly grateful. I must add that they are none of them responsible for any errors of fact or judgment that may appear in this book.

The photographs in plates 7 and 8 were first reproduced in Mrs Hedda Morrison's *Sarawak*, published by Messrs MacGibbon and Kee. I am grateful to Mrs Morrison and the publishers for permission to use them.

I also thank the Syndics and staff of the Cambridge University Press for their continual kindness and help.

STEVEN RUNCIMAN

LONDON
1960

BOOK 1
BORNEO

*The superior figures in the text refer to
notes that begin on p. 268*

CHAPTER I

THE ISLAND AND ITS PEOPLES

'The Island of *Borneo*', wrote Captain Daniel Beekman early in the seventeenth century, '(so called from a City of that name) lies on the North of *Java*, and on the East of Sumatra, and of the Peninsula of *Malacca*. It is situate between the 7 Deg. 30 Min. of North Latitude, and the 4 Deg. 10 Min. of South, under the Equinoctial, which divides it into two unequal Parts.... So that it is in Length 700 miles, in breadth 480, and in Circuit about 2000. It is counted the biggest Island, not only in the *Indian* Sea, but in the whole World, except perhaps *California* in the South Sea.'[1]

The Captain's views on California were not uncommon at the time. He was in no position to know that the as yet undiscovered island of New Guinea was larger than Borneo; and the rest of his information was not so very inaccurate. The huge island of Borneo lies across the Equator in the shape of a rough, uneven quadrilateral. Its north-west coast stretches for some 750 miles down from the most northerly point, Cape Sampanmangio, in latitude 7° 1' north, to Cape Datu, where the coastline turns south by east for some 350 miles, then east by south for about the same distance, to Cape Salatan, in latitude 4° 10' south. The east coast stretches over 800 miles, jutting out just north of the equator to Cape Kaniongang. The north-eastern end of the island is more broken in outline, somewhat resembling the head of a dog facing to the east. With its indentures, none of them very large, the whole coastline measures about 3000 miles. The area of the island is estimated at 284,000 square miles. Except in the north and at certain widely spaced head-lands, the coasts are flat and swampy. The main mountain range runs as a watershed south-west to north-east, on an average about a hundred miles from the north-west coast. Few of its peaks rise above the height of 5000 feet, except in the north, where the mountains pile up to the great tower of Kinabalu, the Chinese Widow, 13,455 feet above sea-level. It is the highest peak between the Himalayas and the mountains of New Guinea. Though most of the mountains are not remarkably high they are rugged and covered in forest and difficult of access. The plains, too, are forest covered, and many of them are swamps that

3

cannot be crossed in the rainy season, except where paths have been made by placing roughly hewn planks on wooden piles.

It is geographically an inhospitable island. Except in the extreme north there are no natural harbours. Ships must shelter in the mouths of muddy rivers, across each of which there is a bar. The rhythm of the tides is variable; and the bars are often too shallow to be crossed by anything larger than a light canoe, and for canoes the crossing is difficult and dangerous. Once the bars are passed, the complex river system provides the only means of communication for many miles inland. Nearly every river has a delta, branches of which may join it to another river. But even so travel is hazardous. Up some rivers there runs a daily bore. The mud-banks in the river-bed continually change their position. Tree-trunks floating down on the current add to the difficulties of navigation. As the traveller penetrates further upstream there are rapids to be faced. The boat may have to be carried past them over a rough path along the bank.

In this low country the scenery is uninviting. To quote Captain Beekman again,

many score Miles near the Sea the Country looks like a Forest, being full of prodigious tall trees, between which is nothing but vast swamps of Mud. At high Water you may sail in a great way among these Trees in several places, but at low Water it is all Mud, upon which the Sun (especially in the Equinox) darting his scorching Beams perpendicularly, raises noisome Vapours, Fogs, etc. which afterwards turn into most violent Showers, that fall more like Cataracts than rain.[1]

Now and then along the river-banks there is a patch of drier land, just above the swamp level. It is there that clearings have been made and settlements founded with a little cultivation. In some places, where the mountains approach the coast, there are isolated hills that rise abruptly out of the swamp-land, whose lower slopes provide a footing for man and his beasts. Further inland the country is scarcely more hospitable but rather more habitable for those who have the energy to clear the tangled jungle. But, without the protective covering of forest, the soil quickly deteriorates.

By the river-banks the vegetation is so dense as to be impenetrable. Away from the swamps the undergrowth is still thick; but it is possible to make a way through it, though progress is slow owing to numerous streams and boggy patches, sudden outcrops of rock or the trunks of fallen trees. Even men accustomed to it sometimes lose their way in it, and it is customary to carry a parang, not so much for cutting through the vegetation as for marking the trees so as to identify the path for the journey back. It is a gloomy place, even when the sun is shining. Little light comes through the great trees, often 200 feet in height, and the saplings that crowd between them. Few flowers are seen apart from orchids and other epiphytes; and the fauna remains invisible and inaudible, apart from the occasional distant call of a pheasant or the cackle of a hornbill. The hill-sides are usually steep, with precipitous rocks. There are a few open spaces where rains have washed the soil away; but the going is laborious, even for those who know the mountain tracks.[1]

There are mineral deposits in the hills and their inaccessibility has tended to create an exaggerated estimate of their riches. But the island on the whole is poor and unproductive, and ill suited to support a large population.

Nevertheless it has been populated from the earliest times. It is only within the last few decades that the archaeology of Borneo has been studied seriously, and only within the last few years that results of value have been obtained. Not far from the coast, in the north of what is now Sarawak, there rises out of the jungle beside the Niah river an outcrop of limestone hills, about a thousand feet high and riddled with caves. In the recesses of the greatest of these caves live a million bats and more than a million swiftlets whose nests of glutinous saliva are the basis for birds'-nest soup; but it has a wide mouth opening on to the precipitous mountain-side, accessible by ladders but out of the reach of the beasts of the jungle. The guano deposits left by generations of swiftlets have for some time been worked; for guano is the only natural fertiliser available in the island. But the mouth of the cave is too light for the swifts; its floor has therefore been left undisturbed. Here, in an atmosphere which is perfectly dry and almost air-conditioned, archaeologists, prospecting in 1954 and working more continuously since 1957, have found traces of human existence dating back to the Middle Palaeolithic phase, of 40,000 to 50,000 B.C. The Upper Palaeolithic, the Mesolithic and the Neolithic phases are all also represented, down to the Chalcolithic phase of about 250 B.C. It is not yet possible to say much about the human beings who lived here. The earliest palaeolithic flaked tools have a likeness to those of the so-called 'Sohan' culture of north-west India. The skeletons that have been discovered in a burial-ground a little further into the cave are some of a people of a mesolithic culture, small in size, even in comparison with the present inhabitants of Borneo, Melanoid in type, and some of a neolithic culture, also small but more Mongoloid in type. The craftsmanship of these people was of a high order. Even in the neolithic period the pottery has a fine finish; and by chalcolithic times there appears pottery in three colours, applied as a sort of glaze, which is far superior to anything produced by the indigenous tribes in the island in more recent times.[1]

To what extent the present-day tribes are descended from these early inhabitants is impossible as yet to determine.[2] Of the tribes which now dwell in the area between the central watershed and the north-west coast, with which this history is concerned, the most primitive are the Punans or Penans. Their numbers are now very small; there are less than 4000 in the territory of Sarawak; but they probably represent a race that at one time roamed over the whole interior of Borneo. They are nomads, living occasionally in caves but usually in lightly built huts, quickly constructed and soon abandoned. Their food is the wild sago and a few other herbs and the varied beasts and birds that fall victims to their blowpipes. Physically, like all the native races in Borneo, they are slightly Mongoloid in facial structure, but they are comparatively light skinned; they are larger boned than many of their neighbours, and strong and healthy; and they are adepts at hunting, moving silently and invisibly through the jungle, and amazingly skilled in the use of the blowpipe. But they are timid and unaggressive. Down the centuries fiercer neighbours have encroached upon their ranging grounds, till now they are restricted to the forests round the upper waters of the Baram and Limbang rivers. Some of them now are taking to a settled life and practising agriculture.[3]

Their immediate neighbours are the Kelabits and Muruts, who seem to have inhabited the northern side of the central watershed longer than most of the tribes there, but to have been driven into the hills by later invaders. The name 'Kelabit' means 'people of the river Labid', while 'Murut' simply means 'hill-folk'. The two peoples are closely related. Physically they too are comparatively fair skinned—and they consider fair skins desirable—and are taller and stronger than the peoples of the plains. They differ from their neighbours in having worked out an advanced technique in irrigation and the cultivation of rice and in dwelling in communal longhouses which do not have separate apartments for the different families. They are now far from numerous; there are less than 2000 Kelabits and less than 4000 Muruts. They only entered into the history of modern Sarawak at the end of the nineteenth century.[1]

The tribes that drove them into the hills are the Kayans and the Kenyahs, who seem to have been originally akin to the Kelabits and Muruts but to have developed along different lines. Both the Kayans and Kenyahs came from the south of the watershed. According to the traditions of both peoples the Kenyahs crossed the mountains some time before the Kayans. They are river-folk, travelling wherever possible by canoe. They have not in consequence the developed leg and back muscles of the Kelabits and Muruts, nor are they as tall; but their dexterity of shoulder and wrist is far greater. They tend to be solidly, even fleshily, built, and are light in colour. When they first arrived across the mountains the Kayans inhabited the middle and upper Rejang valley, as well as the upper Baram, pushing the Kenyahs before them to the north. But now the Kayans themselves have been driven from most of the Rejang lands by the far more numerous Sea Dyaks, and are concentrated in the Baram valley. They number now rather more than 6000 people, and the Kenyahs about 1000 less. The Kayans are a warlike and aggressive race, but with a considerable artistic sense; their crafts are the most advanced among the Borneo tribes. The Kenyahs are a little less pushful. Both inhabit longhouses with separate apartments for the families. They are an aristocratic people, with a high regard for their hereditary chieftains.[2]

There are other small racial communities in the north of the present Sarawak, such as the Bisayas, of southern Filipino origin, living around Brunei Bay, and a few Dusuns, who have spread from over the North Borneo frontier.[3]

Further to the south the oldest communities seem to be those of the Land Dyaks, whose main settlements are on the Sarawak and upper Sadong rivers. They are smaller in build than the tribes of the north and darker in colouring, but stronger than their appearance would suggest. Their villages are not of the pure longhouse type but are composed of contiguous houses, built on piles and sharing a common platform that serves as the village street. They have no hereditary chieftains and lack leadership; but they are a practical and matter-of-fact race, far gentler than their neighbours, who have consistently bullied them throughout history. Many of their communities have in consequence retired to hill-tops, and all are poor. They travel by land rather than by water, though they possess canoes. Till the days of the Rajahs their misfortunes were steadily reducing their numbers; but during the last century they have increased, and now number more than 48,000 souls.[1]

By far the most numerous of the indigenous peoples living to the north of the Bornean watershed are the tribes collectively called the Sea Dyaks or Ibans, of whom there are now close on 200,000 in Sarawak. The name 'Sea Dyak' is somewhat misleading. To the Netherlands authorities all the indigenous inhabitants of Borneo were known as Dyaks or Dayaks. The first English comers to arrive in Sarawak similarly called the non-Malay tribes whom they met 'Dyaks'. But it was soon clear that these were of different stock. The name of Land Dyak was, therefore, given to the tribes whose lives were spent mainly on dry ground, while the tribes who lived on the rivers, travelling almost entirely by canoe, and sometimes venturing out into the sea, were called, rather inappropriately, Sea Dyaks; and this particular group of tribes retained the name. They are now sometimes called Ibans; but that word seems simply to mean 'person', or, in the Kayan language, 'wanderer'. Its use is somewhat recent. Rajah Charles Brooke wrote in 1892 that 'Iban was not known to any of our Dyaks 40 years ago....It is not Dyak except as having of *late years* been taken from the Kayans and Bakatans.' At present the tribes on the Rejang river prefer to call themselves Ibans and those on the Batang Lupar and its tributaries, Sea Dyaks.

The Sea Dyaks are rather taller, stronger and fairer and with more regular features than the Land Dyaks, with whom they have little in common. But they are neither so large in body nor so fair as the Kayans and the other tribes further to the north. They came from south of the watershed later than their neighbours. Their original home was in the centre of the island, round the Kapuas river, where many still remain. They began to make their way through the gaps in the hills leading to the upper Batang Lupar and the Ulu Ai some centuries ago; and the movement has continued steadily till the beginning of this century, combined with a smaller movement back across the mountains. Most of the genealogies and traditions kept by Sea Dyaks, who can often trace their ancestry back for more than thirty generations, tell of continual migrations. It was not until the middle of the last century that they penetrated into the Rejang valley, at the expense of the Kayans. Their need for movement was due to their thriftless methods of agriculture; they would make clearings in the forest and grow rice in them till the soil was exhausted, when they would seek new homes.

They lived in longhouses, often containing some fifty families, under hereditary chieftains; but their aristocracy was less well organised than the Kayans. They were essentially river-folk. As they gradually moved down towards the sea, the Malay chieftains in possession of the coast enrolled them into their pirate companies; and the Sea Dyaks quickly found piracy to their liking. It suited their warlike natures and gave scope to their remarkable skill at handling their canoes.[1]

With the partial exception of the Land Dyaks all these indigenous peoples have many traits in common. The personal status of women is high. There is no difference between the personal status of the sexes, as regards civil rights, the ownership of property and inheritance, though inevitably there is a division of labour. The women see to the household. They cook the food, they brew the *borak*, or rice-beer, they draw the water from the river or the springs, and they tend the gardens close to the longhouse. The men hunt and perform all the tasks connected with the jungle; but both sexes help in the rice-harvest. Much of the life is communal; decisions about hunting and harvesting, as well as major problems such as migration and war, are taken by the villages as a whole. But the economy is not communistic; each individual has his private property. Till recently money was almost unknown. Wealth consisted in the possession of livestock or ornaments and above all in great pottery jars, of Chinese manufacture, some of them as much as ten or twelve centuries old. To own a jar, or more than one jar, is a sign of aristocracy as well as of riches. The jars are used for storing objects and are very carefully guarded. To be forced to surrender one is the severest of punishments. In most of the communities slavery existed. The slaves were war-captives or waifs who had found their way to the settlement, or their descendants. They were usually the property of the chieftain. They enjoyed no civil rights and could only marry within their class; but they were seldom ill treated and generally shared in the life of the community.

The religious notions of these people were simple. They believed somewhat vaguely in a supreme god and in spirits that controlled the sky, the earth and the water. These spirits made their wishes known and gave warnings or encouragement by means of omens, such as the appearance of a beast or bird and the direction of its movement, or by means of dreams; and, to appease them, so that the crops would grow, certain rituals were obligatory and certain taboos enforced. There was a general belief in an after-life, which would be roughly similar to this life. To ensure a happy entrance into it ceremonies had to be performed. Sudden death, especially death in battle, was therefore to be deplored. There were no temples, no holy images and no priests; but many communities possessed a magician, who, among the Sea Dyaks, was usually dressed as a woman and did woman's work, being allowed a 'husband' to perform the male tasks that should have been his.[1]

All these tribes also shared a practice which was to make Borneo notorious. They indulged in head-hunting. It seems that the practice was not very ancient, and various legends were told to explain its introduction. It was certainly widespread by the eighteenth century. To take a head was a sign of virility, and the more heads that a long-house possessed, the greater its prestige and, it was hoped, its prosperity. Heads might be taken from the enemy in battle or from the corpses of the slain, or from some intruder, such as an itinerant merchant, who had offended the community and had thus permitted a breach of the laws of hospitality. Very often some young man would go off by himself to collect a head, in order to impress his comrades or, still more, the young woman that he hoped to marry. Indeed it was above all the women who saw to it that the practice should survive. His victim would then be some wayfarer whom he met on his journey; or he would lie in ambush near some longhouse with which his was on bad terms, to secure the head of one of its inmates. If his trophy was the head of a woman or a child his prowess was so much the higher; for it proved that he must have crept very close to the enemy longhouse. The loss of a head, besides its obvious physical disadvantage, was inconvenient spiritually; for the proper funeral rites could not be performed on a head-less trunk. Its recovery was therefore important; and periodically tribes would make peace with one another and exchange their trophies. If one tribe found itself short in the exchange it would make good the deficiency by including the heads of some of its slave-folk. This growing mania for head-hunting not only provoked needless warfare. It also made it unsafe for anyone to stray far from his home unless he were accompanied and armed; and it discouraged traders from attempting to sell their wares up the Borneo rivers.[2]

The gentle Land Dyaks only adopted this brutal practice on a limited scale. There was another indigenous race, which never adopted it, considering itself on a higher level of civilisation than the tribes of the interior. This was the Melanaus, living along the coast between the mouths of the Rejang and Baram rivers. Originally the Melanaus seem to have been a branch of the Kayans; but their different environment produced different habits. They cultivated the sago-palm; and sago, not rice, was their staple food. Living on the coast they were largely sailors and fishermen, and had some contact with other maritime peoples. Some centuries back they fell under Malay domination and adopted Islam, though somewhat superficially, keeping many of their old superstitions. They began to abandon their longhouses and to live in villages of the Malay type. Physically they are smaller and darker than their kinsfolk in the interior; but this may largely be due to an intermixture of Malay blood and the blood of other seafaring tribes. Their women were considered to be very beautiful and were much sought after for Malay harems.[1]

It is unknown when first the Malays came to Borneo. According to Malay tradition the original home of the race was the kingdom of Menangkabau in Sumatra; but it is likely that its main breeding-ground was Java. From the islands the Malays spread into what is now called the Malay peninsula. In the course of its movements the race became adulterated with Indian and Mongoloid blood, as well as the blood of aboriginal peoples. But there is still a dominant Malay type, smallish in stature and delicately made, with darkish colouring and somewhat Mongoloid features. The chief bond between the Malay peoples is the Malay language, which is basically the same, with local dialects, throughout the Malay world, and which has a kinship with some of the indigenous languages of Borneo, such as that of the Sea Dyaks. Nowadays there is a further bond in the Muslim religion.

Islam came fairly recently to the Malays. They seem first to have been given political unity by invaders from the Indian sub-continent. The Indo-Malay kingdom of Sri-vijaya, based on Palembang in Sumatra, was flourishing by the seventh century A.D., with Hinayana Buddhism as its religion. It reached a high state of civilisation, though much of its wealth was derived from the activities of Malay pirates who were its vassals and who since the fifth century had preyed on Chinese shipping when it attempted to approach the Straits of Malacca. But even before the Sri-vijaya age Indian invaders, both Buddhist and Brahmin, had brought goods, including works of art in the Gupta style, round the Malay archipelago. The great Sailendra Empire of Javaka, which replaced Sri-vijaya, dominated Indo-China as well as the Malay peninsula and the greater islands of the archipelago until the mid-ninth century, when it lost most of its island possessions to an Indo-

Malay kingdom based on Java, the Majapahit kingdom. It is likely that Sri-Vijaya and Javaka each in turn controlled the coasts of Borneo, without, however, penetrating into the interior, while the Majapahit kings were certainly suzerains of the coastal tribes, and during those centuries numbers of Malays settled along the coasts. The Malays of Sarawak itself claim to have come directly from Menangkabau, in the early days of Malay expansion; but the Malays of Brunei, whose dialect is somewhat different, are said to come from the Malay peninsula, at a slightly later date. The ruling families, both in Sarawak and Brunei, boast of a descent from the Sultans of Johore.[1]

To what extent the Borneo coasts were civilised by these Malays under Indian influence is uncertain. Archaeological discoveries include a few ornaments, inscriptions, and statues, including one of Ganesh of the sixth or seventh century, found at Limbang, and one of Buddha in the late Gupta style, dating from about A.D. 800, found at Santubong.[2] It is probable that piracy prevented any constant intercourse between the centres of Indian civilisation and the Malay settlements on the Borneo coast, except at times during the Javaka and Majapahit periods. By the thirteenth century the Indian influence was everywhere on the decline, and a new cultural element was being introduced. Arab traders and missionaries began to preach the doctrines of Islam throughout the Malay world and to receive a ready welcome. By the end of the century the Malays of the peninsula were already converted to Islam, and the newer religion gradually spread round the islands. The Majapahit kingdom lasted till the second half of the fifteenth century, but it had already lost control of Borneo. There the most important Malay state to emerge was Brunei, on the north-west coast, which was to give its name to the whole island. According to tradition, its first Muslim ruler was a certain Awang Alak ber Tabar, who ruled there about the beginning of the fifteenth century. He married a princess from Johore, abducting her on her way to marry the already Muslim Sultan of Sulu, in the southern Philippines. She was a Muslim and he embraced her religion, taking the name of Mohammed. His brother and successor, Ahmed, was the ancestor of the Royal line of Brunei.[3]

The Malays are an aristocratic people, with a reverence for royalty and a high lineage. There were already princely families among them; and now a new aristocracy was introduced from amongst the Arab immigrants. These were the *Sherips*, as they were locally called, who claimed descent from the Prophet himself and therefore demanded and received special respect as authorities on matters of religion. Though they intermarried with the Malay aristocracy, their descendants were given the same privileges and prestige. They did not prove to be a desirable addition to Bornean society. Throughout subsequent history the sherips caused endless trouble owing to their pretensions and their greed.[1]

By the close of the fifteenth century the coast-lands of Borneo were owned by a number of Muslim Malay sultans, of varying power and wealth, all of them owing some sort of allegiance to the Malay rulers of the peninsula and looking westward for their culture, to the Sayyid dynasties of India and beyond to Arabia. The Indian Ocean seemed to have become a Muslim lake; and at its eastern end it seemed that a great Muslim Malay empire was to be established, centred on Malacca.[2]

The swift triumph of Islam in the Malay world was due not only to the decadence of the old Indo-Malay kingdoms, but also to a temporary eclipse of the greatest power in the Far East, the Empire of China. The Chinese had long been interested in both the peninsula and the archipelago: Chinese merchants had been sailing round the islands and through the Straits of Malacca since long before the Christian era. It is impossible to date the first contact of the Chinese with Borneo. Beads of Chinese origin nearly three thousand years old have been found in the island. Chinese coins of the Tsin and Han dynasties— roughly from 200 B.C. to A.D. 200—have been unearthed at the mouth of the Sarawak river, together with some of earlier date. The oldest of the jars still kept in Borneo longhouses date at the latest from the times of the Tang dynasty (seventh to tenth centuries). The first literary mention of Borneo in Chinese seems to be that of the traveller Fa Hsien, who in A.D. 414 described the land of Ye-p'o ti. The island of P'oni or Po-ni, mentioned by several subsequent writers, is almost certainly Borneo; and there is no doubt about the identification of Brunei with P'oni or Po-ni, to which references occur in the histories of the Sung dynasty. We are told that the King of Po-ni sent tribute to the Emperor of China in 977 and again in 1082, and that when a merchant junk passed by Po-ni its captain as a courtesy would send a gift of Chinese food to the King.[3] By this time trade between China and Borneo seems to have been constant. Hoards of Sung pottery have been found, as well as Sung coins. Many of the ancient jars are of this date.[4] There were probably Chinese settlements already round the coast, as at Santubong, on the west mouth of the Sarawak river, and at Kinabatangan, the 'Chinese River', on the north-east coast. The name Kinabalu, given to Borneo's highest peak, also suggests the presence of Chinese. The Mongol emperors of China, who had grand expansionist ideas, seem even to have contemplated the annexation of Borneo. Kublai Khan is said to have sent an expedition there in 1292; and it is possible that the Chinese for a time occupied north Borneo and that the settlement at Kinabatangan was the result of this campaign.[1]

Chinese traders were welcomed by the indigenous peoples of Borneo, who were eager to possess the jars and beads that they brought, while their silks and metalwork and better-class pottery found a ready market with the more sophisticated Malays on the coast. The Chinese for their part bought edible birds'-nests from the caves at Niah and, in the north-east, jungle produce such as rattan and beeswax, and, from the late fourteenth century onwards, hornbill beaks for carving. A Chinese writer reported in 1349 that the people of Po-ni showed great respect and affection for the Chinese. Indeed, if a Chinese visitor became drunk they would assist him most courteously back to his inn.[2] But by that time Chinese influence was declining. The nationalist Ming dynasty was less interested than the Mongols in foreign adventures, and the Majapahit kingdom in its decadence could no longer keep a check on Malay piracy. The rulers of Brunei began to vary their allegiance according to the political needs of the moment. In the middle of the fourteenth century the last great Majapahit king, Angya Wi-jaya, re-established his authority from Sumatra to the Philippines, and the ruler of Brunei used his help in suppressing local rebels. On his death Brunei sent a humble embassy to China, with a consignment of hornbill ivory; but a few years later its ruler paid homage to the Muslim king of Malacca, Mansur Shah. Owing, no doubt, to fear of Muslim aggression from Malacca, Brunei reverted early in the next century to the Chinese connection. Ming records report the arrival of the King of Po-ni, whose name they give as Maradja Kala, at the Imperial Court in 1408. He died when starting on his return journey; his widow and his son, Hiawang, were sent back home. The latter revisited China and sent tribute to the Emperor.[3]

Kala and his son were probably the last pre-Muslim rulers of Brunei. It must have been soon afterwards that Alak ber Tabar adopted Islam and the name of Mohammed. According to the Chinese the King of Brunei was about now 'a man from Fukien who followed Cheng Ho to Po-ni and settled there'. The Brunei tradition is more explicit. The generally accepted version says the second Muslim ruler, Ahmed, married the daughter or the sister of a Chinese magnate from Kinabatangan, called Sum Ping; while an alternative version says that Mohammed's daughter and heiress herself married Sum Ping. The second version is perhaps the more correct. If the princess succeeded her uncle, and if Sum Ping had himself come to Borneo in the train of Cheng Ho, a Chinese ambassador who went on two missions through the Malay archipelago, then it would fit in with the Chinese story. The daughter of this marriage, or, alternatively, of the marriage of Sultan Ahmed with his Chinese bride, married a *sherip* Berkat, an Arab from Taif, who was descended from the Prophet. Their son Suleiman was the ancestor of all the subsequent Sultans of Brunei.[1]

Under Islam the Malays were better organised and more aggressive than before, while the Ming Emperors in China were never deeply interested in overseas colonies. Such Chinese settlements as existed in Borneo seem to have faded out; and it was not till the eighteenth century that the Chinese returned as settlers, to work the goldmines in western Borneo. But the maritime trade remained almost entirely in Chinese hands. Chinese junks in great numbers visited the Bornean ports, especially on the north coast. In Brunei Chinese coins and measures were in general circulation for several centuries to come; and there were a number of resident Chinese merchants there. The connection between the northern coasts of Borneo and the Chinese was never broken; and the Sultans recognised the Chinese as a useful and friendly asset to their lands.

By the beginning of the sixteenth century the interior of Borneo was occupied by a number of tribes with little contact with the outside world, except when some enterprising Chinese trader made his way up one of the rivers with a cargo of jars and beads. The tribes nearer to the coast, such as the Land Dyaks and the Melanaus, were beginning to fall under the domination of local Malay princes. There were Malay sultans established at Brunei on the north-west coast, at Sambas and Pontianak on the east coast, and at Pasir, Koti and Belungan on the west coast. Of these the Sultan of Brunei, whose territory stretched from almost the northern tip of the island down to Cape Datu in the west, was the most powerful; but his authority was not unquestioned. There were princes living on the Sarawak river, of a line as august as his own, who only paid him fitful obedience; while he and his fellow-Sultans all owed some vague allegiance to the Sultan of Malacca. There were still a few rulers in Borneo who were not yet converted to Islam, especially in the extreme north and east of the island; but they were dying out. Islam had already spread to the Sulu archipelago, in the southern Philippines; and the Sultan of Sulu had territorial ambitions in northern Borneo. Islam was as yet a uniting force among the Malays; and it seemed not improbable that if the rulers of Malacca showed sufficient energy they could be the leaders of a great Islamic confederation which would rule the Malay peninsula and the greater islands of the archipelago. Only a prophet could have foreseen that new forces were soon to intervene and change the course of Malayan history.

THE COMING OF THE EUROPEANS

The challenge to the Malay Islamic Empire came from distant lands, of which no Malay had heard. In 1498 the Portuguese Vasco da Gama rounded the Cape of Good Hope; and during the first decade of the sixteenth century Portuguese ships began to frequent the Indian Ocean and to enquire about the islands on its eastern fringe. In 1510 the Viceroy Albuquerque captured Goa and made it the capital of the Portuguese colonial empire. Next year the Portuguese captured and colonised Malacca. About the same time the Spaniards reached the Pacific shores of the American continent and planned to explore the ocean to find a new route to the Indies. The collapse of Muslim power in the Malay peninsula at first enhanced the power of the outlying Muslim Sultans. The Sultanates of Borneo, such as Bandjermasin, Pontianak and Brunei, emerged as entirely independent; and of these Brunei was still the most important. When European sailors asked the name of the whole island they were informed that it was the island of Brunei, or Borneo.

The first European to land in Borneo and record his landing was an Italian adventurer, Ludovico de Varthema. In 1507 he was sailing in a Malay boat from the Moluccas to Java and called at a port somewhere on the south-east Bornean coast. He found the inhabitants a friendly and personable race, pagans, but enjoying an orderly government.[1] The Portuguese Lourenço Gomez seems to have visited the island in 1518.[2] But the first fully recorded visit by Europeans was made by a squadron flying the Spanish flag. Ferdinand Magellan set out from Seville, on the orders of King Charles of Spain, the future Emperor Charles V, with five ships and a mixed crew of Spaniards, Portuguese and Italians, in August 1519. After crossing the Atlantic and Pacific Oceans he himself was killed in a skirmish in the Philippines in April 1521. In July the squadron, reduced now to two ships and without an accepted leader, sailed from Mindanao in the southern Philippines round the north tip of Borneo and put into the harbour of Brunei, the great city which gave its name to the whole island. It spent about a week there. At first all went well. The King of Brunei allowed the crews to buy provisions and gave an honorific reception and many handsome presents to the delegation from the boats. But after a few days, when a fleet of armed praus set out from the harbour, the Europeans, who had probably been indulging in a little thieving, guiltily supposed that they were about to be attacked and opened fire on the praus, capturing four of them, with sixteen chieftains and three noble ladies on board. Then, without waiting for reprisals, they set sail with their captives and spent the next few days raiding whatever vessels they met. This piracy continued till they reached Tidore and the Moluccas.

The Italian, Antonio Pigafetta, who was one of the crew to be received by the Sultan, wrote a vivid description of Brunei. It was, he says, a huge city, built on piles over the water. He estimated it as containing 25,000 families, that is to say, well over 100,000 inhabitants. He was interested in its way of life, the women doing their marketing by boat when the tide was high. He noted the general habit of chewing betel-nut and the intoxicating strength of the arak which was freely drunk. The riches of the royal palace impressed him, with its silk brocade hangings, its gold and china ware, and its great silver cande-labra. He and his fellow-delegates were presented with silks and cloth of gold, in return for the velvet and red woollen cloth which they offered as gifts. The courtiers of the Sultan, though naked above the waist, were decked with jewelled rings and golden daggers. The Sultan himself, who, according to Pigafetta, was called Rajah Siripada, was aged about forty and rather corpulent. Pigafetta's imagination was especially stirred by the report that he possessed two pearls as large as pigeon's eggs and so perfectly round that they could not stay still on a flat surface. He refused to show them to the visitors; but some of the courtiers attested that they had seen them. Ceremonial journeys to and from the palace were made on elephant-back. The inhabitants were all Muslim.

Brunei was the only town in the island which Magellan's company visited. But Pigafetta heard of another great city, inhabited by pagans, whose king, he was told, was as powerful as the Sultan of Brunei, but less proud. He thought that Christianity might be introduced without difficulty there.[1]

Pigafetta saw Brunei at the height of its glory. The Sultan whom he visited was probably the fifth according to Brunei records, Bulkeiah, who flourished in the first quarter of the sixteenth century and married

Map 1. The Far East in the mid-nineteenth century.

a Javanese princess. He was undoubtedly the master of the whole
north-west coast of the island; and the fact that the whole island was
known to the Europeans as Brunei, Burné or Borneo, indicates that
their informants regarded him as its leading potentate. He was in
diplomatic relations with the other Muslim princes of Indonesia, and
probably also with China. Pigafetta noted that the inhabitants used

19   2-2

bronze Chinese coins, pierced and strung together in the Chinese manner, with the Emperor of China's ideogram on them.[1]

When Magellan's ships returned to Europe and accounts of the voyage were published, both Portuguese and Spaniards began to take an interest in the new-found lands. In Borneo the Portuguese led the way. They were already established in the Malay peninsula, where the great Viceroy of the Indies, Affonso d'Albuquerque, had captured Malacca in 1511. There was already a considerable trade between Brunei and Malacca and the Portuguese determined to continue it. In 1526 their admiral, Gorge de Menezes, sailed to Brunei to arrange a commercial treaty with the Sultan. This was successfully achieved. Henceforward there was a steady export of pepper from Borneo to Malacca and on to the West. Borneo also exported sago—a food, so the Portuguese Tomé Pires notes, which is suitable to the lower classes—fish and rice, and gold of rather a low assay value. In return the Borneans imported weapons and cloth.[2]

By 1571 the Spaniards had completed their conquest of the main islands of the Philippine group. This brought them into continual and hostile contact with the Sultanate of Sulu, which owned territory on the Philippine island of Mindanao as well as in north-eastern Borneo. In their search for allies against Sulu they began to take an interest in the Sultanate of Brunei. In 1578 a disputed succession, which followed the death of Sultan Abdul Kaher, gave them an opportunity. An expedition led by Don Francisco de Sande sailed to Brunei and succeeded in placing on the throne a candidate said to be devoted to their interest. But the new sultan was ungrateful; they were unable to maintain any influence at his Court. A second expedition in 1580 produced no better results.[3]

Neither Spain nor Portugal was seriously interested in Borneo. To the former it was merely of potential but indirect value in the control of the Philippines. The latter was more interested in the islands away to the south-east, Timor and the Moluccas. Before the sixteenth century was over two younger powers had entered into competition with them. The English had their attention drawn to the Indonesian archipelago when Sir Francis Drake sailed through the islands on his way round the world in 1579. He paused at the island of Ternate, where he made a successful commercial deal with the Sultan, buying from him six tons of cloves.[4] His adventures aroused interest in England and led to the collection there of information about the archipelago. In 1599 a Petition of Merchant Adventurers presented to Queen Elizabeth I noted that Borneo was a land 'abounding in great wealth and riches' and that neither the Portuguese nor the Spaniards possessed any 'castle, fort, blockhouse or commandment' there.[1] When the East India Company was founded the following year it included the archipelago within the sphere of its operations. In 1609 two attempts were made to set up trading stations in Borneo, at Soekadana on the west coast and at Bandjermasin on the south-east coast. These were half-hearted efforts. The Company was more deeply interested in the Moluccas, further to the east, where it had high hopes of a station founded at Amboyna.[2] But the English were soon outmanoeuvred by the Dutch.

The Dutch East India Company was founded two years after the English, in 1602; but already Dutch ships were sailing Eastern seas in far greater numbers than the English. By the end of the century there was a Dutch merchant-station at Bantam in Java. In 1603 they founded a station at Bandjermasin, but were forced to leave it four years later, after the local inhabitants had murdered the crew of one of their ships. It was soon afterwards that the English came in; but the Dutch took their revenge in 1612 when an organised expedition captured and sacked the town and forced the Sultan to move his government inland, and the English temporarily to abandon their station. They also set themselves up at Sambas and at Soekadana, where they induced the Sultan to close the English establishment. But their tenure was precarious. The merchants of Sambas were all massacred in 1610; the Soekadana station was destroyed in a local war in 1612. It was clear that trading stations dependent on the whim of a local sultan would never be satisfactory. Early in the seventeenth century the Dutch began to attack the Portuguese colonies in the Moluccas and on the Malayan mainland and to capture cities for themselves from the local princes. They took Ternate from the Portuguese in 1607; and the other Portuguese ports fell to them soon afterwards. In 1641 they drove the Portuguese from the mainland by their capture of Malacca. Meanwhile they secured a territorial footing on Java, where in 1611 they founded the city of Batavia, the modern Jakarta. The English, whom they saw as potential rivals, were intimidated by a wholesale massacre of merchants and their families at Amboyna in 1623. By 1650 the Dutch were supreme in Indonesia. After the massacre at Amboyna the English East India Company, having failed to secure any support from the authorities at home, began to concentrate its attention on India proper; though the merchants never forgave the Royal government and threw all the weight of their influence against the King when the Civil War began in England a few years later. Any hope that the Portuguese might have had of recovering lost colonies was finally dashed when the Dutch conquered Ceylon from them in 1658. Thenceforward nothing was left of Portugal's oriental empire except for Goa in India, Macao off the China coast and half the island of Timor. Their ships still traded in Indonesian waters, especially with Borneo, in spite of the Dutch, till the beginning of the eighteenth century, but their influence was ended.[1]

The Dutch had acquired influence over so vast an area that they tended to neglect the more troublesome parts of it. Borneo had proved to be unsatisfactory. After an attempt in 1664 to re-establish trading relations with the Sultan of Bandjermasin failed, they withdrew all their merchants from the island. In 1698 they assisted their vassal, the Sultan of Bantam, to intervene in a war between the Rajah of Landak and the Sultan of Soekadana. Soekadana was destroyed by the allies in 1699 and all the princes of the west coast of Borneo recognised the suzerainty of the Sultan of Bantam and so, indirectly, of the Dutch East India Company. But the princes of the north and east coasts of the island were left to their own devices, which were not very commendable.[2]

The Spaniards were imperialistic crusaders. The first conquistadors were only one generation removed from the soldiers who had driven the last Muslims out of Spain. They and their descendants were consciously fighting for the Faith and for the Most Catholic King who was its chief patron. They were eager to find wealth, but they were missionaries rather than merchants; their aim was to convert conquered peoples to the Catholic Religion and at the same time to extract what riches they could from the conquered country, especially precious metals, in bullion or in coin or plate, to send back to Spain. The Portuguese also had something of the missionary spirit, though it was tempered by a greater interest in commerce; a desire to establish trade relations made them more tolerant of the infidel. But in comparison with the Dutch the Portuguese were amateur merchants. The Dutch were untroubled by missionary ambitions. They had no desire to raise native races to their level as God's Chosen People. They concentrated with single-minded efficiency on the success of their commerce. Like most economic thinkers of their time their outlook was mercantilist.

They saw wealth as a limited commodity; the less others had of it the more there would be for them. They attempted to carry out this policy in Indonesia. It was their aim that all merchandise going to or from the islands, or in between the islands, should be carried on their ships alone. Not only were they determined to exclude the other European powers from the Indonesian trade, but they interfered with the native and the Chinese shipping which for centuries past had sailed round the islands. To keep up prices they freely destroyed spices and other valuable goods for which their ships had no space. With prices thus maintained

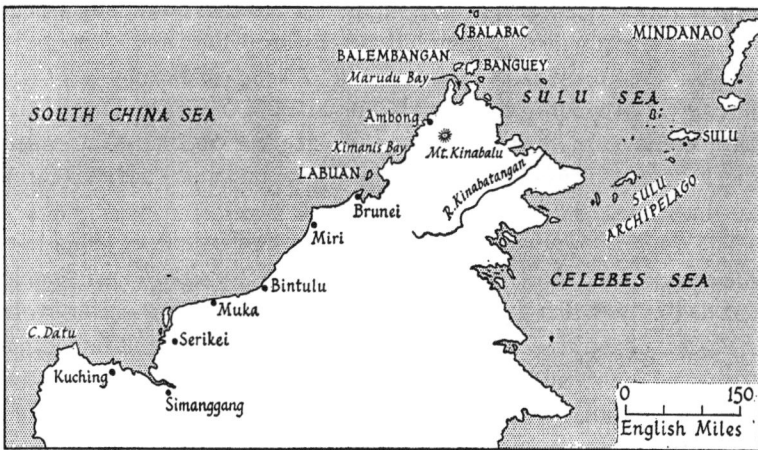

Map 2. The north-west coast of Borneo in the mid-nineteenth century.

artificially high, and with the career of trade officially closed to all except the Dutch, it was not surprising that many ambitious local seamen took to piracy. Piracy was nothing new; there had always been many pirates on the eastern seas. But there was a remarkable increase in the number operating there from the middle of the seventeenth century onwards; and most of them operated from Borneo, particularly from its northern shores. It was an area well suited to them. It was far enough away from the main seats of Dutch authority for police action to be difficult; and should a Dutch fleet appear the pirates could retreat up the winding rivers with their shallow bars, which a prau of small draught could easily negotiate if it knew local conditions and tides but which were impassable to the men-of-war of the Europeans. At the extreme north of the island, far away from any

European fort, there was the superb bay of Marudu, where a whole pirate fleet could assemble unobserved except by the complacent eye of the Sultan of Sulu. Yet much of the China trade passed not far away, while the praus could easily creep round the friendly shores of east Borneo to raid in the Straits of Macassar and even to the Java Sea. Success whetted their appetite. As the eighteenth century advanced the pirates grew bolder and more insolent. The Sultans of Brunei and of Sulu were quite unable to suppress them and preferred to give them unofficial patronage in return for a share of their gains. The pepper trade between Brunei and the Portuguese which, after the Dutch occupation of Malacca, had been continued through Macao, faded out. Chinese traders, who had been ready to challenge the Dutch monopoly, ventured less freely across the sea. The colonies in Borneo had some difficulty in keeping in touch with the outside world. The Dutch were able to police only the lanes along which their own shipping sailed. The British only tried to protect their growing trade with China. It was the small local trader who suffered the most.

The responsibility of the Dutch for the growth of piracy should not be exaggerated. As weapons of western design, more effective than they had known before, began to circulate among the seafaring tribes of Borneo, and as an increase in the value of sea-borne trade became apparent, piracy had ever greater attractions as a profession. But the Dutch policy must bear some of the blame. To Sir Stamford Raffles, who, it must be admitted, was not fond of the Dutch, it seemed obvious that their destruction of native trade was the source of the trouble. The historian Crawfurd, writing in 1820, more broadmindedly blames all the Europeans. 'The piratical character we have attempted to fix upon them,' he wrote, 'might be most truly retaliated upon us.'[1]

In spite of the pirates and the hostility of the Dutch, the English East India Company still hoped to re-establish trade with the Indonesian islands; and Borneo seemed to be the most promising sphere. It was vast, it was presumably rich, to judge from the spices and the gold that it exported; and the Dutch had made little headway there. The Company's station at Bandjermasin had finally been abandoned in 1655. In 1693 the station at Soekadana was reopened, but only for one year; and in 1700 the Company returned to Bandjermasin. But Captain Barry, who was put in charge of the station, and his fellow-Englishmen were truculent and inept in their dealings with the natives and made themselves thoroughly disliked. Seven years later, after the Captain had been mysteriously poisoned, the station was abandoned. In 1714, the Company tried again. Two ships, under Captain Lewis and Captain Beekman, sailed to Bandjermasin. On his return home Captain Beekman wrote an account of their adventures, full of shrewd if not always accurate observations. To be received at all by the local princes the Captains had to pretend that they were independent traders, so unpopular had the Company become. After numerous prevarications and delays they at last made contact with the Sultan, who resided then at 'Caytongee', a hundred miles further up the river. They were hampered by a shortage of goods to present to the Court; they were obliged to provide guns, and men to use them, to help the Sultan put down a local rebellion; and it was only when the approach of the monsoon forced them to announce their departure that they at last obtained the cargo of pepper for which they had been bargaining. In the end, owing undoubtedly to their tact in handling the natives, whom Beekman liked in spite of their commercial morals, the Captains did good business. But they failed to reopen the Company's station. Twenty-three years later, when the evil memory of Captain Barry had faded, the Company was able to return to Bandjermasin for ten ineffectual years. A visiting trader, Captain Alexander Hamilton, found the station ill run and feckless. He reported that the Chief Factor, a Mr Cunningham, was only interested in zoology and not at all in running his factory.[1]

South Borneo proved a disappointment. Even if the Company's servants had been more energetic and more skilful in dealing with the local princes, the hostility of the Dutch, nervous at seeing rival stations threatening their monopoly of the Java Sea, would have made any permanent British settlement there insecure. But by the middle of the eighteenth century Britain began to open up the China trade. Vessels sailing to China in the months of the south-west monsoon, April to October, passed through the Straits of Malacca or the Straits of Sunda and continued their way up the South China Sea, to the west of Borneo. When the north-west monsoon was blowing, in the remaining months of the year, they preferred to take the longer route from Sunda or Malacca round the south and east of Borneo and up through the Sulu Sea. The routes converged near the north-eastern tip of Borneo. In 1759 a young official at Madras, Alexander Dalrymple, who had made a study of old records and charts of the China Seas, persuaded the Company to send him out on a voyage of exploration. He made his way to Sulu and soon was on friendly terms with the Sultan, who was nervous of both the Spaniards and the Dutch and was alarmed by the growth of piracy. In 1761 the Sultan made a draft treaty with Dalrymple. He would allow the East India Company to have the site for a factory in his territory, which included the northern end of Borneo. The Chinese who settled there were to be under British jurisdiction. British and Chinese merchants were to have free trading facilities throughout Sulu territory. The Sultan's merchants warmly supported the scheme, hoping that British protection would enable them to reopen trade with China, in whose markets their goods would, they believed, fetch handsome prices. Dalrymple's subsequent essay in selling Sulu pepper at Canton proved unprofitable, but he remained convinced that the treaty would be worth while, and when he returned to Madras he easily persuaded the Madras government to support him. He was back in Sulu in 1763 with the Company's ratification of the treaty, and the Sultan handed over to him as its representative the island of Balembangan, twenty miles off the northern tip of Borneo.

Reports of Dalrymple's scheme reached London. Even before it heard of the annexation of Balembangan, the East India Company decided to profit by the war with Spain then raging to attack Manila, the capital of the Philippines. In 1763 a British fleet sailed unexpectedly into Manila Bay and easily captured the city. But the Company's hope of bringing the whole archipelago under the British flag was disappointed. News of the capture of Manila only reached Europe after a peace treaty between Britain and Spain had been signed. As this treaty made no mention of Manila it legally reverted to the Spaniards. This failure to conquer the Philippines made a settlement off North Borneo still more attractive; and Dalrymple was soon able to enlarge his success.

He had visited Manila during the British occupation, and there he discovered living in semi-captivity an old man who proved to be the rightful Sultan of Sulu. The acting Sultan, his nephew, was in fact a usurper. Darymple promptly brought the exile back with him to Sulu, to the approval of his loyal subjects; and as the old gentleman had no desire to resume the cares of government and was quite content to let his nephew continue as *de facto* ruler, everyone was happy; and Dalrymple's reputation was higher than ever.

As a result the treaty between Sulu and the Company was amended. The whole north coast of Borneo was now ceded to the Company, from the river Kimanis on the west to the river Kinabatangan on the east, together with Balembangan, Palawan, further to the north, and Labuan (which, however, more properly belonged to the Sultan of Brunei than to the Sultan of Sulu). The old Sultan's son, Seraf ud-Din, was to rule these lands as vassal to the Company.

Dalrymple sailed home to London in triumph. But there he found the Company troubled by internal quarrels and nervous about this vast accession of territory. With some difficulty he persuaded it at least to make a settlement on Balembangan, in spite of protests both from Holland and from Spain. He could not, however, induce the Board to accept his views about the nature of the settlement, and angrily retired from the Company's service. In his place the Company appointed a certain Captain Trotter to establish the factory and then proceed to Sulu to see that the recent treaty still held good, and generally to report on the commercial prospects of northern Borneo. Trotter performed his tasks efficiently. His report was a full and careful summary of the political and ethnological state of the district as well as of its economic potentialities. He recommended that the Company should follow up the scheme, though the Dutch would certainly do their best to hamper it. His report arrived in London in 1770 and encouraged the Company to fit out a ship, the *Britannia*, with £20,000 worth of cargo, under the command of John Herbert, who was to establish the colony and govern it as its Chief Resident. Herbert arrived at Balembangan in December 1773, and at once began to build houses, godowns and wharves. At the same time the Company appointed an Agent to the Court of Sulu, Edward Coles, and another to the Court of Brunei, John Jesse, while William Cornshill was appointed Resident in Palawan.

At first all went well. The display of activity impressed the neighbouring princes; and the chief Sultan of Mindanao sent to Herbert to invite the Company to establish stations in his territory. In 1774 one of the most active of the colonists, Captain Forrest, set out in a ten-ton prau to negotiate with the Sultan and to explore what other islands might offer openings for commerce. His voyage lasted for two years. On his tiny boat, with an all-Malay crew, he reached Mindanao, where the Sultan offered a small island for the Company's use; then he sailed south-eastward, past Halmaheira to the north coast of New Guinea, returning to Balembangan rich with valuable information.

His efforts were wasted. All that was left of the factory by then was a mass of charred ruins. Herbert had not been the admirable administrator that he had seemed. Not content with cheating his employers, the Company, out of £35,000, he, still more imprudently, offended the Sulu merchants, to whom he at first allowed very generous credit in the belief that their crops and raw products were far greater than was the case. When he pressed angrily for payment the merchants became truculent. The pirates of the neighbourhood had deeply resented the establishment of a British settlement at the very entrance to Marudu Bay. They gladly allied themselves with the disgruntled merchants. In February 1775, an armed force of Sulus and pirates landed on the far side of the island. Herbert, who had no idea of the dangers of his policy, was completely taken by surprise. The British and their staff had barely time to escape to their ships. They left the factory to be thoroughly looted and burnt to the ground.

Herbert and his companions retired to Labuan. There he wrote a long despatch to London, minimising the disaster at Balembangan, though he admitted that it was unfortunate. Labuan, he wrote, was a far better site for a station; and he implied that his move thither was an act of wise, premeditated policy. The Company was unconvinced. It was already suspicious of Herbert's accounting; and when it heard the full story and realised that it had lost about £175,000 on the whole venture, Herbert was summarily dismissed. To recoup this loss a frigate, H.M.S. *Dolphin*, was sent under Captain Sir John Clarke to Sulu to demand 40,000 Spanish dollars in compensation. But Sir John's bluff methods were ill suited to negotiations with the Sulus. He offended the Sultan by refusing the gifts offered him out of customary politeness. When the Sultan said that he could only afford 10,000 dollars as compensation, Sir John threatened him with the might of the British Empire; when the Sultan pointed out that Sir John was now in his power, Sir John retorted that if anything happened to him the guns of H.M.S. *Dolphin* would blow the Sultan's palace to pieces. In the end Sir John retired safely to his ship and sailed away, without even the 10,000 dollars which the Sultan might have paid.[1]

Some thirty years later, in 1803, the Company once again tried to establish a factory on Balembangan. But the agents that it sent out failed entirely to make any contact with the Sulu or Chinese merchants. Two years later they abandoned the island, in a state very near to starvation. Marudu Bay was left once more to the pirates.[2]

The attempts of the British to establish themselves in North Borneo had been paralleled by the Dutch in the south of the island, in districts that they had neglected for more than a century. In 1787, taking advantage of a civil war, the Dutch East India Company annexed the whole Sultanate of Bandjermasin. Five years previously the Company had set up its candidate as vassal-Sultan of Pontianak and helped him to extend his authority over much of the west coast, at the same time establishing stations at Pontianak and elsewhere. But, like the British, the Dutch found little profit in the control of Bornean territory. In 1790 the stations along the west coast were closed; in 1797 Bandjermasin and the neighbouring lands were restored to the Sultan. All that the Dutch retained in Borneo, apart from a vague suzerainty, was the small fort of Tatas, at the mouth of the Bandjermasin river.

The British compensated themselves for their withdrawal from North Borneo by the successful foundation of the colony of Penang in 1785. The Dutch withdrawal from the South was due to more serious economic reasons. Holland had entered into the War of American Independence, hoping to share the spoils taken from a defeated Britain; but, instead, the British not only overran Ceylon but their fleet blockaded Java so efficiently that when peace was signed it was difficult for the Javanese export trade to recover its lost markets. Moreover one of the few concessions that Britain obtained at the peace-conference besides the annexation of Ceylon was the opening of the Indonesian waters for traders of all nations. The Dutch monopoly was broken and the British were the chief gainers. Nor were the British the only enemies. Even while the monopoly lasted it was continually broken by the Chinese. Fleets of Chinese junks came every year to Borneo, to buy not only the pepper and gold sought by European traders, but also birds'-nests, bêche-de-mer and sharks' fins, all of which the Europeans disdained; and, with the inexhaustible markets of China far closer than those of Europe and with cheaper overhead expenses and labour, they were usually able to offer the Borneans considerably better prices than the Dutch could afford. So long as the Chinese were in the offing no local prince was eager to commit himself to any commercial arrangement with the Europeans.[1]

At the turn of the century Holland became involved in the French Revolutionary Wars, and a few years later the home-country was overrun by Napoleon's troops and forced to become a vassal-state of the French Empire. As such it was at war with Britain. The British were quick to take advantage of the position. The Dutch East India Company's possessions having passed under French control, it was legitimate to attack them. The Dutch fleet was destroyed in two decisive actions in 1806 and 1807 off the coast of Java. In 1808 a British fleet attacked and occupied the Moluccas. Napoleon had already sent out to Java as Governor-General a Dutch collaborationist whom he trusted, Marshal Daendels, with orders to organise its defences and husband its resources with the object of some day assisting the French in the conquest of British India. Daendels, however, soon found himself completely on the defensive in Java, with few men and no ships to spare. In 1809 he decided that he must close the only remaining Dutch settlement on Borneo, and sent a commissioner to evacuate the garrison from Tatas and hand over the fort to the Sultan of Bandjermasin. The Sultan was alarmed. Unwilling though he might be to commit himself to commercial arrangements with the Dutch, he valued them as allies and protectors who had helped to raise his status above that of the other Sultans in Borneo. If the Dutch were going to desert him for fear of the British, he must win the support of the British. He hastened to send emissaries to the British colony of Penang. The British were not at the moment interested; but a second embassy that he sent to Malacca, early in 1811, received a more gratifying response.

There was a merchant in Malacca called Alexander Hare, a man with self-seeking but romantic ambitions. He had briefly visited Borneo in 1809, on the suggestion of the East India Company. When he heard of the Dutch evacuation of Fort Tatas, he sent two ships to Bandjermasin, hoping to open up trade with the Sultan. The venture came to nothing; but when the Sultan's envoys arrived at Malacca they sought Hare's help, and he introduced them to an acquaintance whom he knew would welcome their proposals, the Agent to the Governor-General of the Malay States, Stamford Raffles.[1]

Raffles was then thirty years old. He had entered the East India Company's service as a young man, and from 1807 to 1810 had been stationed at Penang. During his time there he occupied himself in discovering everything that he could about Malaya and the Indonesian islands. His interests were wide; he studied anthropology, botany and zoology as well as history; but above all he was a political visionary with a remarkable talent for practical administration. He had gone to Calcutta in 1810, where he persuaded the Governor-General of the East India Company's possessions, Lord Minto, that the time had come to annex the whole Dutch colonial empire in the East. He was now in Malacca to organise the invasion of Java. Not only were his agents bringing him reports on the military and political situation in Java, but he was trying to build up alliances with the local sultans throughout the archipelago, so as further to isolate the Dutch. A connection with the Sultan of Bandjermasin and the foundation there of a British factory fitted in well with his schemes. He had long been interested in Borneo. Of all the islands whose political and economic potentialities he had been studying so minutely, it seemed to offer the greatest promise. 'The immense island of Borneo', he wrote to Lord Minto from Malacca in the summer of 1811, 'even the shores of which are yet imperfectly known, contains in its interior a more numerous agricultural population than has generally been supposed.' He spoke not only of the pepper and rattans produced there, but of 'fine wax, birds' nests, deers' horns and tendons, skins and wood'. It was, he declared, 'not only one of the most fertile countries in the world, but the most productive in gold and diamonds'. He estimated the value of its actual export of gold every year at more than half a million sterling. With his eyes fixed on Java and not on the China trade, it was the southern part of the island that interested him most closely; but he added that 'the northern provinces, though more out of the track of general shipping, are not unimportant from a commercial point of view.... The maritime enterprise of these people, though latterly too much devoted to piratical enterprise, could easily be directed into better channels.' He also thought, though he only expressed this in private, that Java if it were conquered might have to be returned to the Dutch when the war was ended, but the Dutch had abandoned Borneo. Any colonies that the British might found there would survive the peace treaty.[1]

Raffles therefore encouraged the Sultan of Bandjermasin; and Lord Minto, when he came to Malacca on his way to conquer Java, gave his approval to the alliance. The Dutch in Java surrendered to the British on 18 September 1811. On Raffles's advice the terms of the surrender made it clear that the Dutch commander was only handing over the parts of Java that his troops still controlled. The west of the island, together with other islands which the British had already occupied or which the Dutch had abandoned, such as the Moluccas or Borneo, were specifically excluded. Raffles wished them to be in a separate category from Java when the time for a peace-treaty should arrive.[2]

Raffles, to whose energy the occupation of Java was due, became its Lieutenant-Governor. One of his first actions was to implement the arrangement with the Sultan of Bandjermasin. Before the end of the month Hare arrived at Bandjermasin, accompanied by an Assistant-

Resident of Dutch origin called van de Wahl, a police-officer with a detachment of Malay police, two doctors, a few clerks and more craftsmen and coolies. His instructions were to assist in the campaign against local piracy, to regulate the trade of southern Borneo and to spread civilisation. It was not a very impressive force for the purpose, but the Sultan welcomed it. After the usual oriental hesitation and delays he signed on 1 October a treaty in which he ceded to the East India Company with full sovereign rights Fort Tatas and the former Dutch territory, the Dyak provinces of South Borneo, together with a rather vaguely defined area comprising most of the petty principalities along the south and east coast which were officially vassal to him. He was released from any treaty obligations to the Dutch; and the arrangement was specially noted as having no connection with the British occupation of Java. The British were to protect the Sultan from all his enemies, European or Asian, and for that purpose were to station a light fleet near by. Any surplus in the revenue was to be divided equally between the Sultan and the British authorities in Java. The Resident's consent must be obtained for the levying of any new taxes or tolls. The pepper monopoly was to continue; the British authorities could cut timber and mine gold and diamonds everywhere except for a few places reserved for the Sultan. The Sultan might appoint no senior ministers without the previous approval of the Lieutenant-Governor of Java.[1]

The treaty was similar to many that previous Sultans had signed with the Dutch and subsequently broken. On neither side was it very exact. The Sultan gave the East India Company a large territory over which he had in fact no control in return for promises of protection which were remarkably vague. But the Sultan seemed content and it was hailed in Java as a diplomatic triumph. Raffles chose to condone the fact that at the same time Hare had made a private treaty with the Sultan which gave him personally and his assignees sovereign rights over an area some 1400 square miles in extent, just south of the capital. Hare was Resident on behalf of the East India Company; but he was also to be a Sovereign Prince. Raffles, who had given Hare permission to trade as a private person, only stipulated that he should be ready to cede his principality to the British authorities with fair compensation should it seem advisable. For the rest Raffles felt grateful to Hare for having brought Bandjermasin to his notice and for accepting the post of Resident and making the official treaty. He saw no reason for curbing

Hare's individual transactions, which might prove to the benefit of everyone.

Indeed, as Hare saw clearly, the treaty would only work well if it produced a financial profit for all parties. The Sultan would not be satisfied with uncertain promises of protection unless meanwhile his wealth was increasing. The East India Company would not wish, in the light of previous experience, to maintain a station which showed a loss. Raffles wished at any cost to preserve the station for purely political reasons; and Hare wished both to make his fortune and enjoy the pleasure of being an eastern potentate. The new colony was started with enthusiasm. Hare had arrived well provided with money; and if he made little distinction between his own and the Government's money, it mattered to no one as long as things went well. He had schemes for increasing the pepper crop and developing rice-fields, and even for making salt-works. A few more Europeans joined him, including a Scotsman almost as ambitious and romantic as himself, John Clunies-Ross.[1]

The Bandjermasin settlement was to guarantee British influence on the south coast of Borneo. Raffles next turned his attention to the west coast. The two important states there were the Sultanates of Pontianak and Sambas, while the influence of the Sultan of Brunei stretched down the north coast almost to the north-west tip of the island. It was in this north-west corner, in the district where Sambas and Brunei influence met, that most of the Bornean goldmines were placed. The mines were worked by Chinese, who had first settled there about 1740 and who by 1760 were rich and powerful enough to set up self-governing communities, known as *kongsis*, which paid only nominal deference to the Malay Sultans. The Dutch had done their best to discourage Chinese immigration into Borneo though they could not prevent it; but since the seas had been opened in 1784, they had given up the attempt. Geographically, Sambas should have provided the outlet for the gold trade. But European merchants had always preferred Pontianak, with its more accessible harbour, to any port controlled by the Sultan of Sambas. In order to find European buyers for their gold and to obtain European goods in return, the Chinese, whether their mines lay in Sambas territory or not, began more and more to use Pontianak. The growing prosperity of Pontianak was naturally resented at Sambas, whose Sultan, finding himself edged out of legitimate trade, began to patronise the pirates. It was a good time for pirates. However responsible the Dutch may have been for the beginning of piracy in

Bornean waters, their warships had been able to control it to some extent. With the destruction of the local Dutch navy by the British in 1806 and 1807 this police-work ended; for the British, with a world-war raging, had not the ships to spare for more than their immediate strategic needs. British commerce soon was to suffer for it.[1]

In 1810, while Raffles was still at Malacca, a British merchant ship, the *Commerce*, had been disabled off the Borneo coast and had drifted on to an island near Lundu. Raffles heard of this and sent a message to the Sultan of Pontianak, asking what information he could give. The answer came that the *Commerce* had been seized by 'the pirates of Serawa, a small dependency of Borneo proper, in conjunction with those of Sambas'. It is in these unpleasant circumstances that Sarawak makes its first entry into English history. Raffles thereupon sent an agent, Mr Burn, to Pontianak to keep watch over British commercial interests, with special regard to the pirate problem, and to establish friendly relations with its Sultan. In the latter task Burn was highly successful. Knowing that Raffles's aim was to tidy up the many small states of the west coast by elevating Pontianak, he was easily able to persuade the Sultan to ask for British protection and a British trading settlement to be established in his city. The station could fly the British flag and contain twenty-four soldiers and would share the land-rents and port-duties with the Sultan. In return the British must support the Sultan against Sambas, and must help him to collect tribute from the Chinese *kongsis* in his dominions. The Sultan further made it clear that he had no obligations towards the Dutch; this arrangement was not to be affected by any possible return of Dutch authority to Java.

Raffles was delighted by it and was ready to join in action against Sambas. Burn had not been so successful in his commission to deal with piracy. He had learnt at Pontianak that the *Commerce* had indeed been captured by a Rajah of Sarawak, with the help of pirates from Sambas. The Rajah had offered to sell the boat to the Sultan of Pontianak. On his refusal to buy her, the Rajah looted the cargo and sent the crew to be sold as slaves at Brunei, with the exception of the second mate, who was put to death. Burn discovered that several other missing ships had suffered a like fate. While he was already at Pontianak the *Malacca*, with a cargo of tin valued at 14,000 Spanish dollars, was captured and plundered by boats belonging to the Sultan of Sambas himself. Sambas was clearly the headquarters of a flourishing pirate connection and must be brought under control.

34

It was not so easy. When, in October 1812, a small naval expedition was ordered to sail up the Sambas river and destroy the town completely, it was unexpectedly attacked near the river mouth by pirates sheltering there and was forced ignominiously to retire. A stronger force sent in June 1813 was more effective. The town was occupied and the Sultan captured and deposed, though the chief pirate leader, Pangiran Anom, escaped into the interior. Raffles followed up the success by administrative measures. In May he had appointed an agent, John Hunt, to Pontianak. In August he sent Captain Robert Garnham as a special commissioner to visit the west and north coasts of Borneo. Garnham proceeded first to Sambas, where he offered to restore the cowed Sultan to his throne on condition that he accepted a British Resident to advise him. He then sailed to Sarawak, where he sent a letter to the Rajah, warning him that unless he amended his ways Sarawak would suffer the same fate as Sambas, and on to Brunei, where the Sultan hastened to show him all deference. Raffles had decided that, except for local coastal shipping, all trade to and from Borneo must be restricted to the three ports of Bandjermasin, Pontianak and Brunei, ports access to which he hoped to be able to police sufficiently well to deter piracy. Part of Garnham's task was to make this policy known to the Sultans. The Sultans who ruled the three ports were well pleased; Garnham met with nothing but smiles at Brunei, while Hunt at Pontianak and Hare at Bandjermasin met with similar local approval. The Sultan of Sambas was in no position to protest. When Garnham returned there from Brunei he found the Sultan ready to accept British suzerainty and to receive a Resident. A treaty was signed giving the Lieutenant-Governor in Java the right to intervene in all fiscal matters in Sambas and, if he wished, to regulate the succession to its throne.[1]

By the end of 1813 Raffles had thus established British authority round all the coasts of Borneo except for the far north-east. He knew that neither the East India Company nor the British Government were enthusiastic about his schemes. He foresaw that it was possible that Java might be returned to the Dutch. But he believed that his arrangements in Borneo would survive and would provide Britain with the nucleus for a commercial empire in the archipelago. Unfortunately his friend, Lord Minto, retired from India in 1813 and was succeeded as Governor-General by a man in closer touch with the Company's and the Government's sentiments, Lord Moira. Lord Moira was alarmed by Raffles's schemes; and when he heard of his Borneo policy he at once wrote to tell him to hold his hand till further instructions arrived. Raffles answered with a memorandum pointing out the necessity for distinguishing between the states that had been dependent on the Dutch at the time of the British occupation of Java and those with which the British had made their own treaties. The latter should not be affected by any retrocession of territory to the Dutch. In reply Lord Moira sent a long despatch criticising the whole of Raffles's policy. If the East India Company were to retain Java, he wrote, there would be no need to indulge in expensive operations in Borneo. If Java were to be returned to the Dutch, then British settlements in Borneo would merely serve to cause friction and could hardly be maintained in the face of Dutch hostility. He did not believe, he added, that the Bornean princes really wanted British protection, and it would cost far too much, in blood as well as in money, to make the protection effective. He would allow the Bandjermasin settlement to be carried on, but the rest must be abandoned. Moreover, the attempt to restrict commerce was illegal and the Government in Java did not possess the means to enforce it. The blockade must be lifted at once. Raffles was forced to obey these orders, which arrived, to his bitterness, at a moment when he could have intervened and set up, he thought, a satisfactory administration at Sambas. The Sultan there had just died, and the Regents were clamouring for a British Resident to take charge. When none was forthcoming the pirate Pangiran Anom was elected Sultan, and Raffles felt obliged to give his approval. Anom was, at least, the most capable of the Sambas princes; but it proved too much to expect him to give up all his old habits.[1]

Lord Moira was only echoing opinions held in London. The East India Company had never been enthusiastic about the occupation of Java and had only approved of it for fear lest the French should establish themselves there and thence threaten India itself. The French were defeated now and the danger was over. Raffles's grandiose schemes might perhaps produce a magnificent profit in the far distant future, but for the moment they were extremely expensive and might well give rise to a number of unsuspected complications. The Company had quite enough to do in the Indian sub-continent to wish to avoid commitments further to the East, particularly in a land such as Borneo in which they had had previous unhappy experiences. The British Government shared the Company's views, but for a different reason. It had decided that a strong Holland was necessary in Europe to safeguard against any further French aggression. Not only were the unwilling Belgians joined to the new Kingdom of the Netherlands, but also some of the former Dutch colonies must be given to it, to ensure its economic welfare. The British had done well out of the Dutch during the late wars. Cape Colony in South Africa, Ceylon, Malacca and parts of Sumatra and the Dutch towns on the Malabar Coast in Asia and Guiana and some islands in the Caribbean had been occupied, as well as Java. South Africa and Ceylon were strategically desirable; the Royal Navy set great store on the harbours at Capetown and Trincomalee. The West Indian sugar-merchants lobbied to retain the greater part of Guiana. The Malabar towns would help to round off the East India Company's mainland possessions; and the British were now well established at Malacca and at Bencoelen in Sumatra. But no one in London was interested in Java. When a treaty between Britain and the Netherlands was signed in August 1814, the Dutch were given back all the colonies that they had held in 1803, with the exception of Cape Colony and Demararaland. This meant that Java, the Moluccas and their other Indonesian possessions passed again to them. Nothing was said about Borneo. When Raffles managed at last to have attention drawn to the settlement at Bandjermasin, of which Lord Moira had approved, it was discovered that no one knew about it at the time that the Convention with the Dutch was signed. Its continued existence could not therefore be upheld.[1]

To Raffles, reduced now to the position of Lieutenant-Governor at Bencoelen, the collapse of his policy was a bitter blow. It was not unexpected; but he had thought that he would at least salvage Borneo from the wreckage. He had not had time to establish agencies at Brunei or Sambas. His agent at Pontianak was obliged to retire. And now Bandjermasin had to be abandoned. Raffles might have grieved less had he realised the peculiar character of Alexander Hare, whom he had sent there. For all his initial energy Hare had not been able to make a success either of the Company's colony or of his own private dominion. The problem was labour. To carry out his schemes and to work his lands he needed a larger supply of coolies than the Sultan of Bandjermasin could provide. The population there was not large; the local Malays were indolent, easy-going men who considered coolie work to be beneath their dignity, while the Dyaks from the interior were unsuited to it. Hare had visited Java at the end of 1812 to secure Raffles's help in recruiting a labour force there. Raffles was sympathetic; and a series of ordinances passed in 1813 invited and then compelled first ex-soldiers, then native-born Javanese to cross to Borneo to work on Hare's plantations. Bandjermasin was further declared to be a convict settlement to which convicts guilty of minor offences could be sent; while women were abducted by Hare's agents to provide wives for the settlers. Though in all more than three thousand labourers of all sorts, mainly criminal, were transhipped to Borneo, they did not form an efficient force; nor was the Sultan of Bandjermasin pleased with the introduction of so many undesirable persons, who, he soon complained, were by their excesses driving his subjects from their homes.

Even had Hare been an experienced planter or a good administrator, his task would have been difficult. He was neither. For all his bright ideas and his skill at persuasion, he was bored by routine work. He saw himself as an oriental potentate and he enjoyed the pleasures which accompanied that role. His energy was devoted to building himself a palace and filling it with slaves and a luscious harem. 'His greatest feature,' wrote his second-in-command, John Clunies-Ross, 'was his licentiousness in regard to all bodily indulgences.' By 1816 both the British factory at Bandjermasin and Hare's own private dominions were in chaos. Little or no pepper was being produced; no accounts were kept; labourers were deserting; the Sultan was, with reason, losing patience. Hare himself found it convenient to spend most of his time holidaying in Java, leaving the settlement to be administered by a triumvirate consisting of his brother John, a man of no ability, John Clunies-Ross, who was loyal but disillusioned, and van de Wahl, whom the others suspected of a corrupt understanding with the Sultan's ministers and who was soon dismissed.

It was only in 1816 that a Commission arrived from the Netherlands to receive back Java from the British. It considered that the Convention which restored to the Dutch all the possessions that they had held in 1803 naturally applied to the Bandjermasin district. The English East India Company had no desire to retain a factory which showed no signs of ever making a profit and were indifferent to its fate. But Raffles's successor in Java, John Fendall, whose duty it was to hand over Java to the Dutch, was worried by the legal problem. The Treaty of 1812 with the Sultan promised him protection against any foreign power, and it had been made in the clear belief that the Dutch had voluntarily withdrawn from Java and neither the Sultan nor the British would be affected by whatever might happen in the future to Java. Moreover disreputable though Hare might be, he had certain rights. The Convention with the Dutch specifically declared that the property of individual persons who chose to remain in transferred territories was not to be touched. Fendall would not hand over Bandjermasin till he knew what the position of Hare's concessions then would be. To add to the complication, the Sultan now suddenly announced that, while he would guarantee the protection of European traders, he wanted the protection of neither the British nor the Dutch. He would govern his country himself. Fendall, who received no instructions from the East India Company about the problem, reported wearily that the retention of the British settlement seemed as impracticable as its transfer to the Dutch. The Dutch on their side, in view of the Sultan's attitude, wanted to negotiate with the British rather than with the Sultan.

Fendall decided to withdraw British forces from the settlement, leaving the Dutch to make what terms they chose with the Sultan. Informing the Dutch Commissioners of his action he sent a Commission of his own to Bandjermasin to supervise the withdrawal and to enquire into Hare's position. The three Commissioners whom he appointed arrived at the factory in September 1816. Hare made it no easier for them by remaining in Java, and his brother John could produce no accounts nor any other records. The Sultan meanwhile decided that he had lost his copy of his agreement with Hare. Eventually the Commission wound up the factory; but the only method of disposing of the labourers imported from Java was to send them back. The Sultan refused to keep them in his lands. It was impracticable to try to send them to Penang or Bengal, where there were penal settlements. So, whether ex-convicts or free—and in the absence of any records kept by Hare it was impossible to distinguish between them—they were shipped to Java, where they caused immense legal and administrative problems for the incoming Dutch Government. The Sultan then changed his mind about foreign protection and made a new treaty with the Dutch. The lands formerly ceded to the British were now ceded to the Dutch, with large concessions for exploiting minerals and timber; the Sultan would appoint his ministers only with Dutch approval and would have no diplomatic dealings with any other foreign power nor grant concessions to foreign traders; and the Dutch would control the succession to the throne. In return the Dutch would guarantee the Sultan against all his enemies, native or foreign, and the Sultan would have complete autonomy over his own subjects. It was a system of indirect rule, which committed the Dutch to the Sultan as much as the Sultan to the Dutch; and it satisfied both parties. Nor did the British authorities object.

Hare, however, objected strongly. But the Sultan had 'lost' his copy of his agreement with Hare; and the East India Company, thankful to be done with Bandjermasin, gave him no support. He crossed to Borneo to tell Clunies-Ross to resist by force any attempt to eject him from his headquarters there at Moloeko, then returned to Java to pester the Dutch, demanding compensation in the form of estates in Java and, when that failed, to petition the Company's government in India to uphold his legal rights. Meanwhile Clunies-Ross prepared to meet by force any attempt that the Dutch might make to take over Moloeko. All Hare's manœuvres were in vain. The Dutch authorities in Java pronounced, a little arbitrarily, that he had no legal claim to his concession, and Lord Moira wrote from India that he would do nothing in favour of a man 'whom we regard as a delinquent'. Hare's reputation and record had thoroughly prejudiced his cause. The East India Company in London subsequently noted in a minute that Hare had some right to compensation. But nothing was done. Clunies-Ross, after some months, retired from Moloeko, leaving it to the Dutch, and sought a better future elsewhere; he ended his life as 'King' of the Cocos Islands. Hare remained in Java, petitioning and agitating, till 1820, when the Dutch expelled him. Some years later he joined Clunies-Ross in the Cocos Islands, but quarrelled with him there over their possession and was forced to leave in 1831. He died in Sumatra in 1833. He was the first Englishman to become a 'White Rajah'; but his experiences were not encouraging.[1]

Though there was official accord in Bandjermasin, relations between the British and the returning Dutch in Indonesia were not smooth. Raffles remained a bugbear to the latter; and his purchase of the island of Singapore in 1819 seriously alarmed them. Spheres of influence seemed everywhere to overlap. Clashes were averted only because the two home governments of Britain and the Netherlands were eager to remain on good terms. A treaty was eventually signed in London in 1824, which gave Britain the Malayan mainland and the Netherlands Sumatra and all the islands 'south of the Straits of Singapore'. The wording was ambiguous; did it refer only to the small archipelago just south of the Straits, or to all the islands? Nearly a half of Borneo lay north of Singapore. Were the British free to colonise northern Borneo? No one knew. Neither the British nor the Dutch plenipotentiaries were anxious to mention Borneo, for differing reasons. They left the inter-pretation of the clause for the future to decide.[1]

Stamford Raffles, the chief architect of the scheme for a British Borneo, remained as Lieutenant-Governor of Bencoelen till 1824. He was a disappointed man. Even his greatest and most lasting achievement, the foundation of a city that was soon to be the trading centre of south-eastern Asia, seemed at first likely to fail. When finally he sailed for home, most of his possessions and the notes that he had carefully collected were destroyed when his ship caught fire. But he never forgot his interest in Borneo. Till his premature death, four years after his retirement, he continued to write of the riches and possibilities of the huge island; and his books found eager readers. Amongst them was a man twenty-two years his junior called James Brooke.

BOOK II
RAJAH JAMES

CHAPTER I

PREPARATION

James Brooke was born on 29 April 1803, at Secrore, in the suburbs of Benares. His father, Thomas Brooke, was a civilian in the East India Company's service, who had risen to be judge of the High Court at Benares. His mother, Anna Maria Stuart, had left her native Scotland as a girl, on her parents' death, to join her brother James in India, where he too worked for the Company. There she met Mr Brooke, who was a childless widower at the time, and married him. They were very happy together; and six children were born to them, Henry, Harriet, Emma, Anna, James and Margaret.

The Brookes claimed descent from the great West-country family of Broke, whose estates had passed long since by inheritance into the house of Warwick. They had been in fact for some generations a family based on London; and the ancestor of whom they were proudest was Sir Thomas Vyner, Lord Mayor of London in 1654, when he entertained Oliver Cromwell at the Guildhall. Elizabeth Collet, Mr Brooke's paternal grandmother, was descended from Sir Thomas's daughter. Thomas Brooke himself was a tall, handsome man, with an old-fashioned courtly manner, well-read and a good talker, though he did not strike his contemporaries as being particularly clever. Anna Maria, his wife, was also good-looking, with blue eyes and a beautiful fair complexion, quiet and shy in her ways, always dressed in simple but expensive clothes. Her children were devoted to her. Of the children, Henry died young in India, as a cadet in the Company's armed forces, and Harriet and Anna died as girls in England. Emma married in 1822 the Reverend Charles Johnson, vicar of White Lackington in Somerset, and Margaret a few years later the Reverend Anthony Savage.[1]

James Brooke was kept by his parents with them in India till he reached the age of twelve. It was usual for British children in the tropics to be sent home at an earlier age, as both health and education were supposed to suffer from too long a sojourn in the East. In James's case neither his health nor his education seem to have been adversely affected; and it is likely that his prolonged Indian childhood gave him a sense that his life belonged to the East. However, in 1815, with the Napoleonic

Wars ended, his parents decided that he needed the discipline of an English school. He was sent to England, to the care of his paternal grandmother at Reigate; but as his guardian his father nominated an old friend, Mr Charles Kegan of Bath. His holidays were to be spent between the two households. At Bath James was very happy. Mr Kegan lived with a number of relatives, including three young nieces with whom James made close friends. He acquired a liking for the West Country which he never lost and which was enhanced when his sister Emma married and settled in Somerset. Old Mrs Brooke's house at Reigate was more austere. Mrs Brooke believed in charity; and James was frequently required to forgo his pudding in order that it might be sent round to an indigent neighbour. He was always allowed his meat course, which was considered necessary for a growing boy; and if the pudding were very attractive he sometimes ate it himself, but never without an abiding sense of guilt.

The discomforts caused by his grandmother's philanthropy were as nothing to those that he experienced at school. The great advantage of the education traditionally given to the British Upper Classes is that anyone who has been through it knows that he is unlikely ever to be so miserably uncomfortable again. James Brooke did not properly appreciate this benefit when he was sent to Norwich Grammar School. Like most boys he was only ready to work on the subjects that interested him. He studied drawing with some enthusiasm; the master was no lesser artist than 'Old Crome'. But in more academic branches of learning he was unsatisfactory; and the Headmaster, Mr Valpy, proud as he was of his pupil in later years, had little good to say of him at the time. But James's schooldays were not wasted. The boys were allowed to go sailing on the River Wensum; and there he learnt how to handle a boat. His force of character impressed the other boys, to whom he seemed a born leader, while his masters were struck by his refusal to tell lies. But, though he made several lifelong friends there, he was not happy, and when, after he had been there for two years, his best friend, George Western, left to go to sea, he decided to run away. A schoolfellow lent him money, and he made his way by coach to Reigate. But he did not dare to enter his grandmother's house, till a servant saw him and told the old lady. She took him in and summoned Mr Kegan from Bath. He arrived in haste and dragged James back to Norwich. But Mr Valpy had had enough of him. James returned happily with Mr Kegan to Bath and remained there till his parents came back from

India a few months later, to settle in Bath on their retirement. James never received any further formal schooling. A daily tutor was tried, but as James had no respect for him he resigned and was not replaced. As James belonged to a family where reading and other civilised pursuits were encouraged, his general education did not greatly suffer.[1]

It had been decided that James should make his career, like his brother Henry, in the armed forces of the East India Company. His Ensign's commission in the Bengal Army was dated 11 May 1819, and a few months later, at the age of sixteen and a half, he set sail for India. He was a satisfactory cadet. Two years later, on 2 November 1821, he received his lieutenancy. He wished to be a cavalry officer. Instead, he was appointed, in May 1822, Sub-Assistant Commissary-General. He disliked the job and was ill-suited for it. A report on his services, while praising his ability, expresses the hope that he will 'receive an early impression of the necessity for steadiness and decision'. He was soon back with the cavalry where, on his own suggestion, he was employed in training a body of volunteer Indian horsemen, to be used for scouting ahead of the main army. The First Burmese War had broken out in March 1824. By the following January James Brooke's troops were ready for action. On 25 January he led them in a charge against the Burmese at a battle near Rungpore in Assam. It was completely successful and James was mentioned in despatches for 'most conspicuous conduct'.

Two days later James and his troops were again in action against the retreating enemy. Once again his charge was successful; but in the course of it he was wounded by a bullet that entered his lung. He fell from his horse and was left on the field for dead. It was only after the battle was over that his colonel recovered his body and found it still alive. James was conveyed to Calcutta, where he lay for some time in hospital. The doctors then insisted that he should be sent home to England for several months' furlough. He was to receive a pension of £70 a year for life.

James arrived at Bath in the summer of 1825 and seemed to be making a good recovery. But early in 1826 his wound broke out again, and he was seriously ill. It was his parents' devoted nursing that pulled him through. The bullet, which had been left in his body, was now extracted from his spine, and was thenceforward kept by his mother as a relic in a glass case on her mantelshelf.[2]

This time his recovery was slow; and his leave was extended till the beginning of 1830. He spent his long convalescence mainly in his parents' house at Bath, reading all that he could find about the East and, in particular, the works of Raffles, and letting his imagination dwell on the great islands that lay beyond the Indian sub-continent. In July 1829, he set sail from London to return to India. But the vessel in which he was passenger, the *Carn Brae*, was wrecked off the Isle of Wight. No lives were lost, but all James's possessions sank with the ship, and the shock and the exposure which he suffered set back his health. The Directors of the East India Company extended his leave for another six months, but warned him that if he did not report for duty in India by 30 July 1830, he would be dismissed from the Service. By Act of Parliament no official of the Company was allowed to be for more than five years absent from his post. Owing to continuous storms early in 1830, when James had planned to sail, no East Indiaman left England. It was not till March that he was able to set out, in the *Castle Huntley*. He had nearly five months in which to reach Bengal, which, in ordinary circumstances, should suffice. But once again the weather intervened. The *Castle Huntley* was first delayed by contrary winds, then becalmed. It was not till 18 July that she reached Madras. In twelve days' time James had to report to Calcutta. The journey by land was impracticable and he soon discovered that no boat was sailing for Calcutta within the time-limit. He had announced his arrival at Madras to the Adjutant-General's office there. Now he asked to be given temporary employment there till he could continue his journey, so that he could be said to have returned to the Company's service in time. He met with a brusque refusal. He was angry and his pride was hurt. Rather than await his dismissal he wrote to Calcutta resigning his commission.

He need not have been so precipitate. His father had been worried by the slow departure from England of the *Castle Huntley*, and he had secured a ruling from the Board of Directors in London that it would be sufficient if James reached Indian soil before the five years were up. An official message was sent to Calcutta ordering Lieutenant Brooke's retention in the service so long as he had complied with this condition. Had he known of this we may presume that he would not have sent in his resignation. But the alacrity with which he made his decision and the lack of regret that accompanied it suggest that he no longer felt in great sympathy with the Company. His reading and his thinking during the long years of convalescence inclined him to dislike its methods and its aims. He had his own ideas about the East.

If Mr Thomas Brooke was worried by the waste of his efforts and by his son's impulsiveness, he never showed it; James never received a word of reproach. James meanwhile booked his passage back to England in the *Castle Huntley*. He liked the ship, and he had friends on board. She was going on to China before returning westward; he would therefore see more of the Eastern World. At the end of August he was at Penang, in September at Singapore, where the *Castle Huntley* remained snugly in the harbour while two typhoons passed by. Early in October he reached Canton, where he remained till the end of the year. He suffered there from a long and severe attack of influenza, during which he was carefully nursed by the surgeon on board the *Castle Huntley*, Mr Cruikshank, already one of his closest friends. From Canton the *Castle Huntley* seems to have sailed straight for England, only pausing to water off the coast of Sumatra and again at St Helena. By the late spring of 1831 James was back with his family at Bath.[1]

James Brooke was an indefatigable and uninhibited letter and journal writer, ready to put down all his passing thoughts on to paper for anyone who chose to see. His frankness was to cause him trouble in years to come. This Eastern voyage was fully described in long letters to his mother and his sister, most of which have survived. They are a curious medley, containing accounts of juvenile pranks and vivid pictures of scenery and of natural phenomena, and of the customs of the countries which he visited. There are passages of philosophical and theological reflection; a reading of the Fourth Gospel leads him to express his doubts about the doctrine of the Trinity; elsewhere he inveighs against religious intolerance. But their most interesting feature is the emergence of his views on Eastern politics. His increasing dislike of the East India Company was perhaps due as much to his admiration of Raffles as to his own experiences; he could not forgive it for its failure to support his hero. But he had his own observations to make. He believed that the Company was neglecting the development of India in favour of the quicker profits to be obtained from the China trade. He was shocked by the humiliations imposed by the Chinese authorities on the Company's merchants in Canton, to which they submitted in the interests of money-making. They should not be so careless of their country's prestige. But this chauvinism was tempered by a sensitive regard for the welfare of the native peoples. Too much association with Europeans did them, he thought, nothing but harm; he had himself remarked in India that the English-speaking Indians were the most unreliable and corrupt. He had no illusions about the native character. The Malays were given the epithet of treacherous, the Hindostanis lazy. He was not attracted by the Chinese. They seemed to him ugly and ungainly, with complexions like corpses; but he wrote admiringly of their industry and their respect for education. But, except for his hatred for John Company and its stifling and short-sighted monopoly, he was not blind to the advantages of commerce. Penang, he thought, should be colonised by independent European planters and traders; it was suitable both because of its climate and because there was only a tiny indigenous population. If Europeans would not settle there, then the land should be parcelled out among industrious orientals. He was always ready to modify his prejudices. After talking with an American missionary, Mr Abeel, he decided that missions guided by Christian precepts 'cannot possibly do any harm, and he must be a heathen who denies the good that might result'.[1]

The years that followed his return to England dragged slowly. His family welcomed him warmly, and his father kept him well supplied with money. But he yearned to return to the East or at least to the sea. He had had long discussions about the future with his friends on the *Castle Huntley*, with Cruikshank the surgeon, James Templar the mate, Harry Wright, Kennedy, whom he visited in Ireland, and a younger boy, Stonhouse, who saddened him by refusing to write to him but whom he visited happily in Scotland. To them he confided his ambition to buy a schooner and go trading in her to some far part of the world. But a schooner cost money and James had no capital. Nor was his father sympathetic. Gentlemen did not go in for trade. To resign a commission in the Indian Army to become the captain of a merchant ship was not, he thought, a move in the right direction. James continued to make plans about his ship. He continued to read about the East, and wrote and published a small pamphlet urging the British Government to be tougher in its dealings with the Dutch. He played with politics and published another pamphlet, anonymously, showing that mere political reform would not be enough to still the present discontents. His only recreation was hunting. He seems to have toyed with the idea of marriage with the daughter of a Bath clergyman, an intimate friend of his sister Margaret, but nothing came of it. About the same time he seems to have met for the first time another young lady who was to be of far greater moment to him in the future, Miss Angela Burdett-Coutts, eleven years his junior and not yet the great heiress that she was to become. She never forgot the impression that he made on her.[2]

In February 1834, James Brooke heard of a promising brig going fairly cheap at Liverpool. He was over thirty; if he were to live the life of adventure that he had planned, he must begin. He wrote from London to his father asking for permission and the money to buy her. Thomas Brooke was old and ill. He disliked the whole idea and at first refused to help his son, but on Mrs Brooke's intervention he yielded. The *Findlay* 'a rakish slaver-brig, 290 tons burden', as James described her, was bought and was filled with a miscellaneous cargo suitable for the Far Eastern market. James persuaded some of his friends from the *Castle Huntley* to join him. Kennedy became Captain and Harry Wright mate. A crew was engaged at Liverpool, and James himself sailed as supercargo.

The voyage was an utter fiasco. They set sail from Liverpool on 6 May 1834. Within a few days James had quarrelled violently with Kennedy. He never was very good at controlling his temper, and he was shocked by the brutal discipline that Kennedy tried to impose on the crew. When the East was reached their merchandise proved difficult to sell. Eventually, at Macao, he sold the brig and the remaining cargo at a loss, paid off Kennedy as handsomely as he could, and himself returned home. The experience had been costly and humiliating, but it was not wasted. James admitted to his friends and to himself that he had been foolish. Another time, he decided, he would have a smaller boat and no cargo, and would be himself in sole control. But it meant another year of waiting. Thomas Brooke was a dying man. Even had he been willing to put up more money his son could not go far away from him at present. James consoled himself by buying a small yacht of 17 tons, the *Eliza*, and cruising in her along the south coast of England, whenever he felt that he could leave his father's side. The cruises were useful in increasing his knowledge of seamanship.[1]

Thomas Brooke died in December 1835. He left his widow a comfortable jointure and to each of his three surviving children the sum of £30,000. James genuinely grieved for him, but the inheritance came at a timely moment. With his mother and sisters amply provided for, James now had money to devote entirely to his own ventures.[2]

He did not wait long before using it. In March 1836, he wrote to Cruikshank to say that he was negotiating for a schooner of 142 tons, called the *Royalist*. Within a month the purchase was concluded. James decided to try her out on a voyage round the Mediterranean. In September he sailed for Gibraltar, with Harry Wright as mate and a temporary crew, taking with him for company his 15-year-old nephew, John Brooke Johnson, his sister Emma's eldest son. They spent the winter and spring penetrating as far as Smyrna and calling in at ports along the North African coast, returning to England in June. He was well satisfied with the ship's performance, and prepared for a longer journey to the Further East.[1]

The preparations were not hurried. Early in 1838 James settled at Greenwich, to be in closer touch with London. He had recently read a book written by the traveller George Windsor Earl on his journey round the coasts of Borneo in 1834. He was much impressed by it; and he remembered and re-read the enthusiastic articles that Raffles had written about the island. Borneo gradually emerged in his mind as his main objective. Having decided on it he set to work to collect all the relevant information that he could find. He met and talked with Earl. He consulted the Admiralty and the British Museum, and found both very helpful, though no one seemed to know very much about the subject. As he was planning large schemes for the future, it would be wise to arouse public interest. He therefore wrote a prospectus of his intentions, designed to procure him, if need be, political and financial support for the future. A summary of the prospectus was published in the *Athenaeum* on 13 October 1838.[2]

It was a wordy but not ineffectual document. James Brooke begins with a brief account of the decay in conditions in the Malay archipelago in recent centuries. He praises Raffles and laments that his policy was not supported. He harshly criticises the Dutch administration, which he considers oppressive, selfish and disastrous. 'We are very certain that the policy of the Dutch has, at the present day, reduced this "Eden of the Eastern Wave" to a state of anarchy and confusion, as repugnant to humanity as it is to commercial prosperity.' That they dominate the archipelago is due to British 'vacillation and weakness' since the removal of Raffles. He then discusses the subjects of Territorial Possession and Commercial Prosperity; which, he says, are inseparable, Raffles having pronounced that a commercial settlement without territory cannot succeed. Territorial possession facilitates administration and breaks down trade barriers; but 'any government instituted for the purpose must be directed to the advancement of the native interests and the development of native resources, rather than by a flood of European colonization to aim at possession only, without reference to the indefeasible rights of the Aborigines'.

His own particular aim would be to inspect Malludu Bay (now called Marudu Bay) in the extreme north-east of Borneo. Its advantages were, he claimed, that it was already a British possession, having been given to the East India Company by the Sultan of Sulu; that there were no great Malay or Bugis settlements nearby; that probably direct intercourse could be made from there into the Dyak interior; that it was well placed with regard to China; and that it formed the western (*sic*) limit of the archipelago. He then discussed the whole position of the archipelago from a broad geo-political viewpoint. The British held Singapore. They had founded a settlement at Port Essington (on the north Australian coast) at the eastern limit of the archipelago; though he would have preferred them to have purchased Timor from the Portuguese, as a better placed Eastern stronghold; and, for further protection to the north, he recommended the purchase of Leuconia (Luzon in the Philippines) from the Spaniards. Both Spain and Portugal would, he thought, be ready to sell or exchange the territories. Meanwhile he would sail to Malludu Bay and make his way up one of the rivers that must debouch there, to discover the great lake of 'Keeny Balloo', of which he had heard, and to open up friendly relations with the Dyaks, and incidentally to study the flora, fauna and mineral resources of the district. He would then proceed to the island of Celebes, the home of the Bugis, who were the great traders of the archipelago, to see if a settlement could be founded there, in an area to which the Dutch had not yet penetrated, and thence sail on to New Guinea, the Aru Islands and Port Essington. He pointed out that his ship, the *Royalist*, belonged to the Royal Yacht Squadron and was therefore entitled to the treatment given to a ship of the Royal Navy.

In an eloquent passage he asked why the Mission Societies in Britain concentrated so exclusively on Africa. Were there no deserving and benighted natives in the East? It is doubtful how much sympathy he had himself with mission-work; his own religious views caused distress to his lady friends at Bath. But he knew that the nineteenth-century British would always show interest and provide money for mission-work, and that might be useful in days to come.

It was an impressive tract. Many of its details were inaccurate. The British claim to North Borneo was vague, to say the least; and Marudu Bay was the chief rendezvous of the Illanun pirates. Its rivers are not navigable and there is no lake at Kina Balu, only the highest mountain in the Indonesian archipelago. Nor were Spain and Portugal likely to part lightly with old-established possessions. But there was no one in London who was better informed than James Brooke. His project roused considerable interest there; and the Dutch Legation hastily sent a copy across to The Hague, to warn the authorities of this dangerous adventurer.[1]

The *Royalist* was due to sail for the East in September 1838. But in August James had a severe bout of illness. In September as the ship was sailing round to the Thames for her final victualling a Dutch vessel ran into her and damaged her; and the Captain's behaviour was so panic-stricken that he had to be dismissed. Finally, towards the end of October, James was satisfied that all was ready. He liked his new captain and his crew. He had found a surveyor to accompany him who had served as such with Captain Fitzroy in South American waters. He was amply stocked with victuals, with goods for barter or presents and with scientific instruments. *Royalist* sailed from London on Thursday, 26 October. He himself prepared to board her at Southampton. But a tremendous gale blew up over the weekend. *Royalist* rode it out in the Downs, but had to put into Ramsgate for repairs. As the weather continued wild, James postponed his departure again. In November he was in London. Early in December *Royalist* sailed slowly down the south coast. James joined her at Devonport; and on 16 December she stood out to sea.[2]

The voyage to Singapore took over five months. Two weeks were spent at Rio de Janeiro and two at Cape Town. It was only at the end of May 1839 that *Royalist* passed through the Straits of Sunda and Banka, and entered the harbour at Singapore. During these months James was able to observe his crew. There were nineteen of them. James had approved of his captain, David Irons, who recognised his authority without question and who shared his hatred of overstrict discipline, but Irons had asked to be relieved of his command at Cape Town. The first mate, Colin Hart, became captain in his place. Hart was an old friend from the *Findlay*, rather a fool, but willing and good-tempered. Andrew Murray, the surveyor, made a good impression at first, as a keen and indefatigable worker; but he indulged in secret drinking and by the end of the voyage was detested by his shipmates for offensiveness when drunk. William Williams, the surgeon and naturalist, was the best educated of the company. But he was dreamy and unreliable, given to self-pity and lacking in stamina. He was marked out for dismissal at Singapore. With the others James was satisfied. James himself took the sights and worked in with his men; but much of his time was spent in reading. He had brought with him all the books on the East that he could muster, as well as other literature. He was particularly impressed by *Oliver Twist*, which had appeared shortly before he left London.

Royalist received a hospitable welcome at Singapore. James had been unwell during the later stages of the voyage; and the ship was in need of repairs. Both were soon restored. Information had already reached Singapore of the aims of the expedition; and the Singapore merchants and their ladies were delighted to entertain the good-looking and well-mannered adventurer. The Governor, Mr Bonham, interested himself in the whole venture and was ready with advice and with information that James had not been able to obtain in London. James listened to him and to anyone else who could tell him about Borneo. He spent nine weeks in Singapore, studying the island and its Chinese and Malay inhabitants; but he was impatient to go on further. On 27 July, with his health fully recovered and with a new doctor, a Dane called Westermann, and a young interpreter called Williamson, who was half-Malay, he set sail again, not for Marudu Bay, but for the river Sarawak, some six hundred miles to the south-west, nearer to Singapore.[1]

THE FOUNDING OF THE RAJ

The province of Sarawak formed the westernmost portion of the territory that remained to the Sultans of Brunei. It had been conquered some two centuries previously and valued because of its gold and antimony mines. The Sultanate had sadly declined since the days of the conqueror, Sultan Hasan, the ninth of the dynasty, who in the early seventeenth century ruled the whole island of Borneo and whose influence extended from the Philippines in the north to Java in the south. Soon after his death the other Sultans of the islands, as well as the Sultan of Sulu, regained full independence; and Hasan's grandson, Muhudin, was obliged to cede the northern tip of Borneo to Sulu, in payment for help in a civil war. The decadence was rapid throughout the eighteenth century. By Muslim custom a throne passes on the death of a ruler not to his eldest son but to the eldest male member of the dynasty. A wise sovereign, such as most of the Ottoman Sultans, guarded against this by putting to death all his brothers and their sons, thus leaving his own eldest son as his undoubted heir. In Malayan lands the late ruler's eldest son was sometimes strongly enough entrenched to seize the throne and eliminate his rivals; but usually the princes and their followers decided the accession by negotiation and intrigue and one or two timely murders.

The throne of Brunei had known many such experiences. In 1839, when James Brooke set sail from Singapore, the Sultan was Omar Ali Saifuddin, a man of about fifty, who was considered slightly weak in the head. His father, Jemal ul-Alam, had been the twentieth Sultan of the dynasty, his maternal grandfather, Khanz ul-Alam, who was also his paternal great-uncle, the twenty-first. He had been destined to succeed his grandfather; but his maternal uncle, Mohammed Alam, surnamed Api, or Fire, had seized the throne. Api was cruel to the point of madness, and brutal to his nephew, though he spared his life, probably because of his near-imbecility. In 1828 Api's sister, Omar Ali's mother, organised a palace revolt, in which Api was captured and put to death. As he awaited the strangling, the form of death reserved for princes, he bade the onlookers observe to which side his corpse would fall. If it were to the left, it augured ill for Brunei. His body fell to the left.

Omar Ali then succeeded to the throne, but, owing to his mental state and the deformity of a small additional thumb on his right hand, he was never formally invested as sovereign and never was able to use the title of *Iang di Pertuan* (the lord who rules) which designated the ruler of Brunei. He had no control over his relatives, who selected another of his maternal uncles, Hasim, as Rajah Muda, or heir to the throne and regent. Soon after his accession a revolt had broken out in the province of Sarawak against the governor, the Pangiran Makota. In about 1837 the Rajah Muda Hasim moved there in order to bring the province back to its allegiance.[1]

Considering the system of government followed by the Sultan and his advisers, revolt was not surprising. The province of Sarawak was governed by corruption and extortion. The Brunei nobles, when they were not intriguing against each other, joined together to extract money and goods from the weaker indigenous races. The Land Dyaks living in the province were especially liable to this treatment. The local Malay chieftains were traditionally entitled to demand tribute from the Dyaks. But they carried their method of the *serah*, the system of forced trade known in all Malay countries, to an intolerable extreme. All the produce of the Dyak village, whether rice or wax or birds'-nests, had to be offered for sale to the chieftain for whatever price he chose to name. If there was more than he wished, his relatives and any other Malays in the district were able to buy the surplus on the same terms. If the produce was insufficient for the Malays' demands, then the deficit had to be met by selling the children of the village into slavery. The Dyaks were also required to buy whatever the Malays wished to sell. A Malay chieftain would frequently send a bar of iron to a village headman and oblige him to buy it at a ridiculously high price. Nor could a Dyak be sure of keeping his own possessions. If his boat caught the eye of a Malay who coveted it, the Malay would cut a notch in the gunwale as a sign that it was now his, and would insist that it be handed over to him in a few days' time. If meanwhile other Malays also fancied it and cut their notches in it, they would have to be given compensation up to the value of the boat. The Land Dyak population, reduced thus to near starvation, was rapidly declining. Those who could retreated into the hills, to be further from the reach of the extortioners.

The Land Dyaks, with their gentle natures, were ideal victims.

Treatment almost as oppressive was given to the Muruts, living on the Limbang, not far from Brunei itself. Fiercer tribes, such as the Kayans and the Sea Dyaks (or Ibans), were handled differently. They could be sold arms and be encouraged to attack their weaker neighbours, on condition that they gave half of the booty to the Brunei government. It was always possible to extort money from a weak tribe by promising protection from a stronger neighbour and then to permit the attack and obtain half the profit. The passion of the Sea Dyaks and their fellow-tribes for collecting heads made them very amenable to such encouragement. With the Sea Dyaks that method could be extended into a wider field. They were coming in increasing numbers over the watershed of Borneo towards the mouths of the rivers of the north-west coast. They were river-folk, accustomed to handle boats. As they approached the sea they learnt from the Malays of the benefits to be extracted from piracy.[1]

Though James Brooke had omitted to dwell on the matter in his roseate prospectus, piracy was rife in Borneo waters. The Malays had a long piratical tradition. The Brunei Malays lacked the energy now to be active pirates, unlike their cousins of Sulu further to the north. The most notorious and enterprising pirates of the time were the Illanuns, who came from Mindanao in the Southern Philippines and who operated under the patronage of the Sultan of Sulu. They thought nothing of voyages of three or four months' duration, and were ready to operate off the coasts of the Malay peninsula or of Java; and their favourite lair was Marudu Bay, which James had hoped to colonise. They tended to avoid attacking European ships, preferring to victimise Chinese or Bugis traders. But in 1838 there had been a considerable battle off the east Malayan coast, when an East Indiaman, the *Diana*, and a British sloop defeated an Illanun fleet which was attacking a Chinese junk. The praus of the Sea Dyaks were not fitted for such long expeditions. They concentrated on the shipping that passed along the Borneo coast, with the full approval of the Brunei government, to which they gave or sold a large proportion of their captures. As piracy increased, honest trade decreased; there was less and less of a market for the produce of the island. More and more of the tribes therefore deserted agriculture to swell the ranks of the pirates. The tribes settled along the Batang Lupar and its tributaries and the Saribas river were already notorious for their piratical habits. If there was not much foreign shipping around, they would raid the tribes living up other rivers.

Occasionally they would even turn against the Malays. In about 1830 the Saribas Dyaks sacked Katubong, then the chief Malay town on the Sarawak river.[1]

It was in the midst of this chaos that rebellion had broken out in Sarawak. Had the governor Makota been content with exploiting the Land Dyaks in the traditional manner, he might have had no trouble. But his exactions were such that nothing was left for the local Malay chieftains, whom he treated with disdain. The great Malay family of Sarawak which provided all the local officials was proud to claim the same exalted ancestors as the ruling houses of Brunei and Johore. When a *pangiran* exiled from Brunei, called Usop, promised to bring them help from the Sultan of Sambas, its members joined with the desperate Dyaks in organising a revolt, which the Rajah Muda Hasim found himself unable to quell. The rebels were known to be seeking help from the Dutch, through their nominal vassal, the Sultan of Sambas. Hasim knew enough of world politics to see that he could counter that by making friends with the British. His chance came in 1838, when a British ship was wrecked off the mouth of the Sarawak river. Hasim heard of the sailors' plight. He had them brought to him, housed them and fed them well, and at the first opportunity sent them back at his own expense to Singapore.

His action made a good impression in Singapore circles. The sailors told of his humanity and friendliness. It seemed to the Governor, Mr Bonham, that here was an excellent opportunity for using James Brooke's expedition to good purpose. *Royalist* should sail to Sarawak to convey to the Rajah Muda the thanks of the governor and of the Singapore Chamber of Commerce and set about establishing British influence at his court. It is likely that at Singapore Hasim's power and personality were overestimated. He was, it is true, official Regent of the Sultanate of Brunei; but at Brunei itself he wielded no actual authority, and in Sarawak he could neither suppress the rebellion nor even control the governor Makota.[2]

It was with high hopes that James Brooke made a landfall on 1 August, and landed later in the day on the western side of Tanjong Datu, the cape that marks the western boundary of Sarawak. He found that the Admiralty charts placed it some 75 miles out, to the north-east. The weather was stormy. It was not till 5 August that he rounded the cape and anchored off the island of Talang-Talang. Meanwhile he surveyed the coast and amended his charts. At Talang-Talang he met a Malay official sent by Hasim to collect turtles' eggs, who told him that a fleet of Illanun and Dyak pirates had only recently left the bay. On 12 August *Royalist* anchored beneath the peak of Santubong, which dominates the western mouth of the Sarawak river, and a boat was sent to the Rajah's residence, some twenty miles up the river. On the morrow a *pangiran* (a member of the higher nobility) arrived with an official message of welcome from the Rajah. *Royalist* then made her way very slowly up the winding river, sounding as she went and once running on to a rock. On 15 August she anchored in the river off the town of Kuching, giving the Rajah a royal salute of twenty-one guns.[1]

Kuching had recently been founded by the governor Makota, after the sacking of Katubong by the Dyaks. It contained about 800 inhabitants, all Malays except for a handful of Chinese traders. The local Malay nobility still preferred to live at Lida Tanah, further up the river. The greater part of the area of Kuching was occupied by the palaces of the Rajah, of Makota and of their attendant nobles. In the Malay fashion the houses were all built on piles on the mud. The audience hall, where James was received on the morning of his arrival, was a large shed, but sumptuously decorated with hangings. It was a formal audience, consisting of little more than polite gestures and the bestowal of presents on the Rajah. But that evening James called informally on the Rajah, who expressed his liking for the English. But were they, he said, really stronger than the Dutch? Which was the cat and which the mouse? James assured him that Britain was the cat. The Rajah was unwilling then to discuss the topic more precisely. But next morning he paid a less formal visit to *Royalist*; and in the evening James received an unexpected call from Makota, who warned him that the Dutch had designs on Brunei and Sarawak. Would Britain intervene if they came? James answered cautiously. He pointed out that the Dutch never attempted to occupy a country till they had already opened up trading settlements in it. The best thing was not to admit any Dutch traders. Makota also mentioned the excellent openings for British traders. James liked both Hasim and Makota. The former seemed to him a timid, indolent and rather pathetic middle-aged man; the latter was younger, better looking and livelier, intelligent and apparently frank.

Both Hasim and Makota assured James that the rebellion was not really serious. So he then asked permission to visit the countryside. Makota had already brought a Dyak from Lundu to visit him; and he had been fascinated to find out what he could from him of his customs and his vocabulary. He was anxious to see Dyak villages for himself. Permission was granted to him provided that he kept to peaceful areas. On 21 August he set out in *Royalist*'s longboat, *Skimalong*, accompanied by two Malay praus, each with a *pangiran* in command. They sailed down the Moratabas branch of the Sarawak river, then turned eastward as far as the mouth of the river Samarahan, up which they began to proceed. Soon they passed from Malay-inhabited territory into Dyak territory; and the *pangirans* begged him to turn back. They could no longer be responsible for him. He returned to Kuching four days later, having enjoyed the scenery and the fauna but having seen little of human native life. A few days later he set out again, to go up the Lundu river and visit the friendly Dyak chief to whom Makota had introduced him. This expedition interested him far more. At Situngong, eighteen miles up the river, he saw for the first time a Dyak longhouse, 594 feet long, housing a tribe of about 400 persons, the Sibuyoh, who seem to have been Sea Dyaks settled in a Land Dyak district. He was hospitably received and shown over the house, but was a little disconcerted to see thirty dried heads hanging from the rafters. However, on questioning the chief he satisfied himself, probably erroneously, that these were only the heads of enemies, taken in open war. His belief was not shattered by learning that a young man was expected to procure a head before he could marry. James went from there on a journey by foot into the jungle, laming himself in the process. He was much impressed when he came upon a small Chinese settlement founded only a few months before, and saw how excellently it was organised.

On his return to Kuching James was obliged to nurse his foot, but it gave him the opportunity for further talks with Hasim. Towards the end of September he prepared to leave for Singapore. He said good-bye to the Rajah and sailed down the Moratabas. At the mouth he took the *Skimalong* to go as far as the river Sadong, accompanied by two *pangirans*, to visit a professed but friendly pirate chief. He was hospitably received by the chief, who talked candidly about his profession, proof of which was visible in the many skulls, female as well as male, that adorned the longhouse. On his return to *Royalist* he said good-bye to the *pangirans*; but a *panglima*, a military captain, remained with a prau to escort him out to sea. That evening, 28 September, the whole party was suddenly attacked by a group of Saribas pirates. The *panglima* was wounded before *Royalist* could fire her guns, which frightened the raiders away. James sent the wounded *panglima* back to Kuching, whereat he received an urgent invitation to revisit the Rajah Muda. He returned by longboat up the river and was entertained with all his men at a sumptuous banquet. Next morning, after an affectionate farewell from his Malay hosts, who presented him with an orang-utan, he returned to *Royalist* and sailed straight for Singapore.[1]

James was well received by the Singapore merchants. But when he reported on his tour at Government House, Mr Bonham was less enthusiastic. It was one thing to discuss the opening of trade relations, but quite another to mention politics. James had been most incautious; what if the news of his conversations came to Dutch ears? James found, not for the last time, that his enterprise was unappreciated by the official world. He was hurt by the rebuke; but it did not change either his opinions or his intentions.[2]

He hoped to return to Sarawak as soon as the war there should be ended. In the meantime he carried out the second part of his project, a voyage round Celebes. *Royalist* sailed from Singapore on 20 November 1839 and returned on 29 May 1840. James enjoyed the journey. It brought him into contact with many interesting and on the whole friendly peoples and their rulers. He saw much beautiful scenery and many remarkable animals and plants. But he came back somewhat depressed, in poor health and with his funds running low. He decided to pay one more visit to Sarawak, to see his friends, then to sail on to Manila and China, and thence to England.[3]

He arrived back at Kuching on 29 August, feeling dispirited and tired. Hasim and the Malay notables gave him a pleasant welcome. But the rebellion had not been suppressed. On the contrary, rebel Dyak forces were now within thirty miles of the town. There seemed to be no prospect of journeys into the interior, and nothing to do at Kuching. Yet whenever he suggested departure, the Rajah Muda tearfully besought him to stay, declaring that there was no one else whom he could trust. He begged James to visit his army, which lay under Makota's command at Lida Tanah, up the river. His presence would encourage the soldiers and awe the rebels. James was interested, and rowed up to the front, in a boat well laden with provisions. He found an extraordinary army, consisting mainly of Malays and a few Dyaks, far readier to quarrel with each other than attack the enemy, and a small, better disciplined force of Chinese. It sheltered behind stockades, with the enemy stockades within shouting distance. Indeed, the hurling of insults formed the main bellicose activity of both sides. Makota and his commanders eagerly ate James's provisions but paid no attention to his advice. He went back to Sarawak to find one of his crew dead and another dying. Once more he decided to leave. Once more Hasim besought him to stay. How could an English gentleman, he cried, desert him now? Moreover, there were signs that some of the Dyak tribes, weakened by starvation, were willing to come over to the government. James let himself be persuaded and returned to the front, making arrangements to have some of *Royalist's* guns brought up the river. The rebels were alarmed. But Makota's apparent liveliness veiled a determination to do nothing. He and his war council would neither attack the enemy nor allow James to negotiate with them. Once again James returned disillusioned to Kuching.

On 4 November James went to see the Rajah Muda to announce his irrevocable decision to depart. Hasim in his distress made one final appeal; if James would stay, Hasim would invest him with the country of Siniawan and Sarawak, its government and its trade, and suggested that he could have the title of Rajah. James was tempted. He was too prudent to accept the offer outright; but he did not say no, and he agreed to stay.

On his return to the army he found it in a better state. Hasim's brother, Bedruddin, a prince somewhat less indolent than most of his kin, had arrived at the camp. James stipulated that he himself must be given supreme command. He found a loyal helper in Bedruddin, who showed both courage and enterprise. There was more activity; and the main enemy stockade was attacked and would have been captured by surprise had not the leader of the Chinese troops chosen the wrong moment to say his prayers out loud. But, owing to Makota's intrigues, Hasim recalled Bedruddin. There were more delays; the army would do nothing more active than build a new fort. But this gave James his opportunity. The fort, manned by Lundu Dyaks, proved difficult to hold against the enemy; a battle had to be fought to relieve it. The rebels were lured out in front of their stockades and James and his English crew, aided by one Malay, an adventurer from Mindanao called Si Tondo, fell on them. They were surprised and fled into the jungle, deserting their camp, their provisions and their ammunition.

After this rout the rebels sought peace; but they would only negotiate with James. When he guaranteed a safe-conduct, a rebel chief, Matusain, came alone and unarmed to the government camp and began parleys. The rebels offered to surrender if their lives were all spared. James said that he could not promise that; it was for the Rajah Muda to decide. But he would use his influence. With that the rebels were satisfied and laid down their arms. They relied on the Englishman.

The Englishman had greater difficulty with Hasim who, encouraged by Makota, had no wish to spare rebel lives. Once again James had to threaten to leave the country; whereon Hasim gave way. Rebel property was confiscated. Wives and children were brought as hostages to Kuching. But no one was put to death.[1]

Next came the question of Hasim's offer. He was only heir-presumptive and regent of Brunei and had no right to alienate Brunei territory. Authority would have to come from the Sultan; and Hasim began to have doubts. He longed to return to Brunei to make sure of his succession. He was losing influence there owing to his long absence. But his influence would diminish further if he were known to be giving away provinces to Englishmen. Yet he could not leave Sarawak in a state of chaos in the hands of Makota, who would undoubtedly provoke a new rebellion. He prevaricated. The only document that James could extract from him was a permit to settle in Sarawak. When James protested, Hasim said this was just a preliminary move, to get the Sultan used to the idea of an Englishman in Sarawak. James began to lose confidence in Hasim.

He had already lost confidence in Makota. Some *pangirans* had to be discouraged by a display of arms from sacking an ex-rebel village; and James discovered that Makota had urged them on. Makota meanwhile retired on a visit to Brunei, to intrigue in the capital. Hasim, fearful of these intrigues, was all the more anxious to follow him, leaving Sarawak in James's safe hands. His intentions were genuine, but he still hesitated over committing himself. At last James said that he must go to Singapore but that he would return if during his absence a house was built for him and a good consignment of antimony collected, and the document regularising his position was prepared for the Sultan's signature. He would bring with him a cargo of goods to barter for the antimony, hoping thus to open up a regular trade. He had made up his mind to settle in Sarawak as its ruler.[2]

Shortly before he left, news reached Kuching of pirate activities off the coast. *A pangiran* sent to enquire returned with a request from the pirate chief to be allowed to pay a courtesy visit to the Rajah Muda. It was suspected that they aimed to capture *Royalist*; but James, who was curious to see them, encouraged Hasim to welcome them. Soon a fleet of eighteen Illanun vessels swept up the river. They were splendid ships manned by fine, athletic men, whose behaviour was perfectly correct. James was able to inspect some of the vessels and to talk with the leaders. They spoke quite frankly of their pleasure in their profession, though they thought that it was not what it had been in their ancestors' times. They had been cruising for three years, and many of their vessels were boats taken from the Bugis. Their conversation made it clear to James that piracy, even more than misgovernment, was the curse of Borneo. It was not enough for the Europeans to protect their own ships and ports if the whole native trade was left open to pirate attacks.[1]

From February to April 1841 James was at Singapore. He was in need of another ship but could find none for sale except for a schooner, *Swift*, which was not very suitable for cargo and extremely expensive. He felt obliged to buy her and filled her with such goods as he could obtain. Mr Bonham, the governor, seems to have been cordial personally, though still distressed at James's entry into politics.[2]

The Dutch, too, were distressed. In November 1840, Mr Bloem, Assistant-Resident at Sambas, wrote to James to protest at his meddling in Borneo politics. Rumours reached The Hague; but, after making enquiries, the Dutch Minister in London reported that Mr Brooke seemed merely to be working for the Royal Geographical Society.[3]

When he arrived back in Kuching, James found no house built for him, no antimony collected and nothing more done about his title. Makota had returned from Brunei as powerful as ever. James found, too, that an expedition of Sea Dyaks, with the connivance certainly of Makota and probably of Hasim, was preparing to raid the Land Dyak tribes and the Chinese settlements. Furthermore, Si Tundo, his loyal friend who had attacked the rebels with him, had been put to death by Hasim's orders. James had two ships to maintain, and, *Swift's* hold being leaky, he was anxious to unload his goods and dispose of them. His anger roused Hasim to action. A house was built with remarkable speed; some antimony collected, and the raiding expedition was forbidden. This last event so shook Hasim that for days he sulked in his house, pleading illness. But he still wanted James's help; and James still wanted to be governor and saw that patience was required. His prestige was high. Both the Land Dyaks and the Chinese regarded him as their deliverer. The latter impressed him more and more; they would be, he thought, valuable allies. In the meantime he collected information about the tribes and customs of the country.[4]

In July news came that a British ship had been wrecked off Brunei and the crew detained by the Sultan. Hasim promised to look into the case but did nothing. So James, after an angry interview with Hasim, decided to send *Swift* to Singapore laden with what antimony had been collected, and *Royalist* to Brunei to ask about the captive crew. He himself would stay alone in his house. He was confident that no one would dare to harm him. On 2 August James was handed a letter written by Mr Gill, chief officer of the wrecked ship, the *Sultana*, saying that he and two others of the crew had been released to go to Singapore, but their ship had been dismasted and they could not proceed for fear of the pirates, and that the rest of the crew, including some women, were imprisoned and harshly treated at Brunei. Soon afterwards *Swift* and *Royalist* both came back. The latter had been badly received at Brunei and forbidden to see the captives; but the former, on reporting the rumour, had induced the Singapore authorities to dispatch the East Indiaman *Diana* to Brunei. Her show of force frightened the Sultan's advisers. The captive crew was at last released.[1]

The incident added considerably to James's prestige. The arrival of the armed *Diana* at Brunei so soon after the discourteous reception given to *Royalist* convinced the government there that he had official backing from Britain; while the reports given by *Sultana*'s crew of his influence in Borneo impressed the Singapore public. James himself was bitterly conscious of his lack of official backing. In a long letter to his mother, written in April 1841 to tell her of his recent adventures, he had wistfully confessed how dearly he would like to be given a knighthood. Could she not bestir herself about it, even though she might laugh? It would so greatly and permanently improve his standing.[2]

Meanwhile proofs of Makota's enmity grew more apparent. James found many of the Malays unwilling to visit him through fear of Makota's agents. When one of the agents tried to poison his Malay interpreter by putting arsenic in his rice, it was time to bring things to a climax. He brought the guns of *Royalist* to bear on the palace, then landed with a small armed detachment and demanded an immediate audience with Hasim. There he reported on Makota's intrigues, which were directed as much against Hasim as himself. He declared that it was Makota's exactions as governor which had provoked the recent rebellion; and he pointed out that he himself was on excellent terms with the Dyaks and the local Malay chieftains, who, if necessary, would fight in his support against Makota.

Hasim was both frightened and relieved. He could not afford to allow a new rebellion with James Brooke as the rebel leader, and he himself distrusted Makota. Stating publicly, and sincerely, that he was acting with a clear conscience, he at last drew up and signed a document assigning to James the government of Sarawak and its dependencies, in return for a small annual payment to the Sultan of Brunei and a promise to respect the laws and religion of the country. The document was duly signed, sealed and delivered; and on 24 November 1841, James Brooke was ceremoniously proclaimed Rajah and Governor of Sarawak.[1]

The Raj was founded. But the new Rajah's position was uncertain. Makota was defeated for the moment, and his adherents publicly abandoned him. But he still exercised influence; his appointment as governor had not yet been cancelled by the Sultan. Hasim stayed on in Kuching as representative of the Sultan, to whom James was tributary. And the Sultan had not yet officially authorised the transfer. Though James called himself Rajah in his proclamations to the people of· Sarawak, he did not yet use the title for external purposes.[2]

No public notice was taken in Britain of the fact that a British citizen had become the ruler of a foreign territory. The Dutch were better aware of it. A report from the Deputy Governor-General of the Indies reached The Hague at the end of 1841 reporting that an Englishman was settling in Sarawak and meddling in the government there. The Sultan of Sambas, who was vassal to the Dutch, was alarmed lest the opening up of Sarawak would damage his trade; and Mr Bloem, the Assistant-Resident there, had therefore given encouragement to the rebels. For this excess of zeal, Mr Bloem had been transferred to another post; for the Dutch authorities, like Mr Bonham at Singapore, did not like their citizens to interfere in native politics. But something ought to be done, the report said, to curb an 'enterprising adventurer, such as Brooke must be regarded'. Nothing however was done. The Dutch were not in a position to indulge in expensive intervention in Borneo, which might also cause trouble with the British Government. James Brooke was allowed to begin his reign without any complications emanating from The Hague or from London.[3]

CHAPTER III

THE BEGINNING OF GOVERNMENT

It is not easy to take over single-handed the government of a strange country. James Brooke had no administrative experience. His commercial experiences had been unfortunate. He was not yet perfectly adept in the Malay language. He had no fellow-Europeans with him, apart from the crews of his ships, *Royalist* and *Swift*; and they were often away, keeping open his communications with Singapore. His ship's surgeon, the Dane Westermann, occasionally stayed on shore with him, as well as young Williamson, the interpreter. He managed to acquire a secretary from Singapore, a former merchant's clerk called William Crymble, who was to stay many years in his service. A boy from the Royal Navy, Bloomfield Douglas, who had joined *Royalist*, was also often kept ashore, being considered, no doubt, suitable for training as an administrator. Meanwhile, a friend called Mackenzie was staying with him; and Captain Elliott of the Madras Engineers visited him in the spring of 1842, and built him an Observatory.[1]

James was not deterred by his problems. He had long ago made up his mind what the general lines of his policy would be. A long pamphlet sent to England in 1842, in the hope of rousing interest and support there, explained his position and his aims, repeating what he had frequently written in letters to his family. He would insist on a just administration; he would protect the oppressed Dyaks; he would encourage the Chinese merchants and would welcome any commerce that was not detrimental to the natives' interests. He would like British trading houses to take an interest in Sarawak and the Church to send a mission there; though privately he believed that the Americans made better missionaries than the English.[2] He quickly gave practical expression to his views by issuing a code of laws, hastily printed in Malay at Singapore. It contained eight provisions. Murder and robbery and such crimes were to be punished according to the traditional laws of Brunei, the *Ondong-ondong*. All men, whether Malay, Chinese or Dyak, were free to trade or work as they pleased and to enjoy their gains.

Roads and waterways were to be open and used without let or hindrance. Trade would be entirely free, except for the government monopoly of antimony ore; but there was to be no forced labour for the government. No one was to molest the Dyaks or try to obtain goods from them at forced prices; if they paid their taxes to the proper officials, they were then free to sell their goods where and at what prices they pleased. Taxation would be fixed and the yearly payments required clearly stated. Regulations about standard weights and measures and a low-value coinage would be introduced. Finally everyone was warned that these laws would be enforced strictly, and anyone that disliked them had better emigrate to an easier-going country.[1]

His first action was to insist on the release of the ex-rebel women and children who were held at Kuching. This delighted the Dyaks but offended many of the Malays. Some Dyak girls had been taken as slaves into Malay households. He was obliged to leave them there. Next, he insisted on the reinstatement of the three leading local Malay princes, who had gone into exile after the rebellion, the Datu Patinggi, the Datu Bandar and the Datu Temanggong, as heads of the Malay community and as administrators over the Dyak tribes. The three Datus, though at first frightened of offending Makota, became James's loyal supporters, much as they resented the restrictions placed on their traditional exploitation of the Dyaks. They were not very efficient administrators; the Datu Temanggong in particular, though cheerful company, was remarkably unreliable. But they knew the ways of the country and James had no one else.[2] With the Chinese his relations were at first excellent. They had been throughout, he said, his great allies. He wished to encourage their immigration, and he admired the efficiency and democratic organisation of their *kongsis*. Soon he had to modify his views. There was one *kongsi* operating in Sarawak territory, the San Ti Qu, who held a charter entitling them to work the gold in the district on the right-hand branch of the upper Sarawak river. Another *kongsi*, the Sin Bok, which had been obliged to leave Sambas territory, asked permission to work in Sarawak and was offered the district on the left branch of the river. The San Ti Qu protested, saying that their charter gave them rights over both branches and forbade any other *kongsi* to work in the country. James summoned the *kongsi* leaders to a conference and discovered that the Chinese translation of the charter had blandly added these points. It needed the threat of force, after two days of useless argument, to induce the San Ti Qu to yield. They saved their face by securing one or two minor concessions, such as the remission of their last year's tribute, which they had not yet paid. After that James had no more trouble with the Chinese for many years. There was a constant influx of Chinese settlers, some from other parts of Borneo and many from Malaya or even China. He welcomed them, but tried to keep watch over their political activities.[1]

The Dyaks were friendly; but a branch of the Singé tribe took this opportunity of defying both James and Hasim. They retired to a mountain-top, and it needed a tedious campaign to reduce them. At last, in September 1842, their leaders, called Parimban and Pa Tummo, were captured. Hasim insisted that they should be put to death by stabbing. James was distressed but felt the penalty to be necessary.[2]

He was already involved in what was to be the major problem of his career, the extirpation of piracy. Early in January he heard that the Sanpro and Sow Dyaks had been attacked by Sadong and Skrang Dyaks, sent by the brother *sherips*, Mullar and Sahap. He was preparing an expedition against the pirate tribes, when one of the Skrang chieftains, Matari, 'the Sun', came to visit him. Matari asked James if he really intended to punish piracy and head-hunting. On being told so, he asked pathetically if he might not have permission to steal a few heads occasionally, and went on begging to be allowed 'just to steal one or two' as a schoolboy would ask for apples.[3] There were more reports of pirate activity in April at the mouth of Sarawak river. James was away from Kuching, up-country, at the time; but Hasim sent the Datu Temanggong, whom Mr Crymble joined, to intercept the pirates. It was difficult for the Datu and Crymble to induce their followers to attack the raiders; but fortunately the enemy retired out to sea. James on his return sailed out in pursuit and managed to overtake them near Talang Talang. It took him some time to locate them but eventually he was able to surprise their two ringleaders, a certain Bedreddin, a *pangiran* who had many relations in Kuching, and the *panglima* Illanun. They were taken to Kuching, where Hasim insisted, against James's protests, in putting both to death by strangling, as befitted noblemen. Bedreddin protested to the last at being killed for merely having himself killed a few Chinese. His companion died in silence. The episode showed the pirates that the new ruler of Sarawak meant business.[4]

The government soon settled down to a rough routine. When he was in Kuching James was accessible in his house to anyone who wished to see him. Whenever it was necessary he himself administered justice, sitting in the large hall of his house with such of the Rajah Muda's brothers who chose to attend on either side of him and the Sarawak Datus at the end of the table. The litigants and their witnesses sat opposite. He found that he had to decide cases from his own estimate of the characters involved. The truth was seldom told, but the lying was inexpert. Witnesses on the same side, if questioned separately, told remarkably divergent stories. But as it became realised that James was prepared to bring in and enforce judgments against the rich and powerful, the standard slowly improved. There were comparatively few criminal cases. The litigation was mainly over loans, inheritance or the title to lands or slaves.[1]

Financial affairs were less easy to sort out. James had no head for figures. The accounts that he kept, or that Crymble kept for him, were an unmethodical jumble. He estimated the revenue of the country sometimes at £5000, sometimes at £6000. Out of that he had to pay the salaries and wages of the administration and his own living expenses, as well as the upkeep of his two ships. It was insufficient. Every now and then he would have to draw on his own dwindling private fortune, through his agents in Singapore. He did not worry overmuch. He firmly believed that the country had enormous mineral resources and agricultural potentialities. In spite of his journeys through the land he would not realise that most of it was either swamp or mountain and that there was little space for the great farms and plantations that he envisaged. He thought that the seams of gold and antimony ore were inexhaustible. He had large hopes of making money out of diamonds. He heard of an old diamond-mine up the Sarawak river at Santah, which he reopened, in a somewhat primitive way, and built himself a cottage nearby. The cottage gave him great pleasure but the mine brought him little profit. The diamonds were few and poor; and he was cheated abominably by Haji Ibrahim, the Chinese Muslim who was his foreman there, an old rogue whom he could not help liking.[2]

The continued presence of Hasim in Sarawak was an embarrassment, as no one quite knew where the authority lay. To James the solution was obvious; Hasim should return to Brunei and take over the government there. He believed Hasim, in spite of his weakness and prevarications, to be a sincere friend to himself and to the British. But Hasim was afraid. During his long absence from Brunei enemies of his, the *pangirans* Usop and Munim, had acquired influence with the Sultan. Recently another British ship, the *Lord Melbourne*, had been wrecked off Brunei and coloured members of the crew were detained there. It also appeared now that the lascar members of *Sultana*'s crew had never been released. James decided to visit Brunei, to have his own position legitimised by the Sultan, to pave the way for Hasim's return there, and to rescue the unfortunate Indian sailors.

In July 1842 James sailed in *Royalist* to Brunei, accompanied by Hasim's brothers Bedruddin and Markarle. Hasim thought that he would never see any of them again and bade farewell to them in tears. On 21 July *Royalist* anchored in the Brunei river and James sent envoys to the town to announce the arrival of himself and the *pangirans*. Next morning, from two o'clock onwards, numbers of Brunei *pangirans* and their suites came from the town to pay their respects, all professing themselves to be friends and admirers of Hasim. Bedruddin landed that afternoon, anxious to ensure that James would be suitably received. He returned next day saying that all was well, both as regards the reception and as regards Hasim's return. On the 25th, laden with gifts, James was rowed in his longboat to the Palace. The Sultan was an ugly, unimpressive little man, with an insatiable appetite for gifts. But he was extremely affable to James, both at the formal reception and at the more private talks that followed during the next week. James was honourably but uncomfortably lodged at the Palace. The Sultan who, to show off his linguistic talents, addressed him always as 'amigo sua' declared himself eager for his uncle Hasim's return and delighted that James should take over Sarawak; and he made no difficulties about the release of the seamen from *Lord Melbourne*. The three lascars from *Sultana* presented a more difficult problem, as they had been sold as slaves. James had to pay 25 dollars to redeem them. The only problem lay in the Sultan's greed. He wanted all the presents James had reserved for the *pangirans*. He could not believe that more gifts were not concealed in *Royalist*. He was only contented when James promised to send the tribute from Sarawak in the form of British goods and foodstuffs, in particular soft sugar which should reach the Sultan before the fast month of Ramadan. With the *pangirans* James was not quite so successful. Munim, the most powerful, was courteous but cold and made excuses not to see him. With Usop, who seemed livelier, James had a candid conversation and hoped, a little doubtfully, that he had made a friend of him.[1]

By 1 August all the business was concluded. The lascars were all safely aboard *Royalist*. The Sultan had entrusted James with a letter for Hasim, cordially inviting him to return to Brunei; and he had written and sealed a document formally recognising James as Rajah of Sarawak. James's title was now unassailable and complete.[1]

James had not been impressed by Brunei. The whole town was built on piles over mud that stank atrociously at low tide. Its population seemed to him to be near 10,000, but, except for the Sultan and the *pangirans*, everyone was very poor. The Palace was large but dirty and tumbledown. Only Usop possessed a clean and well-furnished house. But the scenery was beautiful, and on the bank of the river opposite there was an excellent site for a town.[2]

Royalist finally sailed from the Brunei river on 5 August and ten days later reached Kuching. Hasim was delighted to see James and his brothers back after so successful a mission. On 18 August the Sultan's document recognising James as Rajah was publicly read out, and all present were told that if any of them would not accept the appointment as valid, he must speak now. Hasim then put the question personally to Makota and two of his chief supporters. They hastened to express obedience to the Sultan's decree. Hasim then announced that anyone who disobeyed it would have his skull cleft; whereat ten of his brothers leapt into a war-dance, pointing their daggers at Makota. Happily Makota remained stock still, and no blood was shed.[3]

It was, however, nearly two years before Hasim could make up his mind to move to Brunei. Though ambitious for the Sultanate, he was timorous; he felt safe at Kuching. James now longed for him to go with all his vast clan. They did not attempt to interfere in the government, but their presence weakened it. The Malays, who have a deep respect for Royalty, hesitated to obey James's orders if they seemed in any way displeasing or damaging to Hasim; and the family could not suddenly abandon its lifelong habits of corruption and intrigue. James had little use for any of Hasim's brothers, except for Bedruddin, whom he liked and admired. But Bedruddin would be more useful to him at Brunei than at Kuching.[4]

With his title secure James was ready to obtain more definite support, both political and financial, from Britain. He needed an agent in London; and after some enquiries he appointed Mr Henry Wise, of Melville, Wise and Co., Broad Street, who was highly recommended to him as an able business man and negotiator, energetic, enterprising and honest. His correspondence with Wise satisfied him, though he did not always agree with Wise's schemes. Wise was rather too much a shrewd man of affairs, ignorant of local conditions and needs. But he could learn about them when he came to see the country for himself. Meanwhile he was doing useful work in trying to capture the interest and sympathy of the British Government and of the City.[1]

1843 opened gloomily for James. His friend Mackenzie was desperately ill and all his European staff was away. Westermann the surgeon had just left to retire. It was a relief when *Royalist* returned from Singapore bringing on board a new surgeon, John Treacher, a young man who had sailed round Celebes with James and who was to collaborate with him for many years to come. When Mackenzie recovered, James himself sailed for Singapore. It was two years since he had left Borneo. He wanted to talk to Mr Bonham and to see what help his friends among the merchants there could provide. He spent three months there, from February to May. At first he felt thwarted. In letters sent during the last months to Wise and to such old friends as John Templer he had begged for some show of official interest in his venture. He would like Sarawak to become a British Protectorate; he would be willing to cede it to Britain if he were installed as governor or, if need be, he would himself retire. He pleaded for money to help develop its resources. All he demanded was that the benefit and security of the people should be guaranteed, that there was proper provision for the government and for 'right-minded persons' to succeed him, and that some provision or employment should be given to those who had followed his fortunes.[2] But the British Government appeared only mildly interested, while Wise wanted to found a large company which, James feared, would exploit rather than develop the country. He tried another line of approach. He had learnt when at Brunei that there was coal to be found on the island of Labuan. Surely the Royal Navy would be glad to hear of a coaling-station so conveniently placed with regard to China. Here he was more successful. While he was in Singapore he heard that a naval surveying vessel, H.M.S. *Samarang*, under Captain Sir Edward Belcher, was shortly to be sent to the Borneo coast.[3]

On the last day of April news reached Singapore of a large pirate fleet operating off the Borneo coast. There was a squadron of the Royal Navy at Penang at the time; and Mr Church, Resident Councillor, sent to warn its Commander, Captain Keppel. James, hoping to find an ally in his campaign against the pirates, himself hurried to Penang. Henry Keppel, younger son of the Earl of Albemarle, was an enterprising and independent-minded officer. He took an immediate liking to James, and at once offered to convey him back to Kuching and thence to go pirate-hunting with him. It was the beginning of a lifelong friendship.[1]

H.M.S. *Dido* with Captain Keppel and James aboard reached Kuching on 15 May. Keppel was fascinated by everything that he saw there. He enjoyed his ceremonious visit to Hasim. He was impressed that James had so small a handful of Europeans to help him. Actually the European population of Sarawak had recently been increased. Without consulting James, Wise had bought and sent out another boat, *Ariel*, which arrived under the command of David Irons, formerly of *Royalist*. James was not entirely pleased; but on board was a young connection of his, Arthur Crookshank, whom he gladly took into his service. He had also acquired a pleasant young assistant called Ruppell. In addition, two merchants and their clerk had arrived from London to help James on commercial matters. Their names were Steward, Smith and Maiden. They were joined a little later by a Mr Hentig.

The European community was seldom to be found in its entirety at Kuching. Some members would be on a voyage to Singapore, to sell antimony and other local products and to buy European goods there. James had recently replaced *Swift* by a better boat, *Julia*, for this purpose. Others might be up-country, supervising the mines or seeing to the welfare of the Dyaks. James believed in his officers moving about the country. When Keppel arrived he only met Dr Treacher, Williamson and young Bloomfield Douglas, as well as two ex-able seamen, one acting as armourer, the other, called Charlie, as steward and factotum.[2]

Both Keppel and James were eager to get at the pirates. They had come across pirate ships on the voyage from Singapore. A yacht was due to follow with the mail from London. Keppel thought it wise to send to meet her; but his own pinnace was being repaired. James had recently had a launch built locally, called the *Jolly Bachelor*, in which he had fitted guns. Lieutenant Hunt of *Dido* borrowed her and she sailed down the river. That night she was surprised by pirates who thought her a native vessel. They were driven off, their chief being slain, and the yacht safely escorted up to Kuching. It was clear that piracy was not a figment of local imagination.

After Keppel had been for a few days in Kuching, the Rajah Muda Hasim sent him a formal letter asking for his help against the pirates of the Saribas and Skrang rivers. It is probable that Keppel's commission was to suppress the pirates of the high seas, the Illanuns. But, as the letter pointed out, these Dyak tribes were undoubtedly piratical. They refused allegiance to Brunei or to anyone else and they ruined the coastal trade. James, who may have inspired the letter, successfully urged him to agree, and proposed accompanying him. He believed that to attack the pirate tribes in their native lairs was the only way to reduce them to order.

On the news of the projected expedition the Skrang and Saribas Dyaks prepared to resist. But many of the tribes nearer to Kuching whose record had not been good in the past hastened to promise to be good in the future. Makota took this opportunity to slip away from Kuching and visit his friend Sharip Sahap of Sadong; who promised to release the Sow captives that he still held, sent Keppel a gift of two handsome spears and a porcupine, and invited him and James to a feast whenever they would pass his way. The Malay chieftains at Kuching were alarmed at James joining the expedition. They vainly begged him to stay with them.

This first campaign set the pattern for many to come. It was a motley force. *Dido* provided her pinnace, two cutters and a gig, to which the *Jolly Bachelor* was added, with about eighty men in all. The Sarawak Dyaks provided two boats; Brunei Malays filled another. There were other small boats from Kuching, manned by Malays, and Dyak boats containing about 400 men. The whole force numbered about 700. Keppel and James followed in another gig, and a third, under Lieutenant Gunnell, tried to maintain liaison and discipline throughout the flotilla. Dr Treacher and Mr Ruppell were with him. The expedition left Kuching on 4 June and sailed to the mouth of the Saribas.

The objective was the three fortified villages of the Saribas, Paddi, on the main river, and Peku and Rembas, up tributaries. Rain fell without ceasing. There was daily danger from the bore that sweeps up the river. Where the swamps on either side of the river gave place to firmer ground, bands of tribesmen swooped down the slope yelling and hurling spears at the passing boats. There was one serious alarm when it seemed that the expedition was being attacked in the rear; but the advancing force proved to be Lingga Dyaks, long at feud with the Saribas, who had come to help. They were not of much value, as they preferred looting to fighting. At last Paddi was reached, a longhouse situated at a fork where a tributary joined the river. It was screened by a stockade, and below the fork a barricade was stretched across the stream. The Saribas defended the barricade fiercely, causing several casualties; but once it was forced they fled into the jungle. Paddi was then easily taken and consigned to the flames. The expedition then retired to go up the side-streams to Paku and Rembas. The enemy attacked them as they were passing over some shallows, but in vain; and next day the headmen of Paddi sent to ask for a truce. James interviewed them and warned them that unless they abandoned piracy their houses would be burnt again and the Lingga Dyaks let loose on them. They agreed to reform their ways but said that they could not answer for Paku or for Rembas. The flotilla then proceeded to Paku, which surrendered. The inhabitants were given a similar warning. Rembas put up a stiffer resistance, but was stormed with little loss and looted and burnt, the inhabitants fleeing to the jungle. They too emerged to ask for a truce next day and made similar promises of good behaviour. The expedition was able to return triumphantly to Kuching. Its success made a good impression. Very few lives had been lost; and though the enemy villages had been destroyed no Dyak woman or child had been hurt. James's prestige was particularly high, as the Dyaks all believed that he had stilled the bore, which had never been so small as during those crucial days.

Keppel had hoped to join James on further expeditions; but a message reached him almost at once, ordering *Dido* to the China Station. He and James parted with great mutual regret. Their friendship was never broken.[1]

James's next visitor was less sympathetic. Three weeks after Keppel's departure H.M.S. *Samarang*, under Sir Edward Belcher, sailed up to Kuching. He had come to report officially on Borneo and James was anxious to impress him favourably. But he was less ready to be impressed. On the other hand, the younger members of the crew were charmed by James and his romantic career. From one of the midshipmen, Frank Marryat, son of the author of *Masterman Ready*, who wielded a lively pen and a far from inexpert pencil, we have a good description of the life that Europeans were then leading at Kuching. He had ample time for his observations, for, as *Samarang* was starting to sail down the river to convey Belcher, with James, to inspect Brunei and the Borneo coast, she ran on a rock a mile below the town. As the tide in the river ebbed she fell over to starboard and rapidly filled. The crew had to abandon her till she should be salvaged. James kept the officers in his own house and found houses for the midshipmen, the petty officers and the crew. He entertained them all lavishly and arranged expeditions for them into the country. The midshipmen were not at all pleased when the ship was at last raised.[1]

James was no longer living in the house hastily built for him by Hasim in 1841, which was close to the Rajah Muda's palace in the town. He had moved, just after *Dido's* departure, to a larger building on the opposite, left, bank of the river, where Makota had had his house. It contained one large room, which was his audience-chamber and his dining-hall, several small rooms off it in which his staff and his guests slept, and his own suite of rooms at the side, a bedroom, sitting-room and library, with bathroom underneath. It was built of wood and reminded visitors of a Swiss chalet. Round it were three wooden bungalows, one serving as an annexe to the main house, one inhabited by Williamson, the interpreter, and one by the merchant Hentig. Dr Treacher and Mr Ruppell shared a large house on the other side of the river. These Europeans led a somewhat communal life. They all breakfasted together at James's house at 7 a.m. and met there again for dinner at sundown. James was a genial and considerate host; and visitors were impressed by the comfort and good taste of his residence.[2]

Samarang was raised by local efforts; but the news of her mishap brought ships from Singapore to rescue her. When at last she sailed from Kuching on 23 August, having managed to strike the same rock again but without serious damage, she was escorted by two brigs, H.M.S. *Harlequin* and H.M.S. *Wanderer*, by two East India Company steamers, *Diana* and *Vixen*, as well as by *Royalist* and *Ariel*. It was an impressive fleet that arrived off Brunei six days later. The Sultan was awed by the sight of so many ships. He gave James and Belcher a most courteous reception. He solemnly announced that he bestowed Sarawak on James and his heirs in perpetuity. He begged to have his uncle Hasim sent back to him. He gave a written promise to discourage piracy; he would open his ports to British trade.

James had reason to be pleased with the mission but for one thing. Belcher was not impressed by Brunei and thought it foolish to worry about its future. When James urged him that now was the moment to press for the cession to Britain of the island of Labuan or of Muara promontory, on the coast opposite, he was uninterested. Nor did he change his mind when he saw Labuan, a few days later. He gave it a brief glance, decided that there could not be much coal on it, and sailed on. Smallpox was raging throughout Brunei territory. He wanted to be away.[1]

It was not long after his return to Kuching that James learnt what Belcher had reported. He was furious. Belcher declared the Labuan coal to be unworkable and recommended no action. Further, he called the Sultan of Brunei a savage. James, though he considered the Sultan an unreliable imbecile, was enraged to hear a dynasty and court that had lasted for three centuries called savage.[2] At the same time he was worried by Wise's perpetual demands that a large company to exploit Borneo should be formed.[3] Had he not been able to look round and see the increasing prosperity of Sarawak and his Dyaks 'really quite fat and happy-looking', he would have been sunk in depression. As it was he had a sharp attack of fever over Christmas; and in January he went to Singapore to recuperate. There he had a setback on hearing the news of his mother's death. He had been devoted to her; he had always written to her of his plans, his ambitions and his worries. He had had no idea how ill she was. It was a great shock to him.[4]

To distract himself he decided to visit Penang, having heard that units of the Fleet were there under Admiral Sir William Parker. Parker was very friendly. He expressed himself delighted with the initiative that Keppel had shown against the pirates. He himself was about to send a similar expedition against pirates in Sumatra and he invited James to join it. James gladly accepted. The Sumatran pirates, who were Malays, proved tougher fighters than the Dyaks. They fought for five hours before their stronghold at Murdu was taken; and in the course of storming the stockade James received a cut on his eyebrow and a bullet in his arm. The British sailors loved him for his bravery; but when he met Keppel at Singapore after the fighting was over, he was sharply rebuked. His duty was to govern Sarawak, not to risk his life in Sumatra.[5]

He was delighted to see Keppel, who had hoped to sail to Kuching with him. But *Dido* was ordered to Calcutta first. James had just sold *Royalist*, and he had sent his new schooner, *Julia*, ahead, counting on travelling with Keppel. He was thus left stranded at Singapore till May, when H.M.S. *Harlequin*, under Captain Hastings, was authorised to convey him home. It was time that he returned. On his departure in January, Sherip Sahap of Sadong, egged on by his guest Makota, had built some two hundred boats and now, with his Malays and his Dyaks, and his brother Mullar's Dyaks from the Skrang river, was raiding and blockading the whole coast of Sarawak. He did not dare to attack *Harlequin*, which brought James safely to his capital. But Captain Hastings refused to disobey instructions to return at once, in spite of James's pleading for a short joint-expedition against Sadong. James had to wait the arrival of *Dido* in July. Meanwhile he did what he could to intercept raids, without much success. *Dido's* arrival was especially welcome because on board as a midshipman was James's nephew, Charles Johnson. The East India Company's steamer *Phlegethon* arrived a few days later.

Sahap's stronghold was at Putusan, up the Batang Lupar, not far from the present town of Simanggang. Mullar lived on the river Undup which flows into the Batang Lupar fifteen miles higher up. On 5 August *Dido* and *Phlegethon*, with the *Jolly Bachelor* and a flotilla of Malay boats, moved out from Kuching. Hasim's brother, Bedruddin, insisted on joining the expedition, to the wonder of the Malays. It was unusual for a prince of the Blood Royal to go willingly to battle. Sahap had not expected an attack so soon. Putusan was as yet imperfectly fortified; it fell after a short attack and was put to flames. The Dyaks with the expedition were delighted to be able to collect a number of heads there. Next, Sahap's own residence, two miles further up, was burnt, together with Makota's nearby. Both were sumptuously furnished; and in the latter James recognised many presents that he had given to Makota. Sahap and Makota fled up the Undup river. Despite the barriers erected by Mullar across the river, Keppel's boats forced their way through. The settlement at Undup was destroyed, as well as an encampment further upstream. There was a skirmish nearby, in which Lieutenant Wade of *Dido* was killed; but further advance was impracticable. The expedition retired, leaving Sahap, Mullar and Makota refugees in the jungle. A small expedition was then sent up the Skrang river, which enters the Batang Lupar just above the Undup, led by the Datu Patinggi Ali, and joined, against orders, by Mr Steward the merchant. It was less successful. The Datu's boat was ambushed, and he and Steward and most of their company killed.

When the expedition returned to Kuching, having lost about thirty men, with sixty wounded, it was learnt that Sahap and Makota had gone to seek aid from Sherip Jafar at Lingga. Boats were hastily sent there. Sahap escaped in time, to die soon after as a fugitive at Pontianak in Dutch Borneo. Mullar also fled, but after many years of exile returned home to die. Makota was captured but released and allowed to

I   SIR JAMES BROOKE

2*a*   RIVER SARAWAK AND KUCHING

2*b*   COURT OF THE SULTAN OF BORNEO
(SIGNING THE TREATY WITH ENGLAND)

retire to Brunei; neither James nor Hasim was prepared to order his execution. The campaign made an excellent impression. Soon afterwards the Skrang and Saribas Dyaks sent one of their chiefs, Linggir, to Kuching to announce their submission. They promised to behave better in future, and kept their promise for about a year.[1]

As the flotilla sailed home it was met by H.M.S. *Samarang*. Sir Edward Belcher was more cordial than before and regretted being too late for the fighting. He wished to be of use to James; and, as *Dido* was ordered home to England, James asked for his help in conveying the Rajah Muda Hasim and all his clan to Brunei. Hasim had at last screwed up his courage sufficiently to leave Sarawak; and James was longing for him to go, both to make his own position less equivocal and to have a friend in power at the Sultan's Court. After a visit to Singapore *Samarang* returned to Kuching in October. Belcher had been asked by the Indian Government to look into a rumour that a European lady was held captive at Ambong. This task fitted well with a voyage to Brunei; so he set out in *Samarang* with *Phlegethon* accompanying her, the two ships conveying Hasim and all his brothers, the wives, families and attendants, as well as James and some of his staff. After some hesitation the Sultan received them well. Hasim's enemies at the Court, Munim and Usop, declared themselves willing to accept his authority. James left him there, content though not too sanguine about the future. He induced Belcher to pay another visit to Labuan and found him less discouraging than before; and they sailed together on to Ambong, a wretched village on the North Borneo coast, where no one had heard of the captive European lady. When James returned to Kuching he was altogether in a happier frame of mind.[2]

He now felt supreme in Sarawak. Everyone treated him as unquestioned Rajah; and there were no more intrigues with Hasim behind his back. He spent the next months largely in touring his dominions, and his spare time in writing a treatise on the pirates for the guidance of the British authorities. But he was worried about his position with regard to Britain. He wanted official support, some form of official rank and a guarantee that Britain would interest herself in Borneo. The Navy in the East gave him a *de facto* recognition but that was not enough. His agents in London, both Wise and John Templer, were continually putting his case before the Prime Minister, Sir Robert Peel, and other influential public figures. Yet it seemed to James in Sarawak that they were all ridiculously cautious. The Government wanted to be assured about the resources of the island, with the sort of statistical details that he was quite unable to supply. But the main question, was Britain going to use this wonderful opportunity of opening up Borneo to her influence and her trade, remained unanswered.[1]

In fact more was happening in London than James knew. His name had been frequently mentioned in naval reports. Templer's and Wise's efforts were having an effect. In February 1845 H.M.S. *Driver*, with Captain Bethune in command and Wise on board, arrived at Kuching with a despatch from Lord Aberdeen appointing James as Confidential Agent to Her Majesty in Borneo. The appointment was couched in flattering terms and certainly gave James an official standing, though what exactly it meant was obscure. Bethune also brought a letter from the British Government to the Sultan of Brunei, expressing the intention of co-operating with him against the pirates. James accompanied Bethune to deliver this letter at Brunei. The Sultan received the letter politely and Hasim with enthusiasm. The leading pirate operating off Borneo was now a Sherip called Osman, an adventurer who had established himself as head of a group of Illanum pirates with a base in Marudu Bay. He was in touch with Hasim's chief enemy, Usop; and both of them had sworn to end British influence in Borneo. Osman had publicly vowed to kill Rajah James. Hasim seemed fairly cheerful, but many of his brothers were not; they begged to be allowed to return to the safety of Sarawak.[2]

From Brunei James went with Bethune and Wise to Labuan, which Bethune agreed would make a good settlement, and then to Singapore. During his conversations with Wise he hoped that he had impressed on him the need for patience. It would be impossible and undesirable to get rich quickly in Borneo. The schemes that James had in mind were directed more for the welfare of the local peoples than for the profit of himself or Wise or any London Company.[3]

Admiral Sir Thomas Cochrane, commander of the Far East Fleet, was at Malacca, and James hurried to see him. He shared James's views about the pirates and promised to join him in an expedition against Marudu Bay. Meanwhile James returned in *Phlegethon* to Brunei. They found that an American frigate, the *Constitution*, had just visited the town to offer the Sultan a treaty of friendship in return for an exclusive right to trade and to mine coal in his territory. Fortunately, the interpreter whom the Americans employed was a servant whom James had dismissed for drunkenness. He overstated their demands, which were at once rejected. Had the terms been truly known the Sultan would probably have accepted them, in spite of Hasim's opposition. At the end of July James and Bethune joined the Admiral at Malacca, to escort him to Brunei.

They arrived there with seven ships. The Admiral's first demand was for the release of two British subjects—lascar seamen—said to be detained there. The Sultan blamed their detention on Usop, who refused to come and answer the charge. The Admiral ordered a shot to be fired through the roof of his house. Usop fired back, then changed his mind and fled from the city. His house was occupied and the two captives released. The squadron then moved on to attack Sherip Osman in Marudu Bay.

As the ships entered the bay on 18 August, Osman sent an envoy who asked specifically for James to arrange a truce, but his terms were unacceptable. Next morning twenty-four boats from the squadron, manned by some 550 bluejackets and marines, sailed up the little river on which Osman's fortress was placed. In the fierce battle that followed the fortress was stormed and the enemy scattered. The British losses were six killed and seventeen wounded; the enemies' losses ran into hundreds. Osman himself was mortally wounded and died a few days later in the jungle.

After stopping to visit Balembangan, which both James and Bethune thought inferior as a possible settlement to Labuan, the squadron returned to Brunei. They found that in their absence Usop had made an attempt to capture the city but had been routed by an army led by Bedruddin. Usop had fled to his own estates at Kimanis, across Brunei Bay. There he had been strangled by the local headman, acting on orders sent by the Sultan at Hasim's request. James returned to Kuching feeling far happier. The Marudu Bay pirates had been crushed. Hasim's chief enemy in Brunei had perished. Captain Bethune was preparing a report for London recommending the annexation and settlement of Labuan.[1]

James spent the winter of 1845 happily. Kuching had quadrupled its size since first he had settled there. Trade was beginning to expand. Antimony and gold, though still in disappointing quantities, were being exported, as well as wax and birds'-nests, and the Dyaks were receiving their fair share of the profits. Imported goods were selling well, especially now that Hasim and his clan were gone. Till then a purchaser had always feared that his new possession might be coveted by one of the Malay princes and confiscated. James reported proudly that on one day he sold 400 dozen white china plates and on the next day 100 more. Thanks to the merchants who had arrived the commercial arrangements were now orderly and shop accounts better kept. James was no longer forced to make inroads on his own fortune. He made little excursions from time to time to visit the Land Dyak villages or his cottage at Santah. On New Year's Day there was a grand regatta of canoes. There were amusing episodes, as when he was asked to hear the case of a crocodile, captured after having eaten a man; ought it to be put to death, when it was a royal beast only doing an act according to its nature? There were excitements, as when the Saribas chief Linggir suddenly appeared with eighty armed men and forced his way into James's house at dinner-time, with the clear intent of murdering the company when it rose to leave the table. James whispered in English to a servant to summon the Datus hastily. Soon the Datu Temanggong arrived with thirty men, then the Datu Bandar with eighty. Linggir saw that he was outmanœuvred and slunk back home. When he reached his river he publicly announced that he would have the Rajah's head yet, and displayed the basket that he had made to contain it.

A second unexpected visitor was Makota, who suddenly appeared in Kuching and asked James to lend him money, two thousand reals, or one thousand, or even one hundred, or fifty, or five. James coldly refused, but Mr Ruppell, who was kindlier disposed, lent him three.[1]

James had given the journals which he had kept, on and off, since his first arrival in the East to Captain Keppel; and Keppel decided to publish extracts from them as the greater part of a book describing *Dido*'s exploits. It appeared early in 1846. James was pleased, but nervous about its reception, especially as Wise had warned him that it would do him more harm than good. In the long run Wise was perhaps right. But at the moment the book caught the fancy of the public. It ran almost at once into three editions. From being an obscure settler in the East of whom few outside the Royal Navy had heard, James became quite quickly a national hero.[2] But before he had time to revel in his new fame, he was distracted by ill news from Brunei.

To his regret Admiral Cochrane had not been able to leave one of his ships to keep watch off the Borneo coast. In February the Skrang pirates broke out again and raided some peaceful villages and took some ships. James was expecting a visit from H.M.S. *Iris*, under Captain Mundy, who he hoped would help him to punish them. But *Iris* was ordered to go first to India. In April Cochrane sent H.M.S. *Hazard* to see how things were faring in Borneo. She sailed direct to Brunei; but as she sailed up the bay a canoe with a youth on board intercepted her. He begged the Captain not to proceed as there was treachery afoot but to go at once to Kuching to see the White Rajah, for whom he had a message. He was believed; and *Iris* made for Kuching, where the boy, who was one of Bedruddin's pages, told his story. Soon after Cochrane and James had left Brunei, the Sultan had fallen under the influence of his nominal son Hashim Jelal, who was notoriously not his, and who had married Usop's daughter, and he in his turn was dominated by an adventurer called Haji Seman. Seman played on the Sultan's jealousy of Hasim, who had recently, after the last British visit, been appointed Sultan Muda, or heir-apparent, and at last obtained permission to stage a *coup d'état*. One night, with the Sultan's connivance, the houses of Hasim, Bedruddin and all their brothers were attacked and entered by armed men. Most of the princes were slaughtered at once. Bedruddin drove his assailants off for a while but in despair blew himself up, with his sister and one of his wives, with a keg of gunpowder. Only the slave Jaspar escaped, to carry his last message to H.M.S. *Hazard*. Hasim himself managed to flee, wounded, across the river. When his attempts to parley to save his life failed, he too tried to blow himself up; but, ineffectual to the last, he only wounded himself again. So he took a pistol and shot himself.

The first rumours to reach Singapore of the tragedy added that the Sultan's army was attacking Kuching. When the story reached India Captain Mundy of the *Iris* obtained permission to set sail at once for the East. The Governor of Singapore had already sent *Phlegethon* over to Sarawak; and in her James was able to cruise up the coast and find that the new regime at Brunei had little general support. In June Admiral Cochrane arrived off the mouth of the Sarawak river with a squadron of seven ships, amongst which was *Iris*. The Admiral, with Captain Mundy, went up to Kuching to see James and hear the actual story of the massacre from the slave Jaspar. Mundy, like so many sailors, was enchanted with James, and later was to edit the parts of his journals that were omitted in Keppel's edition. Next day the whole squadron set sail for Brunei. They paused off the Rejang river and James, with the Admiral and Mundy, travelled up the river in *Phlegethon* as far as Kanowit. Sea Dyaks from the Saribas had recently spread up the Rejang and were using it as a base for pirate activity. This unexpected show of force awed them; they rushed to arms at first, but when they were not attacked they hastened to show friendship to the British. On 6 July the squadron anchored off Muara, at the entrance to Brunei Bay. There the Admiral received a letter from the Sultan, brought by two inferior courtiers dressed up as *pangirans*. Omar Ali complained of the discourtesy of H.M.S. *Hazard* in not coming up to Brunei in February. He said that he would receive the Admiral, but only if he came in two small boats. Cochrane did not fall into the ingenuous trap. On 8 July the small boats of the squadron, with *Phlegethon*, moved up to the city. Every bend in the river was fortified with batteries which opened fire. *Phlegethon* was hit below the water-line and damaged, but no other harm was done. When Brunei was reached the Sultan and the Court had fled, with a large part of the population. Two *pangirans* at last were found. One was Hasim's brother Mohammed, who had survived the massacre, though terribly wounded, and had made his peace with the Sultan; the other was Munim, his brother-in-law who, though no friend of Hasim's, disliked the new regime. They confirmed the story of the *coup d'état*. The Admiral destroyed the forts and issued a proclamation inviting the Sultan and his subjects to return, promising that no lives should be taken. The city soon filled up again; but the Sultan remained hidden in the jungle. An expedition penetrated some 30 miles in pursuit of him but was unable to find him.

After a few days the squadron sailed on to Marudu Bay, where the Illunan pirates, encouraged by the Brunei revolution, were active once more. They had destroyed the village of Ambong a few weeks before. The squadron proceeded to attack and burn their two present strongholds on the bay, Tampassuk and Pendassan. The pirates, after some bargaining, fled into the jungle. A few were captured and were identified by some rescued Spanish prisoners from the Philippines.

H.M.S. *Hazard* and *Phlegethon* had been left to guard Brunei. On news that Haji Seman was living in a house not far from Kimanis *Phlegethon* sailed there, to be soon joined by *Iris*, with James on board. After a brief fight Seman's house was occupied. The gardens outside were beautifully laid out and kept by Chinese prisoners, but inside there was a magnificent collection of heads. Seman himself had fled. Once more in Brunei James induced the fugitive Sultan to return. Omar Ali was frightened and penitent. He was made to do penance at the graves of his murdered uncles and to write a letter of grovelling apology addressed to Queen Victoria. He confirmed James in his possession of

Sarawak, giving him sovereign rights without any question of a tribute; and he offered James mining rights throughout his dominions. James, rather embarrassed, accepted, knowing that he could always transfer the rights to the British Government. Munim was put in charge of the Brunei administration, as Mohammed seemed imbecile as a result of his experiences. Munim himself was not much better. He had been fairly active in his youth, but he was ageing and, like most of his kin, indecisive and indolent. James then returned to Kuching. But during the next few months Captain Mundy paid several visits to Brunei, to be sure that all was well. In December authorisation came from the new British Foreign Secretary, Lord Palmerston, to annex Labuan to the British Empire. Captain Mundy told the Sultan that this was the price of his forgiveness by the Queen. There was some argument as the Sultan's advisers thought that some money should be given to Brunei in compensation for the loss of Labuan. But Mundy hinted that the Admiral was not far away and it would be a pity to have to burn down the Sultan's new palace. The Sultan yielded and even offered to come if need be to Labuan for the ceremony of handing over; though he hoped to be excused, as he was such a bad sailor. He was excused. When on 24 December Mundy hoisted the British flag on the island and gave a banquet afterwards, Pangiran Munim was the guest of honour. A treaty was signed between Great Britain and Brunei confirming the cession and giving to the British the task of suppressing piracy along the north Borneo coast. Next May the British government supplemented the treaty by ordering James to sign another, which guaranteed the territories of Brunei. In return none of them were to be alienated to any non-British power or individual without the consent of the British Government.[1]

It had been a tragic year for James, who felt the death of Hasim and, still more, of Bedruddin, very sorely. But good seemed to have come of it. The British had at last taken his advice about Labuan and were thus committed to keeping an eye on Brunei. Just before Christmas he crossed to Singapore to say good-bye to Admiral Cochrane, who was going home, and to meet his successor, Rear-Admiral Inglefield. While he was there he received news from the Sultan of Brunei that Haji Seman had been captured. He wrote back to recommend that his life be spared. Seman was, he thought, no longer dangerous. In May he borrowed the East India Company steamer, *Nemesis*, to go pirate-hunting again against some Balaninis, who were operating off the

Borneo coast; the Dutch authorities had given warning to Singapore of their activities. He came up with them off Muara, capturing three of their boats and releasing about a hundred captives. After visiting Brunei to sign the new treaty, he was back in Kuching in June. Everything there seemed orderly and peaceful, his main problem being to settle the wives and children of Hasim and his brothers, whom he had brought over from Brunei. In July, after leaving the administration in the care of Arthur Crookshank, he returned to Singapore to catch the mail-boat to England.[1]

He arrived at Southampton on 2 October, delighted to see his family and his friends again after seven years. He was equally delighted, though less willing to admit it, to find himself a public hero.[2] The success of Keppel's book made his name and his achievements widely known. The Government was well disposed. The Foreign Office had been repeatedly irritated during the last eighteen months by protests about him coming from the Netherlands Foreign Ministry. In December 1845 the Dutch complained that the settlement of 'le Sieur Brooke' in Borneo had been done with the connivance of the British and was contrary to the treaty of 1824. Lord Aberdeen replied that Mr Brooke had acquired his property in a legitimate and open manner and his efforts had been concentrated on suppressing piracy and spreading civilisation. He was perhaps unfavourably disposed to the extension of Dutch influence in the districts where he had acquired possession; but that was the only charge that could be brought against him. There was no underhand British connivance; and the only operations in which the British had indulged in those waters were entirely lawful expeditions against the pirates. A list of them was given. M. Dedels, the Dutch Foreign Minister, replied that expeditions against piracy were admirable, though it would have been more courteous to invite the Dutch to join in them. But an English settlement on the mainland of Borneo was against the treaty of 1824 because it would inevitably lead to continual collision. If Mr Brooke had only been given by the Sultan of Brunei (who was entitled indeed to make what arrangements he wished for his dominions) a short lease there was no objection, especially as Mr Brooke seemed to have conducted himself admirably; but the gift of the province in perpetuity was a different matter. Lord Aberdeen's reply was unyielding. His advisers could find nothing in the 1824 treaty that prevented a British subject from establishing himself on the north coast of Borneo, that is to say, north of the Equator. The treaty did not give Holland rights over the whole of Borneo; and he saw no reason why

Mr Brooke's settling there would necessarily lead to a clash. Her Majesty's Government would certainly take precautions to prevent that. He ended with a nasty taunt: if jealousies and dissensions were to be made to cease, he asked 'whether such object might not be more easily accomplished by rendering the policy of the Netherlands Government in the Eastern Seas more conformable to the commercial spirit of the day and to the customs of other nations'.[1]

James could therefore feel that he had the support of the Foreign Office behind him. He needed little such assurance. Three weeks after his arrival he was summoned to spend a night at Windsor as the guest of the Queen. Her Majesty and Prince Albert both talked to him most cordially, the latter asking him many searching questions. Amongst the other guests were Sir Robert and Lady Peel; and Sir Robert was markedly affable.[2]

Next the Freedom of the City of London was presented to him at a great banquet at the Guildhall held in his honour, and soon after the Freedoms of the Goldsmiths' and Fishmongers' Companies. A number of clubs, including the Athenaeum and the United Services invited him to become an honorary member. Oxford University gave him the honorary degree of Doctor of Laws. Even his old school, from which he had run away and which had refused to take him back, now organised a dinner in his honour. The Government too showed its official approval of his work, appointing him Governor of Labuan and Consul-General for Borneo at the large salary of £2000 a year. It was also announced that the Queen was pleased to name him as a Knight Commander of the Order of the Bath.[3]

These were probably the happiest days in James's life. He could not but enjoy the honours given to him; and in between the honorific ceremonies he had time to visit his family and his friends, old friends like John Templer and newer friends such as Keppel. He renewed his acquaintance with Miss Burdett-Coutts, and found her deeply interested in his work. He was at his best with the young. When at Oxford for the Encaenia he frequently slipped away to see undergraduate friends, and he had many friends among midshipmen whom he met in naval circles. He was always on the lookout for promising young men who would come and work in Borneo. Now that he had a sovereign state to bequeath he needed an heir. It was about this time that he suggested to his sister Emma and her husband that their eldest son, James Brooke Johnson, should be trained to be his successor.[4]

There was also the question of a religious establishment. Unorthodox though his own religious views were, he always intended that the Dyaks should be given the benefit of the Christian faith, so long as there was no interference with the Muslim Malays. Friends of his had already roused an interest in a mission to Sarawak. In November 1847 a large meeting was held in London, with the Bishop of Winchester in the chair, at which James spoke, describing the life of the Dyaks and asking for subscriptions for the mission. There was a good response headed by Queen Adelaide, who sent £50. The Christian Knowledge Society and the Society for the Propagation of the Gospel in Foreign Parts gave grants; and enough money was raised to start the mission and to support it for four or five years. To lead it a committee set up to administer the fund chose the Rev. Francis McDougall, a former medical doctor who had taken Orders because the young lady of his choice, Miss Harriette Bunyon, had vowed that she would only marry a clergyman. He too addressed the meeting in the Hanover Square Rooms; and the tone of his talk, we are told, 'made Mr Brooke sigh'. But it was hoped that he would be more tolerant when he arrived in Borneo. He and Mrs McDougall set out for Kuching on 30 December 1847, with a small child and with one assistant, the Rev. W. B. Wright. They arrived in Kuching on 29 June, sailing from Singapore in *Julia*, to be followed soon by Rajah James.[1]

The Rajah's visit had been highly successful. But he still had two worries. He had not been getting on very well with Mr Wise. To Wise it seemed ridiculous not to take advantage of the existing interest and enthusiasm. He wished to float a large public company, in which he intended to have half the shares. It would buy Sarawak from the Rajah but leave him to administer it, on a profit-sharing basis. The country would be properly developed, to everyone's financial benefit. He could not comprehend why the Rajah disliked the scheme. Indeed, James's demands for financial support were not easy to satisfy in view of his determination that no one should make money out of the people of Sarawak. Wise was to be allowed to form a company, to which James would give a charter for the exclusive trading rights in Sarawak and Labuan, provided that it raised a capital of £30,000. Wise had to be content with that; but he was resentful, and he had further cause for resentment. James's letters to John Templer had often been hard to decipher; and an enterprising clerk in Templer's office sent some of them round to Wise, hoping that he would be able to identify some of the more illegible names and dates, and not knowing that the letters contained remarks that showed James's growing distrust and dislike of Wise. Wise remained outwardly cordial, but he began to attack James to his cronies.[1]

James's second worry was that, though he was now Governor of Labuan and Consul-General for Borneo, the Government had come to no decision about his status in Sarawak. He was not recognised as Rajah and ruler of a sovereign state. His request for it to be recognised as a British Protectorate was shelved. He seemed to enjoy unofficial recognition; but that offered no security to Sarawak for the future. What would happen if he were to die? The Government's hesitation was understandable. Not only was it difficult to decide on the legal position of a British citizen who acquires sovereignty over a foreign land; but did Britain really wish to be committed to an establishment in Borneo, a country which appeared far more important in James's eyes than it did to the statesmen in London, with all the world to contemplate? The occupation of the little island of Labuan was one thing; it could easily be given up if need be. It was another matter to take over the responsibility for Sarawak.

The Government might hesitate, but it treated the Rajah with respect. When the time came for his departure for the East, it placed at his disposal, for himself and his party, H.M.S. *Maeander*, under the command of his old friend Captain Keppel. She set sail from England on 1 February 1848.[2]

CHAPTER IV

THE YEARS OF TRIBULATION

It was a cheerful voyage. The Rajah was accompanied by a new private secretary, Spencer St John, who was later on to be his biographer. Wise had recommended him, as the son of an old business associate; but the St Johns were beginning to doubt Wise's integrity. Also on board were Mr William Napier, named Lieutenant-Governor of Labuan, with his wife and daughter, and Mr Hugh Low, a botanist who had already spent nearly three years in Sarawak and was now appointed Colonial Secretary at Labuan. The midshipmen on board included James's nephew Charles Johnson and a boy to whom James had taken a fancy, Charles Grant, whom he persuaded to join his service. Though Charles Johnson, who was rather serious, and St John, who was very serious, disapproved, the midshipmen treated James almost as an equal, using his cabin as a club-room. The senior officers were shocked; but James's good spirits charmed everyone. Both he and Keppel were excellent talkers; and St John gives a gay picture of the Rajah dancing a polka with one of the officers, followed by a valse with Mrs Napier. During the voyage the engagement was announced of Miss Napier to Dr Low.[1]

The party was cordially received at Singapore. The official confirmation of his knighthood arrived when he was there; and he was formally invested with the Order by the Governor. He attended Miss Napier's wedding; and a number of dinners were given in his honour. He was back in Kuching in the first days of September. A fortnight later his eldest nephew arrived. Brooke Johnson had already changed his surname by deed poll to Brooke, and was generally, though not yet officially, recognised as the heir to the Raj. The Malays called him Tuan Besar, the 'Great Lord'. Charles Johnson had already left to return home; but the brothers had a few days together at Singapore.[2]

There were other additions to the European community. Charles Grant left the navy and stayed on with the Rajah. Another former midshipman, William Brereton, a distant connection of the Brookes, who had visited Sarawak on board the *Samarang*, joined the service about the same time, as well as a Mr Alan Lee and Mr Henry Steele.

The McDougalls were living in the Court House, while a house and a church were being built for them on a hill just behind the town, given by the Rajah for the perpetual use of the Mission.[1] A few more traders had arrived, including a party who had leased the working of the antimony mines from Wise and his partners. These, however, did not remain in Kuching for long. They had been given the lease without James's knowledge; and he discovered that they had too little capital to work the mines continuously. He therefore cancelled the contract.[2] He had already written from Singapore to Wise repudiating the concession to him and asking for his account for the last three years. As Wise had just founded an Eastern Archipelago Company to exploit Sarawak and Labuan, he was in a difficult position and began to show his resentment openly. James retaliated. In the course of 1848 the firm of Melville and Street went bankrupt and James lost a large sum in it, possibly £10,000. He blamed Wise for having involved him in it. By the end of the year he broke off all connection with him.[3]

Apart from the antimony mines all had gone well during his absence. Arthur Crookshank had proved an efficient, just and well-respected administrator; and there were no disorders to report. James was given a warm welcome by the Malay and Dyak communities. His first action, having received permission from Lord Palmerston to do so, was to provide Sarawak with a national flag, a red and purple cross, out of the Brookes' shield, on a yellow ground. It was hoisted very ceremoniously before the assembled citizens at Kuching, while the band from the *Maeander* played *God Save the Queen*. The Rajah himself flew the Union Jack also at his residence, as Consul-General for Borneo. The flying of these flags inspired a letter of protest from the Netherlands Foreign Ministry to London.[4]

Sarawak was peaceful; but the Rajah's absence had encouraged his enemies in Brunei and the pirates. Makota had recovered influence at the Brunei Court and was in touch with the Saribas Dyaks, to whom Sherip Mullar had returned. Raids were increasing again, not against Sarawak territory but against the peaceful Dyak tribes and the Melanau villages along the coast to the East. James could not deal with the problem at once; he had to go to establish his government at Labuan. He spent two months on the island. His experience was disillusioning. The island on which he had set such store proved to have a very insalubrious climate. He fell desperately ill and nearly all his companions had fever. His letters home grew querulous. Drainage would improve the climate; and good barracks and offices were needed; but he was allowed no labour force and insufficient money. Then he heard to his fury that *Maeander*, which he had hoped would be diverted for his own use, was ordered to the China Station, and he would have to make do with the East India Company's steamer *Nemesis*, when she could be spared from her regular runs between Singapore, Kuching and Labuan. How could he fulfil his Consular duties under such conditions? Moreover, *Maeander* was well suited for use against the pirates, whereas *Nemesis* would be useless for that. In December 1848, while *Maeander* was still at his disposal, he sailed in her to visit the Sultan of Sulu, whom he found friendly and full of promises to repudiate his pirate subjects. From Sulu he went on to Mindanao in the Philippines and was hospitably received by the Spanish Governor of Zamboanga; and he peered into Illanun Bay, the home of the Illanun pirates, whom the Spaniards were quite unable to control. When *Maeander* returned to Labuan at the end of January, Captain Keppel, who had planned the cruise as an aid to convalescence, was delighted to notice how much more cheerful he was. Moreover, the settlers in the island seemed better and happier. But then Keppel and *Maeander* had to proceed to China, and James returned to Kuching.[1]

There he was horrified by the reports of pirate activities. The Saribas Dyaks had acquired a new leader, a Malay known as the Laksamana. During the last three months they had burnt a number of villages and killed some 300 persons. At the end of February they raided the Sadong river, killing 100 of the local Malay population while they were harvesting. They planned to attack the town of Gedong but found it prepared, so sailed away. Their next objective was the Melanau villages round the mouth of the Rejang river. Canoe-loads of Melanau refugees from the Matu and Kalaka rivers began to arrive at Sarawak with tales of devastation. At the end of March, after one attempt to lead an expedition against them had been foiled by the weather, James made use of the arrival of *Nemesis*, under its friendly Commander Wallage, to penetrate into the Saribas country. But most of the pirates were busy raiding. He was able to burn a few of their longhouses but never to come to grips with them. His efforts had little effect; he would have to wait until a larger expedition could be organised. The Navy's help was needed, and was promised for July. In the meantime James revisited Labuan and Sulu, whose Sultan signed a commercial treaty with Britain.[2]

The expedition which set out from Kuching on 24 July was the most successful and most notorious of all that he launched. Admiral Sir Francis Collier had sent H.M.S. *Albatross*, with H.M.S. *Royalist*; and *Nemesis* was available. *Albatross* was too large for use in the shallow pirate waters, but provided her longboats, which set out with *Royalist*, *Ranee* and *Nemesis*. James brought a fleet of eighteen praus, led by his own war prau, *Rajah Singh*. He was joined by over fifty praus manned by the Sea Dyaks of the Lundu and Balau rivers and the Malays from the Samarahan and Sadong rivers. As the force sailed into the mouth of the Batang Lupar it learnt that the Saribas raiders had set out in full strength two days previously for the north. James planned to intercept them on their return, by blocking the three rivers up which they might travel. He and his praus waited just inside the Kalaka river, *Nemesis* and the main force lay in the Saribas, while *Royalist* guarded the entrance to the Batang Lupar.

Late in the afternoon on 31 July a rocket from *Rajah Singh* told the rest of the squadron that the pirate fleet was sighted. It had intended to raid the town of Matu, which, however, it found well defended; and it had only had time to destroy one village before the news of the Rajah's expedition arrived and it seemed wise to return home. Finding the Kalaka river blocked, the fleet swept round the low headland into the Saribas; and there, in the growing darkness, ran straight into the main concentration of its enemies. The battle took place off the sandspit of Batang Maru. The pirates were soon thrown into disorder by the gunfire from *Nemesis* and the smaller naval vessels. They could not escape up the Saribas; and the Rajah's praus came round to cut them off from the open sea. His Malay and Dyak allies, longing for revenge on the tribe that had so long persecuted them, showed no mercy. The pirates fought tenaciously for five hours, under a bright moon. Led by Linggir one group made a supreme effort to board *Nemesis*, but their canoes were overturned and many of them cut to pieces by the steamer's paddle-wheels. At last, after losing nearly a hundred boats and nearly five hundred men, their main force, still about two thousand strong, managed to land on a peninsula some ten miles up the river. The Rajah could have cut them off there and prevented their escape into the jungle, but he thought that they had learnt their lesson. As it was, some five hundred died from wounds or from exposure before they reached their homes.

The expedition followed them up the river to burn once more their stronghold at Paku. It then turned north to sail up the Rejang to Kanowit, where it destroyed some villages belonging to the Skrang Dyaks who had moved there and were raiding their neighbours. It returned to Kuching on 24 August.[1]

The campaign had been remarkably efficacious. The Saribas tribes were crushed, and sent to offer their submission. Though they were unrepentant, it was many years before they ventured to go raiding again, and then on a much reduced scale. The Skrang Dyaks were thoroughly frightened. When the Rajah sent Mr Crookshank to build a fort on the Batang Lupar, close to the mouth of the Skrang river, they too submitted. The fort was built with the help of the friendly tribes of the district and was put under the charge of Sherip Matusain, an old Malay trusted by the Rajah. The local tribes, however, did not trust him and asked for an Englishman. Brereton, then aged twenty, was sent and lived there for several years without a compatriot nearer than Lingga, where another fort was built and put under the charge of Alan Lee.[2]

A new era seemed to have begun. The coastal peoples could grow their crops and harvest them in peace. Coastal trade revived. At Kuching there was an atmosphere of contentment. Mrs McDougall, in spite of a serious illness which nearly cost her her life, wrote happily home about its pleasant social life. The Rajah was At Home every Tuesday evening to the whole British community, with dancing and charades; and the party would end with the singing of the song *Rix Rax*, which acquired the status of the Sarawak National Anthem. The McDougalls were At Home on Thursdays; and once a month the Rajah entertained them to dinner. He frequently invited the children of the Mission school to play in his garden. Young Brooke charmed everyone with his bright, pleasant manners. James had left him in charge when he went off for the Saribas expedition, and he played his part well. But James's health was not good; and he was worried about Labuan and about the commercial position. The Eastern Archipelago Company was not proving efficient. But he hoped to sort it out. He had no idea as yet about what was happening in England.[3]

The British Liberal conscience is a remarkable phenomenon. It is often unattractive and often characterised by smugness, narrowness, ignorance and a certain lack of scruple. But its value has been great. If British colonial policy has changed in the course of the last two centuries from an imperialism that was sometimes commercial and sometimes political into a conception that colonies are trusts to be administered only until the local people are fitted to administer themselves, it is mainly due to the unrelenting efforts of the liberal-minded men of the nineteenth century who kept a constant eye on British overseas settlements, to see that there was no harsh exploitation of native races and no trampling upon their human rights. Societies such as the Aborigines Protection Society played an honourable part in maintaining Britain's good name. Unfortunately, with regard to Borneo the British Liberal conscience showed itself at its worst. In fact James Brooke, though his methods were his own, shared the same ultimate views; no one was more determined than he that native races should not be exploited or oppressed. But his temperament, though liberal in a broad sense, was not akin to that of most Victorian Liberals, with its pious Puritan background. He was an adventurer and, though generous and altruistic, an egoist. He had, moreover, a love for expressing himself in writing impetuously, and not always consistently, and too great a willingness for his writing to be published. Such words as 'Am I really fond of War?—I ask this question of myself, and I answer—Certainly—for what man is not', when removed from their context, were unlikely to please the high-minded. It is not surprising that many honest philanthropists in England found him incomprehensible and even a little outrageous.

Nevertheless it is hard to justify the venom of the attack that was made on him, especially as its chief agent, working from behind the scenes, was neither philanthropic nor pious. Henry Wise was already angry with James for refusing to help him to riches and for criticising him behind his back. This enmity was increased by the misfortunes of the Eastern Archipelago Company. Wise had failed to secure the backing of any respectable merchant-house, owing to the demands that he made about his own salary. The Company was short of capital, and its few backers wanted quick profits. James was not being helpful. He had refused flatly to join the Board himself. He had brusquely turned the Company's lessees out of Sarawak; and though the Company was given early in 1848 the concession for coal-mining in Labuan, the coal was not easy to mine. James Motley, the Company's representative, discovered that the coal near the surface had all been taken by a certain William Henry Miles, a man who had appeared in Labuan in 1847 and set up a dram-shop there and had obtained a two-year lease of mining-rights from Mr Napier. The mines were at the north end of the island.

The Government refused, and the Company could not afford, to build a road to them. Motley found himself short of labour and without any form of police protection. He quarrelled with Napier, which was not difficult, as Napier quarrelled with everyone, including his son-in-law. The Government, which was itself short of money, would not pay for the coal. Fever was endemic. When Captain Keppel came to the island to coal in August 1848, he found little there, and his men had to load it themselves. For all his affection for James, he reported that Labuan was useless as a coaling station. Admiral Collier, who visited Labuan later, was even more damning in his reports. Motley gave up the struggle and allied himself with Miles, who soon found a way of ingratiating himself with Mr Wise and his company.[1]

The attack on James Brooke began on legitimate lines. On 21 August 1848, the day before he was invested with his knighthood at Singapore, the House of Commons was asked to vote money for the upkeep of Labuan, including a salary of £2000 for the Governor. Mr Joseph Hume, Liberal Member for Montrose, an old man whose two passions were the discovery of scandals in the public expenditure and in the colonial administration, said that the salaries were too high. He moved for a reduction, and was supported by Mr Gladstone. The Prime Minister, Lord John Russell, spoke in defence of the motion; whereat a friend of Hume's, Colonel Thompson, rose and said that, while Rajah Brooke was certainly a remarkable man, anyone with a spark of humanity must shudder to read of the massacres perpetrated by the Royal Navy during the operations against the so-called pirates of Borneo. Hume's motion was defeated, and no more was heard of it for the moment.[2]

James himself provoked the next row. He visited Labuan in the autumn of 1849. There he found Napier in the midst of his quarrels. Napier's enemies accused him before James of carrying on trade. Miles had just left and had sold his dram-shop to Napier's clerk, Meldrum; and Napier had guaranteed some of Meldrum's minor purchases. James, rather too precipitately, decided that Napier was guilty. He learnt that Napier had borrowed money from Wise before leaving England. That, too, angered him. He curtly suspended Napier from his post as Lieutenant-Governor. It is true that after Napier's departure Labuan became a happier place. But Napier was in fact innocent of the charges brought against him. Scott, who succeeded as Lieutenant-Governor, was a more capable and more equable man.[3]

It was about this time that the story of the Battle of Batang Maru reached England. To most of the British public it was another brilliant saga of British arms. Hume thought differently. It was Wise who had drawn his interest first to Borneo. When Keppel was publishing James's journals he had consulted Wise about the wisdom of publishing certain passages which seemed to glory in the battles that James had fought with the pirates. Wise advised against their publication but kept copies of the relevant passages. He had sent Hume extracts which, divorced from their context, certainly gave a very bloodthirsty impression. Hume had faith in Wise, who clearly knew a great deal about Brooke and Borneo, and who had, moreover, helped largely in the recent foundation of the Aborigines Protection Society, which seemed equally admirable. He was deeply and sincerely shocked. It was clear to him that this so-called Rajah, whose commercial doings Wise had painted in a lurid light, was using the Royal Navy to massacre innocent savages in order that he might grab their land. Hume consulted Richard Cobden, who shared his ideals and was a far more astute and experienced politician. More ammunition was given to them in 1849, when Captain Mundy published a new edition of James Brooke's journals, including some of the sanguinary passages which Keppel had omitted.[1]

It was not long before Cobden and Hume had an excellent opportunity for airing their views in Parliament. By an Act passed in George IV's reign prize-money was paid to any ship of the Royal Navy that went into action against pirates, at the rate of £20 for every pirate killed and £5 for every pirate present at the action. The Treasury were beginning to find this very expensive, and the Government planned to amend the Act. In future the prize-money would be assessed according to the circumstances of each action. There had already been complaints at the sum claimed by Captain Belcher for an action against Illanun pirates in 1844. The case was only settled in 1849, when he received £12,000; and now over £20,000 was due to Captain Farquhar and his men for the battle of Batang Maru. Sir Christopher Rawlinson, Recorder of Singapore, before whose Court the claims came, asked for £100,000 from the Treasury to cover the sums that he would have to pay out for 1849.

The Bill to reorganise prize-money came up for the second reading on 11 February 1850. Hume and Cobden hastily summoned a public meeting, apparently through the Peace Society, which, in spite of an awkward speech by a certain Captain Aaron Smith, who had himself been a victim of piracy in Borneo waters, empowered them to present a petition to the House, drawing its attention to recent events in Borneo. Cobden therefore intervened in the debate, to say that there was no evidence that the victims of the recent attack had ever indulged in piracy against any British vessel. One of his supporters, Colonel Thompson, intervened to ask, not unreasonably, whether prize-money did not tempt naval commanders to regard innocent tribes as piratical. The Government's answer satisfied the House; but on 21 March Hume moved for papers regarding Borneo. On 23 May the Naval Estimates came up, and included the £100,000 required by the Recorder of Singapore. Cobden rose to assert categorically that the murdered Dyaks had not been pirates. Mr McGregor, who was a friend of Wise and Chairman of the Eastern Archipelago Company, suggested that Sir James Brooke would have to be tried for the massacre. Sidney Herbert, while saying that the prize-money could not be withheld unless the Recorder of Singapore's judgment was reversed on appeal, wanted to know about Sir James's commercial activities. Bright, while not mentioning Sir James, declared that so large a sum should not be paid without exhaustive enquiries. Government speakers supported the Rajah's actions and reputation, and the Estimates were passed by 145 votes to 20. Hume's demand, made in July, for a Royal Commission to investigate Borneo was similarly rejected. Palmerston, as Foreign Secretary, wrote to James to confirm the Government's complete confidence in him. But in fact the Government was a little disquieted, especially as Wise had written a clever letter to Lord John Russell insinuating that the Rajah's proceedings were not quite in order for a servant of the Crown.[1]

James had been unwell after his visit to Labuan in the autumn. In March he went to Penang to recuperate, together with his nephew Brooke, who had also been ill, and the McDougalls. Mrs McDougall had recently lost a child and very nearly died herself. At Singapore James learnt from English newspapers of the attacks being made on him in England. He was deeply hurt and very angry. Though in the salubrious climate of the hill-top in Penang he recovered something of his health and his nerves, St John reported that he was never quite the same man again.[2]

The Government had asked him, in his Consular capacity, to go to Siam to arrange a new commercial treaty between the British and the Siamese. In August 1850 he was ready to visit Bangkok. The mission was a failure. An American mission, sent a few month before, had failed to come to any agreement with the Siamese, who now showed that they were equally unready to oblige the British. James never saw the King, Rama III, who was ill. He only once saw the Chief Minister, the Phrakhlong, and the Supreme Council, the Senabodi. The negotiations had to be done by letter. His demands that British merchants should have rights of residence and property, freedom of worship, no restrictions to their trading and an extra-territorial Consulate, were all rejected by the Siamese. The merchants already, they said, had freedom of worship and no unnecessary trade restrictions. They had to control residence permits as sometimes British merchants behaved badly and they were not prepared to grant any extra-territorial rights. James's demeanour throughout was noticeably haughty, but that seems not to have caused offence. What ruined his diplomacy was that in his exasperation he threatened the use of force and of the British Navy. He himself admitted failure and privately declared that force would be advisable. But it might be better when the old King died. His probable successor, Mongkut, was said to be anglophile and more amenable.

Later, indeed, relations between the Rajah and King Mongkut were cordial. The King sent a state barge as a gift to Kuching, and it was used by the Rajah on official occasions till it was destroyed during the Japanese occupation. The Borneo Company, founded in 1856 to develop Sarawak, soon acquired interests in Siam; and it was to the Company that the King applied for an English nursery governess for his children. The career of Mrs Leonowens, which modern authors and playwrights have so romantically exaggerated, was the outcome of Brooke's mission to Bangkok.[1]

James was back in Kuching in October, well satisfied with the situation there. In December he visited Labuan and was pleased with its progress. But his health was still bad. He felt that he would benefit by another journey to England to recuperate and also to be at hand if more attacks were to be made on him. As he passed through Singapore in January he learnt that Mr Woods, Editor of the *Straits Times*, had been given an official position as Deputy Sheriff. The *Straits Times* had at the time described the battle of Batang Maru as an atrocious massacre and had always taken a malicious delight in reporting every attack on him. James regarded Woods as a personal enemy. He wrote angrily to the Governor to protest. The Governor declined to intervene; and Woods inevitably heard of the protest. At the same time James thought that he had traced the story of the atrocities committed at Batang Maru to Dr Miller, surgeon on *Nemesis*. He persuaded the Admiral, Francis Austen (Jane Austen's brother) to hold a Court of Inquiry, at which Miller denied spreading any reports. The matter was dropped.[1]

The Rajah arrived in England in May 1851, and remained there till April 1853. He had planned to take a cottage at Lyme Regis and to live there in retirement, but in fact he only left London to pay short visits to his family and friends. First he tried once more to have the status of Sarawak clarified. While he had been recuperating in Penang, Mr Joseph Balestier, the unsuccessful envoy from the United States to the Court of Siam, received orders from President Zachary Taylor to make contact and arrange treaties of amity and commerce with Brunei and Sarawak. Balestier therefore arrived at Kuching with a letter from the President to His Highness the Rajah of Sarawak. It gave James enormous pleasure to be recognised by a foreign power; and he always felt warmly grateful to the United States. But in his absence no treaty could be arranged. Moreover, he felt that he must first consult the British Government. Lord Palmerston, to whom he applied, gave him free permission to enter into any treaties that he wished. But still the British themselves would neither recognise him as a sovereign ruler nor undertake to protect him and his country. James's hope of procuring some definite ruling by personally seeing the Foreign Secretary was disappointed, in spite of his recognition by the Americans.[2]

Still more worrying was the renewed attack on him by Hume and his friends, which broke out as soon as he landed. Hume hastened to give notice that he would once more ask for a Royal Commission. On 10 July 1851 he raised the matter in Parliament, armed now with two documents. One was an address organised by Woods and signed by fifty-three merchants of Singapore, thanking Hume for his efforts, declaring that no one of them knew of Dyak pirates and deploring armed action against helpless natives. The other was a letter from William Henry Miles, late of Labuan, roundly stating that the battle of Batang Maru was an unprovoked massacre and complaining that James Brooke was obstructing in every possible way the settlement or trading of any other European along the north coasts of Borneo. With this additional evidence Hume reiterated his charge that the Dyaks were not pirates. His friends backed him. Cobden declared that Sir James fought his neighbours for the purpose of obtaining their land. Thompson said that he who liked could act St George, but he did not himself believe in the dragon. Mr Gladstone was more restrained. He described Sir James Brooke as a truly Christian philanthropist, but felt that, all the same, the question of piracy and its suppression should be examined.

For the Government Mr Drummond had no difficulty in showing that William Henry Miles was not a man to be trusted—he had, owing to a little misfortune, been abroad at the Queen's expense—and that he was too illiterate to have written the letter quoted by Hume. He then produced a letter actually written by Miles, which was misspelt and entirely without punctuation. When the laughter provoked by this document subsided, Mr Headlam read a letter from the Bishop of Calcutta, praising the Rajah's noble work. Lord Palmerston winding up said that he had never heard a debate on which the arguments were so entirely on one side. He quoted reports from Consuls in the Dutch and Spanish colonies expressing the pleasure felt there in the Navy's operations against piracy, and declared that Sir James Brooke emerged from the discussion with his character untarnished and his honour unblemished. Hume's motion was negatived by 230 votes to 19.[1]

Hume and his friends were silent for a while but not inactive. There were weaknesses in the Rajah's case. The fort that he had built to control the Saribas was not in his own territory but on territory that was legally part of the Brunei Sultanate. In his determination to prevent the exploitation of the local peoples he did certainly try to prevent other Britons from settling in Borneo. The publication of his journals by Captain Mundy in 1848 provided his critics with many bellicose passages which Keppel had omitted, and which Cobden read with growing glee. James for the moment was satisfied with the clearing of his name in Parliament. He was delighted to receive a letter from Captain Hastings of H.M.S. *Harlequin*, whom he had criticised in print for not having helped him against the pirates in 1844. Hastings told him that Hume had tried to obtain his support but that he refused to give him any information. He was unperturbed by a speech of Cobden's at Birmingham in November, in which his atrocities were said to throw the atrocities of the Austrian General Haynau into the shade. His chief worry was whether he was going to be sent to Siam again. King Mongkut had succeeded to the throne there; and James was ready to set out in October to visit him. But he learnt that until the late King's prolonged funeral rites were over matters of policy would be neglected.[2]

Hume meanwhile had found a new ally. There was a trader living in Singapore called Robert Burns, who claimed to be the grandson of the poet. In 1847 he came to Labuan and crossed to the mainland, to go on a trading venture up the Bintulu river. On his return to Singapore, he produced an interesting paper on the Kayan tribes with whom he had lived. He had an undoubted talent for anthropology, but he was more deeply interested in money-making. His observations led him to believe that the Bintulu district was rich in minerals. He therefore hastened to ask for a concession from the Sultan of Brunei and for capital from friends in Singapore. The capital was forthcoming and the Sultan promised a lease on condition that the British authorities approved. The matter was referred to Lord Auckland as Governor-General of India; and he consulted the Sarawak authorities. James was in London; and his deputy in Sarawak, Mr Crookshank, wrote to the headmen of Bintulu to tell them to guard Mr Burns's safety, as he came with the Sultan's authority, and to remind them (unnecessarily in Burns's view) that no Englishman had authority to force them to work against their wishes. When he returned to Kuching James followed it up with a letter to the chiefs. The next that James heard of Burns was when he was sued by a Malay from Brunei at Labuan for non-payment of a debt. The case was decided against Burns in his absence. In 1849 Burns asked Captain Wallage of the *Nemesis* to convey him from Labuan to Bintulu. Wallage refused. He had no wish to make a special call at Bintulu and there were many small boats available for Burns. Burns complained to James, adding that he was being victimised. James curtly supported Wallage. Burns did not in fact return to Bintulu. The antimony there was perhaps not as profitable as he had hoped; and the chiefs had not been helpful. He was next heard of up the Baram river. In 1850 three local chiefs wrote to James as Governor of Labuan to say that this trader had arrived and they had hoped to do business with him. But they found that he not only stole people's wives but ordered the local tribes to kill anyone who entered the Baram river, of whatever race they might be. Lieutenant-Governor Scott read the letter and passed it on to James, who wrote back to the chieftains to say that no Englishman who misbehaved enjoyed any protection from him or from the British Government, and that wrong-doing must be punished in every country. Later that year Burns was sued at Labuan for assault by the captain of a ship in which he had travelled. But the crew testified so openly about the lawless behaviour of both parties that the case was dismissed. Burns stayed on at Labuan, making occasional trading voyages to the mainland. His chief cronies there were Miles, till he returned to England, and Meldrum of the dram-shop and his partner Riley.

The letter purporting to come from Miles which Hume read to the House included the story of Burns's victimisation. It is, however, unlikely that Burns drafted it, as he had some knowledge of anthropology, while the letter lumped all the races of Borneo, including the Saribas Dyaks, together as 'Malays'. In August 1851 Lord Palmerston received a letter from Burns himself. It was a more effective statement of his case, which was not without some point. James had no legal right, either as Consul-General or Rajah, to decide who should be allowed to trade in Brunei territory. But Palmerston was perfectly satisfied by the full report that James, at his request, sent to him.

Burns was not to remain Hume's ally for long. In September of that year he set out with Captain Robertson of the *Dolphin* to sell armaments round the coast of north Borneo. Off Marudu Bay he and Robertson quarrelled. The captain was about to sail angrily back to Labuan when *Dolphin* was suddenly attacked by pirates. Burns's head was taken from him, together with those of most of his companions. Eventually the local Sulu governor, an amiable ex-pirate called Sherip Yassan, sent the boat with the few survivors back to Labuan.[1]

Hume was unperturbed. He still did not believe in pirates. Early in 1852 he forwarded to Lord Derby a letter purporting to come from the Sultan of Brunei, full of complaints about the Rajah. When Derby caused enquiries to be made in Brunei, the *pangirans* there said that the letter had been forged by Burns and Motley the previous year in order to embroil them with Sarawak. In March Hume rose in the House to move for copies of this letter and the letter from Burns to Lord Palmerston, and reiterated his charges, citing Miles once more. Henry Drummond in reply produced evidence that Miles was an ex-convict from Australia called Loyd, who had been a fence, a brothel-keeper, a pickpocket, a procurer and a bigamist. But Hume refused to accept the proofs.[2] Meanwhile in Labuan Motley put it about that Burns had been murdered by agents of the Rajah. He himself, however, was killed a few years later with all his family by the pirates whose existence he denied.[3]

James had reason to feel satisfied at his enemies' failure. On 30 April his friends rallied round him at a public dinner held in the City of London in his honour. The list of guests was widely representative; the speeches were full of praise for him; and his own reply impressed everyone by its sincerity. He spoke with pride of his achievements and with hope for the future of Borneo.[1] Before long he realised that the Eastern Archipelago Company had never raised the capital which it had guaranteed to produce under the terms of its charter. He therefore successfully brought an action in the Court of Queen's Bench to vacate the charter; and the verdict was supported on appeal before the Exchequer Court by a majority of seven judges to one.[2] Sidney Herbert was still raising trouble in the House over James's alleged commercial activities. It is true that his position as Rajah with control of certain commercial monopolies in Sarawak was doubtfully compatible with his position as Governor of Labuan and Consul-General. He tried to explain to Herbert in a series of private letters that the two positions did not clash, or, at least, that a government of which Herbert was a member had not thought so. But Herbert declared himself unsatisfied.[3]

At the end of 1852 James was informed that for reasons of economy the Government intended soon to cut down the establishment at Labuan and abolish the post of Governor. He had already announced his wish to resign the post; and he offered to forgo a quarter of his salary till a decision was reached. But on 1 January the situation was changed by the coming into power in England of a coalition government under Lord Aberdeen. It was not a very stable government and it needed Liberal support. The Cobdenite section of the Liberal party was worth conciliating. Hume took advantage of this to distribute round the Government a long open letter repeating all his old charges. James consulted his lawyers about issuing a writ for libel; but they advised against it.[4] Other intrigues were going on behind the scenes. James had already seen Lord John Russell, who was Foreign Secretary till the end of March, to say that he intended to go back next month to Sarawak and that he wished to be relieved of his official appointments. He was told that Lord Aberdeen would like him to retain them. On 15 March Lord John informed the House in answer to a question from Hume, that it was not intended to set up any enquiry on Borneo before Sir James Brooke's departure. He was therefore horrified to hear officially on 30 March, six days before he was due to sail, that the Government proposed holding an enquiry in the East, under Lord Dalhousie, on his whole situation. James had at times pressed for a parliamentary enquiry to be held in London. But an enquiry held at Singapore was a very different matter. He would not be able to produce his witnesses, former Ministers of the Crown and Naval Officers, there so easily; and it would be far more damaging to his prestige. He wrote from Southampton on 4 April to Lord Clarendon, the new Foreign Secretary, to record the propositions which he considered should guide the Commissioners; and he sailed that day believing, as he wrote to Templer, that nothing but good would come from the enquiry. He was as yet prepared to forgive the Government for the somewhat disingenuous manner in which it had sprung the enquiry on him.[1]

At Singapore he learnt further details of the Commission, from information sent by Hume to the *Straits Times*. But it was only long after his arrival in Sarawak that he was informed of the full instructions given to the Commissioners who were to conduct the enquiry. These instructions declared that the Government had never recognised him in any way as ruler of Sarawak; the Commission was to find out his real status and whether it was compatible with him holding offices under the British Crown. It was to decide whether he was or was not a suitable person to decide who were pirates, and whether in fact the victims of his attacks had been pirates. It was to sit only at Singapore and perhaps Labuan. It would not visit Sarawak. Templer, who forwarded a copy of the document to him, had already made a protest to Lord Clarendon on his behalf. James had already written to Clarendon asking for details. Now he angrily wrote again, pointing out that the Foreign Office under Lord Palmerston had recognised his position as ruler of Sarawak, in letters to the Netherlands Government and to himself, and that it was the Royal Navy, never he, who had decided on the piratical nature of the tribes that it punished. The enquiry seemed to raise again the question of the Eastern Archipelago Company which had already been decided in a Court of Law. He asked pertinently about the expenses in which he would be involved, and about the witnesses resident in England whose evidence he considered necessary for his case.[2]

Before an answer could reach him the Rajah returned to Sarawak. During his long absence Sarawak itself had been peaceful. His nephew Brooke was officially in charge and had fulfilled his functions adequately. No evidence survives of the actual structure of the administration. It was fundamentally based on the Rajah's prestige; but the details must have been evolved by the loyal and less-known officials who worked for him. James was no administrator himself. But the country was certainly administered firmly and justly; and the credit for that must go to Arthur Crookshank and his junior colleagues, heroes whose exploits are unsung in history. In particular young Brereton distinguished himself as ruler of the Dyaks of the Skrang and Saribas districts. In July 1852 they were reinforced by an officer who was to outshine them all in ability. Charles Johnson, the younger son of James's sister Emma, arrived to take service under his uncle. His brother Brooke was delighted to see him and have his support. He was at once called the Tuan Muda, the 'young Lord', and was sent to take charge of the district of Lundu, west of Kuching.[1]

Just over the border things were not going so well. The salutary effect of the battle of Batang Maru began to wear off. In April 1851 young Brooke, accompanied by St John and McDougall, sailed in the *Jolly Bachelor* up the Skrang and Saribas rivers and then up the Rejang as far as the mouth of the Kanowit, where they laid the foundations for a fort. It was to control the Saribas Dyaks, who had begun to settle the district and were oppressing the local Melanaus. The site was prepared and a rough building erected, furnished with guns brought from Kuching, and it was left under the charge of Abang Durop, the brother of the Datu Patinggi of Sarawak, who was soon replaced by an English Officer, Henry Steele. McDougall, whose prowess as a doctor was far more effective than his missionary enterprise, kept an enthusiastic journal of the voyage, describing Brereton's primitive but dignified administration of justice at Saribas fort, and Brooke presiding over a peace conference between the Skrang and Lingga Dyaks.[2]

That autumn Brooke went on an expedition with Admiral Austen to punish the pirates in Marudu Bay who had attacked the *Dolphin*. Jane Austen's brother thus avenged Robert Burns's disreputable grandson.[3] Early in the spring of 1853 Brooke heard of a pirate fleet setting out to attack shipping off Sambas, and took the *Jolly Bachelor* and some war praus out to intercept it. It may be that he was deliberately misled; for the real trouble broke out elsewhere. The main agent in reviving Saribas piracy was a chieftain called Rentab. He had, even after the battle of Batang Maru, opposed the idea of any compromise with the Europeans; and he had proved his mettle and won great prestige by conducting a profitable raid against a Chinese village near Sambas and by defeating the praus sent by the Sultan of Sambas and the Dutch to pursue him. He particularly resented the Skrang Dyaks, whose most influential chief, Gasing, had made close friends with Brereton and was now a loyal supporter of the Rajah. With the Tuan Besar away off the coast to the west, it was a good moment for Rentab to attack the Skrang. News of his plans reached Brereton, who summoned Lee from

Lingga to his aid. They collected what loyal Dyaks and Malays they could muster. Lee wished to remain on the defensive in the fort at the mouth of the Skrang. But Brereton insisted on moving to a stockade up the river. When the fleet of Rentab's canoes appeared round the bend of the river, the Malays could not resist attacking them, and Brereton rashly joined them, to run straight into Rentab's main fleet, which was hidden behind the bend. Lee followed to rescue him. There was a sharp battle. Brereton just escaped with his life, but Lee was mortally wounded. Rentab's losses were heavy enough for him to abandon the raid, but he had won a victory of prestige. He retired to build himself a fort on a high hill called Sadok, near the sources of the Skrang and Saribas rivers. Charles Johnson was hastily sent out to replace Lee at Lingga.[1]

James was still at Singapore when he heard of the disaster. It would have to be his first task to punish Rentab. But when he arrived at Kuching in the first week of May, his friends noticed that he looked strange and ill. Next morning it was clear that he was suffering from smallpox. It was a virulent attack. There was no European doctor in Kuching. McDougall, who had a good medical training, had recently gone on leave to England. The Rev. A. Horsburgh, who was in charge of the Mission, read up the medical books in McDougall's library and tried to minister to the invalid. But James was a difficult patient. He did not take kindly to Horsburgh, as Horsburgh sadly confessed. He would only allow such friends as had already had smallpox to approach him. The bulk of the nursing fell on Arthur Crookshank and St John and on his old Malay friend, Sherip Matusain. It seemed for a time that he would not recover; and the anxiety and affection demonstrated by all classes and all races in Kuching was deeply moving. Though the house was in quarantine, Malay ladies would wait there with perfumed water in which he could be washed and cool plantain leaves on which he could lie. In the mosques and Chinese temples as well as in the church there were constant prayers for his recovery. No one in Kuching could doubt the love that his people had for him. At last the fever abated; but three months passed before he could return to normal life. His handsome face was pitifully pock-marked; and he looked far older than his years. But to St John it seemed that the illness had quieted his temperament. He no longer roused himself into such truculent excitement when he talked of the British Government and the Commission of Inquiry.[2]

On his recovery in August, he sailed with St John to Labuan and Brunei. He was well received at Labuan, but thought now that it should be abandoned, as the British Government was not prepared to spend any money on it. At Brunei his reception was splendid. The old Sultan, Omar Ali, had died in 1852. His sons being generally believed not to be really his, he was succeeded by the chief minister, Pangiran Munim. Munim, though married to Omar Ali's sister, belonged himself to a junior branch of the family and was unsure of his position. He was anxious to have the Rajah's full support. James greeted him with marked cordiality, congratulating the Brunei *pangirans* for having chosen their sovereign so wisely; and he made a point of being particularly affable to his old enemy Makota. He had two pieces of business to discuss. The first was to obtain the cession of the Skrang and Saribas districts, in which he had intervened in the past without any legal right. As the area was notoriously lawless and brought in no revenue to Brunei, the Sultan was delighted to oblige him, in return for a small sum and half of any surplus revenue that might be produced from the district. A deed was drawn up giving the Rajah sovereign rights over the coast and hinterland as far east as Kabong, on the Kalaka river.

The Rajah's second task was to obtain from the Brunei Court the letters which his enemies had written to the late Sultan and to Makota. In asking for them he talked too freely and with some exaggeration of the enmity that the British Government was showing him. St John vainly tried to restrain him. The Malays not unnaturally began to have doubts about his position; and Makota declared that the letters were lost. But Makota needed money; and when one of the Rajah's party offered him several hundred dollars, the letters miraculously reappeared. They and the money passed hands at dead of night through the bathroom window of the house where the Rajah lodged. In spite of the damage to his prestige that the Rajah had done himself by his rash talk, the Sultan and his *pangirans*, including Makota, refused to have anything to do with the enquiry. His enemies could obtain no help at all from them. Brunei may have been a centre of corruption; but the loyal friendship shown by its Court to James Brooke at this crisis should not be forgotten.[1]

On his return to Sarawak, James had to face the problem of Rentab. Brereton was still supported by loyal Skrang tribesmen but, with Rentab unbeaten, his position was precarious. At Lingga Charles Johnson was ably bringing order to the district and extracting some revenue from it, in spite of the enmity of two old Malay ladies, Dang Isa and Dang Ajar, who owned most of the land and the population. They were remarkable women, always ready to don men's clothing and lead their dependants into battle, and always ready judiciously to employ poison; and they were indefatigable conversationalists. They called Charles their son while plotting against him. It needed stern action to break their power.[1]

In December James sailed to Skrang and tried to make contact with the Saribas tribes. One of their chiefs, Bulan, was known to be well disposed. But he proved to be so scared of Rentab that he would not commit himself to support the Rajah; and Rentab refused to negotiate. There would have to be a punitive expedition.[2]

Early in the new year, before the Rajah was back, St John learnt from a Malay friend that the Datu Patinggi, Abdul Gapur, was planning a revolt. He had been in the old days one of the leaders of the rebellion against Makota and had welcomed James Brooke's coming. But he had been offended by a reform of the Rajah, which ordained that the three Datus should no longer buy up the goods of the Dyaks, each in his own district, for resale, as before, but should be given a fixed salary. In 1851 he had married his daughter to a certain Sherip Bujang, whose brother, Sherip Masahor, was the *de facto* ruler of the lower Rejang. The Rajah distrusted Masahor and tried to stop the marriage; but the girl insisted; and permission was grudgingly given. This caused further offence to Abdul Gapur, who began to intrigue with Masahor. He was now with the Rajah's army and apparently quite loyal. But St John's informant believed that he had plans to murder the Rajah, the Tuan Besar and the other Europeans in the camp. St John sent hastily to warn the Rajah. Judicious questioning of Abdul Gapur's entourage proved that there was indeed some such plot; and proper precautions were taken. But there was not enough evidence to bring the Datu to trial. However, in June the Rajah appointed headmen for each of the kampongs (or groups of Malay houses) in Kuching, giving them commissions to arrest evil-doers. Abdul Gapur, as senior Malay official, summoned the headmen to his house and took away their commissions from them. He was not going to allow anybody to be made a Datu, he said. The Rajah responded by calling an open meeting of all the leading men of the country. The Datu Bandar, who was the Datu Patinggi's brother-in-law, and the Datu Temanggong, who was his cousin, were told what was to happen and promised their support. At the meeting the Rajah reproved the headmen for giving up commissions that he had bestowed on them, but said that he knew them to be loyal to him. He then turned on Abdul Gapur, telling him that he must submit to the government or die. Abdul Gapur submitted. Then, while he still sat in the Council Chamber, his house was searched for arms. He was allowed after that to go home; but a few days later the Rajah suggested that he might like to go on a pilgrimage to Mecca. He wisely agreed. His offices were given to the Datu Bandar. The title of Datu Patinggi was abolished. When eventually he returned he was still truculent. His relatives refused to go surety for him, so he was banished to Malacca.[1]

So long as the Datu Patinggi was at large James had to postpone any action against Rentab. But in April Brereton planned a small expedition against one of his supporters, a chief called Apai Dendang, whose long-house was at Dandi, on a spur between the Skrang and Saribas rivers. Hitherto campaigns against the pirates had been conducted by water. But to reach Dandi it was necessary to march for several miles through the jungle. Neither Brereton nor Charles Johnson, who came to join him, was used to land warfare. Progress was so slow and difficult, that after one day the two Europeans and the Malay troops allowed their Dyak allies to go on without them. It was a mistaken policy. The Dyaks penetrated to the longhouse, without scouts and in no form of order. Those that tried to climb into it were cut down by the defenders concealed inside. The rest fled back to their leaders, pursued by jeering enemies. But Apai Dendang was inclined to be friendly. He promised to pay fines in compensation for some Skrang Dyaks whom his men had recently killed; and he offered provisions and guides to take the expedition back to the fort at Skrang.[2]

In May news reached Kuching that Charles Grant, who was stationed at Lundu, was ill with smallpox. The Rajah hastened there to look after him. Fortunately it was not a severe attack, and he soon returned with the invalid to Kuching. During his absence there was a scare in Kuching when the powder magazine blew up in a thunderstorm. St John believed that it had been hit by a meteorite. The damage was large, but no lives were lost.[3]

In August the Rajah himself set out against Rentab. The Commission of Inquiry was about to sit at Singapore; and some of his advisers wondered if it were wise to go attacking pirates at a moment when his whole right to attack pirates was about to be questioned. But James had no doubts. He was now the legal sovereign of the district; it was entirely his own affair. And Rentab was a proven pirate. The expedition was planned with care. Rentab was known to be at a fort called Sungei Lang, near the head of the Skrang river. The Datu Temanggong was sent up the Saribas river, to prevent reinforcements reaching Rentab from there. Steele, from Kanowit fort, moved up the Kanowit river to keep the Dyaks there at home. The main force, led by the Tuan Besar, with his brother, Crookshank, Brereton and four other officers, moved up the Skrang. The Rajah went with them for some thirty miles, to a spot called Entaban, where he stayed with the heavier ships which could go no further. The force penetrated to the hill of Sungei Lang and after a sharp battle, nearly lost because the Dyak troops, as usual, attacked too soon, its palisades were stormed and the longhouse entered and burnt. Rentab's losses were heavy and he himself was wounded. But his men carried him away to safety to his almost impregnable fortress on Mount Sadok. The battle was watched with deep interest by Bulan and his group of Dyaks, who were strictly neutral.

It was not practicable to advance against Sadok. The loyal Dyaks, having enjoyed one victory, wanted to go home now; and there were not enough supplies left for a longer campaign. As the army returned to Kuching it was struck by an epidemic of dysentery. Many of the men died. Brooke Brooke was seriously ill for some weeks. His brother, Charles Grant and St John all were unwell. Brereton had been left behind at his fort at Skrang. There the disease attacked him. He died in October, aged twenty-three. He bequeathed his few belongings to the local chieftains. Charles Johnson, the Tuan Muda, was sent to Skrang to replace him and now had the whole Batang Lupar district under his care.[1]

It was time now for the Commission of Inquiry to open at Singapore. It had been ordered over a year ago; and the long delay not only infuriated James but also began to create an atmosphere of boredom about it even at Singapore. The Government of India was annoyed at having to conduct the affair. It took many months for them to find suitable Commissioners who could be spared. Names had to be submitted to London; and Clarendon turned down the first suggestions. At last he consented to the appointment of the Advocate-General of India, Charles Henry Prinsep, and a government agent, Humphrey Bohun Devereux. They arrived at Singapore on 27 August to find that none of the documents from London that were needed for the case, copies of

Hansard as well as letters and affidavits, had come. The Rajah arrived a few days later, travelling in a ship of the Royal Navy.

Few Commissions can have been more haphazard and ineffectual. Of the two Commissioners, Prinsep was highly neurotic, and was, indeed, certified insane a few weeks after his return to India. Devereux was clear-headed but somewhat cynical and impatient of the whole affair. The Rajah was hurt and angry and determined to be truculent; he refused to respond to any friendly gesture on the part of the Singapore authorities and forbade his staff to accept any social invitations. His first action at the opening session on 11 September was to read the protest against the terms of the Commission which he had already sent to Lord Clarendon. But his opponents found the terms equally inconvenient. The only document available for the Commission was the paper drawn up by Hume in London. It accused James Brooke of having settled in Borneo with the sole object of seeking profit by trade, of having meddled in Brunei politics for his own personal ends, of having made cruel attacks on the inhabitants of Borneo on the pretext that they were pirates, but really to subject them to his rule, and of having obtained the assistance of the ships of the Royal Navy and of the East India Company in making these barbarous attacks. It referred to the refusal of Captains Belcher and Hastings to comply with Sir James's requests for aid in these attacks, which were entirely unjustifiable, and to the memorandum sent in by the fifty-three British merchants of Singapore.

Not all of this was relevant. Neither Belcher nor Hastings nor any other naval officer supported Hume's assertions. And the Rajah's enemies proceeded to pile up other irrelevancies. Mr Woods, the editor of the *Straits Times*, insisted on being present at all the hearings in his role as Deputy Sheriff. Prinsep approved, though Devereux demurred, but admitted later that it had been useful. The Rajah thereupon absented himself from the Court and had to be lured back. His behaviour and the continual delays over obtaining papers caused innumerable adjournments. Woods himself and Napier, the ex-Lieutenant-Governor of Labuan, tried to bring their personal complaints against the Rajah before the Court but they were ruled out of order. The Rajah wasted many hours in a close cross-examination of Motley, the employee of the Eastern Archipelago Company in Labuan, who, though his cronies were men such as Burns and Miles, in fact knew very little of what had been going on. The Commissioners' patience was already near to exhaustion before they could reach the two essential points of the enquiry.

First, were the Skrang and Saribas Dyaks pirates? The fifty-three merchants who had signed the memorial to Hume denying the existence of piracy proved hard to trace. Some of the signatories were dead or had left the East. A few, led by a Mr Guthrie, firmly maintained that only Malays were pirates, never Dyaks except under compulsion. Dr Allen—a medical practitioner who had never been a merchant— said that he had signed the memorial without having any views on the matter; but he thought, in view of all the talk, that it would be only fair to James Brooke that an enquiry should be held. Captain Wright of the *Julia* and Thomas Tivendale, a shipwright, both testified that they had promised to sign the memorial in the belief that it favoured the Rajah's actions and had vainly tried to have their names removed when they learnt what it really contained. The memorial was thus discredited. More telling evidence in the Rajah's favour came from other sources. Fifty-nine Chinese merchants at Singapore sent a memorial to the Commission expressing their gratitude to Sir James Brooke for having done so much to make the seas safe for their ships. The ex-Datu Patinggi, passing through Singapore on his enforced pilgrimage to Mecca, was summoned by Mr Woods in the hope that his rancour against the Rajah would induce him to attack his cause; but the Datu firmly declared that the Skrang and Saribas Dyaks were indeed pirates; his own child had been killed in one of their raids. Finally, a Dutch official, Mr C. F. Boudriot, who happened to be passing through Singapore, intervened. The Dutch had no reason to support James, whose presence in Borneo they resented. But Mr Boudriot's sense of justice was outraged. He gave clear and authoritative evidence that he, and every Dutch official in Borneo, regarded these Dyaks as pirates, whose atrocities were unquestioned and whose suppression was vitally needed. Spencer St John, when called upon, added lurid details about the atrocities.

There remained the question of James Brooke's own position. In a final appearance before the Commission, he announced that he had resigned the offices of Governor of Labuan and Consul-General for Borneo, as there had been criticism, and he himself felt that it was now unbefitting as Rajah of Sarawak to continue in those offices. He declared that he had never sought personal gain and had never been a trader who buys and sells for his own profit. As regards himself as an independent ruler he was not quite logical. He had, he maintained, sovereign rights; he could coin money, make war, sign treaties, and he owed these rights to election by the free people of Sarawak and to tenure from the Sultan of Brunei, to whom he did not deny that he paid a yearly sum. He remained a British subject; and if there should be a clash between British and Sarawak interests he would be bound to support the former. He wished Britain to accept a protectorate over Sarawak, as its *de facto* independence was modified by lack of material power. It was not, however, bound by the 1847 treaty between Britain and Brunei, in which Britain guaranteed to suppress piracy in Bornean waters. The suppression of piracy in Sarawak was his own task.

This statement was made on 27 October. It was not till 21 November that the Commission finally closed. Prinsep, who was becoming more and more eccentric, wanted to continue it in Labuan and Brunei; but Devereux was firm. It was costing the government between £800 and £900 a month; and he had had enough. Moreover, the Sultan of Brunei refused to co-operate in any way out of loyalty to his old friend James. Devereux's views prevailed; and each Commissioner settled down to write his report. Prinsep's was short. He thought that James Brooke's actions against the Dyaks had been justified. Their piracy had been proved and more evidence might have been forthcoming had not Sir James Brooke's personal opponents disseminated rumours that witnesses might be inconvenienced or detained. But he thought it unfortunate that Sir James associated himself with savage allies; was it necessary to pursue the pirates up their rivers so fiercely? He held that this association was 'a strong ground against the investing of an individual, holding authority under a half-savage chieftain, with any such official character under the Crown of Great Britain, as that then held by Sir James Brooke'. He found that Sir James had never been a trader in the true sense of the word, but it would be wrong to entrust him with any discretion to determine which tribes were piratical or to allow him to call for the aid of the Royal Navy. His position was none other than that of a vassal of the Sultan of Brunei, though his tenure was admittedly very lax and easy to discard.

Devereux sent in a longer report. He too regarded the Dyak tribes in question to have been clearly proved piratical, and he spoke with approval of Sir James's various actions against them; nor did he regard those measures as over-harsh. Whether Sir James should be entrusted with the discretion to decide which tribes were piratical depended, in his opinion, on whether he held any official position. If Great Britain was to suppress piracy along the north coast of Borneo, as she had undertaken to do by the treaty of 1847 with Brunei, there should be some authority empowered to call upon the help of the Navy; but in his present position Sir James had not that power. He then discussed at some length the status of Sarawak. He could not agree that it was independent, as Sir James claimed. There had not been a successful rebellion against Brunei there, nor had Sir James been properly elected ruler. As Rajah he still paid £1000 annually to the Sultan. How then could he be a sovereign ruler who could freely dispose of his country? Sir James had very properly said that as a British subject he would always put the interests of Britain above those of Sarawak. The whole position reminded Devereux of that of the Court of Directors of the East India Company when they held land in India from local potentates. The questions raised at that time had never been solved; and Mr Devereux did not offer a solution now. He did, however, consider that the Treaty of 1847 applied to Sarawak as a part of Brunei.[1]

In short, the findings of the Commission entirely exonerated James from the charges brought against him. Hume and his friends were silenced, though many years later Mr Gladstone was to make an unkind reference in Parliament to the Battle of Batang Maru. Wise attempted to reopen the issue of the Eastern Archipelago Company by another action against the Rajah, which failed; he too faded from the picture. But the findings were not helpful for the future of Sarawak. The Rajah had been pronounced a vassal of the Sultan of Brunei and in no way entitled to call upon the protection of Great Britain. His prestige in the East was damaged; and there were elements there which did not fail to notice his official isolation.[2]

James himself was at first elated to be clear of the long humiliating episode. On 2 December, the day before he sailed from Singapore for Kuching in H.M.S. *Rapid*, he wrote gaily to Templer that:

> Now is the winter of our discontent
> Made glorious summer by that blockhead Hume,
> And all the clouds which lowered about our house,
> In the dull bosom of the Blue-books buried.

But, once back in Kuching, he began to worry about the status of his country. Letter after letter was sent to Templer asking him to consult the best legal opinions in England on his behalf. He was worried about the cost to himself of the Commission. Templer was to see that every farthing of postage and stationery was to be charged to the Government. He half hoped that he would be asked to reconsider his resignation from his official posts, or at least from that of Consul-General.[1] He was not at all pleased when the following summer he received a polite letter from Lord Clarendon, saying that the Government had refused to accept his resignation till the Commission should be over, for fear of seeming to show prejudice, and in doing so now wished to express its satisfaction with his services. Lord Clarendon further announced that the new Consul-General for Borneo was to be Spencer St John. James at first told St John to refuse the appointment; and St John had difficulty in trying to show that this was meant as a friendly gesture. The appointment might have been given to the new Governor of Labuan, Mr G. W. Edwardes, a man who very soon showed his dislike of the Rajah. As James both liked and trusted St John he reconciled himself to his promotion, but still regarded it as a snub to himself. He would not allow a British Consul to reside in Kuching, so St John moved to Brunei. At the same time he agitated with the British Government at least to give him a steamer, if they would not offer him protection. But this was refused; and he could not afford to buy one for himself.[2]

Further difficulties arose when the British Government issued an Order in Council laying down that all law cases in which British subjects were concerned must be held in the Courts of the nearest British colony. This was an infringement of the sovereign status of Brunei as well as Sarawak. The Rajah refused to countenance it. St John as a compromise suggested that as regards Sarawak the Rajah would guarantee that any such case would be heard under a published law, that no British subject would be inflicted with a punishment heavier than an English Court would give, and that the Consul-General would be summoned to sit among the judges. Thanks to the influence of Lord Grey, who had always been a staunch supporter of the Rajah, the Government accepted the compromise. Sarawak's position was still equivocal, but there seemed now to be good will. The Rajah even found it possible to forgive Hume, when asked to do so in a message from Miss Harriet Martineau. 'I will be as generous as she wishes', he wrote. 'Hume, I am now convinced, was not guilty of anything more than stupidity and perversity.' In this charitable frame of mind James was able to turn to the happier task of devising improvements for the government of his country.[3]

CHAPTER V

THE CHINESE RISING

To Spencer St John's friendly but not uncritical eye the months that followed the end of the Inquiry seemed the happiest in the Rajah's career. He still had his grievances against the British Government. But he was no longer persecuted; his good name had been vindicated; and powerful friends, such as Lord Grey and Lord Ellesmere, were using influence on his behalf. His personal finances worried him; but the country was prospering. He could make further plans for it. The European community was growing; and he found it sympathetic. There were distinguished visitors now and then, whom he loved to entertain. He was an admirable host. Like many men who live too much alone with juniors and subordinates he was apt to resent contradiction and to expect complete compliance with his wishes. But when he was in the company of men whom he liked and respected his manner mellowed. He enjoyed and encouraged argument. He talked freely and well himself, showing the extraordinary width of his interests and his reading. He became a passionate chess player, working out many problems with St John. During the early part of 1855 Alfred Wallace the naturalist spent several months in Sarawak. He was a very welcome guest. St John, who was soon to move regretfully to Brunei, describes with relish weekends spent in the bungalow that James had built at Paninjow or in his cottage at Santubong. James and Wallace would stay up half the night boisterously arguing on matters of religion and science. Wallace was a protagonist of Darwin's theory of the origin of species, while James regarded himself as a modernist Christian. If Charles Johnson were there he would weigh in with crude, pantheistic views, the result, so St John thought, of too much indiscriminate and uncritical reading. McDougall, though cheerful and high-spirited, did not care for intellectual discussion, so the Church would be represented by his second-in-command, Mr Chambers, who was always ready to stand up for orthodoxy. St John enjoyed taking part, as did some of the younger officials, such as a newcomer, Charles Fox; but these young men seemed not to have the same tough educational training as their elders. Neither Brooke Brooke nor Charles Grant cared for these noisy discussions. They preferred the gentler society of Kuching over which Mrs McDougall presided.[1]

Soon the mission ladies lost their status as the only European women resident in Kuching. Mrs McDougall's health had been bad for some years; but she had completely recovered. There seemed no reason why white women should not live healthily in Sarawak. The Rajah did not much like the idea of his officials marrying. Wives, he thought, might distract men from their duty and unfit them for service in the outposts. But when the wives arrived he welcomed them. Mr Middleton, the Inspector of Police, was married by now, with two children. In October 1856 Arthur Crookshank returned from leave with a bride of seventeen, a quiet, sensible girl, whom the Rajah immediately liked. About the same time news came from home that Brooke Brooke, the Tuan Besar, and Charles Grant, who were both on leave, had married, Brooke's bride being Grant's sister, Annie. The Rajah amused himself by ordering furniture for the house in which the young Brookes were to live.[2]

But there was more to do than to entertain guests and to buy furniture. The pirates were quiescent but not suppressed. In April 1855 the Rajah was at Lundu, having heard that Balanini pirates were off the coast. Though none were encountered he was delighted to find the Dutch at Sambas eager to co-operate with him. He began to feel that he was better valued by the Netherlands than by Britain. In June he visited Brunei, in order to discuss the question of the town of Muka. Muka was a small Melanau port on the coast half-way between the Rajah's frontier and Bintulu, from which sago was exported. Nearly all of the crop was carried in coastal vessels to Kuching, where Chinese merchants milled it. The good government of Muka was therefore important to Sarawak. The government recently had been far from good. The Sultan had appointed as its Governor a *pangiran* called Ersat, whose oppression had brought the populace close to revolt. Their champion was Ersat's cousin, Matusin, who was almost as corrupt but more popular locally, as his mother was of a Muka family. Ersat had banished Matusin, but the Sultan had given him permission to return. One day Ersat publicly insulted Matusin, who ran amok and killed Ersat along with one of his daughters. Ersat had been a friend of Sherip Masahor, of Serikei. Masahor collected his local Malays, together with Saribas and Kanowit Dyaks, and marched on Muka. Matusin, besieged in his house, agreed to surrender, on condition that his life and his people's lives were spared. He was, however, warned of treachery and managed to escape with six followers. Next morning Masahor entered the house and massacred forty-five of its inhabitants, mostly women, giving the heads to his Dyak allies. Matusin fled to Kuching and threw himself on the Rajah's protection. The Tuan Muda was sent to Muka, and found that the Dyaks had not only burnt the whole town but had desecrated the Melanau graves, for the gold ornaments buried with the corpses. He returned to Skrang and imposed a fine on Masahor for having called out Dyaks who were the Rajah's subjects, and banished him from Serikei.[1]

As neither Muka nor Serikei were within the Rajah's dominions, it was necessary for James to go to Brunei to obtain permission from the Sultan to restore order. He found the Sultan genuinely cordial, but the misgovernment and corruption at Brunei as bad as ever. The Sultan's chief minister was Makota, who chose prudently to be absent. An opposition was led by Hassim Jelal, the reputed son of the late Sultan. Munim begged James to remain and take over the government in his name or at least to reorganise the Government. This James attempted. He revived the power of the Datus and insisted that Munim appoint Hashim Jelal as Datu Temanggong, to secure his support for the government and counter Makota's influence. The Sultan also agreed verbally to give the Rajah freedom to do as he thought best with regard to Muka and Serikei. James was somewhat surprised to find out a little later that the Sultan had transferred the government of Muka and Bintulu to Makota. It was clear that something more drastic would soon have to be done about Muka if the sago trade was to survive. The Sultan's promise to maintain the new order in Brunei itself proved equally elusive.[2]

Next January, the Tuan Muda, on his uncle's orders, took over Serikei and built a fort there. It was placed under the charge of Mr Fox. In June the Tuan Muda used Serikei as his base for an attack on Saribas Dyaks who had settled on the Jalau river, a tributary of the Kanowit. With a few hundred men, armed mostly with spears, as he only possessed 100 out-of-date muskets and a few rifles, he advanced into country that the Dyaks had thought impenetrable, and by burning the Jalau long-houses alarmed the Dyaks into abandoning raids for a year or two. The task of keeping the Sea Dyaks under control was now almost entirely on his shoulders. It was a hard task. He had to listen to and assess every rumour of hostile activity and usually to take action without any time to call on help from Kuching. He had to work out his own system of jungle warfare, conscious that his few Malay troops were of little use except on water and that his Dyaks would usually act rashly or stupidly unless they were led by himself or by one or two respected Malay chiefs. He was allowed only £30 a month for the upkeep of the district, which now comprised half of the Raj of Sarawak. Though the Rajah valued his work, occasional reproofs would come from Kuching. When during a rice famine on the Batang Lupar he forbade the export of rice and fixed its price, he was treated to a stern lecture on the importance of Free Trade. That he survived was due to his courage, his hardiness and integrity and an almost arrogant self-reliance, which raised him to the rank of a demi-god, both with the loyal Dyaks and with the pirates.[1]

His brother Brooke, the Tuan Besar, was of a gentler calibre. Brooke was popular with the Malays, who respected his good manners and his intelligence, and he was well liked by the Europeans. St John noted with approval his attempts to organise the administration, especially its finances. The Rajah, who had no gift for organisation, looked on gratefully, though occasionally he was alarmed lest Brooke was overspending.[2] The chief governmental reform was inaugurated by the Rajah himself. His friend Lord Grey had suggested to him that it might be useful to establish a Council of State, as an advisory body which should keep him in touch with the opinion of his subjects. On 17 October 1855 a decree instituted the Council, which was to be composed of the Rajah and his two nephews, the Tuan Besar and the Tuan Muda, the Datu Bandar, the Datu Temanggong, the Datu Imam, the religious head of the Malays, and the Tuan Katib, the native Secretary. Its functions were not clearly stated, nor had it a fixed constitutional position, but the Rajah announced that he would inform it and consult it about any major political scheme or development. At its first meeting, a week later, it discussed the question of the jurisdiction of British subjects in Sarawak and approved St John's proposed compromise.[3]

Soon afterwards the growing importance of Sarawak was emphasised by the establishment of a bishopric. According to St John, who did not like the McDougalls, the mission had played very little part in the life of Sarawak. It had done little to spread Christianity among the heathen Dyaks. Only one missionary, the Rev. W. D. Gomes, who was partly of Cingalese blood, was seriously working up-country, having in 1853 started a mission-station among the Land Dyaks near Lundu. The McDougalls seemed to be concentrating on the easier task of converting the Chinese settled in Kuching, many of whom regarded Christianity as a step towards social advancement and governmental favour. The criticism was not entirely fair. The mission was always desperately short of money. Moreover, McDougall was for a long time the only qualified medical practitioner in Kuching, and was called upon to spend on the cure of bodies time that might otherwise have been spent on the cure of souls. Even St John admitted that the mission ran an excellent school for local children of all races; and Mrs McDougall was always ready to take any child however savage into her house. The Rajah liked the McDougalls. He found them kind and cheerful and undaunted, and in no way bigoted. He also felt that as a sovereign prince his capital should possess its own bishop. The Church in England was not unwilling to elevate Mr McDougall. But there were technical difficulties. Could a Bishop of the Church of England hold a see which was not under the British Crown? It suggested that the Bishopric should be of Labuan. But James was not going to have his country dependent ecclesiastically on a British colony. As a compromise it was arranged that Mr McDougall should be Bishop of Sarawak and Labuan, his Sarawak title depending on Letters Patent from the Rajah. In the autumn of 1855 he went to Calcutta to be consecrated by the Bishop, who, it seems, did not entirely approve of this new recruit to episcopal rank; for he wrote to him after the consecration that 'I have taken the liberty to caution you, now that you are a chief pastor and a father in God, against excessive hilarity of spirits. There is a mild gravity with occasional tokens of delight and pleasure, becoming your sacred character, not noisy mirth.' It was, however, the new Bishop's boisterousness that endeared him to most of his flock.[1]

Mammon, too, was now honoured in Sarawak. After his experiences with the Eastern Archipelago Company the Rajah was unwilling to allow any business firm to interfere in Sarawak. But John Templer persuaded him that Sarawak could only be developed by introducing a company with adequate capital. Through Templer's agency Mr Robert Henderson, of Messrs R. and J. Henderson, was induced to raise the necessary capital and found a company, to be known as the Borneo Company, which was to exploit the government-controlled monopolies, such as coal and antimony, to organise the sago and gutta-percha trade, and finance further governmental commercial schemes. It was to be the sole public company permitted to operate in Sarawak. It was registered in May 1856, with Robert Henderson as its Chairman and with Templer on the Board. The Rajah wished St John to be made its managing director in Sarawak but, to St John's relief, not only was he at this moment appointed to the Consul-Generalship, but the Board of the Company insisted on a trained businessman as its local director. It nominated a man of Danish origin, Ludvig Verner Helms, who had been since 1851 in charge of the antimony mines of the country. Helms was a capable if somewhat complacent man; the Rajah could never bring himself to like him, largely because he had had no say in the appointment. But any annoyance that he felt began to be dissipated when the Company bought a steamer to ply regularly between Kuching and Singapore and named her *Sir James Brooke*. She was well armed, as a precaution against pirates.[1]

By the end of 1856 everything seemed to be going well. Even the British Government appeared to be better disposed. The Rajah's main worry was his own health. Continual bouts of fever made him wonder how much longer he would be able to work in the East. He was therefore all the more anxious to secure adequate protection for his country. But he felt on the whole cheerful and hopeful. He was ill again at the end of the year; but a short visit to Singapore restored his spirits. His nephew the Tuan Besar and Charles Grant and their brides were on their way out to join him, accompanied by his niece, Mary Nicholetts, whose young brother-in-law Harry had just entered his service.[2]

Some of his officials in Sarawak were less sanguine. There was one section of the population which, they thought, should be watched with care. James had no prejudice against the Chinese. His own steward was a Cantonese, Law Chek, who had come with a few friends from Hokkien to settle in Kuching, where they soon dominated the commercial life. They were followed by immigrants of Chao An stock, mostly small shopkeepers and wharf labourers, and by Teo Chow, from Swatow, who mainly settled in small farms just outside the town, where they cultivated gambier. In each case there had been one man who organised the immigration; and these three leaders, Ong Ewe Hai the Hokkien, Chan Kho the Chao An, and Law Kian the Teo Chow, were regarded by the Rajah as the heads of the Chinese community and were jointly consulted by him on Chinese affairs. Their presence was generally recognised as an asset.[3]

Less satisfactory were the Hakka Chinese of the great *kongsi* which worked the goldmines round Bau in Upper Sarawak. James had found this *kongsi* in operation when he first came to Sarawak and admired its efficiency. He had hoped that when he obliged it in 1842 to accept the existence of another *kongsi* across the Sarawak river it would in future respect his government. But trouble had not entirely ceased. The rival *kongsi* had faded out; the Bau *kongsi*'s numbers had grown. There had been a large influx in 1850, mainly of refugees from the powerful Montrado *kongsi*, which operated just across the border; but there were also criminals who came to escape prosecution by the Netherlands authorities. This increase worried the Rajah's officials. The taxes paid by the *kongsi* were assessed on a basis of population; but it was impossible to find out exactly how large the population now was. By the late 1850's it was thought to be around 4000; but the Chinese only admitted to about half that number. It was clear, too, that the *kongsi* was heavily engaged in smuggling opium, which was a government monopoly and an important source of revenue. Most worrying of all was the growth of secret societies among the Chinese. In the early seventeenth century a secret society had been founded in China for the purpose of ejecting the alien Manchu dynasty and restoring the Mings. It was called the Tien-Ti Hueh, or 'Heaven and Earth Society', or alternatively, the Sam-Hap, or 'Triad'. In theory its aim was to create a mystical union between heaven, earth and man, which should produce political harmony. In practice it had long been a closely knit political society aiming at material power, strongly xenophobe and ruthless in its methods. It had by now branches all over Nan Yang, as the Chinese call their colonies outside China itself; and a branch had been formed in Borneo, known as the Sam-Tian-Kiau Hueh. Such societies were proscribed in China and in the British and Netherlands colonies. The Rajah's government tried to forbid the existence of the Sam-Tian-Kiau. But the Hueh found friends among certain Malays. The Sultan of Sambas and his nobles, most of whom had been brought up by Chinese nurses, were sympathetic, chiefly owing to their jealousy of the Rajah; and through them the Hueh made contact with Makota and the anti-British elements at the Court of Brunei.[1]

A clash had occurred in 1850. It was discovered that an agent from the Triad Society in Singapore had come over to reorganise the Sarawak Hueh. He was arrested and sentenced to death; and the *kongsi* was sternly warned.[1] In 1852 the *kongsi* at Bau tried to prevent a Government official from arresting a criminal who was a member of the Hueh. The Tuan Muda was sent with a force of Malays and Dyaks to force submission. The *kongsi* thereupon delivered up the criminal. They were ordered to build and equip a fort at Belidah, near Siniawan, and to pay for its upkeep. It was put in the charge of Sherip Matusain and a garrison of reliable Malays. The Tuan Muda also demanded that a hundred muskets should be handed over as punishment but, to his annoyance, the Rajah rescinded the order.[2]

In October 1856 there was trouble between the Chinese and the British in Canton. The Commissioner Yeh publicly promised a reward of 30 dollars for every British hand brought to him. Soon a rumour circulated round the East that the British in Canton had been massacred. The Chinese in Singapore were encouraged to attempt a rising in January 1857, which was easily suppressed. The Chinese at Bau also heard the rumour. They knew too of the Commission of Inquiry into the Rajah's actions; while the Rajah himself gave exaggerated and imprudent accounts of his unpopularity with the British Government. It seemed to the *kongsi* that the British authorities, already involved in a war with China, would not bother to give any help to a Rajah of whom they apparently disapproved. They were irritated with the Rajah's government. On his last visit round the country St John had noticed an enormous growth in the population at Bau and had warned the tax-collectors. Moreover, the legal import of opium had fallen remarkably of recent years; yet it was clear that as much, if not more, was being smoked by the Chinese. It was proved that the *kongsi* was definitely guilty of smuggling. A fine of £150 was imposed on it, with a threat of sterner measures if the smuggling were to be continued. The fine was paid, with undisguised resentment, in January 1857. Arthur Crookshank, in charge of the administration while the Rajah was in Singapore, was worried. He heard rumours of the *kongsi* buying arms. A friendly Chinese whispered to him that the *kongsi* was going to use the erection of a new joss at Kuching during the festival of the Chinese New Year, at the end of January, as an occasion for entering the town armed and staging a *coup d'état*. He sent a hasty message to the Tuan Muda at Skrang to beg him to visit Kuching with some of his troops over the period of the festivities. The Tuan Muda came, and owing to his presence nothing untoward occurred. But he felt a little uneasy when he returned to Skrang, while Crookshank decided to keep a permanent guard on the small forts that surrounded Kuching and to have the garrison of the arsenal alert day and night.[1]

When the Rajah returned, early in February, both Crookshank and the Commissioner of Police, Middleton, warned him of the current rumours. But he could not believe that a handful of Chinese would venture to attack his capital. He dismissed the guard and said that no special precautions were needed.[2]

On 14 February St John, who was at Brunei, discovered a Chinese who had been banished from Sarawak trying to persuade his servants to join the Tien-Ti Society, telling them that all the British in Sarawak were soon to be slain. St John had already noted that Makota was often closeted with Chinese from Singapore and with Malays from Sambas. He was seriously alarmed and planned to send a message to warn the Rajah as soon as possible.[3]

On the evening of 18 February everything was quiet at Kuching. The Rajah was alone in his house, apart from his valet, Charles Penty. He had been ill again and had spent the day in bed. In the bungalow attached to the house were Steele, on leave from Kanowit, and young Harry Nicholetts, on leave from Lundu. There were two other houses occupied by Europeans on the left bank of the river; Mr and Mrs Crookshank lived in one, and in the other were Mr and Mrs Middleton with their two little boys and a lodger called Wellington, a clerk newly appointed to the Borneo Company. All other Europeans lived on the right bank, the Bishop and Mrs McDougall on the Mission Hill behind the town, Helms and the Borneo Company staff by the river, just north of the Mission, and the few other private houses scattered nearby. Crymble, the Treasurer, lived in the main fort, which contained the arsenal and the prison.

That afternoon a Malay trader on his way down the Sarawak river in his canoe had passed some six hundred armed Chinese embarking in boats at Tundong. He recognised them as members of the Bau *kongsi*. When he pleaded that he must warn his family who lived a few miles down the river so that they would not be frightened, the Chinese let him pass. He paddled as fast as he could to Kuching and reported what he had seen to a well-to-do relative, a trader named Gapur. Gapur considered the story absurd, but thought it wise to go round to see the Datu Bandar. The Datu was equally sceptical. He refused to trouble the Rajah at once, as he was unwell, but he promised to go across and tell him in the morning.

Long before morning came, the Chinese had burst on the town. Soon after midnight they landed on the left bank and made straight for the Rajah's house. They first attacked the bungalow. Steele managed to escape, but Nicholetts was struck down as he tried to leave the house. The noise woke the Rajah and Penty. They met in the passage in the dark, and the Rajah at first mistook Penty for an assailant and nearly killed him. Looking from Penty's window they saw Nicholetts's murder. The Rajah at first wished to fight; but their only light went out. So, while the rebels were gathered round Nicholetts's body, they crept out through the bathroom door. The Chinese set fire to the house. Penty, who could not swim, fled into the jungle, where he soon met some friendly Malays. The Rajah ran down to the creek to the east of the house and swam under the Chinese boats moored there. He then made his way to the house of a trusted Malay official.

Other Chinese simultaneously attacked the Crookshanks' house. As they ran out of the door together Mr Crookshank was badly wounded but managed to slip through the crowd, but Mrs Crookshank was struck down and left for dead. The Middletons' house was next attacked. The family tried to escape through different exits. Mr Middleton succeeded, but Mrs Middleton was caught in the bathroom, where she hid in a large water-jar. The lodger, Wellington, had taken charge of the children, but he was struck down. Mrs Middleton then heard one little boy shriek as the Chinese decapitated him. The house was then set on fire and the other child flung screaming into the flames.

While Crookshank and Middleton succeeded in joining the Rajah, the rebels crossed the river. The flames on the far bank had woken the town; and all the Europeans there, six men, nine women and eight children, had fled to the Mission-house, except for Mr Crymble who attempted to defend the arsenal. His garrison was four Malays. He also armed the two inmates of the prison; but one, a debtor, fled at once, and the other, a homicidal maniac, merely succeeded in shooting himself. After a hopeless defence Crymble and one Malay fought their way out. In the other fort the garrison of three Malays charged through the rebels and all survived. In the Mission-house all the men, including the Bishop, had guns and vowed to hold back the Chinese till the women and children could escape into the jungle. But at the first streak of dawn seven of the rebels came to the house and demanded to see the Bishop. They told him that their quarrel was with the Rajah and his officials, not

3*a* 'GASING'S FEAST ON THE BATANG LUPAR'

3*b* 'SURPRISE OF THE PIRATE VILLAGE OF KANOWIT'

4 'MR BROOKE'S BUNGALOW'

with the Mission or the Borneo Company; and they asked him as a
doctor to come to the hospital where some fourteen of their men lay
wounded.

The Rajah meanwhile, with Crookshank, Middleton and James
Penty, had crossed in a Malay canoe to the Datu Bandar's house, where
Crymble and Steele joined them. He tried to organise a Malay force
to attack the Chinese; but it was impossible to collect enough men,
while the women began to panic. So he ordered the women to be
transferred to the left bank, which now seemed the safer side. Then,
with his officers and a party of armed Malays, he went by foot to the
Santubong branch of the river, where they were received hospitably by
the villagers of Sabang, and boats were placed at their disposal.

The Bishop visited the hospital. While there he learnt that Mrs Crookshank had been found to be still alive, and he insisted that the Chinese
should hand her over to him. Mrs Middleton was also rescued. A
Chinese had found her wandering half-insane and brought her to
Mr Helms.

Next morning the Bishop, Helms, Rupell (a private merchant trading
with the Borneo Company) and the Datu Bandar were summoned to
the Court-house. There they found the President of the *kongsi* seated
in the Rajah's chair, with his secretaries round him. Outside, Nicholetts's
head was displayed on a pole, the crowd being told that it was the
Rajah's. The President announced that Helms and Rupell were to
administer the European section of Kuching and the Datu Bandar the
Malay section, both under the sovereign authority of the *kongsi*. The
Bishop intervened to remind the Chinese that they might have killed
the Rajah, but they had forgotten about the Tuan Muda, who would
certainly bring his Sea Dyak warriors to avenge his uncle's death. The
elation of the Chinese was dimmed. They consulted together and
announced that they would inform the Tuan Muda that he could
continue to rule his Dyaks. They would not harm him if he did not harm
them. But they thought it would be wise to retire quickly to Bau with
all their booty. The three Europeans and the Datu were made to promise
that no one should attempt to pursue them and to swear oaths of fidelity
to the *kongsi* in the proper manner, scattering cock's blood over the
relevant documents. Next noon, 21 February, the Chinese ships,
heavily laden with arms, plate, money and other valuables, began to
move slowly upstream. The *kongsi* had attempted to take Helms with
them as a hostage, but he hid himself in the jungle.

There are certain discrepancies in the three main accounts of the rebellion. The Rajah's account is reproduced by St John. It is modest and appears reliable, though it does not reveal the fact that the Rajah was at the moment a sick man who had seen his friends murdered, his home destroyed and his rule collapsing. Helms saw himself as the hero of the hour. When he came later to write his memoirs, he inserted a long description of the episode written by his devoted secretary, Tidman, thus disingenuously avoiding the need of praising himself. The Bishop also seems to have given himself the leading role; but his version is recorded in more modest language by Mrs McDougall. She does not endorse all Tidman's statements, as when he declared that the Chinese wished to make Helms Rajah because he was so universally popular. But both Helms and the Bishop thought that the Rajah had lost his nerve, and each saw himself as the saviour of the country.

The Rajah, when he retreated down the river, had urged his Malay friends not to attack the Chinese till he could return with sufficient force to secure victory. But now that they saw the Chinese retiring, the younger Malays, headed by Abang Pata, the Datu Temanggong's son, could not be restrained by the Datu Bandar. A small party rushed after the Chinese and succeeded in capturing one of their boats. But they were driven off. The Chinese halted their retreat and sent to collect more men, peasants as well as miners, before coming down again to wreak vengeance on the town.

Meanwhile the Bishop had crowded the women and children of the Mission into Rupell's schooner and sent them down the river. The ship was too heavily laden to go out to sea. They were disembarked at a village near the mouth. Helms emerged from the jungle to join his employees in another boat, which moved down the river; while the Bishop himself went in pursuit of the Rajah, whom he found at the mouth of the Quop river, and whom he angrily persuaded to return to Kuching. The Rajah agreed reluctantly; he had very few men with him and he knew that it would be wiser to wait for the Tuan Muda and his Dyaks. When the boats containing the Rajah, the Bishop and Helms came into sight of Kuching, they found that the Chinese had returned in full force and were burning the Malay quarter. The Rajah's men attacked but were hopelessly outnumbered; and the Rajah wisely decided to retreat again. The Bishop was angrier than ever, 'If the Rajah deserts his country', he cried, 'I must look after my diocese'. He insisted on returning to the town and trying to collect arms from those Malays whose houses had escaped the holocaust. Helms remained cautiously on his boat in the river, but some of his staff joined the Bishop. As the Rajah's boat passed by, Helms declared that he heard him shout out: 'Offer the country on any terms to the Dutch.' This may be true; but it is more likely that the Rajah was advising what should be done should he himself perish. In any case, with the irascible Bishop trying to collect arms and proclaiming that everyone had forgotten him, and with the Rajah fleeing down the river, Helms saw himself as the only sane European left. He was, he thought, for the moment *de facto* Rajah. It was now 23 February.

At the mouth of the river the Rajah arranged for Malay boats to take the women on to Lingga, where they would be safe. He was prepared to follow them and wait there for reinforcements. The Tuan Muda had been lying sick of a fever at Skrang when a Dyak burst in on him crying that the Rajah was slain and the Europeans driven from Kuching. He roused himself and ordered his boat, to find that on all sides Dyak boats were assembling to take vengeance on the Rajah's murderers. As the large flotilla sailed along the coast it met the boat conveying the Mission ladies to Lingga. The Tuan Muda learnt that his uncle was alive, but the Chinese were still in possession of Kuching. Rumours soon reached the Rajah that the Dyaks were at hand; but he was to find a speedier deliverance. As his boat approached the mouth of the Samarahan smoke was seen on the horizon. It was the *Sir James Brooke* returning on her regular passage from Singapore.

The Rajah at once boarded her; and she sailed up the river, escorted by his own boats, and followed close behind by the Tuan Muda and the first of the praus from Skrang. Helms and his Borneo Company officials were picked up on the way. As the steamer swung into sight of the burning capital, the Chinese manned the forts and opened fire. But they had carried off the ammunition for the guns and had only nails and scraps of iron to use. As soon as the *Sir James Brooke* turned her guns on to the town, the Chinese panicked. Many of them were now on the left bank, to burn the Malay kampongs there. The Dyaks landed, destroyed their boats and pursued them into the jungle. Few of them survived. The main Chinese forces, on the right bank, retired by land to Lida Tanah, where they had left their boats. Belief in the invincibility of their joss which they carried with them preserved some sort of order; and at Lida Tanah they attempted to make a stand. A Malay attack led by the Datu Bandar drove them from their positions.

Henceforward their retreat became more and more desperate. They paused at Bau only to collect their womenfolk and portable belongings, then moved as fast as they could travel to the frontier of Sambas. The men surrounding the joss kept good order to the last; but the Chinese were no match in jungle warfare for the Tuan Muda's Dyaks, who harassed them on all sides. The Land Dyaks joined in the harassing. Had it not been for the arms and ammunition looted from Kuching, few Chinese would have survived to cross the border. As it was, many perished on the journey; and of those that reached Sambas territory many were killed by the Chinese *kongsis* there. By the beginning of March the only Chinese left in Sarawak were the shopkeepers and labourers in Kuching and a few farmers and peasants in the close neighbourhood; and most of them thought it wise to leave the country.[1]

On 28 March, when all was over, H.M.S. *Spartan*, with Captain Sir William Hoste, arrived in Kuching, to protect British lives and property. But Sir William admitted that he had no authority to fire a shot in defence of the Sarawak Government. The Netherlands Government were much more friendly. On the news of the rising the Governor of Pontianak at once despatched a gunboat and troops to give the Rajah whatever assistance he might need. They arrived too late to be of value. But the Governor then went to considerable trouble to recover as much as possible of the loot taken from Kuching and carried over the frontier, in order to return it to the Rajah. It is not surprising that the Rajah began to wonder whether he ought not to place his country under Netherlands protection. But in fact, when the story reached Britain, there was great sympathy for the Rajah there. *The Times* pointed out the responsibility of the British Government and said that it was fortunate that the rebels had not been able to read recent Parliamentary Debates. Even the Liberal *Daily News*, while refusing to repudiate its previous strictures, expressed its admiration for the Rajah's popularity amongst his Malay and Dyak subjects.[2]

The failure of the Chinese rebellion strengthened the Rajah's Government in eliminating the *kongsis*. They had been a continual threat to the State, which had derived small benefit from their mining activities. Their disappearance made the remaining Chinese communities far more law-abiding. It was noticed that although from 3500 to 4000 Chinese had been killed or left the country, the revenue raised from Chinese in Sarawak was higher after 1857 than before. There was far less tax-evasion and far less smuggling. It had, moreover, been gratifying to see that not only the Malays and the Land Dyaks, but so many of the Sea Dyaks had remained loyal to the Rajah in spite of the apparent collapse of his power. But the unfortunate results were greater. It implanted into the Brookes a suspicion of the whole Chinese nation, and it seemed to justify the latent racial dislike felt by the Malays and the Dyaks for the Chinese. Though it was still realised that the Chinese could be useful members of the community, it was long before they were made to feel welcome in Sarawak.[1]

The material damage that Kuching had suffered was vast and costly to repair. The Malay town was quickly rebuilt. St John, when he visited Kuching in July, was surprised to see so few traces of the devastation. Even the Europeans were already installed in temporary houses. All of them had lost many of their possessions; and the Rajah, the Crookshanks and the Middletons had lost everything; though a few odd pieces of plate found their way back, thanks to the Dutch. The loss that the Rajah found hardest to bear was that of his library, which he had collected lovingly and which was now entirely burnt. The rehabilitation put a heavy strain on the finances of the country. All that remained of the Rajah's private fortune went to re-equip himself and his officials. The growing prosperity of the country had received a serious setback. The effect on the Rajah himself was bad. He had been through a ghastly ordeal, while suffering from a bout of malaria. The anxieties that he had endured and the horrors that he had witnessed left their mark. The Bishop and Helms might hint that he had behaved in a cowardly fashion, forgetting that each of them had sworn allegiance to the *kongsi*; but it was remarkable that he had acted with so much prudence and good sense. But the strain told on him. Friends, such as St John, noticed that he had lost his old buoyancy of spirit. He was no longer capable of the bursts of optimism and gaiety that had characterised him in the past, even after the humiliating experiences of the Commission of Inquiry. He had always been moody; but his moods were all melancholy now. His natural generosity and friendliness survived but were interrupted by bouts of touchy suspicion and fury. Soon it would be whispered that he was no longer quite sane.[2]

CHAPTER VI

THE CLOSE OF THE REIGN

The storm was followed by a brief period of calm. The Rajah's friends rallied round him. A subscription was raised to pay for his immediate needs, to which the Borneo Company contributed £1000. His old school at Norwich sent him a sum to be spent on books and Cambridge University gave him copies of all the recent publications of the University Press. Various acquaintances poured other books on him; but most of them, St John thought, volumes for which they had no further use themselves. In April Brooke Brooke arrived with his wife and his sister and Grant and his wife. The Rajah, who was at once charmed by Annie Brooke, installed the young couple in the house rebuilt on the site of his old house. He himself moved into a bungalow belonging to Mr Rupell, where Charles Johnson would join him when visiting the capital. This gentle young society suited his weary mood. But some onlookers thought the presence of the ladies regrettable. In the old days local chieftains would come and call on the Rajah every evening. Now they kept away. In particular the Tuan Besar seemed to have no intimate friend among the Malays or the Dyaks.[1]

As a token of gratitude to the Malays the Rajah decided to pardon the leading offenders, the old Datu Patinggi and the Sherip Masahor. The one was allowed back to Kuching and the other to Serikei. Many of his officials were uncomfortable about it, but the Rajah's clemency had often proved right in the past; and they did not like to protest.[2] In June he permitted the Tuan Muda to go on another expedition against the pirate Rentab. Charles penetrated to Rentab's stronghold at Sadok but was forced to retire.[3] In September the Rajah went with St John to visit the Sultan at Brunei. He hoped to make some arrangement about Muka and the sago district, but nothing was achieved.[4] In October he left for England, leaving the Tuan Besar in charge of Sarawak. He had not been home for over four years, and he wished both to straighten his finances and to make another attempt to come to an arrangement with the British Government. Moreover, as he wrote to Templer, it was his wish that his nephew Brooke 'may again take his proper position and administer the Government.... The change which must be at my death I am desirous should be prepared for, if not effected, whilst I yet live.'[1]

He arrived in England at the end of 1857. His reception was friendly, even from the Government. Both Lord Palmerston, the Prime Minister, and Lord Clarendon had been impressed by St John's reports from Borneo. Joseph Hume was dead and Cobden no longer interested; and Lord Grey had been working behind the scenes. The Rajah attended a levée where the Queen and Prince Albert singled him out for notice. He remade friends with Miss Burdett-Coutts, a friendship that was henceforward to be the most important in his life, though it began quietly enough, with an invitation to call one evening, soon followed by another to dinner, to meet the Duchess of Cambridge and Princess Mary. He was delighted to see his family and such old friends as Templer again.[2]

But then things went wrong. He himself was largely to blame. He became truculent and suspicious. Early in the New Year Palmerston offered the protectorate for which the Rajah had been agitating for so long. James refused the offer, unless the Government would compensate him for all the money that he had spent in Sarawak. It is true that his only private income now was his India Army pension of £70 a year; and his argument that the British would take more interest in a country in which they were financially interested was sound. In vain his friends, like Brooke's father-in-law, Mr Grant of Kilgraston, urged him to accept the protectorate at once and leave the financial haggling till afterwards. The Government then suggested setting up a naval base in Sarawak, thus giving the country the naval protection that he so ardently desired. He refused the offer out of hand, till his finances should be settled.[3] He was slightly more amenable when asked if Sarawak would absorb Indians exiled from India for their participation in the Mutiny. He agreed to accept any that were not Muslims. Some Sikhs and Hindus were sent. Their descendants are still in Sarawak, respected members of the community.[4]

It says much for Palmerston's and Clarendon's patience that they continued to negotiate with the Rajah. His intransigence defeated his own ends. In February 1858 Palmerston's Government fell, and Lord Derby became Prime Minister. Derby was an anti-imperialist Tory with a dislike for foreign commitments. When it was pointed out to him that there were British subjects in Sarawak who needed the protection of their mother-country, he replied that that was exactly why he disapproved of adventures such as James Brooke's. In spite of James's influential friends, amongst whom Miss Burdett-Coutts now took the lead, he would offer neither a protectorate nor a loan. James was cheered by invitations to address meetings all over the country, even in the Cobdenite stronghold, Manchester, where he twice spoke in the Free Trade Hall and was cordially received. But nothing was achieved. A deputation of his supporters, which interviewed Lord Derby at the end of November, met with a curt refusal of any kind of help.[1]

The Rajah had other troubles. Soon after his arrival in England he met a young man who claimed to be his illegitimate son. The history of Reuben George Brooke is obscure, and only of importance to Sarawak in its effects on the relations between the Rajah and his heir. Nothing is heard of the boy before 1858, though, if his tombstone is correct, he must have been born in 1834. The Rajah seems genuinely to have believed him to be his son, though he would never give his reasons. His sister, Margaret Savage, who had no children of her own, believed him; but the Johnsons were incredulous. They inclined to think that the Rajah had been tricked; while other friends seem to have suspected that the young man was some new protégé and that James was using this unconvincing excuse for justifying his interest in him. James wrote promptly to his nephew in Kuching telling him of Reuben George's existence and suggesting that he might send him out to work in Sarawak. The Tuan Besar's answer was almost hysterical. The Rajah clearly intended to deprive him of his inheritance, and the humiliation was more than he could bear. James wrote him gently and affectionately, explaining that his obligations towards Reuben George in no way interfered with Brooke's rights and expectations. But he began to have doubts about Brooke's good sense and his loyalty. The Johnsons ultimately accepted Reuben George as a relative; but, after this first year, he played very little part in the Rajah's life. He never went to Sarawak, and eventually died in 1874 in a shipwreck while sailing to Australia. He, his wife and his children had been left £5000 in the Rajah's will.[2]

More seriously disquieting was the Rajah's own health. On 21 October, just after he had made a speech at Manchester, he suffered a stroke and a brief bout of paralysis. His recovery was speedy and apparently complete; but the attack was alarming.[3] When news of it reached Kuching the Tuan Besar, still fretting about Reuben George, decided to visit England. He himself, a few days before he heard about his uncle, had lost his wife in childbirth. It was a serious loss; for

Annie Brooke was a calm and wise young woman whom everyone liked and respected and whose influence over her moody husband was admirable.[1] On his way to England he received a letter from his uncle in which the Rajah talked about retiring. If he could receive £10,000 and a pension of £500 to £700 a year (with £200 a year settled on Reuben George after his death), he would abdicate; and Brooke could carry on the government. Brooke therefore arrived in England in February full of hope that he would soon be Rajah.[2]

The main problem, as both the Rajah and Brooke realised, was money. The Rajah was dependent upon whatever sum could be spared from the Sarawak treasury; and, since the Chinese rebellion, there was very little to spare. The Borneo Company had advanced £5000 for the immediate repair of the damage; but the Borneo Company was not doing well. It had tried to open a coalmine on the Sadong river, without employing a trained mining engineer. The enterprise had been a costly failure. So many Chinese had emigrated after the rebellion that there was a serious shortage of unskilled labour, especially in the wharves. Remembering their duty to their shareholders, the Directors now pressed for repayment. To the Rajah their conduct seemed 'discourteous and avaricious'. He never forgave the Company, nor did his successors. He did not, indeed, possess the money.[3]

While he lay ill of his stroke his friend, Thomas Fairbairn, who knew of the financial position, conceived the idea that a Testimonial Fund might be raised from amongst his admirers, to compensate him for all that he had lost. If £20,000 could be collected the Rajah would no longer be dependent on Sarawak; he would be free to retire whenever he chose. Brooke, when he arrived in England, was enthusiastic. He believed from his uncle's letters that if the sum were found the Rajah would abdicate and he would succeed. Miss Burdett-Coutts thought otherwise. She considered the Testimonial Fund undignified, and she saw no reason why the Rajah should abdicate. She considered that if he held on it might still be possible to arrange for a British protectorate and British financial responsibility. She herself generously offered to loan the Rajah the £5000 that he needed to pay off his debt to the Borneo Company. He accepted it gratefully as a business transaction, offering the revenue of the Government antimony mines as security (a security which her solicitor, Mr Farrer, clearly thought inadequate; but he was used to her acts of generosity).[4] The Rajah's most pressing anxiety was thus relieved; but he did not know his own mind. At times his gratitude to Miss Burdett-Coutts and his respect for her judgment led him to listen to her advice. But at other moments he felt tired and longed to be free of it all, either by abdication in Brooke's favour or else by handing over the country as a gift to the British Government. Brooke did not know what to think. His uncle, he believed, had promised him the inheritance; yet he seemed to consider alternative plans. His parents urged Brooke on. The first thing, he thought, was to make a success of the Testimonial Fund. But the contributions were inadequate. Brooke tried to interest Miss Burdett-Coutts; but he talked too much of his uncle's retirement and his own succession to please her. By May 1859 Fairbairn decided that a public appeal must be made for the Fund, though it was to be done as delicately as possible. In spite of his efforts only £8800 was raised. The Rajah took it into his head that the Borneo Company was to blame; its Directors wished to keep him subservient to them. He was further infuriated when the trustees of the Fund, Templer, Fairbairn and A. A. Knox of the Foreign Office, decided to keep the money in trust, giving the Rajah the interest only. Templer knew well that the Rajah was hopelessly unbusinesslike and capable of acts of unwise generosity. He and his co-trustees may also have wondered whether his mind had not been slightly affected by his many worries and illnesses. It seemed to the Rajah that Templer, who was a director of the Borneo Company, as well as a trustee of the Fund, was the villain of the piece. His suspicions were aroused against him.[1]

It must be confessed that Miss Burdett-Coutts did nothing to help the Rajah's relations either with Templer or with his nephew. She was a possessive and autocratic woman; she had no wish for anyone else to exercise influence over her friend. She seems to have encouraged his resentment against Templer; and she clearly already disliked Brooke. The Rajah was beginning to have doubts about Brooke's capacity as an administrator. In the summer of 1858, while he was still in Sarawak, Brooke had intervened high-handedly at Muka, fining some of the inhabitants, although it was in Brunei territory, and proposing to his uncle that the area should be forcibly annexed. The Sultan complained to St John, who protested privately but firmly to the Rajah. James ordered Brooke to be more cautious in future. Then there had been complaints from the Borneo Company that Brooke was unhelpful and it was difficult to work with him. Having no affection for the Company, James upheld his nephew over this. Finally there was trouble over a doctor whom Brooke had engaged on a three-year contract when in London in 1856. He left Sarawak in 1858 declaring that Brooke had misled him and demanding his full three-years' salary. The Rajah decided that the doctor had a good legal case and must be paid, hard though it was to find the money. These episodes had not troubled the Rajah at the time; but in retrospect they took on importance.[1]

In fact, things had not been going well in Sarawak. There was a trade slump, mainly due to the absence of so many Chinese. Illanun and Balanini piracy along the coast had recommenced; and the Royal Navy would not intervene, even when a Spanish girl was captured and forced into a pirate-chief's harem. It was a Spanish affair, not ours, said Captain Sir William Hoste to St John. The Tuan Muda led two successful minor expeditions up the Saribas in the spring, but failed in a new attempt against Rentab in the summer. The only piece of really good news was the death of Makota in November, when he was trying to abduct girls for his harem from a village up the coast from Brunei. He had constantly worked against the Rajah; his elimination came as a relief.[2]

While the Rajah and the Tuan Besar haggled in England, Sarawak was left in the charge of the Tuan Muda. He, like his brother, was tempted to act high-handedly at Muka. Pangiran Matusin was quarrelling there with Pangiran Dipa, the son of Ersat whom he had murdered, who was supported by the Sultan's representative, Pangiran Jahil. Matusin was having the worst of it, so the Tuan Muda went to his rescue and imposed a fine on Jahil. Once again the Sultan complained to St John and once again St John protested to the Rajah, reminding him of the loyal friendship shown him by the Sultan at the time of the Commission. The fine was eventually returned.[3] During the spring of 1859 sinister rumours spread round Borneo. It was said that the Rajah was in disgrace with the Queen of England and would have been put to death but for the intervention of Sultan Munim. Then in June it was rumoured that all the Dutch in Borneo had been massacred. Several Malays hinted to the Tuan Muda that he should keep a watch on Sherip Masahor at Serikei and on the ex-Datu Patinggi at Kuching. But he paid no great attention to the warnings. He had however visited Kanowit on his way to Muka, and had felt something wrong with the atmosphere. So he had left Fox, the resident at Serikei, at Kanowit, to support Steele, who commanded the fort there. Suddenly the news came that Steele and Fox had been murdered in cold blood in the fort by Kanowit tribesmen. The Malays of the garrison were untouched and apparently did nothing to help the Englishmen. The Kanowits owed some sort of allegiance to Sherip Masahor, who professed himself deeply distressed. When the murderers came down the river to Serikei he arrested the leaders and had them executed.

The Tuan Muda hurried to the Rejang to investigate the tragedy. With him came a force of Malays and Dyaks, including the ex-Datu Patinggi—the Datu Haji, as he was called since his pilgrimage to Mecca—whom he did not like to leave behind. Masahor asked to join him as he went up the river. The Tuan Muda stayed for a time at Serikei, hoping for reinforcements from Skrang which never came. The more he investigated the affair the more disquieted he became. There had undoubtedly been a widespread plot in which not only the Kanowits but the Banyoks, another tribe that owed allegiance to Masahor, and many of the Malays of the Rejang were involved. Masahor was outwardly courteous and co-operative; but he had been a little too prompt in putting to death conspirators who might have had interesting evidence to reveal. Abang Ali, a Serikei Malay in whom the Tuan Muda rightly had confidence, had hurried to Kanowit immediately after the murders and had found it deserted by the garrison and burnt. He had no doubt about the complicity of Masahor's Malay followers, many of whom he discovered in hiding and killed. The Tuan Muda himself ordered the death of the Banyok chieftain, Tani, who protested his own innocence but made it clear that he had known about the conspiracy. When he reached Kanowit the Tuan Muda executed the fort-men for gross dereliction of duty. He then attacked the Kanowit tribesmen, aided by his old enemies the Saribas Dyaks, who had settled nearby and hated their neighbours. But the Kanowits were good jungle fighters, who used poisoned arrows. It was only after considerable losses that the Tuan Muda was able to burn their houses and disperse them into the jungle. He then rebuilt the fort and left it in the charge of Abang Ali and a garrison of his choosing.[1]

When he returned to Kuching the Tuan Muda found his friends wary and suspicious. One by one the loyal Malay chieftains, led by the aged Datu Temanggong, came to him and urged him and all the Europeans to wear arms. They were all armed, they said, because they did not trust their neighbours. Even the Datu Imam, who as a religious man should be unarmed, revealed that he wore a kris underneath his robes. The Dutch authorities sent warnings that there was some large conspiracy afoot. The Tuan Muda took precautions. The European houses were kept well guarded and the fort garrisons put on the alert. It was not long before the Datu Haji came into the open. He had stayed behind at Serekei to consult with his friend Masahor. Thence he moved to Lundu, where he told the local Malays and the Land Dyaks that there was soon to be a general massacre of the Europeans all over Borneo, and if they did not join in it they would suffer afterwards. The Dyak chieftain, Badong, was impressed and promised to help. It was arranged that they would march some night on Kuching and set fire to a few houses. When the Europeans came out to see what was happening it would be easy to kill them all. However, a Dyak crept to Kuching to tell the Tuan Muda. Next morning the loyal Datus assembled representatives of the whole Malay community of Kuching in the Malay Court-house, where the Datu Bandar revealed the plot and demanded the Datu Haji's punishment. It was unanimously agreed. On the following day the Datu Haji arrived from Lundu, to put the last touches to his plot. He was met with the news that he was to be sent under escort to exile in Singapore.[1]

But the trouble was not over. Rumours of plots still multiplied. The Rajah's officials were dispirited. All the good relations that they seemed to have created with the local populations seemed to be melting away. Only Kuching remained solidly friendly. Even there the nervous tension was high; and the Bishop, to St John's contempt, decided that it would be prudent to take his wife and family away on leave. It was, he said, all an anti-Christian movement led by his Mohammedan rival, the Datu Imam, a man who was in fact of unimpeachable loyalty to the Rajah's regime.[2]

The climax occurred early in 1860. An impostor named Tunjang gave out that he was the Datu Temanggong of Brunei and heir to the Brunei throne. He toured Brunei and Sarawak territory, helped by Sherip Masahor, spreading disaffection, and summoning all the Malay chieftains to join him. Among the chieftains summoned was Pangiran Matusain, whose known instability made him a likely supporter. Matusain believed that the summons came genuinely from the Datu Temanggong, but nevertheless reported it to the Tuan Muda. He consulted with the Sarawak Datus, who were convinced that the real Datu Temanggong of Brunei was not involved. From the letter to Matusain it was possible to unravel the plot. The impostor had ordered the Malay chiefs to join him on the Sadong river. They were then to march across the frontier into Netherlands territory, to raise the tribes along the Kapuas river, including the Malays at Pontianak, near its mouth. The Dutch would be massacred; and they would then turn and attack Kuching from the rear, while Masahor led an expedition up the Sarawak river to join them in its destruction.

The Tuan Muda hastily sent Matusain to Pontianak to warn the Dutch, and one of his British officials, Mr Hay, to try to intercept the impostor before he could reach the Sadong. Hay was too late; Tunjang had already crossed the frontier, and was being received as a prince in the upper Kapuas. But the Dutch rushed troops up to Sangau, where they surrounded and captured him. His followers melted away; and he himself was taken to Batavia, to end his days in jail. There he was joined by the Datu Haji, who had hopefully slipped away from Singapore to welcome the successful rebels at Pontianak. He discovered his mistake when the Dutch arrested him as he landed. Both he and Tunjang confessed that Masahor was the prime mover in the plot.

Masahor meanwhile came sailing in two well-armed praus to the mouth of the Sarawak river. There he met the Tuan Muda coming down the river in the *Jolly Bachelor*, with a few small praus manned by his Malays, on his way to the Sadong to restore order there. He saw that the plot had misfired and meekly agreed to follow the Tuan Muda. When they reached Semunjan, some twenty miles up the Sadok, the Tuan Muda received uncontestable evidence from the local Malays of Masahor's complicity. He heard, too, that his own life was threatened; Masahor had offered a life pension of 300 reals a month to anyone who killed him. He struck first. But his troops were Muslim Malays to whom the person of a Sherip, a descendant of the prophet, was sacrosanct. They sunk Masahor's praus and killed many of his men, but they let him slip away into the jungle. He escaped to Muka, then returned to his home at Serikei to collect more men. The Tuan Muda collected a force of Dyaks and hurried to Serikei. Masahor fled back to Muka, leaving his houses at Serikei and Igan to be burnt and his property to be confiscated. His power seemed to be broken. With their leaders gone, the lesser conspirators hastened to make their peace with the government. Confidence was restored in Sarawak. It was not so easy to eject the Brookes after all.[1]

The Tuan Muda had acted ably and bravely. But it had been a strain on him. While he was engaged in fighting the conspirators, the Dyaks up the Skrang and Saribas had resumed their raids. Rentab was still at large and more active than ever. It was time that the Rajah or the Tuan Besar came out to take over the government. The news of the conspiracy had deeply distressed the Rajah. He was proud of his nephew Charles and wrote to him: 'I will not praise you, for words fall flat and cold, but you have saved Sarawak.'[1]

It seemed clear that if only the British Government had accepted a protectorate over the country none of this need have happened. The Rajah thought it more than ever necessary to find a protecting power; and for once his nephew Brooke agreed with him. At his uncle's request Brooke opened tentative negotiations with the Netherlands Government, whose attitude in recent years had been friendly and co-operative. But Holland was not in a mood to add to her colonial commitments. The Indies were proving costly and troublesome, and Borneo in particular offered more anxiety than profit. She politely turned down the Tuan Besar's suggestions. The Rajah thought next of France as a protecting power; but the Tuan Besar was less enthusiastic. The Tuan Muda felt strongly against the idea of offering the protectorate to any foreign power and he seems to have convinced his brother. The Rajah grudgingly gave up the negotiations that he had started with the Emperor Napoleon III. He blamed their abandonment on Brooke's lack of co-operation unfairly, for he was also moved by the disapproval of Miss Burdett-Coutts.[2] She, however, accompanied her expression of disapproval with a generous gesture which delighted the Rajah. She offered to buy him a steamer for the use of the Sarawak Government. He would no longer be dependent for communications with Singapore on the Royal Navy or the Borneo Company. The steamer was built on the Clyde and was ready in October 1860. The Rajah named her the *Rainbow*, as a symbol of hope. Meanwhile he bought himself a small house on Dartmoor, called Burrator, in which to spend his declining years.[3]

Brooke had returned to Sarawak in April. He was engaged to be married for a second time, to Miss Julia Wilstead, and seemed happier and calmer, though his relations with his uncle were a little uncertain. He was not wholly to blame. Soon after his arrival he received a letter from the Rajah saying that if the Testimonial Fund raised enough money he would retire and that he was having the abdication papers prepared by his solicitors. In August the Rajah wrote again, now saying that so long as he himself lived, whether as Rajah or as Rajah Tuah (retired Rajah), Brooke could not be free of his control. Brooke could not find out in fact what his position would be. But in the meantime he was kept busy in Sarawak. He wrote to Miss Wilstead to break off his engagement; but she had set out for the East already, and did not receive the letter until she was already married to Brooke, who felt unable to send her back. The marriage fortunately proved very successful.[1]

St John had recently gone home on leave. During his absence his post as Consul-General at Brunei was given to the Governor of Labuan, the Honourable G. W. Edwardes. He strongly disapproved of Sarawak and the Rajah. Knowing this, Masahor came to Brunei to see him and easily persuaded him that he was a much wronged man, the victim of Brooke imperialism. Meanwhile the real Datu Temanggong of Brunei was sent to Sarawak by the well-meaning Sultan to say that Muka was now open again for Sarawak trade. The Tuan Besar was a little suspicious, and decided to follow the Sarawak sago-ships himself with his brother and three armed schooners. As he had expected, the trading vessels were refused admission into the river. When the Tuan Besar came up he tried to open negotiations with Pangiran Nipa, the official governor. When he sent a boat to cross the bar at the mouth of the river, it was met with shot from a battery on shore. Thereupon the Tuan Besar's ships entered the river and he landed with a small force, while the Tuan Muda tried to move the ships higher up the river, which was defended by booms. It was a difficult operation, but at last the boats were manœuvred to a position above the town, while the Tuan Besar's small force cut it off from the sea. But their troops were too few for them to occupy the town itself. They sent for reinforcements from Kuching. When at last these arrived they prepared to advance. But the very next morning, when everything was ready, a messenger came to the Tuan Besar saying that the East India Company's ship *Victoria*, with Mr Edwardes on board, was at the mouth of the river and that if hostilities did not cease at once she would send a broadside into the Sarawak camp. The Tuan Besar was obliged to comply with the order. The Tuan Muda descended the river while Pangiran Nipa's men in the town jeered at him and fired at him. The brothers went out to see Mr Edwardes, who berated them for their inhuman treatment of Masahor and their interference in Brunei affairs. He had, he said, the Sultan's authority to intervene, though he did so in the name of the Queen. The Tuan Besar retired under protest, accompanied by shiploads of the local inhabitants who had helped him and feared Masahor's vengeance. But he insisted first that Mr Edwardes should sign a paper promising to destroy the forts at Muka, to open up the trade and to see that no reprisals were taken against Masahor's enemies. Mr Edwardes did not honour his promises. The day after the Sarawak flotilla had sailed away he returned to Labuan, leaving Masahor in full control of Muka.

The episode was disastrous in its immediate effects. Masahor felt that he could do as he pleased, having the local British authorities on his side. The sago trade remained at a standstill, to the heavy loss of the sago-growers and of the merchants of Kuching and Singapore. When Helms of the Borneo Company came with Crookshank in *Victoria* to Muka two months later they could achieve nothing. Indeed, Masahor would have fired on the ship had not Pangiran Nipa prudently dissuaded him. Worst of all, Mr Edwardes's action seemed to confirm all the rumours that the Rajah was in deep disgrace with his Queen. The newly recovered security of Sarawak was shaken again. But in the long run it did good. When the news reached London everyone was horrified. St John, for all his sensitivity about the rights of Brunei, had no illusions about Masahor. He hurried to the Foreign Office to protest against his deputy's folly. He was respected there, and his views carried weight. Lord John Russell, the Foreign Secretary, wrote out at once to the Tuan Besar to apologise and to thank him for having acted with such self-restraint. St John's protests were echoed by the Singapore Chamber of Commerce, which sent an indignant message to Lord John. Sympathy with the Rajah increased. It was felt that his position had been made intolerable. Lord Palmerston, the Prime Minister, sent him word that, though his advisers were doubtful whether Sarawak was really independent of Brunei and he could not, therefore, accept a legal Protectorate over it, the Sarawak Government could, by applying to him personally, obtain whatever naval or other help it might require.[1]

St John cut short his leave to return to Brunei, and the Rajah decided to travel out with him. He brought with him his youngest nephew, Henry Stuart Johnson, who was to be known as the Tuan Bongsu, the 'youngest-born lord'. It was a pleasant voyage. James was at his best with St John. Even when they disagreed he never quarrelled with him. They reached Kuching in February 1861. The Sarawak Council was summoned, and St John explained to it that Edwardes's action was repudiated by the Queen's Ministers. He went on to Brunei. There his task was harder. The Brunei Court had been enchanted by Edwardes's attitude. It had raised hopes that the whole of Sarawak might be recovered. But Sultan Munim, though by now almost imbecile, had moments of good sense; and he liked and trusted St John. By April, when the Rajah came to visit Brunei, the old relationship was restored. It was easy to persuade the Sultan that Muka was nothing but a worry to him. It would be wiser to cede it to Sarawak for a sum down and a pension for the rest of his life. He agreed to hand over the coast and hinterland as far as Kadurong Point just north-east of Bintûlu.[1]

Lest Masahor should make trouble, St John went to Singapore and secured the aid of H.M.S. *Charybdis* and 200 bluejackets and marines. He sailed in her to Muka and occupied the town without resistance. The Rajah joined him there with a considerable force a few days later. Pangiran Nipa and his friends were sent to Brunei. Masahor, for whose life St John interceded, was exiled to Singapore. He lived on there till 1890, on a small pension from the Sarawak Government, which he supplemented by shipbuilding. Now and then he would try half-heartedly to stir up trouble in Borneo; but his power was broken. The Rajah remained for a month at Muka. He was happy there, busy all day long arranging for the repair of buildings, making regulations to ensure order, hearing lawsuits, and being accessible and affable to everyone. The sago trade revived at once, bringing a new prosperity with it. After building a new fort and installing Mr Hay as resident, he moved on to reorganise Bintulu and build a fort there. In August he was back in Brunei with St John, for the last visit that he was to make there. The final papers about the cession of Muka were then signed.[2]

With his uncle and his brother back, the Tuan Muda was able to return to Skrang and his Sea Dyaks. There was much to be done there. While Masahor was at large his agents had gone round the wilder tribes encouraging their raids; and Rentab was still operating from Mount Sadok. Throughout the summer of 1861 the Tuan Muda led expeditions up the rivers; and in September he prepared to attack Rentab in his stronghold with a force consisting almost entirely of Dyaks. He was experienced now in jungle warfare and left nothing to chance. Rentab's friends were alarmed and began to desert him. He himself refused the terms offered to him. The Tuan Muda's troops moved relentlessly on, through country which his gunnery expert, ex-Sergeant Lees, who had seen service in India and China, thought the worst in the world, with tracks only fit for monkeys. The mountain-top was reached at last. Rentab fought bravely, but more and more of his followers faded away, and he was himself at last forced out of his burning fortress which, like an active volcano, illuminated the countryside for miles around. Most of his possessions were rescued and taken in triumph to Kuching. Broken and humiliated, he retired to a longhouse on the river Entabai, where he died a few years later.[1] His fall did not entirely reduce the Dyaks to subjection. For many decades to come occasional expeditions were needed to curb their head-hunting raids. But never again were they a severe menace to the security of the state. Instead they were able to play a part in keeping order. In 1862 a field force known as the Sarawak Rangers was founded, with Dyaks as well as Malays enrolled in its ranks. It soon became a predominantly Dyak force.[2]

News of the fall of Sadok came to cheer the Rajah a few days after he had returned to England. He had left Kuching at the end of September, 1861. A few days previously, in response to a correctly worded request from his nephew Brooke, he had installed him as Rajah Muda, or heir apparent. In the speech that he made on the occasion, in the excellent Malay that he now spoke, he told the assembly of all that he had tried to do for Sarawak; he introduced Brooke as his heir on whom would now fall the burden of government, for he himself was old; but, he said, he would return among them whenever it was necessary, if danger threatened them. It was a moving occasion. St John, who was present, was deeply affected.

During all his visit the Rajah's relations with Brooke had been cordial. They agreed entirely over internal affairs; and Brooke seemed sympathetic with the Rajah's desire for a protecting power. The new Mrs Brooke was a steadying influence. Brooke could also confide in St John as an old and trusted friend of the family. The Rajah had left Kuching in a happy and hopeful mood. He had St John again as company on the voyage; for St John had just heard of his appointment as Her Majesty's *chargé d'affaires* in Haiti. St John was delighted to see him joking and laughing again as he had not done since the days of the Chinese rising.[3]

The Rajah's good mood outlasted his return to England. He was pleased to be back at Burrator, where he spent more and more of his time. To St John's disapproval he kept inviting unsuitable young men to stay with him, in the vain hope of training them for the Sarawak service. He saw more of Miss Burdett-Coutts and in April accompanied her and her companion, Mrs Brown, on a visit to the International Exhibition at Paris. He had his worries. His nephew Charles, who was on leave, was with him in Paris and had not been a success with the ladies. His breach with his old friend Templer was now complete; he believed that Templer had publicly described him as being insane.[1] Later he thought that Templer had been inspired by Bishop McDougall, who therefore also fell into deep disgrace. His annoyance with the Bishop increased when in May 1862 St John published a book on his experiences, called *Life in the Forests of the Far East*. In it there was a chapter criticising the Sarawak mission for concentrating on Kuching and doing too little for the up-country Dyaks, and for being thoroughly unpractical about its finances. This roused a storm of protest in ecclesiastical circles; and St John was both publicly and privately abused. The Rajah was furious, as he shared St John's views. He prepared an acid pamphlet for St John to publish under his own name, amplifying the criticisms. It put an end to the controversy; and the Mission was soon reformed, though not fully till McDougall retired and was succeeded by his second-in-command, Chambers, who privately agreed with St John though, being related by marriage to the McDougalls, he publicly supported the Bishop.[2]

James had been toying with the idea of putting Sarawak under the protection of Belgium and was negotiating with the heir to the Belgian throne, the Duke of Brabant. He did not much like the Duke when he met him; and Miss Burdett-Coutts, while admitting that the British Government would probably not object to so minor a power becoming protector of Sarawak, made no secret that she herself thought the idea silly. Yet when the negotiations had to be broken off because the Rajah Muda took it upon himself to write to the Duke from Kuching repudiating them, James felt annoyed.[3] It was as well that they came to nothing. Not only was the Duke of Brabant later, as Leopold II and ruler of the Congo, to show that he was not a suitable man to deal with native races, but, thanks to the hard work of Miss Burdett-Coutts's friends, the British Government was seriously considering a protectorate. John Russell, now Earl Russell, favoured one, though some of his colleagues and advisers were lukewarm. At last John Abel Smith, M.P. for Chichester and an old friend of Miss Burdett-Coutts, arranged that the Governor of Singapore, Colonel Cavanagh, should visit Kuching and send in a report on the feasibility of a protectorate.[4]

In Sarawak the government was going well. But the Rajah Muda was in an unhappy state. In April one of his sons, Annie's elder boy, died. On 6 May the second Mrs Brooke died after giving birth to a daughter. The Tuan Muda, whose health after ten strenuous years was showing signs of strain, had gone home on leave in February; the Grants had gone with him. Brooke had had no one to whom to turn except the McDougalls, whose advice was not always wise. But at this juncture the Bishop very sensibly suggested that he should distract his mind by going on a voyage of inspection to Muka and Bintulu. He set off, together with the Bishop, in *Rainbow*, with *Jolly Bachelor* following. Helms accompanied them as far as Muka. While Helms was at Muka a squadron of Illanun pirates appeared off the river and landed raiding parties. Helms sent a canoe, which managed to evade them, to Bintulu to warn the Rajah Muda. He turned at once and after an hour's steaming came upon three pirate praus. There was a sharp fight; but *Rainbow* succeeded in ramming all three boats. There had been some 240 pirates on board, of whom only nineteen escaped. Thirty-one were captured; the rest were killed. With them were nearly 400 captives. One hundred and forty of them were killed by the pirates or drowned before they could free themselves from their chains, 194 were rescued and taken abroad the Sarawak ships. The others swam ashore. Before the praus sank, much of their stolen treasure was salvaged. These praus had been part of a flotilla of eleven, which had dispersed. None of the others approached Sarawak waters, except for one, which began to operate at the mouth of the Rejang but was discouraged when a boat-load of its warriors was lured into attacking an apparently defenceless Melanau canoe which proved to be full of fighting-men.

The Illanuns had learnt their lesson. It was their last raid off the coasts of Sarawak. Brooke was cheered by his victory and the Bishop was thoroughly delighted by his experience. He had helped to man the guns, and it had been with great regret that he had been obliged to go below to tend the wounded. He wrote a glowing account of the battle which he sent to *The Times*. He was surprised and horrified when at once there was an outcry in British religious circles. Fighting bishops might have been all very well in the days of the Crusades; but Victorian evangelism did not at all approve of them. He was sharply reprimanded by his fellow-ecclesiastics. The Rajah, on the other hand, who liked the Bishop's pugnacity, thought rather more kindly of him.[1]

Once back in Kuching, Brooke fell a victim again to his depression. Masahor still had friends in Kuching, and their line was to go gossiping about the town saying that the Rajah intended to hand over the whole country to the British or to some other foreign power and to leave it to its fate. Brooke heard these rumours and felt his suspicions returning.

At this moment Colonel Cavanagh arrived from Singapore to make his report to the British Government. Brooke received him so cordially that the Colonel felt that he could show him all his confidential papers. Amongst them was a report from St John. St John had not shown it to the Rajah. It had apparently suggested that the Rajah should be given by Sarawak the sum of £40,000 in 5 % stock, as he would have to provide for Brooke should the British Government not continue him as Governor. He emphasised that this was merely a suggestion, should the Government contemplate taking over the country. Brooke at once leapt to the conclusion that the Rajah, St John and the British Government were leagued together to deprive him of his inheritance. As soon as Cavanagh had left he took up his pen and wrote to his uncle:

I hesitated not one moment, but resolved to take my own course, and assert my rights and those of the people of Sarawak. Rajah, you must blame yourself. You have overstrained the bow of my patience, and it has broken at last; we must try our relative strength, and all I can say is, that if I prove the stronger I shall always bear in mind that you were the founder of Sarawak, that you *are* my relative, and that you *were* my friend. I don't write this in anger, but in calm determination.

At the same time he wrote to the British Government breaking off all negotiations with it and signing himself 'Rajah of Sarawak'. A few days later he wrote again to his uncle in a rather milder tone, making it clear that he believed that the Rajah intended to hand over Sarawak to be a British colony, and declaring that he himself would do everything to prevent this 'absolute sale of Sarawak', and that the officials and people in Sarawak would support him. This second letter reached the Rajah before the first. It disquieted him sufficiently, though he thought that it could be 'regarded with calmness and met with derision'. When he received the earlier letter he found it impossible to remain calm.[1]

It is possible to sympathise with Brooke. His position was equivocal; he did not know whether he was or was not ruler of Sarawak. His uncle's promises had been contradictory; sometimes he was abdicating, sometimes not. Brooke did not feel that he was being informed about negotiations going on in England, though he, more than anyone, would be affected by them. And he felt strongly against the possible abandonment by the family of a country that he had come to love, and to which he had personally contributed such money as he possessed. But his behaviour was foolish and unbalanced. He should have known his uncle better and made allowance for his inconsistencies. He should have borne in mind that his uncle was the founder of Sarawak, but for whom he would have had no inheritance of which to be robbed. He should have realised that it was in fact impossible for the Rajah as long as he lived to dissociate himself entirely from Sarawak, or for the people of Sarawak to dissociate themselves from the Rajah. His unwise and hysterical behaviour at this crisis unfitted him to become a potentate.

That, certainly, was Miss Burdett-Coutts's view. She encouraged the Rajah to go out at once to Sarawak, and lent him the money for his passage. His nephew the Tuan Muda, whom the Rajah had recently requested to adopt the surname of Brooke, seems to have pleaded for his brother, but to no avail. He was told to make his choice and wrote unequivocally 'I pledge my faith to support you. I condemn my brother's acts and have told him so.' He offered to go out to Sarawak with his uncle. They left England on 15 January 1863 for France, to embark at Marseilles. With them travelled a young friend of Miss Burdett-Coutts called Charles La Touche.[1]

Before leaving England the Rajah changed his will. His previous will had left Sarawak to Brooke and his heirs and, failing them, to Charles and his heirs. Now he cut them both out of the inheritance. His new instrument begins with the words: 'I leave, commit and devise unto Angela Burdett-Coutts of Stratton Street, Piccadilly, in the County of Middlesex, Spinster, the Succession to the Raj of Sarawak.' It was a strange legacy to offer to a middle-aged spinster. Yet there was some sense in it. Apart from the Rajah himself, Miss Burdett-Coutts was the chief creditor of the Raj; and she would have the means to pay off its other debts. He did not contemplate her emigrating to the East and setting up a Court there. On his voyage out he wrote to her that she should offer the country first to England, and if after a month England did nothing, then to the Emperor of the French. She had the quixotic fancy of offering it, if it had to go to a foreign power, to Greece. But the Rajah wrote back that Sarawak could protect Greece quite as well as Greece could protect Sarawak. And, indeed, it is interesting to imagine the scene at Athens if the young king, George I, newly arrived in his small and impoverished kingdom, had suddenly found himself presented with an expensive colony in the distant East.[2]

The Rajah arrived at Singapore on 23 February. Next day the Rajah Muda arrived in *Rainbow*. His brother went to see him, bearing a letter which was to be given to him if he did not submit unconditionally. In it the Rajah disinherited and banished him but promised to consider his case again after three years, at his brother's urgent request. The Rajah Muda submitted at once. At midday the next day he came to see his uncle. His brother was present, also Mr La Touche, who seems to have kept a sort of watching brief for Miss Burdett-Coutts. Brooke once more announced his submission, and said that he would like to go away and travel. He tried to justify his actions, which, he said, were his alone. No one in Sarawak was involved in them. The Rajah answered sternly and sharply. At the end Brooke was in tears, and the meeting broke up abruptly. The uncle and nephew never met again.

Next day a series of notes passed between them, in which Brooke agreed to return to England with a pension of £500 a year, in return for the money that he put into Sarawak. The Rajah promised to reconsider his case at a time of his own choosing.[1]

When the Rajah arrived at Kuching on 7 March he was given a tumultuous welcome, except by the Bishop and the Borneo Company. He found that Brooke had indeed involved no one else in his actions; so he merely informed the Council and the leading citizens as well as his own officials of what had passed. They all agreed that no further publicity was necessary or advisable. But the Malay sense of propriety was horrified at the idea of a nephew defying his uncle who had been a father to him. The Rajah told the Council of his wish for a British Protectorate; with which everyone concurred. He then settled down to administrative duties, trying to restore concord within the Mission and working out a scheme for a National Bank and one for organised Chinese immigration. As a recreation he went on a voyage in the *Rainbow* in search of pirates, but failed to find any.[2]

Meanwhile, the Tuan Muda went up-country. Beyond the Dyaks, between the upper Rejang and the coast, lived the tribes of the Kayans, who as raiders and head-hunters could give points to the Dyaks. Some of them had been implicated in the Kanowit murders; and the annexation of the Muka territory had brought the Sarawak Government into closer contact with their raids. The Tuan Muda collected some 500 boats from the Sea Dyak tribes, who till recently had been at feud with each other. With three European companions, his brother Stuart, Watson, his deputy at Skrang, and Sergeant Lees, he ascended the Rejang, making his way past the Balaga rapids into wild country where no white man had ever been before. The Kayans fled before him into the jungle, leaving their houses to be burnt; but, seeing him advancing relentlessly, their chiefs sent to offer their submission. He returned to Kanowit. There in

August a great assembly of the tribes was held; the Tuan Muda calculated that some 25,000 people were represented. The Kayans promised allegiance to the Rajah. Over a ceremoniously killed pig they swore peace with their hereditary Dyak enemies. Kenyah tribes from further afield were there, seeking the protection of the white man and the trade that followed in its wake. One of the last of the actual murderers of Steele and Fox was handed over, tried and executed. Now at last the Rajah's authority was recognised throughout his domain.[1]

The Rajah was well satisfied. But soon his general contentment was disturbed by news from England. Brooke had been brooding on his grievances on his voyage home. When he arrived, unwise friends, including, it seems, his parents, urged him to assert his rights. He petitioned a number of public men; he circulated a statement putting forward his claims. He threatened to sue the Rajah about enterprises in Sarawak in which both of them were financially concerned. He had a case. He had given all his private money to the country. He could show letters from the Rajah which promised the latter's abdication and implied that Brooke was now in sole control of the country. But the Rajah never had in fact actually abdicated; and to most people it seemed that Brooke should have shown greater respect and gratitude to his uncle. Then, characteristically, Brooke felt that he had gone too far. He sought the mediation of Miss Burdett-Coutts. But she had never liked him, and she thought it weakness to forgive one's enemies. She would not see him and did her best to keep his uncle's wrath against him alive.[2]

In Kuching the Rajah reacted strongly. He sent a short letter to Brooke saying that he disinherited him for the crimes that he had committed against the State and the Rajah. He summoned the Council again and declared Brooke deprived of all his rights and dignities and an outlaw, though, once again, in deference to the Council's wishes, he issued no public pronouncement. The Malay leaders sent a formal letter assuring the Rajah of their undivided loyalty. While Miss Burdett-Coutts wrote to him inflaming him against Brooke, his sister, Emma Johnson, wrote bitterly reproaching him for his cruelty to her son. The Tuan Muda also was attacked by his mother. His position was difficult. He had been fond of his brother and had agreed with him in much disliking the idea of a foreign protectorate for Sarawak or of its absolute cession to Britain. But he felt that his loyalty and his obligations to his uncle came first. His brother Stuart Johnson followed his lead.

Of the European officials in Sarawak, only one, Mr Hay, resigned in support of Brooke.[1]

Having settled things as best he could in Kuching, James Brooke said good-bye to Sarawak for the last time on 24 September 1863, the twenty-second anniversary of his proclamation as Rajah. The farewell ceremonies moved him deeply. The Bishop, with whom he was reconciled, presided over a banquet attended by all the Europeans; and he took leave of the heads of the native communities in a great meeting in the Court-house. He recommended to them the Tuan Muda, who was to govern in his name.[2]

As he was sailing back to England a telegram reached him with the good news that the British Government at last recognised Sarawak as a Sovereign State. It was not all that he had wished, but at least it cleared his own position. The British could no longer refuse a protectorate on the ground that he was vassal to Brunei. Moreover, the British could now send a Consul to Kuching. They appointed a certain Mr Ricketts. But he found so little work to be done there that he advised that only an honorary Vice-Consul was needed. The advice was taken, and a local English merchant, Mr Martin, was installed.[3]

The Rajah lived for nearly five years after his return. Most of his time was spent at Burrator. He joined happily in the life of the neighbourhood, helping everyone, as far as his means and his failing health would allow. But he kept constant touch with his nephew in Sarawak. When Miss Burdett-Coutts decided to start an experimental farm there he gave her eager encouragement and had the land-laws amended to permit it. She was given a piece of land near Quop. The Tuan Muda was somewhat embarrassed by her enterprise. First she wanted to have an Anglican Mission independent of the Bishop attached to it, then favoured giving the management to Moravian missionaries. The manager who was eventually put in proved a failure, and the management was transferred to Mr Martin, the Vice-Consul, in association with the Tuan Muda. Though it never proved profitable, it played its part in helping in the development of pepper-growing in Sarawak, a crop which the Rajah rightly thought would be of benefit to the country.[4]

He was still worried about its future. He feared that if, when he died, Brooke were to arrive there the country, ignorant of the true nature of the quarrel, would accept him. In fact Brooke's health was rapidly deteriorating and there was little likelihood that he could ever go East again. For a time the Rajah toyed with the idea of forming a Sarawak Company, to exercise the sovereign rights on the analogy of the East India Company, and went so far as to work out a constitution. Then he believed that cession to the British Crown was the proper solution. At one moment this seemed feasible; but he held up negotiations by insisting on being repaid himself for all the money that he had sunk into the country and on proper compensation for his nephew the Tuan Muda. By the time that he was ready to yield on these points the British Government was less enthusiastic. In the last year of his life he was negotiating vainly with the Italian Government in the hope of securing if not an Italian protectorate, at least Italian capital to develop the country. Miss Burdett-Coutts gave up her rights as heiress in 1865, when the Rajah settled the country on the Tuan Muda, unless other arrangements should be made.[1]

As a sign that Brooke rule was to endure he busied himself with an issue of stamps which should bear his portrait. It was his last work in connection with his Raj. The stamps only appeared after his death.[2] Of his old friends, St John would come and see him whenever he was in England; and Arthur Crookshank spent much of his leave in 1866–7 with him. He had a partial reconciliation with his sister, Emma Johnson, and even wrote in friendly terms to Brooke, but Miss Burdett-Coutts saw to it that the truce did not go very far. Nor did she approve of his desire to make up his quarrel with Jack Templer. His willingness to see the Templers again nearly caused a breach with her. Her open distrust of Charles Brooke, whom she disliked almost as much as his brother Brooke, caused another temporary coolness. They were close to a quarrel again when James began to write letters to the press in support of Bishop Colenso. It infuriated him that a distinguished clergyman of liberal views should be persecuted by the hierarchy. But Miss Burdett-Coutts preferred law and order. There was a definite breach in December 1867, when her companion Mrs Brown deliberately insulted the Rajah's loyal friend, Mr Knox. When the Rajah defended Knox the ladies showed their displeasure and refused to be appeased. Nevertheless he had found great comfort in her friendship, and he could never forget how generously she came to his rescue when he and his country were near to financial ruin.[3]

In December 1867 the Rajah had a serious stroke at Burrator. St John and Crookshank were with him, and Miss Burdett-Coutts hurried to take lodgings nearby, mainly to see that the Johnson family did not have access to him, in which she was supported by St John. He recovered, but was never the same again. On 6 June 1868 he had another stroke. On 11 June, early in the morning, he died. He was buried, as he wished, in Sheepstor churchyard, a few miles from his beloved Burrator.[1]

If there is any meaning in the word greatness, James Brooke was a great man. He had his faults and his weaknesses. He was touchy, impatient, inconsistent and imprudent; and in his later years his mental balance did not always seem secure. He was a poor administrator and incompetent at finance. His judgment of men was often poor. He liked publicity; and his passion for publishing his letters and diaries led him into trouble because of their very frankness. But he possessed the undefinable gifts of personality and charm. No one who knew him disliked him, though some might be exasperated into quarrelling with him. He loved people in general and usually received their love. For simple races he felt an instinctive sympathy and affection. It was by a series of accidents that he found himself the ruler of an oriental state; but this would not have happened had he not been endowed with the qualities that most impress the East. His integrity awed the Malay chieftains, who had little of their own yet saw it as admirable. His burning sense of justice came as a blessing to the miserable Land Dyaks and all the other poor folk oppressed by extortion and raiding, whose lives he so profoundly changed. The Oriental's intuitions are quick and sound; he soon detects hypocrisy and false friendliness, mean-mindedness and prejudice. James Brooke may have been berated in England for his savagery towards harmless natives; but in fact he was more liberal than most of his critics. No one hated intolerance and injustice more than he did; no one sought less for personal gain. The measure of his greatness is shown by the love and veneration that his subjects gave to him and that their descendants still give to his memory. Looking from Kuching to the strange peak of Santubong, which rises from the sea near the spot where first he set eyes on Borneo, they will tell you that the outline of the summit is the outline of his profile, lying in repose but still watching over the Raj that he created.

It was, nevertheless, a disorganised and impoverished state that he handed on to his successor.

BOOK III
RAJAH CHARLES

CHAPTER I

THE NEW REGIME

News of the Rajah's death was telegraphed at once to the agents of the Sarawak Government in Singapore. There was no boat bound for Kuching in the harbour, so a sailing boat was hired to convey the telegram on to the Tuan Muda. He thought it more seemly not to announce the end of the reign until the mail steamer, which arrived on 25 July, brought an official notification. The grief among all the communities of the population was deep and sincere. Flags remained at half-mast till Saturday 3 August when, in accordance with his uncle's last wishes, Charles Brooke, the Tuan Muda, was proclaimed Rajah in his stead. The people of Kuching were assembled, with as many representatives from the outlying districts as could be collected; a proclamation was read, and the new Rajah's flag saluted. He waited to take the oath till 11 October 1870, when the General Council met for the first time in his reign. But his rights as Rajah were respected and unchallenged from the moment of the proclamation.[1]

The new Rajah had in fact governed the country since the departure of his uncle nearly five years earlier. But James, so long as he lived, liked to be consulted about all main decisions, and he kept a watchful, if not always realistic, eye on the finances of the country. Moreover, till within a few months of his death, there was no certainty that he would not make such arrangements for its future that there would be no succession to his title. Charles's position had not been easy; but he had filled it modestly and loyally and yet with energy. When he took over the government on his brother's disgrace and his uncle's final retirement, he was not well known in Kuching nor very popular there. Since 1852, when he had first come at the age of twenty-three to work in Sarawak, he had spent most of his time up-country, seldom with a fellow-European to keep him company. He had had little opportunity and little desire to acquire social graces; it was only seldom that he had been able to converse with anyone of his educational background. But he was a voracious reader, and he made his own deductions from what he read. St John, when he used to meet him at his uncle's, complained that these deductions were often jejune; but at least his opinions were entirely his own, and, as his experience was enlarged, they grew worthy of respect.[1] He had recently, in 1866, published a book in two volumes on his life in Sarawak, for which Rajah James wrote a preface. The work was written with little literary elegance, but it gives an extraordinary, vivid picture of life in an out-station in the early days of Sarawak, with its loneliness, its austerity, its constant alarms and constant bouts of sickness, and the hardships that were involved whenever an expedition further up-country was required. It also gives an unconsciously vivid portrait of Charles Brooke. He taught himself to have few material needs. 'A good book, even a novel, and a profuse perspiration are indispensable in this country for health and happiness', he wrote. He asked for little more than that himself and found it hard to believe that any European should ever expect more. Like his uncle, he was without physical fear, but he was far cooler in an emergency, with a self-control that was akin to his austerity. His anger could easily be aroused, and it was all the more terrible for being restrained. His indulgence was reserved for the Sea Dyaks. He had no illusions about them. Of the Sea Dyaks of Lingga he says that they 'had that general and most disagreeable idea that white men only came into their country for the purpose of making them presents'. But he took the trouble to understand their customs and their outlook; and in his dealings with them he was scrupulously just. They could not deceive him nor corrupt him nor deflect him from his purpose. He could not arouse among the native tribes the almost romantic affection that followed Rajah James wherever he went. Charles inspired awe and admiration, which are, perhaps, a better basis for government.[2]

Such a man was not likely to be very popular among the European community. Some of his published views were a little startling, as when he maintained that the most suitable population for developing a tropical country would be one derived from intermarriage between the European and the native races.[3] The English ladies in Kuching did not agree with him. His brother Brooke, with his charming, friendly manners, had been a favourite with them; Charles struck them as being farouche and ill at ease in their company. He had met Miss Burdett-Coutts when he was on leave; and she had definitely disliked him, on the grounds that he seemed to dislike her. But her judgment was not unprejudiced; she disliked all Rajah James's relatives; and her social training had not taught her to understand a young man who had spent most of his life alone in the jungle. Even Spencer St John, much as he admired Charles's energy and ability, had little liking for him.[1] But there were, amongst his uncle's officials, men who understood him better. His standards were rigid and unbending; and he was relentless with those who failed to come up to them. But he was capable of thoughtfulness and great generosity. An occasional twinkle in his eye belied the general impression that he was never amused. He had his romantic side; there were whispers of gallant adventures in his youth and even in later life. He was devoted to French literature, though his taste in it was somewhat undiscriminating. He loved music, though his performances as a singer were apt to embarrass his more sophisticated listeners. He rode well and was at his happiest in the hunting field. It used to be said that an official who wished to gain his favour must either speak French, play a musical instrument or be a good horseman. Men such as Arthur Crookshank, his uncle's oldest assistant, understood him and gladly accepted his authority. Throughout his long reign he had no lack of loyal and trusted servants.[2]

He had already introduced reforms into the administration. He had been largely responsible for the creation of the Sarawak Regiment in 1862. In April 1865 he set up a General Council, the Council Negri, the object of which was to bring the chieftains from the provinces into the government. It consisted of the chieftains of the tribes of the various districts, together with the chief European and Malay officials of Kuching and the European Residents, and was to meet at least once every three years, to endorse any major political decision or constitutional development and to discuss plans for the future. Its membership was elastic; as more tribes settled down to orderly government their chiefs were invited to join it. It did not always meet at Kuching. Its first meeting, in June 1867, took place at Sibu.[3] The country was now divided into three Divisions. The first consisted of Sarawak proper, that is to say the basins of the Sarawak, Sadong and Lundu rivers, the second of the Batang Lupar basin, and the third of the Rejang basin and the coastal area up to the Brunei frontier. Each Division had its European Resident, who reported directly to the Rajah. Under the Resident were Assistant Residents, in each of the main centres of population in the Division, with junior officers to help them, some of them recruited from the local communities. Their numbers slowly increased with the spread of orderly administration. Each Resident maintained a Divisional Council, attended by the local chiefs. These chiefs, or *pengulus*, were appointed by the Government, which almost invariably chose the accepted head of the tribe, unless he were too old or too young or otherwise unsuitable. Each village, whether Malay, Melanau, Land Dyak, Sea Dyak or Kayan, had its hereditary or elected head, who was responsible for maintaining order and paying taxes. The Supreme Council, which now met monthly at Kuching, consisted of the Rajah or his deputy, the Resident of the First Division and three or four of the leading Malays.[1]

The resident of the First Division acted as Chief Secretary of the Raj; and the Division, outside of Kuching, was administered by a Second Class Resident. The number of European officials working at Kuching was gradually increasing. A notice on 1 March 1873 lists the maximum monthly salaries to be paid to officials. Besides the Residents, who received a maximum of $350, the Second Class Residents at $230, and the Assistant Residents at $150, the Treasurer and the Chief Medical Officer received $300, the Military Commander, the Head Magistrate and the Shipping Master $200, a First Class Naval Commander and a First Class Naval Engineer at $150, a First Class Treasury Clerk at $120; and there were junior clerks receiving $80 a month, with Second Class Naval Commanders and Engineers, a Police Superintendent and sergeants of companies and storekeepers at the same salary. The dollar was fixed at 4s. 2d. of English money. The salaries were not princely, but the cost of living was low. One dollar would buy six chickens and twenty glasses of gin. There was a gradual rise in salaries during the next decades. In 1880 the Rajah tried to obtain a new Naval Commander on an initial salary of £300 a year—$140 a month—rising to a maximum of £400 a year—$160 a month. In that year cadets entering the Rajah's service were offered $80 a month.

The conditions of service were severe by modern standards. On joining an official was allowed £40 for his passage from Britain. After ten years' service he was allowed two years furlough on half-pay, with $300 for his passage home and out again. After another five years he could have a year's furlough on half-pay, but with only $200 for his passage, and the same again five years later. After twenty-one years of service he could retire and receive a pension of half his last salary, paid in dollars, for the rest of his life. If he asked for leave for urgent private reasons, the Government decided at its discretion whether or not to grant him any passage money. In the case of sick leave; after five years' service he would receive $200 for his passage and half-pay for six months. If he had not completed five years he only received his passage money. A new cadet had to possess a certificate guaranteeing his good health; and if he had to be sent home owing to illness soon after his arrival, he or his family were expected to pay all the expenses of his journeys.

There was no form of marriage allowance; and except in special circumstances officials were not to marry until they had spent ten years in the service, or fifteen years if they were stationed up-country. A cadet who came out in 1910 with a wife and two children without mentioning their existence was not permitted to take up his post but was, as a concession, offered a minor job in Kuching. The Rajah did not welcome the presence of European women, who, he felt, might distract his officials from their work and spoil their relations with the local inhabitants. He had no objection to an official possessing a native mistress so long as he acted discreetly and did not show undue favours to her family. Children of such unions, though some of them might feel resentful of their origins, were usually fitted into the junior posts in the administration and formed a useful element in the community.[1]

Justice was administered by the Rajah in person, assisted by the Head Magistrate. The British Consul was entitled to be present were a British citizen involved in a suit. The Malay Datus dealt with civil cases which concerned only Malays; and there was a Chinese Court to deal with Chinese civil cases. Cases between Dyak tribesmen were settled by the local headman, or, if more than one tribe were involved, before the local Resident or Assistant Resident. Criminal cases came before the Rajah or his Residents. The customary law of the community or the tribe was followed as much as possible; but the Rajah, with the assistance of the Supreme Council, considered himself entitled to modify the law in the interests of good administration. For example, the Malays submitted to a change in the Muslim law of inheritance, which they had hitherto followed, to bring it closer to modern notions of equity. The laws of the State were not yet codified; but in general the Rajah and his Courts consulted the law of British India when in doubt. The Rajah was sometimes criticised for attending the courts in person, as that meant that there was no Court of Appeal. But his guiding principle was that the ruler must be at all times approachable. If he were to exclude himself from Court, he wrote in 1870, he would withdraw himself from hearing the complaints, either serious or petty, of his people; and that would tend to a want of sympathy and knowledge between the rulers and the ruled. He made it a fixed rule that all of his subjects could have free access to him; and he listened with patience and understanding to their problems and grievances. Even when he did not grant them their desires, every one of them could feel that the Rajah had given him his full attention. This personal relationship was the basis of the government of the country.[1]

Rajah Charles inherited a country that was considerably in debt. Rajah James had been no financier; and to rehabilitate the country after the Chinese rebellion had been costly. Charles was forced to practise strict economy. Next to the late Rajah, whose heir he was, Miss Burdett-Coutts was the chief creditor. Half of the £5000 advanced by her to the late Rajah was paid off quickly, and the remainder when Charles transferred the house and estate of Burrator to her in 1871. James had left it personally to Charles, hoping that he would use it as a rest-house for Sarawak officials when on leave; but he considered that an extravagance. As James had paid £2800 for the house and spent £1500 on its improvement, Miss Burdett-Coutts was well paid for the £2500 which she was still owed. With James dead, she was no longer interested in Sarawak. In 1872 she sold the experimental farm at Quop. It had not been a great success.[2]

In 1870 the State Revenue was $122,842; but in 1871 it had risen to $157,501, and by 1880 to $229,718; and it steadily rose henceforward, reaching over a million dollars early in the twentieth century. It was derived mainly from fees received for the farming out of opium, arak and pawnbroking and from royalties on minerals, especially antimony. The Malays paid a yearly tax of $2, only those serving in the Rajah's forces being exempt. The Dyaks paid a tax of $3 for each family, bachelors paying half the tax, and members of the militia being excused it. But the collection of the capitation taxes was always uncertain. In 1870 the State expenditure was $125,161. Though it increased during the following years its rate of increase was smaller than that of the revenue. By about 1877 there was a credit balance; and the revenue exceeded the expenditure thenceforward, till the outbreak of the Japanese war.[3]

This was all the more remarkable because the country was not proving to be the goldmine which Rajah James had envisaged. The mineral deposits were none of them large. The production of gold and of diamonds was meagre, and the antimony was not proving inexhaustible; the cinnabar was disappointing, though of good quality, while coalmining had proved far from successful. Of the agricultural products not quite enough rice was grown for the needs of the population, but sago from the newly annexed Muka district was exported in some quantity. Attempts to grow tobacco and sugar-cane, tea and coffee were made but had to be abandoned. Gambier was a more profitable crop; but the Chinese now preferred to cultivate pepper, with increasing success. Rubber-planting was introduced rather later in Charles's reign and was to become the most important agricultural industry. A little money came in from the sale of turtle eggs and, later, from birds'-nests for soup. Both in mining and agriculture most of the experiments were conducted by the Borneo Company, which did not in consequence show a profit till close on the end of the century.[1]

Rajah Charles shared his uncle's disappointment with the activities of the Church in Sarawak. Too much attention was paid to Kuching and too little to the Dyak tribes; and the work of such admirable missionaries as Dr Gomes at Lundu and Mr Chalmers was inadequately supported, he thought, by the diocesan authorities. They were not entirely to blame. It was hard to find missionaries who were ready to face the severe life that an up-country post involved; and the Society for the Propagation of the Gospel, on whom the burden of paying for the Church in Sarawak fell, was not rich enough to expand its work as far as it would have wished. Charles never much cared for ecclesiastics. Right at the end of his reign he wrote in a private letter: 'Personally I think Bishops are a bit of a nuisance out here.' Bishop McDougall had resigned in 1867. After some delay his second-in-command, Dr Chambers, was appointed in 1870. He was less genial and less popular than his predecessor while Mrs Chambers was nicknamed Mrs Proudie. The Rajah had liked him before his elevation; but in his first sermon as Bishop, urged on by his wife, he took it upon himself fiercely to denounce the morals of the Rajah's British officials. This so annoyed the Rajah that for some time the relations between Church and State were severely strained. The breach was encouraged by Mr and Mrs Crookshank, who disliked the Bishop and his wife. A better feeling was restored after the Crookshanks retired three years later.[2]

The Rajah's rule was intensely personal. He insisted on rather more paper-work than his uncle had required. In a letter written in 1880 about a possible candidate for his service he declared that

Australia and New Zealand are not good schools generally for a man coming to this country. In those countries they get accustomed to a wild out-of-door life, whereas the life here is sedentary and I may say slow, more of office in description and not suited to the tastes of any man fond of field sports, except where there is marching inland to be done, then the country to be got over is perhaps the stiffest in the world. We require good accountants, to write well and have a good practised education.... If a knowledge of surveying and some idea of forms of official routine can be added, so much the better.

Indeed, with the spread of order, the district officer was now seldom required to go on expeditions far from his station. Most of his time was spent in his office, where the local inhabitants could count on seeing him. He had to send regular reports to the Rajah, who complained if they were too long. He had to keep accurate accounts, and to be scrupulously exact and punctual in all financial dealings. Instructions written by the Rajah himself told him how to treat the men under him, how to stow arms, how to organise sentry-go. He must show deference to the local chiefs and always consult them, even if he does not take their advice. In his own comportment he must be simple but dignified; he must not have particular familiars or favourites among the local inhabitants, but must avoid any tendency towards despotism. He was warned against making jokes, as they were seldom understood. As often as possible the Rajah would himself tour the country to see how his orders were carried out. His visits were something of an ordeal for the district official. Such luxuries as the possession of an armchair earned a prompt and angry reprimand. An officer should either be working at his desk or out inspecting his area or else asleep in bed. But good work was noted and commended.[1]

In spite of the increased paper-work, the administration was still very informal. Many important decisions seem to have been made by word of mouth and never recorded, or by personal letters from the Rajah. During the first decade of Charles's reign the records are full of gaps. No copies of his correspondence earlier than 1880 have survived. Were it not that a semi-official newspaper, the *Sarawak Gazette*, appeared for the first time on 26 August 1870, and continued to appear roughly every fortnight, to coincide with the arrival of the Singapore mail-steamer, it would be difficult now to discover what was happening in the country. The *Sarawak Gazette* was first intended mainly to give the citizens of Kuching the news from the outside world, but later concentrated more on local news. After 1876 it only came out roughly once a month.[2]

At the time of Charles's accession Sarawak was enjoying a period of peace. Occasional expeditions were still needed to restrain the Sea

Dyaks of the interior from head-hunting excursions. In 1866 a Saribas chieftain called Balang attempted to trap and murder Mr Cruikshank, the local Resident. A force had to be sent to punish him. In the summer of 1868, just before his accession, Charles led an expedition against the Delok Dyaks on the upper Batang Lupar, to punish them for causing trouble along the Netherlands frontier. In October 1868 there was a curious incident at Muka, when prisoners lodged in the fort took advantage of the commandant's absence on an afternoon walk and the carelessness of the garrison, Sepoys from India, to seize the building and murder an English merchant lying sick there. But they did not attempt to hold the fort; and as they fled with their loot they were overpowered by the local population. By the beginning of 1869 the Rajah considered that he could safely leave the country to pay his first visit to England for more than five years.[1]

When at last Rajah James bequeathed the succession to Charles he suggested that Charles in his turn might nominate as his heir his nephew, Brooke's only surviving son, Hope. Brooke himself had died a few months after his uncle in 1868.[2] But Charles had no intention of passing on the inheritance to a boy over whose upbringing he had no control. He wished for sons of his own. He might disapprove of his officers marrying, but matrimony was clearly his duty. The main object of his voyage to England was to find a wife. He had few friends there; but he remembered that in his childhood he had played with a first cousin, three years older than himself, called Lily Willes Johnson. She had inherited a fortune from her French grandmother, Baroness de Windt, and had since married a Captain Jennings, who took the name of de Windt. She was now a wealthy widow living in Wiltshire. It seems that Rajah James had suggested to Charles that here was a suitable bride for him, calculating, perhaps, that the lady was mature enough to be unlikely to cause any interference with Hope's ultimate succession. Charles wrote a friendly letter to Mrs de Windt, enclosing a gift of Sarawak diamonds. In return he was invited to stay with her.

One summer day he arrived for his country visit, dressed incongruously in a frock coat, with a top hat. The de Windt family was impressed by his appearance; he was not tall, but erect and spare, with a handsome bony face, piercing grey eyes and a large greying moustache; but Mrs de Windt, her elder son and her daughter Margaret, then aged nineteen, found him formidably taciturn. It was only with the sixteen-year-old Harry that he would talk freely about his Raj. He seemed lonely; so when the de Windts left England later in the summer to tour the Tyrol they invited him to join them. Early one morning, as Margaret was playing the piano in their hotel sitting-room at Innsbruck, the Rajah entered and handed her a piece of paper on which he had written:

> With a humble demean
> If the King were to pray
> That You'd be his Queen,
> Would *not* you say *Nay?*

It was his proposal of marriage. Margaret laughed at first, then, seeing that he was serious, she accepted him, to the dismay of her family. They were married quietly on 28 October 1869.[1]

It was a curious marriage. The Rajah was twenty years older than his wife. He was probably never in love with her; but she was a tall, fair, good-looking and intelligent girl who, he thought, would make a good mother for his children and a good figurehead for Kuching society. Nor was she in love with him; but she was bored at home, she admired him, and the venture attracted her. She was to have a hard life. The honeymoon gave her a foretaste of the future. It was spent at Burrator. As they stopped for the first night of their married life in a hotel at Exeter, the dinner that the Rajah provided for his bride consisted of bread and butter, while he partook of grilled pheasant legs and two glasses of sherry. Luncheon next day consisted of dry biscuits, as he disapproved of wasting money on bad meals in English inns. So it went on. Through their long married life he expected her to share in the austerities that came naturally to him. As he was entitled by the law of the time, he took complete control of her money. It was only when he was spending money himself on his one self-indulgence, buying horses and hunting them, that he would allow her to replenish her wardrobe. Her enthusiasm and high spirits fitted ill with his natural taciturnity. He could not see that her accomplished piano-playing was on a different level from his somewhat tuneless rendering of Victorian ballads. To the last her extravagance distressed him. He could not agree with her that the good name and prestige of Sarawak were harmed if its Ranee and her children lived a life of cheese-paring economy. His correspondence is full of pathetic letters to her begging her to reduce her expenses and keep within her allowance, though he paid her debts scrupulously and promptly. But she loved Sarawak deeply, and he was grateful to her for it. They had their many coolnesses and long periods of separation, but they respected each other; and their mutual loyalty, though it differed in kind, was genuine and strong.[1]

The Rajah and Ranee arrived in Kuching in April 1870. Three months later they moved into the Astana, the palace that had been built for them close to the site of James's bungalow which had been burnt during the Chinese insurrection. The Astana, which is still the Government House today, is eclectic in style, with a Gothic tower forming the entrance, and on either side great wings with high-pitched roofs of wooden shingles, with reception rooms and bedrooms all on the first floor, supported on whitewashed brick arcades, with the kitchens and, at the time, the bathrooms on the ground floor. Minor alterations have since been made, and the building has more than once been redecorated, but its outward appearance has changed very little down the years. The Ranee has described in her books the life led at the Astana during the first years of her married life. There were tea-parties for the whole European community on Tuesdays. Now and then there were dinner-parties, followed by music. To her chagrin, no one ever asked her to show off her remarkable musical skill on the battered Erard piano; but the Rajah's vocal rendering of *La donna è mobile* was much admired by everyone except his wife, while the Medical Officer ended the evening in enquiring in a liquid tenor 'Oh, don't you remember sweet Alice, Ben Bolt?' When the Rajah was away up-country, the Ranee would entertain the leading Malay ladies, and even, to the disapproval of old Datin Isa, the Datu Bandar's wife, would hold classes to teach them reading and writing.[2]

During the early years of their married life the Rajah would some-times take his wife with him when he journeyed up the rivers into Dyak or Kayan country. Hitherto it had been difficult for the Europeans to make any contact with the women of the tribes; but when she was present the women would shyly appear and make friends with her. Her kindliness and her sincere pleasure at visiting the native villages and meeting the inhabitants were of great value in building up the atmosphere of general good-will. At times she had a harder task, as when she was left alone with a handful of fort-men at Simanggang, while the Rajah went on a campaign further up the Batang Lupar, and suddenly a party of Kayans appeared, having come from the Upper Rejang, in order, as they said, to join the Rajah, but more probably to see what raiding they could do while he was occupied up the river. The Ranee by a mixture of firmness and bluff kept them under control till the Rajah returned. Though the Rajah was not an easy husband and would coldly snub her enthusiasms, those were happy days for her, especially as her young brother, Harry de Windt, came out to be his brother-in-law's aide-de-camp.[1]

But her main task was to provide heirs for the Raj. A daughter was born in 1870 and twin sons early in 1872. But twins are unlucky in the East. After the birth of a premature stillborn baby and recurrent attacks of malignant malaria, the Ranee's health broke down. The Rajah took her and the children away in September 1873, to return to England. When they passed through Singapore cholera was raging there. As their liner sailed up the Red Sea the three little children were stricken and died, all within one week. The Ranee remained in England for over a year. There, on 30 September 1874, a new son was born, Charles Vyner Brooke, who was at once proclaimed Rajah Muda, heir-apparent. He was left behind under the care of the first Rajah's old friend, Mrs McDougall, when the Rajah and Ranee returned to Sarawak in the spring of 1875. A second son, Bertram, known as the Tuan Muda, was born in Kuching in August 1876, and a third son, Harry, the Tuan Bongsu, in England in 1879. The succession was now well assured.[2] That same year the Rajah's nephew, Hope Brooke, came of age. The Rajah wrote to him offering him his friendship and an allowance of £200 a year, but adding that he was to 'remember not to open anything like discussion, which can lead to nothing and do no good'. Hope Brooke accepted his advice and remained on good, if not cordial, terms with his uncle and his family for many years to come.[3]

These years saw an almost complete pacification of the country. In May 1870 a force of Kanowit Dyaks under their chief, Lintong, attempted to capture the fort at Sibu on the Rejang, but were repulsed. A few months later the Rajah led an expedition up the Katibas river to punish Lintong, who was captured and made to live for some years under supervision at Kuching. He had been in the past a supporter of the Brookes, and his eldest son, who was killed in the attack on Sibu, had been a close friend of Mr Cruikshank, Resident at Sibu. But he could not give up his old habits so easily. Now, however, he learnt his lesson. When he returned to his tribe some years later it was as a loyal servant of the Raj. He became a *pengulu*, and died of snake-bite in 1887. The incorrigible raider-in-chief, Balang, was also captured during this campaign. He was taken to Kuching and put to death for the many murders for which he was responsible.[4]

But the Kanowit and Katibas Dyaks were not yet pacified. Another expedition in 1871 was sent against them. After their villages had been burnt many of them were moved to an area more easily controlled, further down the Rejang. Even there they continued their raids, attacking the peaceful Dyaks of the upper Batang Lupar. They attempted to escape punishment by retiring into the Ulu Ai, close to the frontier. The Rajah followed them there in 1875 and temporarily cowed them. After another expedition the following year the remainder of the Katibas were resettled nearer the coast. In 1879 a Skrang Dyak chief, Lang Endang, started to raid his neighbours on the Kantu river. He was ordered to pay a fine and attempted to ambush the Government Officers sent to collect it. He was sharply punished and reduced to submission.

It was impossible as yet entirely to eradicate head-hunting in the outlying districts. The women of the tribes were largely to blame; for no girl cared to marry a man who had not proved his manhood by acquiring a head. But nearer to the centres of government the tribesmen began to discover that the practice did not pay; watchful officers were prompt to punish it by exacting a heavy fine or, if need be, by a military expedition. Gradually the areas were enlarged in which a villager could wander from his village without the certainty that, should he meet anyone better armed than himself, his head would be forfeit.[1]

Another traditional custom which the Rajah set himself to reform was slavery. Slavery had existed from immemorial time in Borneo. The owners tended on the whole to treat their domestic slaves well, though now and then there were instances of savage cruelty. Agricultural slaves were more in the position of medieval serfs, with certain traditional rights. They were obliged to work for their masters before they could work for themselves and they kept only a small proportion of the crops that they grew. But their private lives were free of interference. Among the Dyaks there were a few captives who were slaves; but the Dyaks preferred defeated enemies in the form of decapitated heads. Both the Melanaus and Kayans possessed slaves, whose treatment was arbitrary. Girl slaves were sacrificed whenever a new longhouse was to be built or when an epidemic threatened the district. When a chief died, a number of slaves were tied to the posts on which the coffin rested and were left there to starve to death.

The Rajah moved cautiously. A sudden prohibition of slavery would have caused chaos and brought no happiness. He did not even advocate an open discussion of the problem. In a circular issued a few months before his accession, he remarked that, amongst the Malays at least, the existing system was easy-going and many slaves were unofficially liberated through the indifference and kindly carelessness of their masters, who might, were the subject aired too freely, remember rights and claims that were at present half-dormant. But, with the consent of the Supreme Council, he gradually made regulations to improve the slaves' conditions. A slave-girl who had sexual intercourse with her master or a member of his family was automatically freed, and her children were born free. Cases of ill-usage of slaves could be brought before the Courts. The import and export of slaves was forbidden, and offenders were heavily fined. A slave was allowed to do paid work for his own benefit, and the money that he earned could go to buy his remission, the price of which, in 1877, was about £6 sterling. Any sale or transference of slaves within the country had to be registered; if this were not done within a certain period of time the slave was automatically freed. This seems to have happened frequently in the case of agricultural slaves. Many Malay chiefs in the past had sought divine favour by liberating slaves on their death-beds. They found now that they could obtain the Rajah's favour by liberating them during their own lives. Of the slaves themselves, the more industrious worked hard to buy their freedom, while the lazier, protected by the law, did so little that many masters found it more efficient and no more expensive to employ hired labour. There were still cases when the Chinese sold superfluous daughters to Malays and later to Dyaks; but gradually the girls were brought up not as slaves but as adopted members of the family. Slavery unofficially existed for another decade; but all the time it was withering away and soon ceased to be a social problem. In 1883 the Rajah introduced a Bill arranging for the manumission of all slaves within five years. In 1886 he withdrew the Bill as being no longer necessary.[1]

The eighteen-seventies thus saw a steady growth in the internal peace and prosperity of Sarawak. The Rajah's relations with the Netherlands authorities over the frontier were good. There had been trouble not long before the Rajah's accession when, twice, Dutch gunboats had seized Sarawak merchant-ships on the plea that they were engaged in piracy; but on both occasions the merchants were exonerated after a protest from Kuching. The Dyak tribes on either side of the frontier were almost perpetually at feud with each other; and the Rajah kept in constant touch with the Dutch Resident at Pontianak in an attempt to restrict their warfare. There were times when the Rajah and the Resident did not agree over the methods to be used; the Dutch system of administration was so different from that of the Brookes that occasional disputes were inevitable. The Rajah's correspondence is filled with letters to Pontianak on measures to be taken over frontier incidents. He was averse to joint expeditions of Dutch and Sarawak forces, as two forces differently organised and trained, and composed of tribes that were jealous of each other, would not easily work together. Where tribes that strayed across the frontier were in need of discipline, it would be better, he thought, that the Netherlands and Sarawak should take it in turn to administer the punishment. He found the Dutch very ready to co-operate with him. There was none of the hostility that had been shown early in his uncle's career. The Netherlands Government had accepted the existence of Sarawak, perhaps the more willingly because Great Britain's acceptance of the Raj was less whole-hearted. In 1871 the Rajah and Ranee paid an official visit to the Netherlands Resident at Pontianak and were treated as reigning princes. Netherlands officials were at all times welcome at Kuching.[1]

In all, Rajah Charles had good reason to be satisfied with the first decade of his reign. It was nearly brought to an end in April 1877, when he narrowly escaped drowning in the river Rejang, at the mouth of the Balleh river. His launch, the *Ghita*, was caught in a cross-current and forced to the bank. He snatched at a branch of an over-hanging tree to push her off; but the branch snapped and he was swept into the stream. He was already unconscious when a boat from Balleh fort managed to pick him up. Had he died then, no one can tell what would have happened to Sarawak. But he recovered without ill effect and survived to deal with the two great and interwoven problems that continued to worry himself and his realm, its relations with Great Britain and with Brunei.[2]

CHAPTER II

GREAT BRITAIN AND BRUNEI

The death of Rajah James and the accession of Rajah Charles had been duly and officially reported to the British Government; and Charles had been acknowledged as sovereign ruler of Sarawak. But the British Foreign Office still regarded the Raj with some suspicion. Recognition of the Raj had been granted by Lord Palmerston and Lord Russell. But the former died in 1865 and the latter fell from power in 1866. Lord Derby's Government, which succeeded, was less friendly; nor was the Liberal Government of Mr Gladstone more amenable. The status of a British subject who was also a sovereign ruler embarrassed the authorities. In 1875 the Foreign Secretary wrote in a letter to the Rajah of his 'anomalous jurisdiction'; and when some years later still the Rajah applied to attend the Queen's levee he was, to his anger, summoned as Mr C. Brooke, with Rajah of Sarawak added in brackets.[1]

The attitude of the British Government was affected by two difficult questions. First, there was the colony of Labuan. James Brooke did inestimable harm to himself and to his successor when he successfully advocated Britain's annexation of Labuan. Labuan had not proved a success as a British colony. Its only asset, apart from its meagre seams of coal, was that it provided an orderly entrepôt for merchants trading along the north Borneo coast. But as Sarawak grew in prosperity and pushed its frontier north-eastward, Labuan lost its unique position. Merchants preferred to use Sarawak ports. Once the personal tie connecting Labuan with Sarawak was broken, jealousy increased. The Governors of Labuan tended to dislike the Rajah and sought above all to prevent him from extending his territory or his influence over Brunei. Mr Edwardes's unfortunate intervention over Muka in 1860 typified their attitude. His successor, Jeremiah Callaghan, had been more amenable; but in 1868 the governorship was given to an able, ambitious and cantankerous Irishman, John Pope-Hennessy. Soon after his arrival he married the daughter of the Chief Secretary, James Brooke's old friend, Hugh Low, then quarrelled irrevocably with his father-in-law. He was known locally as the Pope and was famous for his inability to endure criticism. Anyone who ventured to question his regulations was promptly lodged in gaol, were he Malay, Chinese or British. It was said that when an admiral visited Labuan in 1870 the only official in the island who was not in prison was the Governor himself. On the admiral's report an enquiry was set up. Next year Mr Pope-Hennessy was removed; but his extravagances were attributed to the climate and, after the manner of the British public service, he was given a better job elsewhere.[1]

The presence of this active and arrogant man in Labuan was not likely to improve relations between the colony and Sarawak. And, unfortunately, since Spencer St John and Governor Edwardes had left the scene, the post of Governor was now combined with that of Consul-General for Borneo. Mr Pope-Hennessy was, therefore, the representative of the British Foreign Office in Borneo and was responsible for maintaining the relations between Britain and Brunei, as fixed by the treaty of 1847.[2]

The chaotic condition of Brunei was a permanent irritation to the Rajah. Sarawak merchants who attempted to trade in Brunei territory found themselves continually hampered by the greed and corruption of Brunei nobles. The Sultan had no control over the wild tribes of the interior who lived officially under his jurisdiction. It was impossible to suppress raiding and head-hunting in Sarawak territory if offenders could receive reinforcements from over the frontier and could retire there. Attempts to bring Kayans of the upper Rejang to order were bound to fail as long as their fellow-tribesmen in the Baram valley, in Brunei territory, were undisciplined and free. Early in 1868, just before his accession, Charles Brooke had proposed to the Sultan of Brunei that he should cede the Baram districts to Sarawak in return for a suitable annual payment. As the Sultan was receiving practically no revenues from the Baram tribes and would never be able to assert his authority over them, the proposal seemed reasonable. But Sultan Munim did not agree. His pride was hurt by the suggestion that he should part with more territory, nominal though his rule might be. He had had an admiration and some affection for Rajah James; but Charles had already offended him by his high-handed actions over Muka some years before. He had offended him again in 1867, when the Sultan had sent letters to Sarawak which were carelessly sealed. The Supreme Council at Kuching decided that this was a deliberate insult, probably rightly; for the Malays on the Council knew the minds of their fellow-Malays. In consequence the Sultan was sent only a third of the money due to him till an apology should be forthcoming. There were, moreover, *pangirans* at his Court who owned estates along the coast between Bintulu and the mouth of the Baram and who did not relish the prospect of coming under the sterner rule of Sarawak.

The Sultan appealed to Mr Pope-Hennessy for protection against Sarawak aggression and referred him to the treaty of 1847. Pope-Hennessey wrote to Charles, offering to arbitrate in the matter. Charles replied angrily refusing the suggestion. He could not understand why the Governor should support a government so 'debased, sordid, exacting and unreliable' as that of Brunei, and he wrote to the Foreign Office to complain that the Governor was under the influence of the Sultan and to declare that he was ignorant why matters concerning the Sarawak and Brunei governments alone should require interference from other parties. But the Foreign Office supported Pope-Hennessy and forbade the transaction.[1]

The British Government's sensitive desire to protect Brunei from Sarawak is hard nowadays to understand. Even the Governors of Labuan could not pretend that Brunei was anything but chaotic and corrupt. To support a weak State against a more powerful neighbour may be an act of gallantry in the high Liberal tradition. But, curiously, it was under Conservative governments that the Foreign Office showed the strongest opposition to the Brookes. Nor was this opposition quite logical. The treaty of 1847 forbade the Sultan to alienate any of his territory to a foreign power or the subject of a foreign power without the consent of the British Government. But the Foreign Office, though it had acknowledged Rajah James and his successor to be rulers of Sarawak, had refused to pronounce whether the Rajah was in fact independent of Brunei. If he was not, then any cession to him of Brunei territory was a purely internal affair. And, in any case, he was a British subject and was not, therefore, affected by the clauses in the treaty. The cessions of territory made in 1853 and 1861 had been effected without any reference to Britain, whose approval had been given subsequently without demur.[2]

Mr Pope-Hennessy's departure from Labuan was greeted with relief by his subjects there and with satisfaction in Sarawak. His last public statement had particularly annoyed the Rajah. He had said in a speech before the Labuan Legislative Council, with reference to Sarawak, that 'the policy promulgated thirty years ago by some enterprising and benevolent Englishmen, that the Dyaks could be civilised and that Europeans could conduct the details of trade and administration in the

5*a*   A MALAY VILLAGE

5*b*   A DYAK LONGHOUSE

6   SIR CHARLES ANTHONY BROOKE

rivers of Borneo had proved to be visionary'. But his successor, Henry Bulwer, though better liked in Labuan, carried out the same policy towards Sarawak.[1]

Brunei rule was not popular with the Kayans of the Baram. The tribes high up the river had openly defied the Sultan since 1870; and a small expedition that he had sent up the river that September had been forced to retire in ignominy. In 1872 Rajah Charles sailed up the Baram in his yacht, *Heartsease*, taking with him the Ranee, to show that his intentions were purely peaceful. It seems that he made no attempt to ask the Sultan's permission to visit his territory; but the Sultan learnt of his plan and sent agents to try to prevent the Kayan tribes from receiving him. In spite of their efforts the Kayans proved friendly. The Rajah was hospitably entertained at a village called Batu Gading, four days' journey up the river. His object had been not only to sound the feeling of the tribes, but also to see whether it was safe for Sarawak traders to operate there. He decided to encourage trade. But next year some Sarawak subjects were murdered by Kayans. Charles asked the Sultan to fine the guilty tribe. His request was granted; but the Brunei officials did not venture to penetrate up the river. Instead, they fined the guiltless and more docile tribes near the sea, extorting double the sum that the Rajah had suggested, in order that the Sultan and each official should have his share. It is possible that they hoped incidentally to embroil the Rajah with the Kayans; but the Kayans were not deceived. A few months later the Sultana died; and, as custom allowed, the Sultan sent a commissioner to collect a contribution from his subject tribes to pay for her obsequies. The official who came to the Baram for the purpose read out the Sultan's order to the assembled chiefs and left it with them, knowing that none of them could read. Unluckily a Sarawak official, Mr Brooke Low, visited the district a few days later; and the chiefs showed him the paper, complaining of the high sum that they had been forced to pay. Mr Low read it and discovered that the official had in fact charged twice as much as the Sultan had ordered. Such incidents enraged the tribes up and down the river. By the spring of 1874 they were all in open revolt against the Sultan; who could do nothing to restore his authority. He therefore realised that, after all, it would be wise to cede the district to the Rajah in return for a fixed revenue.[2]

Once again, the British Government refused to countenance such a deal, even though the Sultan himself was amenable. Governor Bulwer had already warned London against what he called 'the restless aspirations of the Sarawak Government for territorial aggrandisement'. The Rajah then suggested that the British should extend a protectorate over the whole of Brunei in order to restore order, or that, alternatively, Sarawak should take over the protectorate. The Foreign Office curtly refused to consider either suggestion. Two years later the Rajah tried again, asking that the clause in the 1847 treaty forbidding the Sultan to alienate territory should be rescinded, if it was held to apply to him. Once again he was snubbed; and the Foreign Office reply was all the more insulting in that it was carelessly addressed to Sir James Brooke. Governor Bulwer had recently been succeeded in Labuan by H. J. Ussher who wrote to London complaining that the Rajah had held back some $3000 due to the Sultan because of the non-payment of debts owed to Sarawak traders by nobles of the Brunei Court, but had offered to forgo the claim in return for the cession of the Baram. Governor Ussher feared that 'this aspect considerably diminished the integrity of the transaction'.[1]

In the end better relations between London and Kuching were achieved owing to a series of events over which the Rajah had no control and of which he strongly disapproved. In 1850 the United States, to the embarrassment of the British and of Rajah James, had made a treaty with Sultan Omar Ali of Brunei, giving it the rights of a most favoured nation. The treaty had never been followed up till 1865, when a certain Mr Claude Lee Moses appeared in Brunei with documents announcing him to be Consul for the United States. How Moses, who was a cashiered seaman from the American Navy, had obtained his papers is unknown. He had borrowed money in Singapore to pay for his passage to Brunei; but he impressed the Sultan. Within a few days of his arrival he obtained from the Sultan and the Pangiran Temanggong of Brunei a personal ten-year lease of a large part of North Borneo, including the islands of Balembangan, Banggi and Palawan, which were not in the Sultan's gift. In return he promised a yearly rental of $9500. Having obtained the concession he hurried off to Hong Kong to raise the money to pay for it. In October he sold his rights to a company to be called 'The American Trading Company of Borneo', whose President was an American merchant, Joseph W. Torrey. His partners were another American, Thomas B. Harris, and two Chinese, Lee Ah Sing and Pong Am Pong. They were to found a colony in North Borneo, for which Moses guaranteed the protection of the American flag, in return for one-third of the profits. Torrey then went with Moses to Brunei. At the sight of his dollars the Sultan invested Torrey with the titles of Rajah of Ambong and Marudu and Maharajah of North Borneo. With ten Americans and sixty Chinese Torrey moved up the coast to Kimanis Bay where, in December 1865, he founded a settlement called Ellena. The British authorities in Labuan were disquieted for a time but, sensitive though they were over the 1847 treaty whenever Sarawak was concerned, they made no official protest to the Sultan against this remarkable concession. They seemed to have calculated that the colony of Ellena was unlikely to prove a success.

They were right. Thomas Harris, who had been nominated Chief Secretary, died the following May and was commemorated by a tombstone 'erected by H. E. the Rajah as a tribute of respect to the memory of an old, faithful and esteemed friend'. Meanwhile His Excellency Rajah Torrey had quarrelled with Moses and had borrowed sums from Chinese merchants in Labuan, which he could not repay. He fled to Hong Kong, pursued by one of his creditors. By the end of 1866 the colony had disappeared and the colonists had drifted over to seek work in Labuan. Moses, who had not been paid by Torrey, followed him to Hong Kong but could extract nothing from him. He returned to Brunei with a party of German adventurers, who took one look at Ellena and departed again, leaving him alone and penniless in his Consulate. His spirit was undefeated. He sent his family to Labuan and then set fire to the Consulate. When it was burnt down he went to the Sultan and demanded compensation. The Sultan refused to make any payment; so Moses complained to his Government. But the United States gunboat which came to investigate the affair was not prepared to support him. Moses moved across to Labuan in 1867 and from there took passage home to America. He was drowned on the journey. Torrey went soon afterwards to New York, where he tried in vain to raise money for the moribund American Trading Company of Borneo. The United States Government toyed for a time with the idea of establishing a naval base on Banggi Island; but it rebuffed suggestions made to it by Torrey.[1]

Meanwhile other European countries began to take an interest in North Borneo. In 1870 an Italian man-of-war, the *Principessa Clotilde*, sailed into Labuan Bay, and her Commander, Captain Racchia, announced to Governor Pope-Hennessy that he had come to prospect for the site of a penal settlement. On his return to Italy he recommended to his Government that one should be established on Gaya Bay, a little

12-2

to the north of Kimanis. When the news of the proposal reached Labuan, Governor Bulwer wrote anxiously home to warn of the damage that the proximity of Italian criminals might do to the morals of the citizens of Brunei; and London prepared to complain to Rome. Protests, however, were not needed, as the Italian Government abandoned the scheme. A greater threat came from Spain. For centuries past the Spanish authorities in the Philippines had tried to assert their control over the Sultan of Sulu, to whom the northern tip of Borneo and the north-eastern coast undoubtedly belonged in theory. In 1873, in pursuit of this aim, the Philippine Government attempted to impose a blockade on all Sulu territory, to the fury of the British and German merchants of Singapore, who controlled most of the Sulu trade. As a result of diplomatic pressure made on Madrid by London and Berlin the blockade was abandoned; but in 1876 the Spaniards occupied Jolo, the main town of Sulu. Two years later, in July 1878, the Sultan of Sulu admitted Spanish suzerainty over all his territories, including those on the Borneo mainland and the islands nearby.[1]

In fact, he had already disposed of those particular territories. Two rival groups had been competing for his favour. A young Scotsman, William Clarke Cowie, employed by the German firm of Karl Schomburg of Singapore, founded, together with Schomburg and another trader, Captain Ross, a small company called the 'Labuan Trading Company', whose object was to smuggle guns and other contraband into Sulu, receiving in return barter goods from the islands and from North Borneo. Cowie occasionally visited Hong Kong to dispose of these goods. There one day he received a demand from Torrey for a 10 per cent export duty on them. Having thus learnt about Torrey's concession, he tried to persuade his partners to buy up Torrey's rights. They refused; and the Labuan Trading Company soon afterwards came to an end. Cowie then acquired a ship of his own and traded in partnership with the Sultan of Sulu, trying in the meantime to block the transfer of any other concessions in North Borneo.

He had, however, a formidable competitor. Herr von Overbeck was born in Lippe Detmold in 1831. After a varied career, much of it spent as a whaler in the Bering Sea, he settled in Hong Kong and became local manager for the opium firm of Dent Brothers and Consul for Austria-Hungary, for which he was rewarded with an Austrian barony. The Baron first heard of Torrey's concessions in 1870. Soon afterwards he visited Europe and interested friends in London and Vienna in a scheme to take them over. Money was advanced; and in 1875 Overbeck bought Torrey's rights in the American Trading Company, on condition that the original lease, which expired that year, was renewed by the Sultan. Torrey and Overbeck then sailed together to Brunei to arrrange matters with the Sultan. Unfortunately for them the Acting Governor of Labuan and Acting Consul-General for Borneo was Hugh Low. He considered that the concessions were contrary to the terms of the 1847 treaty, and he advised the Sultan to refuse them. The Pangiran Temanggong, who owned property in North Borneo, was more obliging. On being paid $1000 he renewed the leases for another ten years. But the Sultan would not endorse the document and Low pronounced it worthless. An Austrian warship that came to Labuan a few months later was informed by Low that the American Trading Company had no legal existence in Borneo.

The Baron returned disappointed to Europe. His money was running out and his friends there refused to advance any more to him. But when in London he met the young head of the firm that had employed him in the past, Dent Brothers. Alfred Dent was interested, and agreed to finance him up to the sum of £10,000. With this backing Overbeck once again slipped quietly across to Brunei with Torrey and reopened negotiations with the Sultan. He was now more fortunate. There was a new Lieutenant-Governor in Labuan, an ambitious young man called William Hood Treacher. He considered that Overbeck's scheme might be used to further the interests both of Great Britain and of himself. He encouraged the Sultan to listen to Overbeck's offer, but advised Overbeck to negotiate for an entirely new lease, adding that there should be a clause making the concession subject to the approval of the British Government, so as to satisfy the terms of the 1847 treaty, and a clause stipulating that it would not be transferred to a citizen of a foreign state without British consent. Overbeck's intention, however, was to sell the concession when it was obtained and so he had the restrictive clauses omitted in the final agreement which he made with the Sultan and the Pangiran Temanggong on 29 December 1877. In it the Baron was created Maharajah of Saba (the old Malay name for Northern Borneo) and Raja of Gaya and Sandakan, with powers of life and death over the native populations, ownership of all the produce of the country, the right to coin money, make laws, levy taxes and custom duties and all other rights usually exercised by a sovereign. In exchange he would pay the Sultan $12,000 annually and the Pangiran Temanggong $3000.

The area over which he was to rule consisted of all Borneo north of a line drawn from Kimanis Bay on the west to the Seboekoe river on the east.

Much of this area, as the Baron well knew, did not belong to the Sultan of Brunei but, nominally at least, to the Sultan of Sulu. So, after pausing at Labuan to ask for Treacher's forgiveness for having omitted the clauses that he recommended, he sailed for Sulu. There, in January 1878, he signed a treaty with the Sultan which gave him, in return for a yearly rent of $5000, sovereignty over all the territory between the Pandasan and Seboekoe rivers, with the title of Rajah of Sandakan and Datu Bendahara. He obtained his concession just in time; for eight months later the Sultan of Sulu admitted the suzerainty of Spain.[1]

The concessions to Overbeck alarmed both the Spanish and the Netherlands Governments. Both protested; but neither was prepared to follow up their protests with decisive action. Eventually in 1885 Spain agreed that she had no territorial claims on any part of Borneo. Dutch hostility led to one or two minor incidents on the east coast of North Borneo; but in 1884 Britain and the Netherlands agreed to set up a joint commission to fix the boundaries between the lands ceded by Sulu and Netherlands Borneo. The present frontier of North Borneo was eventually fixed in 1912, at some twenty miles north of the Seboekoe river. The United States also made a protest, based on her treaty with Brunei in 1850. But the protest had so little legal foundation that it was quietly dropped.[2]

Far more active and persistent objections to the concessions came from Sarawak. For some years the Rajah had been trying to annex the comparatively small territory of the Baram. But, though the Sultan of Brunei had more than once agreed, the British Foreign Office consistently forbade the deal. Now an Austrian subject had obtained concessions from the Sultan far larger in area and far more drastic in nature than Sarawak had ever claimed, and had done so in direct violation of the 1847 treaty; and the British Government had not only turned a blind eye, but its local representative in Labuan had actively encouraged the deal. Moreover, the deal had been concluded that a vast part of Borneo might be exploited by merchants. The Rajah considered that he had been treated most unfairly and, worse, that the interests and welfare of the native races of Borneo were seriously threatened. As soon as he heard of the concessions he hastened to Brunei and demanded an interview with the aged Sultan; to whom he angrily pointed out that the tribal chiefs in the ceded territory had been neither asked to approve of the transaction nor even informed of it. He then crossed to Labuan to see Treacher. The interview was not a success. According to Treacher he lost his temper and declared that the Sultan had no right to alienate the territory and that he himself 'intended to proceed up the Coast and stir up the minds of the natives against the Baron'. Consequently, whenever later any chieftain attempted to oppose Overbeck's successors, Treacher determinedly saw the sinister influence of Charles Brooke in the background.[1]

It was, indeed, useless for Charles to attempt to seek for sympathy from the British Foreign Office so long as Treacher was its man on the spot. Treacher was committed to the concessions and probably was already planning to use them to enhance his own position. He had blandly forgiven the Baron's disingenuity in omitting the clauses that he had suggested to safeguard the rights of the British Government. He also personally disliked Brooke, a feeling which the Rajah returned. Nor would a direct appeal to the Foreign Office in London help Sarawak; for the Permanent Under-Secretary, Sir Julian Pauncefote, was an old friend of the Dent family and eager to support Alfred Dent's schemes. So when the Rajah wrote to London to complain that the concessions were contrary to the clause in the 1847 treaty which had so often been cited against himself and to express his fears that they would not benefit the native peoples, Pauncefote minuted tartly and unhistorically that 'Raja Brooke is evidently incensed with jealousy of Raja Overbeck, but considering that his uncle annexed large portions of the territory in defiance of the treaty which he now cites against the Dent–Overbeck concession, the objection comes with bad grace from him'. The Foreign Secretary wrote to the Rajah that Her Majesty's Government, having no reason to fear for the rights and liberties of the native populations, would 'regret to learn that any action had been taken by any Foreign Government prejudicial to the private interests of the British capitalists concerned'. Meanwhile Treacher sent a letter to the Rajah scolding him for attempting as a British subject and a vassal of the Sultan of Brunei to interfere with a transaction of his overlord's. It is to be feared that the British Foreign Office and its advisers were not very strong on logic.[2]

The Rajah also found that he had the City of London ranged against him. The policy of the Brookes to keep the great merchant houses out of their territory resulted in their having no friends in the City, apart from the Directors of the Borneo Company, who themselves sometimes resented the Rajah's authoritarianism. The City merchants were far more ready to sympathise with the Dents. On this matter the Borneo Company, nervous lest a new North Borneo Company might infringe their monopolies, gave full support to the Rajah, even to the extent of promising to lend him £20,000, to be used to induce the Sultan of Brunei to revoke the Dent–Overbeck concession and lease the whole land as far north as Marudu Bay to Sarawak. But the Rajah soon realised that this was impracticable; the British Government would never permit it. Instead, he approached the Sultan once more about the cession of the Baram basin. In December 1878 the Sultan agreed to hand over the entire district to him for an annual payment of $4200. Once again James asked London for permission to conclude the deal. He found an ally in the Colonial Office, which was not comfortable about the sale of potential colonial territory to a Merchant Company. The Colonial Secretary, Sir Michael Hicks-Beach, considered that 'Rajah Brooke would appear to have strong claims for consideration, as his government has now been firmly established for many years, and has been conducted with success'. But the Foreign Office would not agree. It must refer the matter, it said, to Treacher at Labuan, which was tantamount to forbidding it entirely. As might have been expected Treacher sent an almost hysterical despatch advising against the trans-action. He declared that the Chinese merchants in Labuan and the merchants of Brunei were bitterly opposed to the scheme, as it would divert the trade of the Baram from themselves to Sarawak, and that the Sultan himself had only agreed for fear that if he refused the Rajah might withhold the annual payments due to him. In fact the trade of the Baram was non-existent, while the Sultan was out to get the best bargain that he could and naturally would not appear too eager. The fact that the peoples of the Baram were showing their active determina-tion not to remain under the Sultan's rule conveniently escaped Mr Treacher's notice. On his advice the Foreign Office again forbade the deal.[1]

The Rajah could do nothing except hope that the North Borneo enterprise would prove a failure. At one moment his hopes seemed near to realisation. Probably on Pauncefote's advice, Alfred Dent decided to secure his concession by having it administered by a company with a charter from the British Government confirming its sovereign rights, an idea that was at once reactionary and revolutionary. He induced a number of eminent men, business magnates, former public servants and members of Parliament, to sign a memorandum asking the Government to confer a charter, on the grounds, reminiscent of James Brooke's arguments in favour of the annexation of Labuan, that the control of North Borneo by British interests was necessary to protect the flank of the growing trade with China. Amongst the signatories was James Brooke's old friend Harry Keppel, now an admiral. The Foreign Secretary, Lord Salisbury, was sympathetic, but other matters occupied his attention. He took no action. Then, as 1880 dawned, it was clear that a General Election was in the offing and that it would be won by the Liberals. Dent was alarmed. The delay had used up much of his capital. He offered to sell out his interest to Baron von Overbeck. The Baron tried to raise money in Austria and Germany to buy him out. It is interesting to speculate how, had he succeeded, the British Foreign Office would have reacted to so blatant a flouting of the 1847 treaty. But he failed; and Dent, being unable to sell, was obliged to buy. With the help of his friends he acquired all Overbeck's interests, and, further, paid a sum to Joseph Torrey, who was then in Bangkok, to obtain the shadowy claims of the American Borneo Company. With Overbeck and Torrey out of the picture, Dent's company was purely in British hands.

The new Liberal Government was not so hostile to Dent's scheme as he had feared. Urged on by Pauncefote, the new Foreign Secretary approved of the grant of a charter; and the Prime Minister, Mr Gladstone, concurred, though later he forgot about his concurrence and would have liked to cancel it. Indeed, the charter bore signs of its Liberal origin. The new North Borneo Company, an association to which Dent had transferred all his rights for the sum of £120,000, was granted sovereign rights over the territory conceded to Overbeck and to Dent by the two Sultans. But its foreign relations were to be handled by the British Government, and it was to remain British in character and domicile. It must guarantee to abolish slavery in its lands, to respect native religions and customs and to administer justice in accordance with native law. It must take the advice of the British Government whenever proffered; it must offer free facilities in its ports to the Royal Navy; and its chief local representative must be approved before appointment by the British. In return it did not even receive the promise of military protection from Britain in times of war. This charter was granted by an Order in Council dated August 1881, and published in

November. The first Governor of the company's territory was Mr Treacher, formerly Lieutenant-Governor of Labuan, who was seconded for the purpose by the British Government.[1]

Charles Brooke could not look on the establishment of the new State with approval, especially when he learnt who was to be its Governor. But the British Government now dealt more fairly with him. Even Pauncefote at the Foreign Office realised that the cession of Baram could no longer be forbidden. In January 1882 the Sultan of Brunei was informed that the transfer of the territory was approved by Her Majesty. Five months later Charles Brooke visited Brunei and was received by the Sultan with every mark of friendship and esteem; and the agreement conceding the district for an annual rent of $4200 was signed. Much as the aged Sultan would have liked to protract negotiations in the hope of raising his price, he yielded with the traditional Malay dignity and grace.[2]

The subsequent history of the Chartered Company belied the Rajah's worst fears. The local officials showed a regard for native interests almost as devoted as that shown in Sarawak, though they had the doubtful advantage of being rather more bureaucratically organised. The Company did not achieve the commercial success that its promoters had expected. For a long time its shareholders received an infinitesimal return on their outlay. Instead of the exploitation of the native tribes by greedy merchant adventurers, the problem was, rather, to find capitalists ready to provide money for the development of so unpromising a territory. But, at least so long as Treacher governed the country, Charles Brooke could not forgive its existence. In the summer of 1883 he paid an uninvited visit to the territory and wrote to Sir Frederick Weld, the Governor at Singapore, that he thought it all 'an inflated idea'. But he tried to keep his sense of justice. When one of his ex-officers, J. B. Cruikshank, took service with the North Borneo Company, he wrote to promise him that his pension would still be paid, unless he took part in some action which was clearly unfriendly to Sarawak.[3]

In May 1884 there was an armed revolt against the Sultan along the Limbang river, which flowed into Brunei Bay just south of the capital. Both the Rajah and Treacher had agents in Brunei, busily trying to obtain other concessions from the Sultan or the *pangirans*. To Treacher it seemed clear that the Limbang revolt was organised by the Rajah's agents; but more probably it was spontaneous. The local inhabitants, exasperated by extortion from Brunei, saw how the people of the Baram were benefiting from Sarawak rule and wished to follow their example. The rebels marched on to the capital. To protect his palace the Sultan had to borrow twenty-four rifles from Labuan; and only the arrival of a British gunboat saved the city from being overrun. The British Acting Consul-General patched up a truce; but it was quite impossible to recover control of the rebel territory. In December some Sarawak traders were murdered by Murut tribesmen on the Trusan river, further east along Brunei Bay. The Rajah was then in England. His deputy, Mr Maxwell, protested to the Sultan and the Pangiran Temonggong, who admitted that they were powerless to punish the murderers and themselves suggested that Sarawak should take over the district for a suitable rent of $4500, to go to the Pangiran Temanggong, whose property it was. Maxwell agreed, subject to the Rajah's approval; which was given when the Rajah returned early in 1885. The Rajah's officials then entered the Trusan district and in a short time established their authority over the Muruts there. Treacher, who was still acting Consul-General until a successor should be appointed, protested. He was at the time negotiating to secure the Padas river basin and the Kalias peninsula for North Borneo. But at the same time he honestly reported that the inhabitants of Limbang were determined not to return to the Brunei fold and would accept any form of British rule, including that of Sarawak.[1]

In May 1885 the old Sultan died, aged nearly a hundred. For all his weakness and inefficiency he had preserved some sort of authority in Brunei itself. His successor was the Pangiran Temanggong Hashim Jelal, the reputed son of the former Sultan Omar Ali. But his legitimacy was so widely doubted that many *pangirans* and local chieftains refused to recognise him. Unsure of his position, and with no money other than the rents that he received from the concessions to Sarawak and North Borneo, his only practical policy was to play off his neighbours against each other. Even as Regent he was doing so efficiently. As the Colonial Office reported confidentially to the Foreign Office that same month: 'If something is not done soon to cool the exasperation of Messrs Brooke and Treacher, there will not be a *pangiran* left in Brunei.'[2] At the close of 1884 Treacher had obtained Padas and the Kalias peninsula for a rental of $3000, after sending heavy bribes to members of the Regent's harem. He then expelled the Pangiran Kurim, who owned much of the land there and who happened to be a Sarawak subject.[3]

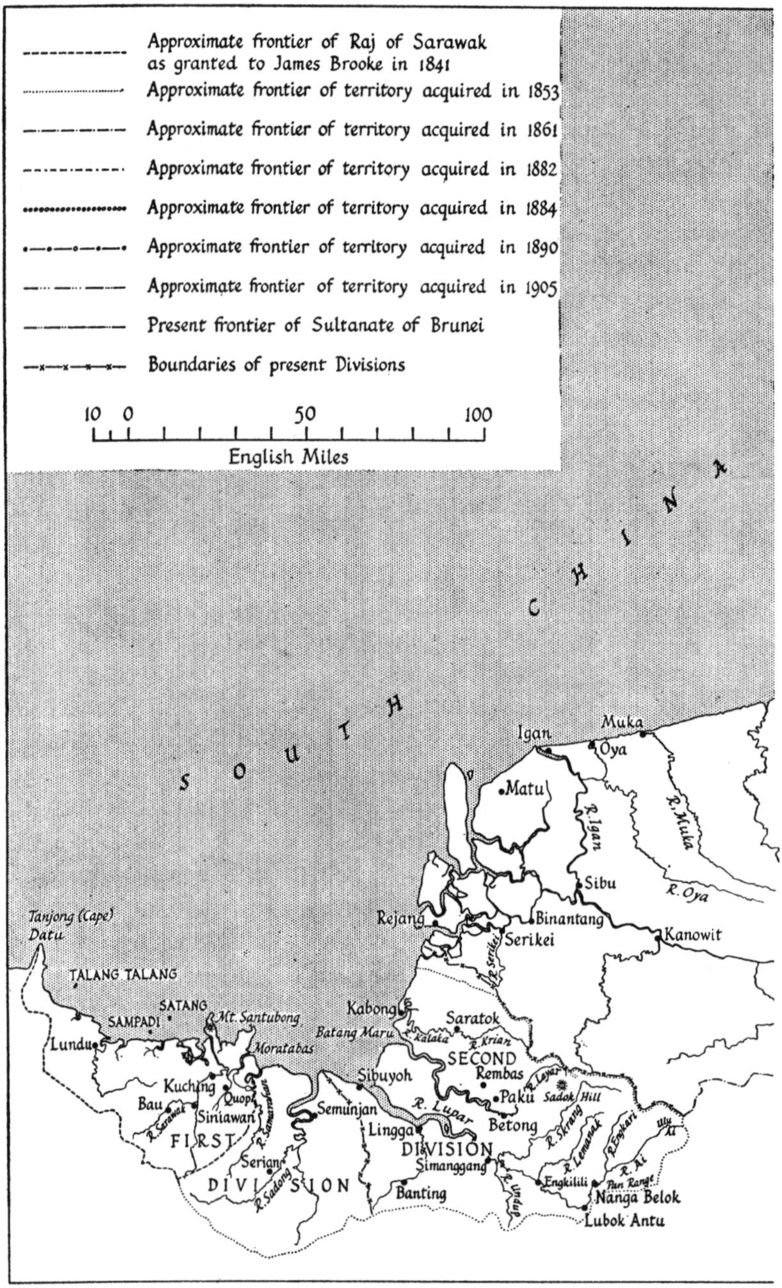

Map 3. Sarawak and Brunei, showing successive boundaries.

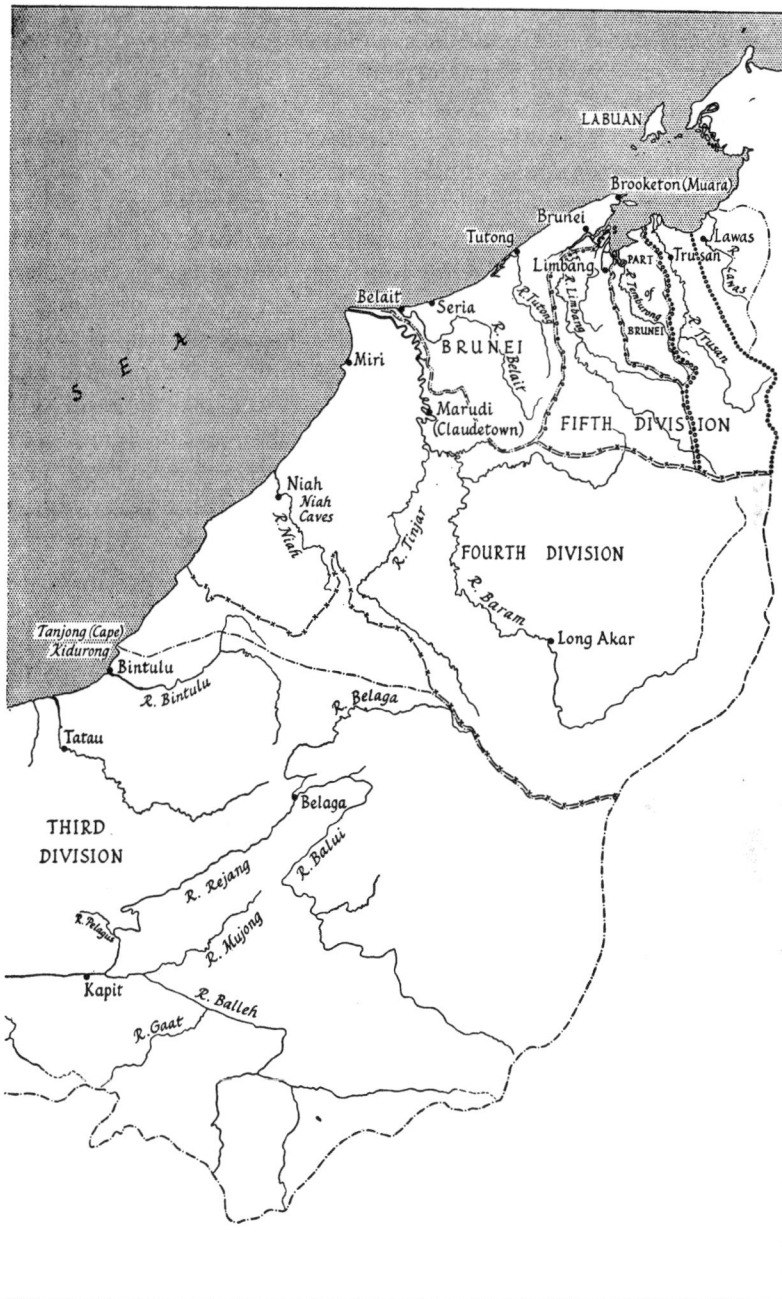

LABUAN

Brooketon (Muara)

Brunei

Tutong   Lawas

Limbang   PART Trusan

Belait   Seria   of

BRUNEI

R. Belait

Miri   BRUNEI

Marudi   FIFTH DIVISION
(Claudetown)

Niah
Niah
Caves   FOURTH DIVISION

R. Niah   R. Tinjar

R. Baram

Tanjong (Cape)   Long Akar
Kidurong
Bintulu

R. Bintulu   R. Belaga

Tatau

THIRD   Belaga
DIVISION

R. Rejang   R. Balui

R. Pelagus   R. Mujong

Kapit   R. Balleh

R. Gaat

S   E   A

In November 1885 the Limbang population again rose in open revolt and threatened Brunei. The new Sultan invited the Rajah to Brunei and begged him to put down the revolt. The Rajah refused to intervene in order that Limbang should be handed back to Brunei misgovernment. His attitude was thoroughly correct; but his agent in Brunei, Mr Everett, went rather far in privately encouraging the Limbang peoples to expect positive support from Sarawak. Relations worsened next year, when the Sultan refused to punish the murderers of a *pangiran* who was a Sarawak subject.[1]

At this time a new British Consul-General, Dr Leys, was appointed. He reported in favour of the cession of Limbang to the Rajah. The Brunei *pangirans* with property there were in favour of it, as the only means of obtaining any rents from their tenants; and he thought that the Sultan, who obtained no money from the district, would agree. If something were not done soon, the Limbang peoples would certainly march again on Brunei.[2]

The Government was prepared to take this advice. But Treacher was not yet defeated. The North Borneo Company arranged for a question to be asked in the House of Commons, on the grounds that the Rajah had forcibly seized Limbang against the formal protest of the Sultan, of the native chiefs and of the Malay *pangirans*. The Rajah had, it was true, recently been to Limbang and issued a proclamation there telling the people not to attack Brunei, but promising to protect them if they were attacked. Meanwhile they should resist transference to any other flag. Leys now admitted that the Sultan was not so ready to yield Limbang, but, he said, it was 'obvious to everyone: (1) that the Brunei Government cannot control the Limbang people; (2) that the cession of the river to Sarawak would pacify the Limbang people, content the great majority of the Brunei Rajahs who have interests in the river and bring about immediate peace; (3) that the only one who prevents the cession taking place is the Sultan, supported by the British North Borneo Company'. The Foreign Office was still ready to agree to the cession, as well as to confirm the cession of Padas to the company. But now Treacher and his friends started a campaign against Dr Leys. It resulted in the appointment of Sir Frederick Weld, Governor of Singapore, to enquire into the whole situation above Leys's head.[3]

Some such enquiry was necessary. Not only was the situation in Brunei full of danger; but both France, and, still more, Germany were showing an unwelcome interest in Borneo affairs. But Weld was not the right man to conduct the enquiry. He knew Malaya, where British policy was based on supporting the local Sultans; and he fancied himself as an adept at making friends with these rulers. Sultan Hassim was delighted. Here was a man who apparently believed all that he said and who allowed him to insult Dr Leys with impunity. Soon, in June 1887, Weld telegraphed to London that all was well in Brunei and in Limbang. It was only necessary to appoint a British Resident to advise the Sultan at Brunei and to govern Limbang in his name. On his return to Singapore he followed up his telegram with a report on the same lines, adding that Brunei should become a Protectorate. Leys, smarting under Weld's treatment of him, asked pertinently who was to pay the Resident's salary. He also reported that the Sultan had promised to cede Limbang to Sarawak at the end of October 1887, for a payment of $20,000, if he received no other money before that date. The Foreign Office ordered Leys to forbid the cession, while Weld wrote from Singapore to complain not only of Leys but also of the Rajah's agent, Everett, who had been pressing the Sultan with somewhat inaccurate threats. Leys and Everett were officially reprimanded, while the Rajah telegraphed to the latter to tell him to stop all negotiations with Limbang. Meanwhile the North Borneo Company urged the Foreign Office to establish its Protectorate over Brunei quickly, to save it from Sarawak aggression.[1]

Although Mr Davies, the North Borneo Company's Resident on the West Coast, sent in through Weld an ingenious proposal for the payment of a British Resident to govern Limbang—a post which, with Weld's support, he coveted for himself—London decided that the expense would be too great. Both the Foreign Office and the Colonial Office came to believe that it would be better to cede Limbang to Sarawak after all; but the Sultan must not be forced against his will. It was, however, decided not only to establish a Protectorate over Brunei, but over North Borneo and Sarawak as well.

The Rajah was delighted. For many decades he and his uncle before him had pleaded for protection. In October 1887 he eagerly sent the Foreign Office his proposed draft for the Protectorate. It contained seven points. Britain would give Sarawak protection against foreign enemies. It would not interfere in the internal administration. It would guarantee the succession of the Rajah's son and future heirs and in the case of a minority would accept as regent the Ranee or anyone else whom the Rajah appointed. It would appoint a Consul-General to Sarawak. Sarawak would maintain its own armed forces. Sarawak would send all foreign communications, except those dealing with local frontier matters, through the British Foreign Office. All the remaining territory belonging to Brunei Bay would be given to Sarawak.

The Foreign Office replied with its own draft the following May. This consisted of six clauses. Sarawak was to be an independent protected state, with no interference in its internal administration. Any dispute as to the succession to the throne was to be referred to Her Majesty's Government. Relations with all foreign powers, including Brunei and North Borneo, were to be conducted through the Foreign Office. British consular officers were to be appointed to Sarawak. British subjects, shipping and commerce were to receive most favoured nation treatment. There was to be no alienation of territory. The Rajah in Council accepted all these terms, with the exception of the third, which was emended to allow matters of frontier administration to be decided locally. The emendation was approved. The treaty embodying the Protectorate was signed by the Rajah in Council on 14th June 1888, and returned countersigned from London in September. At the same time the Rajah was created a Knight Grand Cross of the Order of St Michael and St George.[1]

Brunei became a Protectorate that same September, though the Sultan refused to admit a British Resident to advise him, and, for reasons of economy, the British Government acquiesced in his refusal. A treaty setting up a Protectorate over North Borneo was signed about the same time, to the relief of the Chartered Company, on which no further administrative restrictions were placed but which could now feel secure against foreign aggression. The Governor of Singapore became High Commissioner for the Borneo Protectorate.[2]

The establishment of the Protectorate caused great satisfaction to the Rajah: and it implicitly confirmed his possession of the Trusan district. But the problem of the Limbang remained unsolved. Dr Leys, whose health had been broken by his humiliation at the hands of Sir Frederick Weld and the Sultan, retired on prolonged sick leave. His successor as Acting Governor of Labuan and Acting Consul-General, A. S. Hamilton, reported his belief that the Sultan would be glad to be rid of Limbang, but to save his face he must be requested by Britain to cede it.[3] But nothing was done. In the meantime trouble flared up again between the Company and the Rajah. The North Borneo Company coveted a small area on the Kalias peninsula, the Damit river, just opposite to Labuan, which had not been included in the original concession, nor had its boundaries been fixed. It belonged to a Brunei princess, whose brother, the Pangiran Shabandar, administered it with little regard to the probable frontier. The Company decided to eject him by force; and for that purpose the agents hired Dyak warriors from Sarawak territory without informing the Rajah. It moreover used Labuan as a base for its operations without informing the Acting Governor; who returned home one afternoon to find some of these Dyaks drying the heads of their victims on the lawns and flower-beds of Government House. Hamilton, who was a testy ex-naval officer and stone deaf, was not amused. But by now the Company had overrun the small territory; and Hamilton was sufficiently appeased by an appeal from the Company for his arbitration. He allowed the annexation of the Damit by the Company, on the payment of ample compensation to the Pangiran and his sister. The Rajah was less forgiving. He could not condone the employment of Dyaks, to whom he was trying to teach peaceful ways, on such an expedition. He was disappointed when the Pangiran did not pursue the matter further and sue the Company for heavy damages.[1]

Meanwhile the Rajah had personally acquired a small area of land in Brunei. William Cowie, who had been a pioneer in obtaining concessions in North Borneo, and who was later to become Managing Director and then Chairman of the British North Borneo Company, had acquired from the Sultan a lease of the tip of Muara peninsula, at the western entrance to Brunei Bay. There was coal there, and he was working it. He was not at the time on good terms with the Company, though later he was to claim to be its true founder, and, in honour of the Rajah, he had named his coalmine and the village that grew up round it Brooketon. It was not a profitable venture. Early in 1887 Cowie decided to cut his losses and offered his concession to the Rajah. The Rajah hesitated. At last, in September 1888, he agreed to buy, perhaps more from fear that otherwise the North Borneo Company might take it over than from any great faith in its potentialities. The Sultan of Brunei made no objection; he had sold the lease for a capital sum to Cowie, so was no longer financially interested. The British Government approved, so long as the Rajah bought as a private individual and not as ruler of Sarawak. But he was permitted to administer the settlement with his own officers and police, though in the Sultan's name. A *pangiran* appointed by the Sultan, but paid by the Rajah, kept nominal watch over Brunei interests. Cowie had run the colliery in a haphazard manner. The Rajah bought up-to-date equipment for it and installed experienced managers. But it still continued to lose money; and the capital expenditure was never recovered. When at last a British Resident was appointed to Brunei, the question of the administration of the district was re-opened. The Rajah was ordered by the Resident to withdraw his police, and an export duty was placed on the coal. Angry letters passed between the Rajah and the British authorities. Soon afterwards the development of the newly discovered oil-fields weakened any interest in coalmining. Eventually, in 1921, the Third Rajah, with some relief, handed the district back to the Sultan. The colliery was abandoned, and the village around it was overrun by the jungle. Nowadays there is little to show where Brooketon once stood.[1]

Early in 1890 the people of the Limbang district took matters into their own hands. For six years they had refused to admit the Sultan's officials into their land or to pay taxes to Brunei. Now they hoisted the Sarawak flag and invited the Rajah to take over the territory. The Rajah was ready for the call; for his agents kept him well informed about the situation along the river. He hastened there and on 17 March issued a proclamation assuming the responsibility for the government, 'unless Her Majesty the Queen of England may see fit otherwise'. The British Government hesitated for nearly a year before giving its complete approval to the annexation. The British Consul, Trevenen, was sent to enquire if the people of Limbang really wished to be annexed. Satisfied on that point the Foreign Office insisted that the Rajah should pay the Court of Brunei the sum of $6000 a year, adding that if for three consecutive years the Sultan refused to accept this indemnity, it would be forfeit. The Sultan protested, even telegraphed personally to Queen Victoria. When his appeal failed, he firmly rejected the indemnity. But, as he explained privately, this was not so much from wounded pride as from a desire to punish two recalcitrant ministers. The Pangirans Bandahara and Di Gadong were by virtue of their offices entitled to the main part of the revenues from the Limbang and therefore to the indemnity. By refusing to accept the indemnity, which they could not receive without his permission, he could give concrete and effective expression to his displeasure.[2]

The acquisition of the Limbang district by Sarawak left the Sultan with merely Brunei town itself and the coastal districts as far west as the mouth of the Baram. He also kept two enclaves, the Temburong valley, between the Limbang and the Trusan, and the small Lawas valley, between the Trusan and the Chartered Company's territory.

Meanwhile the Chartered Company was appeased by a decision in London that the Governor of North Borneo should also be Governor of Labuan, under the ultimate authority of the Colonial Office. This arrangement lasted till 1906, when the Colonial Office resumed direct control, somewhat to the relief of the Company, which had found the administration of the island a difficult and thankless task.[1]

Even without the complication of Labuan the North Borneo Company had been passing through a bad period. There was a general trade depression in the East in the years following 1890. North Borneo was not proving so productive as had been hoped. The main export was now tobacco to America; and this was severely hurt by the high tariff policy adopted there in 1893. Many of the Directors lost faith in the Company and resigned, including the first Chairman, Sir Rutherford Alcock, and Lord Brassey. Lord Brassey, who had spent some time in Borneo waters in his yacht *Sunbeam* in 1887, proposed a scheme by which the British Government should amalgamate its Protectorates in Borneo and Malaya with the Straits Settlements into one large colony. He believed that anyhow the British Government should take over North Borneo, paying off the shareholders by the gradual sale of land there, or if the British Government was not prepared to act, that the administration should be handed to the Rajah of Sarawak, of whose system of government he spoke and thought very highly. A new Board of Directors, of which Admiral Keppel was a prominent member, was impressed by Lord Brassey's views. As Her Majesty's Government would not intervene, the Rajah was approached. But he believed that if the whole administrative system in North Borneo were reformed, there would be a saving of about $30,000 yearly. He was, therefore, prepared to take over the country if he could issue bonds to cover shares up to a total of £500,000. He would guarantee the shareholders a dividend of 1 per cent, to be raised proportionately as soon as the revenue exceeded $210,000, his estimated cost of the administration. But he must have the right to buy out the Company by taking over the whole share capital paid up at the amount of transfer but not exceeding £500,000. He would take over all liabilities; and if at any time he or his heirs failed to fulfil their obligations, the Company could foreclose, or Her Majesty's Government could appoint an administrator. His offer came before a General Meeting of the shareholders in February 1894. In spite of Lord Brassey's advocacy, the Company's lawyers advised strongly against the proposal. It was rejected by a large majority. But the Company was empowered to offer the Rajah the Governorship of the territory. He refused the offer at once. It seems that he had not been enthusiastic even about his own proposals, which, indeed, would have provided him with more work and worry than he could well manage. Nor had the shareholders cause to regret their decision. By 1896 the worst of the depression was over, and the territory at last began to produce a dividend.[1]

It was not North Borneo but Brunei which the Rajah dearly longed to absorb. In 1899 the inhabitants of the Belait and Tutong districts, between the Baram and Muara, rose in revolt against the Sultan. Their chiefs hoisted the Sarawak flag and sent a deputation to Kuching to invite the Rajah to take over their land. Hardened by experience, the Rajah was cautious. Early next year the Pangiran Bandahara of Brunei, who had always been a friend of his, urged him to move his forces into Belait; but the British Consul, Mr Keyser, forbade him.[2] The revolt continued, in a desultory but occasionally bloodthirsty war. A new British Consul, Mr Hewett, recommended early in 1903 that the Rajah be allowed to annex Belait and Tutong; but the Foreign Office, on the advice of Joseph Chamberlain, the Colonial Secretary, again decided against the cession. Hewett reported that the Sultan, who had recently embarrassed everyone by appealing to the Sultan of Turkey and offering to hand him all his possessions, including Limbang, was really willing to accept the offer. There was oil in the territory in question; and Hewett thought that it would be wiser to give it to the Rajah rather than let the Sultan keep it. He received no thanks for his suggestions. Instead, the Colonial Office recommended that he be moved and a Resident appointed for Brunei. Sir Frank Swettenham was anxious to have this done.

Meanwhile the Rajah made another offer to the Sultan. He proposed that he should annex the whole territory of Brunei, with the exception of Brunei town. The Sultan and his heirs should continue to receive the cession moneys due to them. In addition the Sultan should be given $1900 monthly, and his successors $500 monthly after his death. The Pangiran Bandahara and the Pangiran Pamancha should have $500 monthly and their heirs, after their deaths, $250. $10,000 should be paid at once to the Sultan and $5000 to the two Pangirans. The coal royalties from Muara should be paid to the Sultan till the existing agreement expired. The Sultan and the Pangiran Bandahara should retain their flags and the salutes due to them. This offer was reported to the Foreign Office in July 1903. Swettenham, when asked his views, said that Brunei was not really in so chaotic a state as people said; but he thought that the Sultan might well accept the offer if the money payments were slightly raised. But neither the Foreign Office nor the Sultan would commit themselves, though during the next summer the Sultan was trying to raise a loan from the Rajah. He had recovered some control of the Belait and Tutong districts, but found it almost impossible to raise any money from them.[1]

In 1902 the Chartered Company had purchased the lease of the Lawas river, thus bringing their frontier down to that of Sarawak. Unfortunately the *pangirans* from whom the lease was bought were not in possession of the district, which had been occupied for many years by the Pangiran Abu Bakir. He announced that he would yield his lands only to the Rajah of Sarawak. Both sides appealed to Swettenham as High Commissioner. He upheld Abu Bakir's claim to the land but also upheld the lease. To appease the Pangiran the Company invited the Rajah's nephew, Brooke Johnson, who had been Treasurer in the Sarawak Government, to administer the district. This did not work satisfactorily. By the end of 1904 the Company decided to make a generous gesture and transfer the concession of Lawas to Sarawak. In return the Rajah gave over to the Company such shadowy rights as he had to mining concessions on the west coast of North Borneo, which he had acquired from Cowie at the time that he purchased the lease of Muara. The Foreign Office gave permission for the transaction; and Lawas formally became part of Sarawak on 12 January 1905.[2]

As a result of the arrangement relations between the Chartered Company and Sarawak took a turn for the better. There was still a spirit of rivalry; but the bitterness was gone.

The Rajah was, however, to find Lawas as difficult to govern as the Company had done. The *pangirans* who claimed estates there were still active and were well armed with documents. Meanwhile Brooke Johnson had obtained personal concessions from the Pangiran Abu Bakir. The Rajah was horrified that one of his officials, who was, moreover, his own nephew, should have acquired a private interest in Borneo territory. His son, the Rajah Muda, who had been sent to take over the territory, was reproved for not having been more strict with Brooke Johnson. The Rajah loudly repudiated all connection with his nephew and even took his name off the list of patrons of the Sarawak Club so long as Brooke remained a member. In the end the Foreign Office advised him to pay compensation to Brooke, while he had to promise to recognise the *tulin* rights of the Brunei *pangirans*. But he soon brought orderly government to Lawas. It had been a notorious slave-market till the Chartered Company took it over. He completed the Company's work in ending the slave-trade.[1]

With the acquisition of Lawas Sarawak reached its ultimate limits. The Rajah had added to his personal possessions in Brunei by the purchase from the local landowner of Kota Batu, between Muara and Brunei town, on the site of the ancient capital of the Sultanate. But this purchase caused some resentment, as the site contained some of the tombs of the Sultans and their families. After some discussion the Rajah offered the land back at the price which he had paid for it.[2] No more Brunei territory was to go to Sarawak. The Rajah's proposals for the future of Brunei remained under discussion for some years. But towards the end of 1905 the British Government decided in favour of appointing a British Resident to Brunei and preserving the integrity of the Sultanate. By the terms of an agreement which came into force at the New Year, 1906, the Sultan was obliged to accept a British Resident and to consult with him on all matters concerning the external relations and internal administration of Brunei, except only for religious affairs. His income and those of the chief *pangirans* were guaranteed by the British Government. Sir Frank Swettenham had long advocated this solution and even believed that were it to be achieved the Rajah ought to give back Limbang to the Sultanate. In fact there could be no question of returning Limbang against the wishes of its people. Swettenham warned London to expect heavy opposition to the whole scheme from the Rajah and, to a lesser extent, from the Chartered Company. But though the Rajah expressed his disappointment, and though Mr Cowie, now Chairman of the Chartered Company, wrote to the Foreign Office regretting that the Rajah's proposals had been rejected, the strongest opponent to the appointment of a Resident was the Sultan himself. He made it known that he would just as soon have accepted the Rajah's terms.[3]

If we look back in the light of later events, it is difficult not to regret the decision of the British Government. The system of appointing a British Resident to advise local Sultans worked well enough in the Federated Malay States. But the history and circumstances of Brunei were different. The specialist advisers employed by the Government were men trained on the Malayan mainland, who never quite understood that the problem of Borneo could not necessarily be solved by the methods that they had found successful. Brunei in 1905 was not a viable state. For many years it was in a trough of bankruptcy. Then the discovery of oil made it inordinately and disproportionately rich. Any attempt nowadays to integrate the British territories in Borneo is sorely handicapped by the decision to preserve Brunei made in 1905.

Even though the Rajah accepted the settlement, the Foreign Office remained deeply suspicious of him. In the spring of 1906 it became clear that Sultan Hashim was dying. When in early May the Rajah arrived in Brunei, the British Resident telegraphed in alarm to London to say that his presence was undesirable, and reported later that the Rajah seemed to have been intriguing with the Pangiran Bandahara, and that he had secured possession of certain unspecified documents. The Resident was told to assure the people of Brunei that cession to Sarawak was not being considered. It is probable that the documents secured by the Rajah concerned the rights of the *pangirans* in territories already ceded to him, about which he was eager to have correct information. At the same time he no doubt hoped that his friend the Pangiran Bandahara would succeed to the throne, to which by old Muslim custom he was entitled as Senior Prince of the Blood Royal. But, on the advice of the British Resident, when Hashim died the throne was given to the late Sultan's young son, Mohammed Jelal ul-Alam, with the Pangiran Bandahara as Regent.[1]

Towards the end of 1907 the surveillance of affairs in the Borneo Protectorate was transferred from the Foreign Office to the Colonial Office. The Rajah had usually found the Colonial Office the more sympathetic of the two Ministries, at least until the time of Joseph Chamberlain. On the whole the change improved Sarawak's relations with London.[2]

Meanwhile the Rajah's personal position had been officially settled. In 1888 the Inland Revenue had enquired, somewhat ignorantly, of the India Office whether the Ranee's income was liable to tax. The India Office passed the question on to the Foreign Office, which pronounced that the Rajah was the Ruler of an Independent State, and therefore the Ranee was not liable.[3] Even after the Protectorate was established a few months later he was still so considered. He was pleased when the Grand Cross of St Michael and St George was bestowed on him. But the personal side of the problem did not worry him. When in England he avoided official life as far as he could; and though he felt some irritation at being addressed on official occasions as Sir Charles Brooke, it was more because he felt that to be an insult to Sarawak than because he desired a fixed precedence. But the Ranee, living mostly in England, found her equivocal social position rather inconvenient, quite apart from the question of the prestige of the Raj. Soon after the accession of King Edward VII she caused strings to be pulled at Court. The King took an interest and proclaimed that Charles Brooke should be recognised by the Court as Rajah of Sarawak and be given precedence there immediately after the Heads of the Indian Native States. The Rajah was pleased at first; but when the Ranee wrote to him to boast of her part in the matter, she was severely snubbed. 'Dearest Margaret,' he replied, 'I must confess that the King's notice of my position has fallen 50 per cent in my estimation, as I thought he had paid me the honour without being in any way solicited...such world-like ambition does neither the country nor myself an atom of real benefit.' Nevertheless his sense of respect for the King led him to apply to attend a levee when he was next in London, in order to be received officially as Rajah. He was offered a baronetcy in the 1912 New Year's Honours, but refused it. He did not approve of hereditary titles, he said.[1]

The Rajah's whole attitude towards Brunei has sometimes been criticised. It appeared to many members of the Foreign Office at the time, and to many writers of more recent date, to show little more than a crude lust for territorial expansion. They were inclined to doubt if Brunei was in as hopeless a state as the Brooke propagandists maintained, or if the populations in the districts that he was so eager to annex really wanted to be under his rule rather than under the rule of their own compatriots, to whom they were used, and to wonder whether the revolts in his favour in districts such as Limbang were really spontaneous and not the result of hard work by his agents. It is certainly true that many of the Malay upper classes were not at all willing to pass from Brunei to Sarawak rule; but most of those Malays were in a position to benefit by Brunei corruption. An English visitor who was at Miri in 1872 had an argument with a local Malay, who said to him: 'Look how the Sarawak people are fined for the slightest offence, and the fine goes to the Government, while here, except for the *serah* we rarely fine people unless it be for some grave offence, and the fine goes to the injured party.' Indeed, the greater efficiency of the Rajah's administration was not always pleasing to the Malay taxpayer. But the humbler people, who were for the most part not Malay, found the *serah*, which obliged them to dispose of their produce through the landowner, an almost intolerable burden; and further enquiries revealed that in that very year the *pangiran* who owned Miri had extorted $9000 from the local inhabitants. The races other than the Malay certainly welcomed their transference from Brunei to Sarawak; and many of the Malays shared their views.[1]

It is, however, true that Rajah Charles dealt with Brunei with little regard to the pride and sensitivity of its ruling classes and that to this day his high-handedness has left a certain legacy of resentment. Spencer St John, in the short life of Rajah James which he published in 1890, felt it his duty to express his disapproval of 'the action of Sarawak in seizing by force any part of the Sultan's dominions'. He was referring in particular to the annexation of Limbang, and he believed that had Charles been more tactful, he could have achieved his object 'without violating any principle of international law'. In the past, Rajah James had always been more gentle and more courteous in his dealings with Brunei and, in spite of the stern action that he took there on occasions, the Malays continued to regard him as a friend. Charles was more impatient; he also knew much more clearly what he wanted. Experience had taught him that too much courtesy led to endless delays and postponements. He knew that his Government was to the advantage of the subject races, and he was not to be deflected. Whether his methods were unwise or morally wrong, his motives were for the good of Borneo; and he achieved most of his objectives. Even St John admitted in a private letter to him that 'if the Foreign Office could understand how the Brunei Rajahs govern Limbang, they would make no objection to your taking it over'. Mr Helms, the former Manager of the Borneo Company, who was not always uncritical of Brooke rule, wrote after a visit to Limbang, when its fate was in the balance, that 'the present state of things in this river is very deplorable, and unjust to the natives, who sit on the rail, uncertain who will be their master, anxious to give allegiance to Rajah Brooke's government, but dreading lest they should be handed back to their old taskmasters'. 'For the sake of humanity' he hoped for an early transference of the district to Sarawak.[2]

A gentler and more tactful Rajah might have maintained happier relations with Brunei and caused less lasting resentment there; but, in view of the hesitation of the British Foreign Office, he would have been obliged to leave whole areas of country under the chaotic and oppressive government of the Brunei *pangirans*. Charles Brooke believed it his duty to rescue the native population from such a fate, and he believed that they looked to him for rescue. He acted on those beliefs; and it would be rash to presume, out of sentimentality, that he did wrong.

CHAPTER III

TOWARDS PEACE AND PROSPERITY

Speaking to the Council Negri at their session of 1891, Rajah Charles recalled the thirty-nine years that had passed since he entered the Sarawak Service. They could be divided, he said, into three equal periods. During the first thirteen years, from 1852 to 1865, he and his fellows had devoted themselves to the work of suppressing head-hunting among the Dyaks. It had been a life of carrying arms and keeping watch and ward against subtle enemies. During the second period, which began roughly the moment when he took over the government of the country, military expeditions had still been necessary, but the time had also been spent in the peaceful pursuits of giving and amending law and establishing its supremacy. During the third period, from 1878 to the year in which he spoke, the rough and perilous life of the past was no longer required; he and his old comrades 'could sit in their armchairs and attend to the political business and commercial progress of the country'.[1]

The last remark was disingenuous. The Rajah never sat in an arm-chair himself and rebuked those of his officers who possessed such a luxury. Nor was it quite true that military expeditions were entirely unnecessary. But, apart from the Lang Endang expedition of 1879 and the Bukit Batu expeditions of 1881, and trouble in the Kadang hills from 1884 to 1886, there were no disturbances that could not be settled by a local officer and his handful of police, till towards the close of the century the adventurer Banting raised a revolt in the Ulu Ai. And such risings as occurred were not now set in motion by a deliberate refusal to accept the Rajah's authority but by a resentment of his attempts to stop raiding and head-hunting between rival tribes. The existence of the Raj was never threatened; but vigilance was still needed if the Rajah's subjects in the outlying districts were to live in peace and in security. But meanwhile peace and security were creating a welcome rise in revenue.[2]

Far more than in the First Rajah's time the government was centred on the Rajah. James had not been an administrator; it had been men such as Crookshank who had built up the administrative machine. But Charles kept the whole administration tightly in his hands. The personnel was still small. In 1884 a French visitor, Edmond Cotteau, reported that 'thirty Englishmen, no more, govern and administer the country, and that with only a few hundred native soldiers and policemen, and almost without written laws. A handful of men of a strange race is blindly obeyed by 300,000 Asiatics: to what must we attribute this great result if not to the justice and the extreme simplicity of the Government?'[1] M. Cotteau's estimate of the population of Sarawak was exaggerated; but he was right when he spoke of simplicity and justice. The justice, it is true, was somewhat arbitrary. Up-country the Rajah's officials administered it according to local customary law, modified only by the Rajah's orders on matters such as slavery. In Kuching the Rajah himself was the fount of justice, and, as far as possible, every case came up before him in person, or before his appointed deputy, were he absent. He administered it partly according to the customs of the people involved, partly according to the codified Indian Law, and partly according to his own common sense. The results would often have horrified a modern judiciary. Once, for example, during a police prosecution for petty theft, he sentenced a young Chinese, who had been present at the time of the arrest but who was clearly unconnected with the crime, to a short prison sentence. When questioned by the Ranee on the ethics of the sentence, he answered that the young man had not been able to produce in Court anyone who would vouch for him. That meant that he could not be employed in any honest occupation; and a spell of hard work in prison would be good for him.[2] Such arbitrary judgments were not unusual. Yet no section of the community, not even the Chinese, seems to have regarded him as other than a strictly just man. Nor did anyone, except for an occasional European observer, show dismay because there was no appeal from his judgments. Civil cases between Malays continued to be heard in purely Malay Courts. For cases between Chinese, Chinese advisers assisted the magistrates until, in 1911, a Chinese Court was established. It dealt only with marriage and inheritance and disputes between business partners, but was also a Court of Appeal from local Courts on matters of debt and bankruptcy.[3]

The simplicity of the administration provides problems for the historian. A minimum of records was kept. Residents of the Divisions were required to send a regular report to the Rajah, containing an outline of the chief civil and criminal cases that occurred in their district, together with an account of any social or economic event of interest; but long reports were not welcomed. The Rajah kept copies of most of the letters that he wrote. But many decisions were taken by word of mouth, when district officers visited Kuching or when the Rajah went himself on tours of inspection. District officers sent in reports to the Resident of their Division, many of which were forwarded on to the Rajah.

The Residents were Europeans, though a Malay might temporarily be appointed to a Residency. The district officers were sometimes European, sometimes Malay and sometimes of mixed origin. For most of the eighteen-eighties the fort at Kapit, at the junction of the Rejang and the Balleh rivers, was in the charge of Domingo de Rosario, the son of the First Rajah's cook, a Portuguese from Malaya of eclectic origin; he had been born in the Astana kitchen. His letters to the Resident at Rejang, though written in a unique English, give a typical account of the problems that a district officer had to face. Cases of heads or slaves taken on raids occur at intervals. It was the officer's task to see that both were surrendered to Authority. He heard minor lawsuits, and often needed the Resident's advice, as when 'Jukand a fort-man is going to bring up a case against the sergeant for abetting adultery with his wife'. When he convicted anyone for some crime he would wait for the Resident to pronounce the sentence. He had to keep an eye on merchants trading in his district. This was not always easy. In January 1884, Rosario writes to the Resident: 'Sir, Rumours are spreading about here that Raj Metain and Abang Latip was murdered some where about Pois while going down. I hope this is not true and if it does I will not be surprize at all as they are an awful swindler cheating Dyaks right and left.'[1] Or there might be rumours of forthcoming inter-tribal raids to be reported, or false rumours to be quashed. The Dyaks were apt to become dangerously excited if they believed that the Government was going to send an expedition against some tribe that they disliked. Finally, it was the officer's business to collect the poll-tax from the Dyaks and to deal efficiently with defaulters. These journeys were amongst the more pleasant episodes of the officer's life. The coming of the white man provided an occasion for festivities in the longhouses, whose inhabitants paid the tax without demur, unless the season was bad.

Problems still arose when tribal customs and the Rajah's law were at variance. A typical case was reported from the Baram in 1886, when an unmarried Kenyah girl who became pregnant and refused to reveal her lover's name was left to starve in the forest. The head chief of the district was surprised to be fined 10 pikuls of rice for causing her death, but he paid.[1]

Life in such out-stations was still lonely, and required the officer to have good health and strong nerves. But there was no longer the physical danger of the past. After the episode at Sibu in 1870 there was no further attempt to storm a fort or murder a European officer. It was only on expeditions against recalcitrant tribes that a European risked shedding his blood. Forts were nevertheless still necessary. Several were built during these years. The fort at Kuching was rebuilt and named Fort Margherita, after the Ranee, whose second name, Alice, was given to the fort at Simanggang, and whose third name, Lili, to a new fort at Betong. At Kabong a fort was built in 1878 and called Fort Charles, after the Rajah. It was washed into the sea in an inundation in 1893 and rebuilt a little further inland. Up the Rejang a fort was built at Belaga, begun in November 1883, and finished six weeks later, and called Fort Vyner, after the Rajah Muda. There was already a fort at Kanowit, Fort Emma, called after the Rajah's mother, and at Muka (Fort Burdett, called after Miss Burdett-Coutts). The fort built at Bintulu was called Fort Keppel, after the First Rajah's old friend. The Rajah liked to name places after his relations, his officials and his friends. The administrative centre which was founded on the Baram river was called Claudetown, after the first Resident of the new Division, Claude de Crespigny, and the fort there called Fort Rose, after the second Resident, Dr Rose. The fort on the Trusan river took its name of Fort Florence from Mrs Maxwell, whose husband was acting as the Rajah's deputy at the time when the Trusan district was offered to Sarawak.[2] These forts were simple affairs, built of wood or rough stone, with armouries and quarters for the fort-men below and on the first floor an office and crude living quarters for the district officer. Only when the district was entirely pacified could the officer move out into a house of his own. Wives were not encouraged to live up-country. The Rajah liked the forts to be as uniform as possible. The model which he thought should be copied was that at Simanggang. New precedents were to be avoided if possible.[3]

In Kuching life was growing steadily more comfortable. The

European community was still small. When in 1887 the Rajah entertained all the resident Europeans to dinner, only five ladies were
present.[1] The bachelor gentlemen enjoyed themselves. Several were
reprimanded or down-graded for drunkenness, others for appearing in
public with their local mistresses. Many officers were perpetually in
debt to the Treasury or to the Post Office. Others, against the law,
used government employees or prisoners in their houses or gardens.
But the firm hand of the Rajah was steadily imposing order and
decorous behaviour.[2] Living was cheap. Shoes cost about 2s. 6d. and
shirts 10s. in 1887.[3] The Europeans were allowed, perhaps mistakenly,
to import rice and spirits free of duty. Comfortable houses were
being built. There was complete security. Gerard Fiennes, who came
out that year to tutor the Rajah's sons, wrote home that he slept with
every door and window in his bungalow open. He reassured his
parents, too, about the health of the city. 'Fever', he wrote, 'beyond
the common heat fever is almost unknown, as a strong tide up the river
and a daily heavy shower wash away all impurities and keep the town
far sweeter than most English towns'. A slip of flannel worn round the
waist was, he thought, the only precaution necessary for avoiding
sickness.[4] Occasional epidemics of cholera still sometimes swept through
the Malay kampongs and the crowded Chinese bazaars. There were bad
outbreaks in 1874 and 1877 and again in 1888, but the Europeans were
not affected. The last serious outbreak was in 1902; but only one death,
of a Chinese, was recorded then.[5]

Kuching was growing in size. At the end of 1888 the township was
officially enlarged to include the whole area within a two-mile radius
from the Court-house.[6]

The Malays were still the most numerous and prominent community
in Kuching. The heads of the community sat on the Council Negri with
the Rajah and the Resident of the First Division. The number of Malay
Councillors slightly varied; in 1870 there were four, in 1875 five. The
recognised head of the community was the Datu Bandar, Haji Bua
Hasan. His father had been Datu Patinggi at the time of the First
Rajah's arrival. His brother-in-law was the rebel Datu Patinggi, Abdul
Gafur, after whose exile the title remained in abeyance till 1937. His
elder brother had been Datu Bandar till his death in 1865, he himself
had been Datu Imam till he succeeded his brother. He died in 1906
at the age of about ninety-five. His wife, Datin Isa, was a lady of great
character and a close friend of the Ranee. She was a stickler for old-

fashioned customs and moral standards, and was much distressed when
the Ranee instituted classes for reading and writing for the younger
Malay ladies. The Malays have a great respect for royal and noble birth.
It was considered fitting that the high Malay offices should remain in
the Datu Bandar's family. The Malays appreciated their part in the
government. Malay was an official language in the Raj, and Islam the
official religion. Except in outlying districts where the Brunei *pangirans*
still had some influence, they remained devotedly loyal to the Brooke
dynasty.[1]

Few Dyaks were as yet to be seen in Kuching. Some Land Dyaks
came in from the neighbourhood to market. The Sea Dyaks kept to
their own districts. But the chiefs of peaceful tribes were given
considerable administrative powers and were expected to keep their
people in order; and for meetings of the General Council they would
be summoned to Kuching and entertained at the Astana. After the
annexation of the Baram, Kayan chieftains would also apppear. Gerard
Fiennes was delighted to meet at the Astana one evening in 1887 'a
funny old file, one Dian, a Kayan chief. . . . He came in clad solely in
tattoo marks and a "chawat" or waist cloth.'[2] The main problem that
the Dyaks presented to the Central Government was the control of
their migrations. They moved when their simple agriculture exhausted
their land, and continually pressed down towards the coast. An order
signed by the Rajah in 1903 forbade them to settle in the coastal lands
between Kadurong and Miri, which was to be reserved for Melanaus,
but it was difficult to enforce the order.[3]

The Chinese community was growing in size. Chinese immigration
had come to a standstill after the rising in 1856; and many Chinese had
left the country. Rajah James before his death tried cautiously to
reintroduce immigrants. In a letter to Miss Burdett-Coutts, written in
April 1863, he reported: 'I have some details of the Chinese immigration scheme. Our funds are not large enough to enter into it upon a
large scale, and common prudence dictates that we should not throw
a mass of Chinese, whose antecedents are far from inspiring confidence,
into a peaceful country. I propose therefore making a trial by locating
from 500 to 2000 and allowing the plan to grow gradually to its full
proportions.'[4] It is uncertain how far James was successful in his
efforts. By 1871 there were close on 5000 Chinese in Sarawak. They
controlled the sago refineries and much of the commerce was back in
their hands. When a Chamber of Commerce was founded in Kuching

in 1873 they formed the leading section. The Rajah had already ordained that there should be a Chinese magistrate sitting in the Debtors' Court. In 1878 a large area was allotted to Chinese merchants for pepper growing.

Immigration was still fitful and unorganised. Most of the immigrants came direct from China; but a Chinese Imperial law forbade emigration from the Empire. It was not repealed till 1894, though it had not been strictly enforced since 1860. In 1880 the Rajah arranged for 500 Chinese to settle on the lower Rejang. He undertook that the Government would provide sufficient land for the settlers, with a monthly allowance of rice and salt; that it would engage to keep open communications by steamer with Kuching and would transport goods on reasonable terms, and would build a police station to protect the settlement and interpreters to help them and generally to see to their welfare. In return the settlement must be permanent. He obtained settlers on these terms; and the settlements, after some initial difficulties, prospered and attracted other immigrants. By 1887 there were at least 7000 Chinese in Sarawak. Some of them had already moved up the Rejang to Sibu. There were only thirty Chinese in Sibu in 1883, but two years later they were prosperous enough to give the Resident, Mr Bampfylde, a handsome signed testimonial to thank him for his help in settling them.[1]

The Rajah was impressed by the energy and industry of the settlers. In 1900 he made new efforts to find settlers for the Sibu district. The Sarawak Government signed an agreement with a certain Wong Nai Siang, from Foochow, and his partner Lek Chiong, to introduce 1000 adult Chinese into the Rejang area. Not more than half were to be brought before 30 June 1901, and the rest within the following twelve months. $30 was to be advanced by the Government for each adult and $10 for each child, two-thirds of which were to be paid through the contractors at Singapore and the remainder when the party passed through Kuching. The immigrants were to arrive within four months of receiving the instalment at Singapore. The loan would be paid back at the rate of one-fifth each year for five years, beginning at the end of their first year. The Government would pay for all passages and provide not less than 3 acres of land for each adult, free of rent for twenty years, then at a quit-rent of 10 cents an acre, and compensation should the Government need to reoccupy the land. The settlers would grow and market such produce as they pleased, but rice should be the first objective. The Government would provide landing-places and paths and assist in the transport of goods. It would guarantee the settlers' protection from any hostility on the part of the natives. The settlers might have a few muskets, to protect their land from wild pigs. There must be no sale of opium or gambling without permission. The Government would recognise the head man, or Kang Chew, recommended by the contractors. His actual duties were to be defined later. Finally, after two years if all was working well, the same contractors could arrange for further parties of settlers. But sureties had to be given.[1]

The first batch arrived early in 1901. There were seventy-three of them, all Christians, glad to leave China after the anti-Christian movement there connected with the Boxer rebellion. Five hundred followed a few days later, in February, and 500 more in March, actually ahead of the agreed date. The Government did not object. Atap huts were provided for them. It was all very primitive at first; there were deaths from snakes and scorpions, and the jungle was hard to clear. Without the help of a Methodist Missionary, Mr Hoover, the settlement might have collapsed. But it survived, and entered into a period of high prosperity when rubber-planting was introduced in 1906. These settlers were Foochows, nearly all of the Wong clan.[2]

The Government made another agreement in March 1901, to introduce Cantonese to the Sibu district. Five thousand were to come altogether, in ten annual batches of 500. The contractors were paid $5 for each adult. The first batch arrived later in the year, led by an earnest Methodist called Wong, who, to the relief of the Government, strongly disapproved both of opium-smoking and gambling. In 1911 there was another influx of Chinese Methodists, when a missionary called Brest brought a large party of Henghuas. The result of all this immigration was to turn Sibu from being a small village into the second town of the country.

There was in addition considerable privately organised immigration. Successful settlers would send for their relatives. Very few ever returned to China. Children were born to them in large quantities. Within half a century from 1870 the Chinese population of Sarawak was multiplied by more than ten times its original number.

Each Chinese group or settlement was organised under its Kang Chew. He was appointed by the local Resident and acted as liaison between the Resident and his people. He had the monopoly of selling pork, arrack and opium to the settlement, as well as controlling its gambling and pawnbroking activities. For the most part the Chinese were allowed to keep their customary law, except in matters that were repugnant to the Government, such as the sale of children. The Chinese customs as regards marriage, divorce, inheritance and intestacy were continued, but needed registration or endorsement by a government magistrate. The State, however, made its own rules where another community was involved. For instance, Chinese fathers could not dispose of their illegitimate children by indigenous women; the mother kept custody if she were deserted. Marriage between those of different religions, even if they were of the same race, had to take place in a registry office; and the Government laid down the rules for divorce in such cases. Many of the Chinese were Christians; and there was a steady flow of conversion. There were a few Chinese Muslims; but a large proportion retained their ancient beliefs. There was still a tendency among the Chinese to join secret societies. Whenever these were discovered they were firmly suppressed.[1]

The Chinese were not considered as being one of the indigenous races of the country; and they were neither given nor promised as yet any official part in the Government, though an increasing number of Chinese clerks were employed in Government Offices. But they were given the personal protection accorded to all citizens. Their indefatigable energy and enterprise soon made them the richest community in the country. Though this did not add to their popularity among the other races, their lot was secure and not unhappy. A few might wish for larger opportunities for exploiting the up-country tribes than a watchful government allowed them. But if a venturesome Chinese trader lost his head to some Dyak or Kayan hunter, his relatives could be assured that if possible his murderers would be punished.

There was a small Indian community in Kuching. Some were the descendants of the Sikhs and Sepoys introduced by Rajah James after the Indian Mutiny, and were employed as policemen or in the Militia. Some were merchants, chiefly engaged in the cloth trade, who had settled there. Most of them were Muslims and were, therefore, administered according to Islamic law, along with the Malays, though purely Malay customary law did not apply to them. There was also a Tamil labour force, consisting largely of Christian converts.[2]

Christianity was slowly spreading. All through his life the Rajah was inclined to be critical of the management of the Anglican mission. He thought that too much time was spent in converting the Chinese in Kuching, many of whom accepted Christianity, he suspected, in order to ingratiate themselves with the Europeans; and he deeply resented any attempt by the hierarchy to interfere with the morals and habits of his European officers. But he was annoyed when the *Sarawak Gazette* published an article criticising the mission. His relations with Bishop Chambers improved; but they were never cordial. With Bishop Hose, who succeeded to the see in 1881, he was more friendly. But the see now had Singapore added to it, somewhat to the Rajah's annoyance; and the Bishop was obliged to spend half his time out of Sarawak. During the early part of his episcopacy his chief deputy in Sarawak was Archdeacon Mesney, who had been a missionary at Banting. The Rajah liked him and gave him the post of Government Chaplain, which entitled him to a salary from the Government. The post was abolished when Mesney retired in 1897.[1] His successor as Archdeacon, Mr Sharp, was a man of great energy and devotion, but lacking in tact. The Rajah thought him too High Church, and was both scornful and angry when he organised 'a night procession with all sorts of absurdities'. The Archdeacon would also interfere with the Sarawak Rangers in their barracks, trying to force attendance at church on them. The Rajah was even angrier when a missionary at Lundu wrote articles for the Singapore Press criticising Sarawak. The culprit must be sent away. The Archdeacon also founded a Chinese Institute for his converts, which the Government had reason to suspect of a connection with a secret society. Sharp was much upset when his leading Chinese helper was exiled.[2] The chief bone of contention between Church and State was over the marriages of converts. The Rajah continually complained that zealous missionaries rushed converts to the altar, forgetting that a certificate from the local government officer was needed. These hurried marriage ceremonies were not always desirable, he thought; and his magistrates were wiser on the subject than young missionaries. When Bishop Hose retired in 1908, Archdeacon Sharp was considered a likely successor. He loved the country; and his two sisters had done good work in the mission schools. But the Rajah would not allow it. 'Sharp wants it', he wrote to the Archbishop of Canterbury, 'but I won't have him in my territory.' The Archdeacon was disappointed and hurt, but accepted the veto with dignity; while the Rajah, who was not vindictive, gave him some generous and needed financial help on his retirement.[3]

The Rajah was particularly annoyed when the funds collected for the Church in Sarawak were diverted in part to Singapore. He was relieved when, on Hose's departure, the see was restored to the original size. The next Bishop, Dr Mounsey, was appointed only to Sarawak and Labuan. The Rajah did not care much for Bishop Mounsey, whom he considered narrow-minded about other Christian sects. He was furious when the Bishop requested him to intervene in the private affairs of his unmarried employees. They were, he replied, 'no worse than those living in the cities of Europe, notwithstanding numerous Churches and zealous clergymen'. He was proud, he added, of the men in his service. When the Bishop returned to the charge over concubinage, he was told that the Rajah recommended 'those who wish to improve the human race to commence in the West'. Bishop Mounsey retired in 1916.[1]

He approved more wholeheartedly of the work of the missions up-country, so long as the missionaries co-operated properly with his officers. By the end of the century there were mission stations at Quop, in Land Dyak country, and four in Sea Dyak country, at Lundu, Banting, Sabu and Sebatan. There had been more; but there were not enough missionaries to occupy them, and the churches were falling into ruins. The devoted labours of the earlier generations of missionaries, men like Gomes, Perham, Chalmers and Mesney, who had founded the stations, were not being carried on. By 1912 there were only three Anglican clergymen working in Sarawak outside Kuching, two English-men and one Chinese, at Banting, Sabu and Quop. There were not enough funds to provide for more; and critics murmured that too large a proportion of the money sent out sparingly by the Society for the Propagation of the Gospel was spent in Kuching. Bishop Mounsey tried to improve matters by founding a Borneo Missionary Association, to supplement the work of the Propagation of the Gospel. But many years elapsed before there was enough money to enlarge the staff. The schools run by the Mission received a grant from the Government; but they could not be maintained if there was no one to take charge of them. By 1912 there were not more than 6000 Anglican converts in Sarawak; and most of these were Chinese in Kuching.[2]

Ever since the days of the Spaniards and Portuguese the Roman Catholic Church had taken an interest in Borneo; but its early efforts to convert the Muslim Malays met with failure. In 1857 a Spaniard, Father Cuateron, founded a Mission at Brunei and Labuan. He was, however, adventurous rather than pious; and his methods both of raising and of spending money were hardly consonant with his priestly office. When he had lost most of his funds in wild speculations, his churches were closed and he himself faded away. In 1880 the Catholic Bishop of

Salford, the future Cardinal Vaughan, asked permission to start Missions in Sarawak. The Rajah replied that he had no objection so long as they kept to districts where the Anglicans were not operating, and so long as they did not attempt the conversion of Muslims. He would like, he said, a French or Italian gentleman to start the Mission; but he approved of the first Vicar Apostolic, Thomas Jackson, a former army chaplain, who spent the money given him as a testimonial after the First Afghan War on promoting his missions. The Roman Catholics were allowed to make their headquarters in Kuching, but were assigned the Third Division for their missionary work. The Rajah recommended that they should operate there from Kanowit. They were later, in 1901, allowed to found a Mission on the Baram, in the Fourth Division. By 1908 there were eleven European priests, two lay brothers, and eleven Nuns or Sisters of Charity in Sarawak.[1]

The Methodists reserved their attentions to the Chinese at Sibu and down the Rejang, whose settlements they had helped to organise. They too enjoyed the Rajah's goodwill.[2]

In an interview which he gave to a British journalist in 1908 the Rajah aired his views about missions and religion in general. 'We have two large Missions at Kuching,' he said, 'a Catholic Mission and a Church of England Mission, and they do excellent work in the way of education; but I do not think that Christianity has, so far, benefited the Dyaks. The Mohammedans are a fine people, and they never try to make converts. I have no fault to find with the Mohammedan religion; it displays no fanaticism in Sarawak; it is generous, reasonable, and admirably suited to the Eastern minds. I allow no one to meddle with my Mohammedan subjects, and I would turn out any missionary neck and crop who interfered with them.'[3]

The Rajah approved of education within moderation. In a pamphlet which he published in 1907 he asked: 'Are we doing the right thing towards the education of the native races? Can no means be found by which to endeavour to raise them as fitting inhabitants of the soil?... We stuff natives with a lot of subjects that they don't require to know, and try to teach them to become like ourselves, treating them as if they had not an original idea in their possession.' He was doubtful whether the Dyaks were yet ready to leave home to go to schools, as it only made them feel out of place and unhappy when they returned to their longhouses. When in 1909 he found that some young Dyak girls had been brought to Kuching, he ordered them to be returned home.

'I can't say that I am in favour of the education of native girls unless it is done by their own people and without the separation from their relatives', he wrote.[1]

Nevertheless he was ready to give support to the schools founded by the Missions. There had been a school attached to the Anglican Mission since McDougall's early days; and it had gradually grown in size. The old buildings were inadequate. In 1886, owing to Bishop Hose's labours, with some help from the Government, a new boys' school was completed; and the old building served as the girls' school till funds could be found to rebuild it. By the beginning of the next century some 300 boys and 60 girls were being educated by the Anglican Community, in spite of perpetual shortage of staff. The Roman Catholics obtained permission to found a school at Kuching after their arrival. The Rajah, though not enthusiastic, offered $200 towards its building and $200 a year towards its upkeep. He offered the same yearly sum for the upkeep of a Roman Catholic school at Kanowit, with a gift of $50 for its building. The Roman Catholic school quickly increased in size and soon slightly outstripped the Anglican, largely because staff was more easily available. Both schools had a large proportion of boarders and were run on the lines of a simple English public school. The pupils were mostly Chinese. But, as the Rajah insisted that religious education should not be compulsory, soon a few Malays began to send their sons there. There was also a small Roman Catholic girls' school, attached to a convent.[2]

The first Malay school was opened by the Rajah in 1883; and a second was founded soon afterwards. These were staffed by Malays and did not attempt to do more than give a sound grounding in elementary subjects. They were followed in 1903 by a Government High School, open to all races and staffed by Chinese, Malays and Indians, and by two Government-run Chinese Schools. In the provinces, both the Anglicans and the Roman Catholics ran five schools each, with the aid of small grants; and the Methodists had their school at Sibu. The Malays had no schools outside of Kuching, though in every village the local Imam held classes for boys in the mosque, when the rudiments of Koranic education were taught. The Chinese had small schools in most of their settlements. If there were more than sixteen pupils, a small grant was given to them. A few Dyaks were beginning by the end of the century to send their boys to Kuching, while the Mission schools in the provinces catered mainly for Dyaks and other up-country races.

By contemporary standards these educational facilities were adequate; but the ambitions of early educationalists were curbed by the Rajah's determination that education should not disrupt the traditions of the country.[1]

The health services were somewhat primitive. Kuching had a hospital and a Government dispensary; but there was a shortage of doctors and nurses. It was only in 1870 that a Government nurse was appointed, at a retaining salary of $8 a month, but with extra pay when she had work to do. Several years elapsed before she received additional help. In the meantime the ladies of the Missions assisted her as best they could. The Missions ran small hostels for visitors who fell sick. There was only one European medical officer till the end of the century. District officers were expected to have some knowledge of medicine and to keep an eye on the health of their districts. Kuching had a piped water supply and an adequate drainage system by the end of the century. Sibu was provided with a hospital, a converted shack, and a Medical Officer only in 1913. Its drains were appalling; but fortunately floods washed the town clean twice a year. A lunatic asylum was built at Kuching in 1909.[2]

Outside of Kuching there were no roads. All transport was done by water. The Government kept a small but increasing number of steamers and launches so as to maintain communications between the chief centres of population; and the Borneo Company assured communications with Singapore and the outside world. These were set back in 1896, when the Company's steamer, *Rajah Brooke*, the second successor to the *Rajah Brooke* of James Brooke's day, was wrecked on a voyage from Singapore to Kuching.[3] A telephone was installed in Kuching in 1900 and was soon extended to Upper Sarawak. A telegraphic cable was already open to Singapore. Telegraphic communications were established within the main centres in Sarawak early in the twentieth century.[4]

The Rajah was, however, unwilling to indulge in expensive public works until he was sure that the country's finances could stand the cost. These he watched with a careful eye and with growing satisfaction. By 1880 the revenue had risen to $229,718; by 1900 it was $915,966, and in 1907, just before the Malay dollar was reduced in value to 2s. 4d., it was $1,441,195. Expenditure also had risen, from $203,583 to $1,359,247. But there had been a favourable balance every year. The public debt was steadily reduced and was wiped out in 1905. At the end of 1907 the Government balance was just over $800,000, and its only liability was for notes in circulation, amounting to $190,796.[1] Gratifying though these figures were, there was not much money for capital expenditure; and some of the Rajah's private enterprises, such as the coalmine at Muara, never proved successful. He himself, as his uncle's heir, had been the country's chief creditor, once Miss Burdett-Coutts's loans had been repaid. But after the debt to him had been settled he derived the smallest possible income from the country. He had no money outside the country. Its revenues, therefore, paid for his home in England and for his family, whose extravagance he desperately tried to curb.[2] The Ranee believed that it would be damaging to the prestige of Sarawak were she to live meanly, while two of his sons ran now and then into debt. The whole government was run on strictly economical lines. Though the cost of living was beginning to rise, salaries were barely raised. Any form of extravagance was regarded with disapproval.

Most of the revenue continued to come from the Government interests in mining and from the farming-out of monopolies. Many of these were held by the Borneo Company, which was still the only European Company allowed into the country, and which served as the Rajah's bankers. But, with the spread of order and prosperity, taxation began to bring in appreciable sums. The mines continued to disappoint the authorities. A small but fairly steady amount of gold was produced; but the antimony, which had been in earlier days the Government's main source of wealth, was gradually being exhausted. By the end of the Second Rajah's reign it played only a small part in the economy. But agricultural products were improving. Pepper plantations were growing in size. Gambier for a time was a prominent export, though it was grown less and less as the twentieth century advanced. Sago, grown in the Muka district and milled in Kuching, was one of the main exports. As the Dyaks became more settled they learnt to harvest illipe nuts. Timber, in which the Government was directly interested, was growing in importance as an article of export. The advent of rubber trees in 1905 made a tremendous difference to the agricultural economy. All these products were liable to awkward fluctuations in price; and some crops such as the illipe were notoriously unreliable.[3] But, though the value of exports might vary and farmers dependent on one crop only might pass through unhappy periods, the general economy of the country was healthy. The growth of prosperity inevitably meant a growth in imports. All machinery and manufactured goods, even cloth, were brought from abroad. In some years it was necessary to import rice. But the exports seldom failed to pay for the imports. It was only after 1898 that the Borneo Company began to make any profits from Sarawak. Till then it had depended for profits on its operations in Java and Malaya, and, above all, in Siam. But by the turn of the century it could justify to its shareholders its operations in its original sphere.[1]

Progress was slow; and the Rajah's aversion towards great business houses led critics to believe that he was a narrow reactionary with regard to his country. He himself maintained that he would welcome foreign capital, if he could be sure that the investors would deal fairly with the native peoples. The test came when oil was found in Borneo. In 1895 the Rajah received information that oil, some of it of good quality, was to be found at Miri, close to his frontier with Brunei. There were at first conflicting reports about its possible development. In 1897 he was inclined to believe that it would not be worth while to explore further. But early in the next century it became clear that the deposits would be worth working, though many of them were in Brunei territory. By 1909 there was enough oil to justify the Rajah in negotiating with the Shell Oil Company to found a subsidiary company to exploit it. At the Annual General Meeting of Shell next June, Sir Marcus Samuel reported the find of oil at Miri and the concession granted without payment by the Rajah. The Sarawak Oil Company, financed by Shell, moved in soon afterwards. In 1914 Sir Marcus announced that the production of oil in Sarawak amounted to 200 tons a day. A small royalty was paid to the Sarawak Government on every ton. Unfortunately, in the long run, the oil, like much else in Borneo, was to prove disappointing. The best wells were found to be over the frontier, in territory that the British Government had wilfully left to Brunei; and even they seemed not inexhaustible. But meanwhile the finances of Sarawak benefited from the find, and from the Rajah's willingness both to encourage the development of the wells and to allow capital in for the purpose, on the understanding that there would be no attempt to exploit his subjects.[2]

His rule was, indeed, a superb example of enlightened despotism. He was the government, but he was neither obstructionist nor illiberal. The prosperity and peace of Sarawak was his reward.

CHAPTER IV

THE ENLIGHTENED DESPOT

No life of Charles Brooke has ever been written. His career lacked the romantic glamour of his uncle's. James was a splendid adventurer, fond of publicity, capable of inspiring devoted friendships and passionate quarrels, creative in his ideas but careless over humdrum details. His was the conception that gave birth to Sarawak, a state in which a handful of disinterested Europeans should guide a number of indigenous Eastern races to live together in amity and growing prosperity without interference with their traditions and customs. Sarawak could not have been created without his peculiar genius; yet, in spite of the work of eager and loyal helpers, he left it impoverished and precarious. It was his nephew who ensured that the experiment should not fail.[1]

Charles was in every way a contrast to James. He hated publicity. He was reserved in manner and hard to approach. The long years that he had spent in the jungle, alone with his Dyaks, had taught him to do without friends. He preferred his books and his thoughts. He was not intellectual. The books that were his chief solace were popular French novels; and his taste in music was a perpetual grief to the Ranee. But he was a clear thinker and an acute, if remote, observer of the world's political scene. Above all, he was an administrator.

In administration his only fault was that he was too active. There was not a detail in his government that he did not personally supervise. We find him deciding himself on what marble slabs should be used for the fish stalls in Kuching market or how in detail the new doctor's house should be decorated. We find him himself ordering music from Messrs Hawkes for the Municipal Band, and dismissing the conductor when he thought the performance was inadequate. 'The band somewhat worse last evening', he wrote in 1910 to the Resident of Kuching, 'and the programme very badly chosen. I can't stand this any longer and I now direct you to inform Master de Vera that he is to do no more duty and he will retire on pension, if one is due, at the end of the month.' The band, indeed, was one of his favourite creations. He personally decided on what occasions and where it might play. Chinese towkays might apply for it at suitable times. He liked it to play some dance music but preferably operatic pieces or 'more solemn pieces by good composers'.[1]

Another of his creations, in which he was deeply interested, was the Sarawak Museum, which he founded chiefly for zoological specimens, but which was to embrace anthropology and folk-art. He took immense pains to secure adequate curators. He was interested also in horticulture and proud of the Astana gardens. Towards the end of his reign he was absorbed in making a railway to run south from Kuching. He himself supervised much of the laying of the track and decided upon the engines and coaches to be used. It was opened in June 1915, when five miles of track were ready. Two more miles were ready that August; and it reached the tenth mile by 1917. There were trucks to carry passengers, at 2 cents a mile; but it was mainly used for bringing agricultural produce into Kuching.[2]

It might have been better had he not been so eager to keep everything under his control. Up-country his officials were expected to use their initiative; and hard work and enterprise were noted and commended. But in Kuching itself his pervasive presence stultified the men who worked for him. They were allowed little initiative and no independence of action. As he grew old it was said that to obtain his notice and secure advancement it was necessary to attend all the concerts of the band, where he was inevitably to be found. But in fact he was very conscious of all his subordinates, their circumstances and above all their misdemeanours. If any of them were sick, the Rajah decided whether he should resign and leave the country; if any died, the Rajah himself saw that the widow was given a suitable pension. If any misbehaved, the Rajah wrote to reprimand him. It cannot have been easy to work for him; but he commanded such respect and admiration that few men voluntarily left his service before their time was up.[3]

When he was in residence in Kuching his life fell into a regular pattern. He would rise early and walk in the Astana garden and do a little work in his study; then, at nine o'clock, he would cross the river. A little group of officials would be waiting on the landing-stage to greet him and would form up in procession behind him as he walked, under a ceremonial but tattered yellow umbrella, carried by a sergeant of the Sarawak Rangers, to the Court-house. A Malay retainer carrying books and a paper umbrella in case of rain brought up the rear. The Resident with four Datus were lined up there to greet him. After shaking each by the hand, he would visit the Treasury and the Resident's office, then would be accessible to anyone who wished to see him, or, until he grew older and deafer, would move to the Court-room to preside over the judiciary. At the end of the morning he would walk back in procession to the landing-stage, and go home for his luncheon. He liked to go, on horseback or on foot, in the late afternoon to inspect whatever public work was on hand. Sometimes in the evening he entertained guests. His dinner-parties for the Europeans were stiff affairs; and everyone was relieved when, at an early hour, he curtly dismissed the gathering. He was more at his ease when he entertained Malays or Dyaks; and he would talk freely to visitors from Europe if they showed a serious interest in the East.[1]

He disliked pomp. Only on rare official occasions, such as his Birthday Parade, did he appear in uniform, when he wore the dress of a Knight Grand Cross of St Michael and St George. Ordinarily he wore a blue serge coat and white trousers, and usually a white helmet with a magenta-coloured puggaree round it. A similar puggaree sur-rounded the felt homburg hat that he sometimes sported. He usually carried a long silver-topped cane and kept a fresh sprig of honeysuckle in his button-hole. But he liked his officers to look well dressed. Early in his reign he ordered all of them to acquire uniforms—a tunic, trousers, sash, belt and cocked hat. He was anxious that his likeness on copper coins and on stamps should be correct. He had no need to insist upon being personally treated with respect; no one would have dared to do otherwise. But he demanded that junior officers should address their seniors as 'Sir'. A certain formality seemed to him necessary, though personally he liked to escape from it all.[2]

He was often away from Kuching. He enjoyed tours of inspection round the country; and he loved to retire for days on end to his bungalow near Mount Matang or, still more, to Simanggang, up the Batang Lupar, in the Dyak country where he had spent so much of his youth. Once Sarawak was fairly peaceful he went regularly to England in the winter to enjoy two months of hunting. For some time he leased a house near Swindon, Purton House; then he bought Chesterton House, near Cirencester, which remained his English home for the rest of his life.[3]

It was a lonely life; and he did not wish for it to be otherwise. After the early years of their married life he seldom saw the Ranee. Her health had never been good when she was in Sarawak; and while her sons were at school in England she stayed there to be with them. She spent some months in Sarawak with the two elder boys in 1887. There followed a period when her son Bertram, the Tuan Muda, was seriously ill for some years, and she did not like to leave him. Meanwhile the Rajah had become accustomed once more to a bachelor life and content with it. When in 1895 she suggested bringing Bertram out to Sarawak he gave permission, on condition that she paid for the passage-money out of her own income; and he himself left for England a few weeks after her arrival. Even when she was in England she seldom stayed at his house. She lived herself in London or in Surrey, entertaining a large circle of friends. She was particularly fond of literary celebrities, who all enjoyed her company. There was never any open breach between her and the Rajah. They corresponded with each other freely and affectionately; they used to appear together on formal occasions; they would meet to discuss the children's welfare.[1]

To the last she remained devoted to the interests of Sarawak. But the Rajah was often alarmed by her enthusiasm. When she proposed writing the history of the country, he hastened to send a letter discouraging her. 'I don't think you are the right person to do it', he said, 'as however good your book may be it would be looked upon as not an impartial account.' But he was glad to sponsor the book she wrote called *My Life in Sarawak*. He was loyal to her after his fashion. To his son Vyner, who had complained of her apparent preference for her other sons, he wrote of her that she had at heart the real interests of Sarawak, 'much more so than any other person excepting myself'. But to his son Harry, whom she somewhat spoilt, he wrote: 'I dread your mother's methods in England regarding myself and Sarawak more than any enemy in the West, and I have written about this more than once, but my pen is useless in that direction.' It is possible that the family treated some of his political ambitions with more amusement than respect. The boys' tutor, Gerard Fiennes, writes from Kuching in 1887: 'The Rajah is still away.... No one knows what his little game is, but I strongly suspect that he is at Brunei trying tooth and nail for the cession of the Limbang.' Fiennes also noted that 'the Ranee proposes, the Rajah disposes'.[2]

With his eldest son Vyner, the Rajah Muda, the Rajah's relations were not good. Vyner was appointed to the Sarawak service in 1897, at the age of 23. He served at Muka and at Sibu; and from 1904 onwards he was left in charge of the country whenever the Rajah himself was away in Europe. The Rajah seems always to have thought him a little easy-going and extravagant, and not quite serious enough; but he had no cause for complaint. After the Rajah Muda's marriage in 1911 matters became worse. The Rajah did not care for his daughter-in-law and she returned his dislike. He suspected her of having a bad influence on the Rajah Muda, encouraging him to be extravagant and pleasure-seeking and insubordinate. The letters that passed between father and son were often acrimonious and bitter. They reached a climax in 1912, when the Rajah Muda discovered that orders had been given to receive his brother, the Tuan Muda, with the same ceremonial honours that were accorded to him. He suspected a plot to disinherit him. Neither he nor his wife made any secret of their anger. The storm blew over. The old Rajah had too strict a sense of propriety to repudiate his heir, though he wished the Tuan Muda, whom he trusted, to be associated as far as possible with the government after his death. The Rajah Muda apologised to his father; but the apology was accepted somewhat grudgingly; 'there are hard things to forgive and impossible to forget', the Rajah wrote to him. The Rajah had previously talked of retiring from the government, retaining only the control of the finances and the administration of Muara. Now he said that he would rule till his death. But a few months later, in February 1913, he once again told the Rajah Muda that he would abdicate in December, so long as the local Council considered the transference of power a safe move. But Vyner must guarantee to spend two years without a break in the country. The suggestion came to nothing. Indeed, in the whole story there is a curious echo from the later years of the First Rajah. The Rajah Muda was still left in control during his father's absences. But his functions and his income were carefully regulated. He had a salary of £6000, £5000 paid at home and £1000 in Sarawak, with a monthly entertainment and travelling allowance of $200 while he was in the country. While the Rajah Muda was living in the Astana he was required to pay for his cook and kitchen staff, his valet, and all servants other than the butler and his boys and the outdoor staff. He had also to provide his own wine, liqueurs and cigars, though the food was supplied by the State. The Rajah Muda was especially forbidden to communicate directly with the Secretary of State for the Colonies. Everything must be done through the Rajah, or through the Sarawak State Office in London, which the Rajah instituted in 1912. When the Rajah was absent from England, this Office was under the Tuan Muda. Above all, the Rajah tried as much as possible to prevent the Ranee Muda from visiting Sarawak.[1]

The Rajah and Ranee both agreed in preferring their second son, the Tuan Muda, whose life was made embarrassing in consequence. Devoted though he was to Sarawak, he had no personal ambition to rule it and was eager to be of service to his brother, who, however, could not help suspecting that he was in league with his parents against him. The Rajah Muda's suspicions were not surprising. The old Rajah openly rejoiced when the Tuan Muda's wife, the Dayang Muda, gave birth to a son, while the Ranee Muda only produced daughters. He was always far more affable to the Tuan Muda's children than to the Rajah Muda's. His two daughters-in-law saw him in a very different light. While the Ranee Muda later wrote, 'what an unscrupulous and inhuman man this Second Rajah of Sarawak was', or, again, 'he was hated and feared, flattered and cajoled, until he lost all sense of the outside world', the Dayang Muda wrote with obvious sincerity of 'the dear old Rajah'.[1]

The Rajah's youngest son, Harry, the Tuan Bongsu, played little part in the story. His extravagance as a young man distressed his father; and when he grew up and married, his wife's ill-health added to his need for money. She died soon after giving birth to a son; and her husband followed her a few years later before he had much chance to prove his worth.[2]

The Rajah had good reason to be distressed by his family's liking to spend money. In 1903 his family solicitor, Mr Booty, failed, involving the Brookes in considerable financial loss. The Rajah was scrupulous in seeing that the beneficiaries of the family did not suffer; and, though the Ranee accused him of misappropriating her funds, he continued her allowance of £3000 a year. He himself economised strictly for some time. Fortunately Sarawak was in a state of growing prosperity.[3]

Except in the Ulu Ai, round the upper waters of the Batang Lupar and along the frontier in the East, Sarawak was also at peace. But there trouble had broken out in 1893, started by a remarkable Dyak adventurer, called Banting, who, though of humble origin, established himself as a leader of the Batang Lupar Dyaks, and allied himself with the chieftain Ngumbang. He kept up a long tribal war with the Dyaks living between the Rejang and the frontier. In May 1894 the Rajah himself led an expedition up some of the southern tributaries of the Rejang to punish the raiders, but without lasting results. In 1897 Banting was attacked at his village of Delok. His son was killed and the village burnt. This, combined with the failure of a raid that he made on

Dyaks near Lubok Antu, kept him quiescent for a time. But early in
1902 he started again to attack peaceful Dyak villages. The Rajah
determined to punish him thoroughly and put into the field the largest
expeditionary force that Sarawak had yet seen. It was larger than he
intended, as some 12,000 Dyaks insisted on joining it, in addition to
a strong contingent of Sarawak Rangers and Malays. It was led by the
Rajah Muda and Mr Deshon, Resident of the Third Division. In June
the force moved up the Batang Lupar, planning to block every path
that led from the Ulu Ai. But as it lay at Nanga Delok cholera broke
out in the camp. Many of the soldiers died, especially among the
Dyaks, who hastened to hurry homewards in order to bury their dead
in their own villages, away from the depredations of head-hunters.
About a thousand of them perished. The Rangers and the Malays,
themselves reduced by illness and death, were forced to retire. It was
a tragic and disastrous episode; and though later in the year Mr Bailey,
the Resident of the Second Division, led forces which burnt villages
belonging to Banting's followers on the Engkari river, and some
belonging to Ngumbang on the Pan range, the rebels were undismayed.

In March next year the Rajah in person led an expedition up the
Batang Lupar, with about 2500 men. He did not press very far as he
heard that Banting and Ngumbang were willing to negotiate their
submission. It was an illusory hope. They continued to raid their
neighbours. So the following June two columns set out from Simanggang. One under Mr J. Baring-Gould pushed up into the Pan range
and there defeated the rebels, while the other, under Mr H. L. Owen,
marched up the Engkari river and destroyed the villages there, without
meeting the enemy. The Rajah had taken a deep personal interest in the
expedition and set detailed instructions about the order of march to be
followed. Picked Dyaks were to go in the van, then the Sarawak
Rangers, followed by the Malay troops, with the Europeans in their
centre, and the other Dyaks on the wings. A march should not start
before 7 a.m., so that the troops could be properly fed; and it should
halt at about 2.30 p.m., to give them time for making a satisfactory
encampment. If possible the Dyaks should be kept from trying to rush
an enemy stockade. It was better to devastate the country around and
wait till the following morning for the attack. The Europeans must keep
together; and all the more caution was required if the enemy did not
seem to be at hand. It was better not to stay more than three days in
enemy country. This campaign cowed most of the rebel chiefs into

submission; but Banting and Ngumbang stayed out. In 1906 both of them offered their submission but changed their minds. However, in 1907, finding that their followers were drifting away they consented to attend a peace-meeting at Kapit, where, in the presence of the Rajah and the Rajah Muda, all the Ulu Ai Dyaks agreed to end their feuds with the Dyaks of the lower Batang Lupar. Once again Banting went back on his word. At a meeting held at Lubok Antu to cement the peace he demanded a fine of jars from the loyal Dyaks, and on their refusal took to the hills again. It needed a destructive expedition led the following year by Mr Bailey, after the Rajah Muda had refused the leadership, to bring him finally to heel. Thenceforward he caused no more trouble.[1]

Banting was the last of the great rebel leaders. There was still an occasional trouble-maker. Later in 1908 a Malay called Pangiran Omar, living on the Netherlands frontier, encouraged the loyal Dyaks to defy the Rajah's authority by selling them charms which would preserve them against danger. He was arrested by the Dutch authorities; and a small expedition up the Sadok river punished some of his followers. But in March 1909 a certain Masir disseminated similar charms among the Lingga Dyaks and induced them to try to ambush the Resident. They were repulsed and later punished.[2] After that episode there was no more fighting in the First and Second Divisions. For some years past, even in spite of periodical unrest, the letters between the Resident at Simanggang and his subordinates are mostly concerned with details about building houses and gardens, or disciplining the Rangers better, or verifying accounts, with only an occasional warning about the untrustworthiness of some chieftain or the unwisdom of indulging some tribe.[3]

There had been some warfare in the Trusan district soon after its annexation by the Rajah; but it had been easily quelled; and the Fifth Division, consisting of the Lawas and Trusan rivers, enjoyed complete peace. The Kayans and Kenyahs in the Fourth Division were better disciplined than the Dyaks. Once their chiefs accepted the Rajah's authority there were no more disorders. Only rarely did the Government have to intervene to end some inter-tribal feud, particularly between the Kelabits and Muruts. On one such occasion, when the two tribes, as a token of their peacemaking, exchanged the heads that had been taken in the past, one Kelabit chieftain found that he was one head short of the promised number. He therefore killed a slave to make up the deficiency. He was hurt and surprised to be fined for it.[4]

It was only in the Third Division, up the Balleh river, that trouble continued for some time. This reached a head in 1915, when a group of young Dyaks on the Gaat and Mujong tributaries of the Balleh started to commit murders wherever they could find defenceless victims. Fellow-Dyaks, Chinese traders, visiting Kayans and primitive Ukits were among those whose heads were taken. A strong punitive expedition early that spring reduced their activities; but many of the culprits retired to the upper waters of the Gaat and defied the Government for several more years.[1]

But on the whole Rajah Charles in his old age could look at his country and be satisfied. He was active to the last. In 1912 he lost the sight of one eye as the result of a hunting accident; but his remaining eye was as watchful as ever. He was growing deaf; but it was unsafe to presume that he ever failed to hear what was said in his presence. In 1914, when the First World War broke out, he was in England. He returned to Kuching at the end of the year, earlier than was his usual habit. Sarawak itself was barely affected by the war; but certain controls of prices were considered necessary, and a certain tightening of the regulations, though the Rajah protested against the censorship imposed at Singapore, which was inconvenient for communications between London and Kuching. His own vigour seemed undiminished. The last letter copied in his Letter Book is a lively complaint to Archdeacon Small, whom he suspected of trying to invade the territory allotted to the Roman Catholic Missions. 'You seem to know more about the country than I do', he wrote. In the autumn of 1915 he went to his beloved Simanggang for a few weeks' rest. There, he wrote, he was passing his time in reading and writing, with a two-mile walk every evening. But he was now 86 and beginning to feel his years.[2] In September 1916 he formally handed over the administration of the Dyaks to the Rajah Muda. At the end of October he fell seriously ill. Early in December he had recovered sufficiently to sail slowly to England round the Cape of Good Hope. He appeared to be better when he reached London and went down to Chesterton House. But in April he was ill again. He died on 17 May 1917, a few weeks before the 88th anniversary of his birth. He had reigned for nearly fifty years.[3]

Few rulers have achieved so much; and few rulers have possessed so remarkable a personality. Charles Brooke was essentially an autocrat, who appeared to the outside world to be a determined enemy of progress.

He had his own ideas of progress, which sometimes seemed revolutionary to those who knew him well. 'The Rajah is extremely nice and kind', wrote Gerard Fiennes in 1887, 'but a fearful Radical.' He always considered himself a Liberal in politics. In 1888 he applied to join the National Liberal Club when it should be opened.[1] He disapproved strongly of the Boer War in 1899. The remarkable pamphlet, *Queries, Past, Present and Future*, which he issued in 1907, showed a fierce dislike of the type of Imperialism dominant at the beginning of the twentieth century. 'Why now should we be deluged with flags, Union Jacks and pennants dangling over churches, schools and other edifices', he asked. 'Are these the right signs of brotherly love and good will?' He criticised the attitude of the new generation of colonial officials. 'All our possessions are too much Anglicised. Where good and friendly feeling—I might almost say love—existed in the early part of the last century, when black and white were combined in feeling, there has been a falling-off, a separation, in consequence of the English developing into higher civilisation—as it is termed—among themselves with wives and families and European luxuries, and so it has happened that though we govern, we only do so by power, and not by friendly intercourse of feeling.' He foresaw the consequences. 'My own opinion is that before we reach the middle of the century all nations now holding large Colonial possessions will have met with severe reverses....' 'India', he said, 'to a certainty will be lost to us', and he believed that Canada, Australia and New Zealand would soon be 'independent, under their own flags, and with their own laws'. He was often accused of being anti-Chinese; yet he wrote that 'intellectually the Chinese are our equals, are physically as strong, and, I believe, as brave; with surprising industry, energy and activity in commercial enterprise...'. 'The desire of the Chinese is to rid their country of Europeans.' Indeed, if he gave the Chinese little share in the administration of Sarawak it was from fear lest their enterprise might tell to the disadvantage of the other races in the country. His solution for part of the problem was, as it had been half a century earlier, that the Europeans who wished to settle in the East should mix their blood with that of the natives. A mixed race would be better fitted for the life there. To his officials he said that his policy was 'to veto such native usages as are dangerous or unjust, and to ingraft western methods on Eastern customs by a gradual and gentle process, always granted that the consent of the people was gained for such measures before they were put into force'. Of his own government he said elsewhere: 'I place complete confidence in my people. I could not govern Sarawak as I do, if I did not take their advice on all possible occasions.' He was critical of the Dutch for not trusting their subjects in Java and Sumatra. 'Consequently they fail and will always fail.'[1] He, as he said to his daughter-in-law, the Dayang Muda, had a 'wise country, for its laws are based on emotion as well as spiritual needs'.[2]

His words were sincere as well as wise. Autocrat he might be, but he was no reactionary; he was a man of generous, unprejudiced and far-sighted views, and with the will and self-control to carry them into practice. Modern Sarawak is his memorial, far more than the monument that stands outside the Court-house in Kuching.

BOOK IV
RAJAH VYNER

CHAPTER I

YEARS OF PEACE

The Rajah Muda was in Sarawak when news of his father's death was telegraphed to Kuching. One week later, on Thursday, 24 May 1917, Charles Vyner Brooke was proclaimed Rajah. His brother, the Tuan Muda, came out in August to join him, and the new Ranee arrived in May next year. His formal installation as Rajah took place on 22 July 1918.[1]

The old Rajah intended to rule Sarawak even after his death. In his will he repeated for the last time the principles according to which he had governed and which he wished his successors to maintain. He had feared lest the new Rajah would wish to spend too much time and too much money in England. He urged him to remain in Sarawak for at least eight months of each year and warned him that the First Rajah when he founded the State of Sarawak 'never entertained the idea of thereby founding a family of Brookes to be European millionaires'. He recorded with pride that the Raj and its finances were flourishing, and he hoped that the methods which he had employed to achieve this would be continued. He did not entirely disguise the fact that he would have preferred to be succeeded by his second son. He therefore directed that 'no material developments or changes in the State or in the Government thereof and no new works such as public works...shall be initiated by my son Vyner without first consulting my son Bertram'. The Tuan Muda was also to carry out the duties of Rajah and administer the new Government whenever the new Rajah should be absent in England; and when the Rajah was in Sarawak the Tuan Muda should preside over the Sarawak Advisory Council in Westminster. The Tuan Muda was to be known as the Tuan Besar—a title which in fact he never assumed— and was to be paid the same respect as was shown to his eldest brother.

I raise my second son to this position [the will ran], hoping that he will by his extended experience be an additional safeguard against adventurers and speculators who would desire to make profits out of the country without regard to its real welfare. And I fervently hope that my two sons will see the necessity of acting together to keep intact and develop the resources of the country which has been brought to its present state by myself and my faithful followers after so many years of devotion to it.[2]

The fears of Rajah Charles did not seem to be justified. There was no marked change in the system of government. The European officials who had served his father served the new Rajah and were given the same responsibilities and the same trust. The same cordial relations with the Malay and other communities existed; and occasional operations were still needed against head-hunters in the interior. But there was a change in the atmosphere. Rajah Vyner was very different from the formidable, austere, hard-working autocrat who had died. He had a fine presence and great dignity, when it was needed; he could chill unsuitable familiarity by a glance from his cold blue eyes. But in general he was affable and easy-going. He enjoyed the pleasures of life; he was generous and more human in his contacts. But to some of the older generation he seemed a little frivolous and less selflessly devoted to his task.[1] There was now, too, for the first time for many years, a hostess at the Astana. The new Ranee was lively and clever. Like her mother-in-law she took a great interest in her adopted country and wrote books about its history and the charm of its peoples. But she liked to enjoy herself in her own way and gave an impression of being out for her pleasure. Under the new regime which she and the Rajah personified, life was much gayer for the Europeans in Kuching; but some critics felt that there was a general relaxation of standards.[2]

Rajah Vyner did not follow with exactitude his father's injunction that he should spend at least eight months of the year in Sarawak. At first his comings and goings were rather irregular. In 1919 he was away for almost the whole of the year. Later he settled down to a more regular routine, spending the winter months in Sarawak, leaving in the spring and returning in October. The Ranee and their three daughters were usually with him for about half his sojourn in Kuching. During his absences the Tuan Muda would take over the government, usually arriving from England a few days before his departure. Under the Tuan Muda, even if he were accompanied by one of his daughters, life in the Astana was quieter. The Tuan Muda preferred not to occupy the Astana itself but lived simply in the bungalow attached to it, using the palace only for entertaining. To the older generation he seemed to represent his father's ideals more than his brother; his habits were austere and he liked to journey as often as possible into the interior. The two brothers worked well enough together. If the Rajah had been hurt to find that his parents trusted his brother more than himself, he was not a man to harbour personal resentment; while the Tuan Muda showed unceasing deference to his elder brother and was careful to emphasise that his was a junior role. It was, however, observed that recommendations made by the Tuan Muda were seldom adopted by the Rajah.[1]

Economically and socially the country continued its steady progress. The First World War had affected Sarawak very little; but there, as elsewhere, a relief from tension was felt when the war was ended. The years that followed were prosperous. The State revenue was just over $1,700,000. In 1921 it was up to $2,900,000. It fell a little in 1922, owing to a drop in the price of gold; while the coalmine at Brooketon showed a heavy loss. But it rose again and in 1929 reached the height of nearly $6,700,000. During the world slump in the 1930's it fell again; in 1933 it was only just over $3,500,000. Then it rose once more, to reach nearly $7,500,000 in 1940. Fluctuations in the price of rubber, which was now one of the main crops, and of pepper were reflected at once by the revenue; while the increase in revenue later on was largely due to the development of the oil-fields near Miri. In 1927 there was a yearly production of 700,000 tons of oil, which was about the same amount as in 1914. Ten years later the amount was doubled. In 1934 an experiment was made to restrict the output of rubber by what was known as the 'tapping holiday'. It proved ineffectual; and control by individual assessment was introduced in 1937. After some difficulties at first, owing to its complication, it succeeded in providing greater stability in prices.[2]

Expenditure also increased. Public services were developed. The railway, so dear to the late Rajah's heart, was reorganised, and it was possible after 1920 to travel along its ten miles after dark. Roads round Kuching and Miri were improved. A wireless station was set up at Kuching, which was working well by the end of 1912. By 1925 there were eight wireless stations in the country. Three more were added that year, and seven more in 1926. The station at Kanowit was installed in 1927. Hospital and dispensary services were slowly improved. In 1925 a government dentist was appointed. A new Leper Settlement was founded, as a memorial to the late Rajah. That same year an expert government printer was engaged and brought out from England, and the first aerial survey was attempted of the country.[3] Periodically there were disastrous fires which raged through the old wooden bazaars in the provincial towns. In 1928 both Simanggang and Sibu bazaars were destroyed, the latter causing damage of some $2,000,000. But these disasters were not wholly harmful; for the authorities were thus enabled to rebuild the bazaars in a less attractive but less inflammable and more sanitary style. Sibu, which was developing fast, was provided after its fire with an up-to-date drainage system.[1] In 1924 a branch of the Chartered Bank of India, Australia and China was opened in Kuching, to the great satisfaction of individuals and of business firms there. Hitherto such banking facilities as had been necessary had been performed by the Government or the Borneo Company.[2] Not all the planned improvements were fully realised. A Government air-service, inaugurated in January 1929, had to be abandoned in June. The airfields were not yet suitable; nor was the meteorological service adequate.[3]

The cost of living was rising. In 1919 it was estimated that wages had risen 50 per cent since 1914 and that foodstuffs were up to 100 per cent dearer. A report sent to the Colonial Office in London on living conditions in Sarawak in 1928 estimated that a European official working in Kuching had to spend $200 a month, or $130 if he lived in the provinces. Government officials paid no rent for their houses, and there was no income-tax. In Kuching the regular wage for a cook or houseboy was from $25 to $30 a month. Gardeners and grooms charged a little less, chauffeurs a little more. Salaries were not very high; but it was possible for an official who was not unduly extravagant to live comfortably and even put a little money by.[4] There was certainly no lack of applicants for the Sarawak service. Recruits were chosen informally. They were often the relatives or friends of former officials or of men personally known to the Brookes. But any youth who liked the prospect could apply to the Sarawak office in London. There was a prejudice in favour of boys from the West Country. If his application sounded well and if he gave a good impression when interviewed by one of the senior Sarawak officials or by the Rajah or Tuan Muda in person he would be appointed without more fuss. It was rumoured that the Ranee liked also to have a chance of inspecting the candidate, to be sure that he would be a social asset to the community. It was not till 1934 that, on the shocked insistence of the Colonial Office in London, a competitive examination was introduced.[5] There had, indeed, already been signs that the authorities in Britain were looking with interest but some disfavour on an administration which so happily dispensed with the proper trappings of bureaucracy. Two Labour Members of Parliament, Mr Thomas Griffiths and Mr Grundy, who visited Kuching in 1921, reported certain criticisms. The latter believed, with some reason, that it ought to be possible to appeal from the Rajah's Court to a higher authority. The former considered that the country should be developed more fully and more quickly and not be merely used, as he worded it, to make the Brooke family rich.[1]

It is possible that Kuching did at this period give an impression of easy-going amateurism. The austere atmosphere of the previous reign was ended. There were more wives resident there now, and a new Club was opened in 1920 for their relaxation. The Ranee, whenever she was at the Astana, organised dances and amateur theatricals. A cinema was built by the Rajah, who called it the Sylvia after her and found it a profitable investment.[2]

There were legal reforms. In 1922 the Indian Penal Code was incorporated in the official Laws of Sarawak, so far as it was applicable. In 1924 a Sarawak Penal Code was introduced, based on the Indian Code. The Rajah's judicial duties were reduced in 1928 by the appointment of a Judicial Commissioner, Mr T. M. L. Stirling Boyd, who was raised in 1930 to the rank of Chief Justice.[3]

Office hours were not very arduous; the hard work was mainly done in smaller stations up-country. A serious-minded Swede, Eric Mjöberg, who was Director of the Museum from 1922 to 1925, was horrified by what he saw. After his retirement he published a book, which is full of inaccuracies and prejudices, but which vibrated with indignation at the laxity of Kuching life. 'Here we take it all easy', he was told, so he said, on his arrival; and he found that no one was in his office except between 9 and 11.30 a.m. and 2 and 3.30 p.m. The Rajah struck him as a man of goodwill who did his best, but was fond of pleasure and incapable of decisions. He listened when one talked to him and said: 'I see, I see', while his thoughts wandered. His government was one of incoherence and personal favouritism. The Ranee shocked Mr Mjöberg by making up her lips in public. She would not allow the ladies of Kuching to wear yellow, a colour reserved for herself. His chief venom was directed against the Chief Secretary, Mr J. C. Moulton, who was appointed in October 1923, when the post was instituted, replacing that of Resident of the First Division. Moulton, who had long connections with Sarawak and had recently been Curator of Raffles Museum at Singapore, was, according to Mjöberg, notoriously lacking in morals and scruples. Under his aegis 'unprintable things' happened in Kuching society. It is possible that Mjöberg's enmity was due to professional jealousy and also to an attempt by Moulton to prevent him from removing a number of specimens when he retired. Moulton died during an operation for appendicitis in June 1926; whereat Mjöberg triumphantly added a paragraph saying that he had been obliged to commit suicide.[1]

The 'unprintable' things seem merely to have been the possession by several of the officials of local mistresses drawn from the indigenous people. This was, in fact, far less dangerous to the well-being of the country than a growing tendency amongst the newly-come wives towards a 'Mem-sahib' attitude with regard to non-Europeans, whom they tried to exclude from their Club. Such behaviour ran counter to the whole tradition of Sarawak and was kept as far as possible in check. But the growth of the European community meant that there was a little less social intercourse than before with the Asians.[2]

Many of the figures who had played a part in Rajah Charles's reign disappeared during the early years of Rajah Vyner's. Bishop Mounsey had left Sarawak even before the old Rajah's death. His successor, Bishop Danson, arrived in April 1918. The Datu Bandar, Mohammed Kassim, son of the former Datu Bandar, died in July 1921, while on a pilgrimage to Mecca. He was succeeded by his son, Haji Abdillah. The Datu Hakim died the following month. The Datu Temanggong, brother of the Datu Bandar, died four years later.[3] The Sultan of Brunei, Mohammed Jelal-ul-Alam, died in 1924, to be succeeded by a son aged eleven, Ahmed Tajmuddin. When the young Sultan came of age seven years later the Rajah handed back to him Muara and the coalmine at Brooketon, the lease of which Rajah Charles had bought in 1888. Its return was a friendly gesture, and prudent at the same time; for the coalmine had proved an expensive failure and was to be abandoned.[4] Many of the older Sarawak officials had gone home; many had died. In 1923 Mr A. B. Ward, who had joined the service in 1899 and had risen to be Resident of the First Division and Chairman of the Committee of Administration, retired. In 1929, Mr Baring-Gould, who had joined the service even earlier, died, a few weeks after Dr Charles Hose, who had been for many years Resident on the Baram.[5] New offices were created. It was on Mr Ward's retirement that the post of Chief Secretary was instituted. A new Department of Trade was inaugurated a few months later. In 1929 a Secretary for Chinese Affairs was appointed. He and his successor were Chinese-speaking. They dealt with the Chinese community through the *Kapitans* or headmen.[6] Soon there were no officials left who remembered the old days before the turn of the century and before Rajah Charles had completed his task of bringing peace and security to the country.

Even now there were still riots and still a few rebels. In 1923 a riot in Miri broke out when a Javanese labourer wounded a Chinese. The Police and the Sarawak Rangers had to open fire, to control the crowds. Thirteen rioters were killed and twenty-four wounded before order could be restored. There were occasional isolated murders in the provinces, and occasional cases of amok, as in 1926, when a Dyak policeman killed four Chinese at Sibu. More seriously, there were still a few tribes in the Ulu Ai and up the tributaries of the Rejang river who refused to submit to the Rajah and abandon their feuds and their head-hunting. The rebels on the Gaat river had been severely defeated in 1915, but by 1919 they were again defying the Government. An expedition accompanied by the Tuan Muda and commanded by G. M. Gifford, Resident of the Third Division, set out from Kapit in April. The rebel villages were burnt and the rebel leaders fled over the frontier into Netherlands territory. There they were arrested and handed to the Sarawak authorities. The four ringleaders, whose names were Blikau, Gila, Unyat and Kunjan, were put into gaol in Kuching. Their followers were settled on the Igan river, where they could be supervised.[1]

The activity of the Government impressed the tribes of the interior. The Ulu Ai Dyaks, though they had officially submitted to the Raj in 1909, along with the Engkari Dyaks, still maintained their feud with the Skrang, Layar and Lemanak Dyaks, who were their neighbours to the east. Their raids had continued; and the Skrang had made counter-raids. Now they decided to make peace. In August 1920 the Rajah in person came to Simanggang to attend a ceremony of the tribe known as *Palit Mata Sapu Moa*, which means 'Dry the eyes and wipe the face'. As a sign that the feud was over there was an exchange of old jars. The Ulu Ai Dyaks gave up twenty jars and the Engkari ten, in return for ten each provided by the Skrangs, Layars and Lemanaks. After the formal transference of the jars the whole company settled down to uninhibited festivities.[2]

Four years later an even greater and more significant peace-making ceremony was held. Feuds between the Sea Dyaks of the Rejang and its tributaries and the Kayans, Kenyahs and Baloi, whom they had gradually displaced, had been going on for many decades, in spite of the Government's efforts to keep them in check. There was particular enmity between the Dyaks and those of the latter tribes who lived over the frontier in Netherlands territory. In 1921 matters had come to a head with the murder of fifteen Dyaks in the river Iwan, beyond the frontier. Both the Sarawak and the Netherlands authorities were determined that the warfare should cease; and the tribes themselves were weary of it. But the general reconciliation was difficult to plan. There were local differences in custom between some of the tribes, in particular between the Dyaks and the Kayans. After preliminary meetings at Long Nawang in Netherlands Borneo it was decided that the formal reconciliation should take place at Kapit and that Dyak customs should be followed.

On 13 October the Rajah, who had been visiting England, returned to Kuching. Three days later he unveiled a monument to his father, which stands outside the old Secretariat Building. Then he prepared to set out to fulfil a task which the old Rajah would have regarded as a far more fitting memorial. During the second week of November hundreds of Dyaks assembled at Kapit. The Rajah himself arrived in his yacht *Zahora* on 12 November, to be greeted with the firing of guns in his honour and the war-cries of the assembled tribes. Next evening ninety-seven boats containing 960 men from over the frontier arrived at the mouth of the Balleh river, which flows into the Rejang just above Kapit. They had come over the watershed; and three of their men had been drowned in the rapids high up the river. With them was the Netherlands Civil Comptrolleur of the Apoh Kayan district, together with Captain Molenaar of the Netherlands Colonial Light Infantry and a Sundanese bodyguard. The officials were received by the Resident of the Division, with a guard of Sarawak Rangers, next morning. Then the warriors from over the border paddled in their canoes four abreast down the Rejang, raising their paddles in salute as they passed the Rajah's yacht. Other Dyaks and Kayans came in from neighbouring districts. That evening there were more than four thousand warriors encamped round Kapit. The following day was spent in visiting and in feasts. The ceremonial peace-making took place on the 16th. Pigs were sacrificially slaughtered in vast numbers; and the leading chieftains on each side rose one after another to pray that peace should be preserved and to curse those who should try to re-open the feud. Then the Rajah rose to thank those who had brought about the reconciliation and to warn his subjects that it must be maintained. The Netherlands Comptrolleur gave a similar warning to his people. Finally the Rajah made gifts to the leading chieftains on each side. He presented a valuable ancient jar to the Dyak Pengulu Koh and to the Baloi leader Tama Kilu, and a gong to each of their deputies. The whole impressive ceremony ended with a genuine feeling of goodwill.[1]

The peace had been largely due to Pengulu Koh, a man in his fifties who was now the recognised leader of the Dyaks of the Rejang. He had been born in Netherlands Borneo in about 1870, his family having fled there after taking part in Rentab's revolt. But his grandfather had returned with him while he was still a boy and had bought some land near Song from the local tribesmen for the price of two slaves. It was on the edge of what was still Kayan and Kenyah country; and when his uncle was murdered by Badang Kenyahs he avenged his death by taking seven Kenyah heads. For this he was outlawed, but eventually travelled to Kuching to make his peace with the Rajah. He was fined 1½ piculs, the equivalent roughly of $43. Afterwards he accompanied the Government forces on expeditions up the Rejang and the Balleh, and finally settled near Kapit, where he took to planting rubber. His noble birth, his adventures and his personality soon made him a leading figure amongst the Dyaks; and the Government named him a *pengulu*. In gratitude for his work over the reconciliation he was now appointed Pengulu Temanggong and was acknowledged as the senior Dyak chieftain. He enjoyed his rank for over thirty years, till his death in 1956.[2]

This splendid reconciliation ceremony ended the chief inter-racial trouble in the interior. For some years there was almost complete peace; and when trouble occurred again it was due to economic rather than tribal causes. Many of the Dyaks had now taken to growing rubber and other jungle produce. When in 1929 and 1930 the prices that they could obtain for their produce dropped disastrously there was general discontent; and it was difficult to make the people in the remoter districts understand that the Government was not to blame for it. The dissatisfaction was greatest in the lands up the Kanowit and Entabai rivers. The malcontents found a leader there in a certain Asun, a *pengulu* who was soon to be degraded for his rebellious attitude. It was necessary in 1931 to send an expedition up the Kanowit to arrest Asun. A few of the malcontents were taken and brought to Kuching; but Asun and his leading followers escaped into the jungle. The Tuan Muda, who was administering the country at the time, went in person up the Kanowit river to meet him. But Asun was truculent; he decided to continue the revolt. In his report on his interview the Tuan Muda suggested that difficulties were largely due to the shortage of responsible European officers in the out-stations and the presence of too many clerks who insisted on all regulations being punctiliously carried out. With little or no money coming to them from the sale of their crops, the tribesmen found it hard to pay their taxes; and the clerks were not empowered to offer them a respite, nor were they people who could talk with friendly authority to them and explain matters with the easy good manners and jokes that the Dyaks loved. At the end of the year Asun offered to negotiate. Blockhouses were built and garrisoned round the disaffected district, isolating it. Asun's attempts to persuade the Dyaks of the Batang Lupar to join him failed. Eventually, in December 1932, he gave himself up to the authorities. He was sent to a comfortable exile at Lundu.[1]

As an outcome of Asun's rebellion a group of young Dyaks banded together to go head-hunting. There were never more than thirty of them; but, though they were outlawed, they were not entirely rounded up till 1941. Their victims were not very numerous. Three Chinese were murdered on the upper Rejang river in the spring of 1934; and a party of Malays and Kayans were attacked on the Pelagus in August, and a few of them were killed and their heads taken. The head-hunters retired into the Katibas area. There the Government surrounded them with a series of blockhouses. Patrols killed two of the outlaws and captured a third that year. Four more were killed the following spring and others were captured later in the year. By 1936 it was no longer necessary to garrison the blockhouses. The few remaining rebels remained quiet in the depths of the jungle. The last four gave themselves up in the autumn of 1940, trusting in the Rajah's clemency. To the irritation of his law officers, he pardoned them, delighted that head-hunting should have ceased before the centenary of Brooke rule should be celebrated. There had been a few other isolated cases in 1939, the worst being when a Chinese family near Song were attacked. But the murderers were soon captured and sentenced to death. By 1940 anyone could wander through Sarawak with no fear that his head would soon adorn a longhouse. It was no mean achievement to have eliminated a custom so deeply ingrained in the Borneo peoples.[2]

As a sign of the growing security the Sarawak Rangers were disbanded early in 1932, after seventy years of active and gallant existence. The Constabulary, to which a military section, known as Force B, was added, was sufficient now for maintaining order.[3] The Rajah had

7   THE SARAWAK FOREST: ON THE SLOPE OF MT SEPALI
(THIRD DIVISION)

8*a*   THE RIVER BALUI (UPPER THIRD DIVISION)

8*b*   KELABIT LONGHOUSE

already given symbolic expression to the maturity of his Raj by founding on his birthday, 26 September 1928, an Order, the Star of Sarawak. Rajah Charles would have considered such a thing frivolous; but the Order gave pleasure to its recipients. The Chinese community was particularly gratified because its leader, Ong Tiang Swee, was created one of the original members.[1]

Peace and progress continued, with old figures disappearing and new figures entering on the scene. Bishop Danson retired in 1931, to be succeeded by Bishop Noel Hudson. The Anglican Church in Sarawak had moved away from the low evangelical atmosphere at Bishop McDougall's death. Neither Rajah James nor Rajah Charles would have approved; but it may well be that an increase in ritual gave greater spiritual satisfaction to the converts; though Methodism flourished among the Chinese on the Rejang; and, many years later, the wild Muruts were to become staunch adherents of an austere evangelistic body.[2]

On 1 December 1936 the Ranee Margaret died in England, aged 86. Forty years had passed since last she had visited Sarawak; but she was, and still is, remembered there for her courage, her kindliness and her charm. In the early days she had played a leading part in making the rule of the Brookes beloved by the women of the country; and in her latter years, though her husband sometimes disapproved of her methods, she did her best to see that Sarawak was well regarded by the authorities in Britain.[3]

Two months later her daughter-in-law, Ranee Sylvia, who was equally anxious to serve her country but whose tastes were more modern, travelled to Hollywood to discuss the possibilities of making a film for which Sarawak should be the setting.[4]

In April 1937 the title of Datu Patinggi was revived and given to the Datu Bandar, Haji Abdillah. Later that year Bishop Hudson left Sarawak after a popular episcopate, to be succeeded by Archdeacon Hollis.[5]

Such news items were now the most important features of the *Sarawak Gazette*. There were no grave crises to record. The country had recovered from the slump, and its agriculture was flourishing. Oil was pouring from the wells at Miri; though, with a bitter irony, it was becoming apparent that the richer oil-wells in the district lay over the frontier, in the lands which the British Government had preserved for the Sultanate of Brunei. From being almost a bankrupt patch of territory Brunei was on the way to emerge as one of the richest States in the East. However, its growing prosperity benefited its neighbours. All seemed to promise well for the future, at least if Sarawak would remain in isolation from the rest of the world.[1]

But there were gloomy prophets who not only foresaw war in Europe but feared that the conflagration might spread all over the Eastern world. And there were other prophets who wondered about the personal destiny of the ruling dynasty.

CHAPTER II

THE END OF THE DYNASTY

It was the tragedy of the Brooke family that its members, for all their talents, their energy and their public spirit, found it difficult at crucial moments to agree among themselves. The first Rajah's bitter quarrel with his eldest nephew had threatened at one time to wreck the Raj. The Second Rajah's ill-concealed distrust of his son and heir had never become a public scandal but had caused acrimony within the family. The Third Rajah also was to be involved in disputes with his kin.

It is impossible for an historian to pass judgments upon family disputes. Personal relationships are so often affected by intimate matters that never are put on record; and family letters contain passages written in the heat of the moment and never intended as a permanent statement. Yet, when the future of a country is concerned, such disputes cannot be entirely ignored. The historian must try to give the known facts fairly and objectively, in an attempt not to criticise but to explain.

Rajah Vyner and his Ranee had three daughters but no son. By the law of Sarawak, which embodied the testaments of the first two Rajahs, the succession was limited to male members of the Brooke family. Rajah James, when he left the succession to Charles, entailed it on his sons, according to the usual rule of primogeniture, and failing his sons, those of Charles's younger brother, Stuart; though Charles was empowered, if he wished, to nominate his eldest brother's son as his heir. Charles bequeathed the succession to his sons and their male issue in order of primogeniture, failing them to his brother Stuart's son and his male heirs, and failing them, to the British Crown. Rajah Vyner's heir was, therefore, his brother the Tuan Muda. But the Tuan Muda was only two years younger than the Rajah; and his health had not in the past been robust. The next heir was his son, Anthony Brooke, born in 1912. In the event of the Rajah's death it seemed likely that the Tuan Muda, if he survived, would renounce his rights and that Anthony Brooke would be the next Rajah. It is melancholy for a man to possess a great inheritance to which his own issue is debarred from succeeding. A nephew is not the same as a son; and though the Rajah was never given to harbouring resentment, he had had cause for jealousy in the past at his parents' preference for his brother; and it was ironical that the Raj should pass in the end to his brother's child. The Ranee seems to have felt about it even more strongly than the Rajah. His nephew was, after all, no blood relation of hers. She tried tentatively to sound opinion to see whether the succession might not be transferred to one of her daughters, or at least to her eldest daughter's son. The Rajah did not share her optimism. He accepted Anthony as his heir; but he could not help regarding him with some criticism and mistrust.[1]

Anthony Brooke entered the Sarawak service in 1936, going to serve as a district officer in the Third Division. He showed at once that he was seriously interested in his prospective inheritance, that he had strong views about its administration and that he was fearless in expressing them. It was easy to prophesy that he would not always be in agreement with his uncle and that there would be a clash. At first, however, the Rajah accepted his nephew as his ultimate heir. In March 1939 Anthony Brooke was appointed Rajah Muda and was so created at a ceremony on 9 April. The title, while it did not legally constitute him as heir-apparent, implied that he would in fact succeed to the Raj and would in the meantime act as the Rajah's deputy whenever the Rajah himself were absent. When the Rajah left for England a few days later, the Rajah Muda took over the Government.[2]

The outcome was unfortunate. Some of the older officials were suspicious of the Rajah Muda, whose outspoken views were not always popular with them. In particular he made no secret of his belief that the administration was over-centralised. Four senior officers, including the Chief Secretary and the Chief Justice, happened to retire in June. Inevitably, in spite of denials, rumour attributed their retirement either to dissatisfaction with the new regime or disagreement with particular measures. The Rajah Muda had drawn the Rajah's attention to certain irregularities in the service and had earned his thanks for it; but that seems to have aroused some dissatisfaction. Soon afterwards a new post, that of General Adviser, was set up, and a house was set aside for the new incumbent. The Treasurer and his office considered that the Rajah Muda was too generous with the Government's money in providing for its furnishing. About the same time the Rajah Muda advanced money out of the Treasury to clear the debts of one or two officials. The Rajah Muda himself considered that as his uncle's deputy he could use the Government's money as he thought best.[3]

The outbreak of war in Europe in September 1939 brought the Rajah back to Sarawak. He arrived early in October. Towards the end of the month the Rajah Muda, who was engaged to be married, left Kuching to meet his bride, who was flying out from England. At Rangoon, where the marriage took place, he received orders from the Rajah to proceed to England. With the Rajah's permission he spent a honeymoon in Sumatra, then flew on to Europe. His mother was at Athens at the time, and he paused there to see her. There he received notice from the Rajah that a proclamation issued in Kuching deprived him of the title and rank of Rajah Muda, on the grounds that he was 'not yet fitted to exercise the responsibilities of this high position'.

The matter might have been of importance only to the Brooke family had it not been for the atmosphere of uncertainty that the incident created among the public. The Rajah was certainly within his rights to abolish a title that he had created if he felt that its holder had exceeded his powers. But the title had been equivocal. It suggested that Anthony Brooke was now the accepted heir to the Raj. Legally it was not so definite; the Tuan Muda remained, as he had always been, the heir-presumptive. But the legal position was not appreciated by the ordinary citizen of Sarawak, who naturally believed that the whole future of the succession was now in question. There were further complications. The Rajah was known to be talking about retirement. The Ranee was rumoured to be seeking to change the line of succession. Above all, the outbreak of war, though as yet it had little effect on material life in Sarawak, added to the nervous tension.[1]

Doubts about the succession seem to have inclined the Rajah to consider whether his position should be divested of some of its powers and responsibilities. To many people an autocracy was already an anachronism; the whole world was moving towards what is called, often without semantic accuracy, a more democratic way of life. The British authorities were less prepared to allow a British citizen to have absolute dominion over a tract of land that might well prove to be of strategic or economic importance, especially in times of war. The appointment of a General Adviser, coming from Britain, was a step towards closer British control. The Rajah himself was tired. Had he possessed a son his attitude might have been different; but, being human, he could not feel so strongly about an inheritance which would probably pass to a nephew with whom he already had sharply disagreed. He also had an adviser on whom he greatly relied, a strange figure called

Gerald MacBryan, who flits disquietingly through the last pages of the story of independent Sarawak.

Gerald MacBryan was a man of great personal gifts, handsome, clever, persuasive and brilliant as a linguist; but he gave an impression of ambition, unscrupulousness and a curious instability. He had entered the Sarawak service from the Royal Navy in 1920, and was given a post in the Third Division. Owing largely to his talent for languages, he played a useful part in helping to negotiate the peace-making between the Dyaks and Kayans at Kapit in 1924. In 1926 he resigned from the service but returned privately to Kuching in the following year and was soon reinstated. In 1929 the Rajah made him his Private Secretary. The post of Chief Secretary fell vacant; and no successor was appointed for some months, during which it seemed to many officials that he was running the country. Their dissatisfaction brought about his resignation the following year. He then passed on to Australia, where he was married. He next appeared in Sarawak in 1935, allegedly on his way from England to Australia to obtain a divorce. He was asked to leave the country, but was granted permission to stay long enough to see certain friends. While there, he announced his conversion to Islam. He then left with a Malay girl, whom he married according to Muslim rites at Singapore. She accompanied him to London and thence on a pilgrimage to Mecca. The journey was described, on information that he supplied, in a book by Owen Rutter called *Triumphant Pilgrimage*. In it MacBryan is given the pseudonym of David Chale: but there was no attempt to hide his identity. His photograph, in Haji costume, provides the frontispiece. The book showed clearly that it was his ambition to become a leader of the Muslims in the Far East, with his headquarters in Sarawak.

In 1940 the Sarawak authorities allowed him to return with his wife, in order that she might see her people. The war had broken out and, as he was of military age, his British passport was endorsed with an order requiring him to report back in England before the end of 1940. The passport was somehow lost while he was in Sarawak, and a Sarawak passport issued to him. In August of that year he was given a post at the Sarawak Museum. In December he was taken by the Rajah with him on a journey to Limbang. In January 1941 he was appointed Political Secretary, with a place on the Supreme Council, and soon afterwards became once more Private Secretary to the Rajah, who was clearly fascinated by his intelligence and his persuasive charm, in spite of his past history. It was popularly believed thenceforward that the Rajah's subsequent actions were the outcome of his influence.[1]

The year 1941 was to see the centenary of Brooke rule in Sarawak. In spite of the war in Europe the country was prospering. In 1940 the Rajah had made two gifts, one of a million dollars and one of half a million, to Great Britain out of his Treasury; and early in 1941 he presented another million dollars. By the Treaty of 1888 Great Britain undertook to protect Sarawak from foreign enemies; and it seemed right and honourable that Sarawak should make a financial contribution to the British war effort. That Sarawak could afford the contribution was a tribute to its well-being. So long as the war confined itself to Europe and the Near East, there was no reason why the well-being should not continue. The country's exports, oil, rubber and foodstuffs, had increased in value; and though imports were also dearer the balance was favourable. Discord within the Brooke family was stilled. Anthony Brooke had returned to the Sarawak service and was working as a district officer at Serikei. After a hundred years the Brooke experiment seemed fully to have justified itself. Apart from the still distant war nothing should have spoilt the rejoicing in its centenary.[2]

In March 1941 the Rajah issued a proclamation announcing that he proposed to celebrate the centenary by divesting himself of his absolute power and establishing a Constitution for Sarawak. As a preliminary step, on 31 March a Committee of Administration was set up, under the presidency of the Chief Secretary, to which the Rajah delegated his authority till the Constitution be enacted. At the same time an agreement was signed providing for the Rajah's future financial position and the allowances paid to members of his family and officials hitherto dependent on his privy purse, and for the payment of a sum to clear off what might be considered his financial obligations to the State and to compensate him for the loss of his rights. The details were kept private. This was probably a mistaken policy, for it inevitably gave rise to rumours that the Rajah was selling his birthright, and that perhaps some of his advisers were doing well out of the bargain.[3]

The Constitution itself was issued on 24 September 1941, when the week of Centenary Celebrations had already begun. There had been difficulties. The Rajah had invited criticism of his proposals; and he had hoped to settle once and for all uncertainty about the succession by naming his nephew, the ex-Rajah Muda, as his heir. But when his nephew refused the honour on the ground that his father, the Tuan

Muda, who was the legal heir-presumptive, was still alive and had not renounced his rights, and when he further sent in a long and detailed criticism of the Constitution proposals, the Rajah was not pleased. A technical misdemeanour, due to a misunderstanding, when Anthony Brooke left his present post without obtaining due permission, was the excuse for dismissing him from the Sarawak service. The Rajah then tried to persuade the Tuan Muda to accept nomination as heir under the new Constitution. Rajah Charles's will, which the Rajah had sworn at his accession to honour, required him to consult with his brother before making any changes in the government of Sarawak and had also laid down the line of succession to the Raj. The Tuan Muda's loyalty to his brother kept him from publishing the fact that his consultative rights had been ignored; but he saw no reason for altering their father's plan for the succession. He was already heir-presumptive, and the position was clear. But if, under the new Constitution, the Rajah could nominate an heir, he could presumably degrade his nominee; and the position was once more uncertain. In spite of the Tuan Muda's protests the Rajah announced officially that he was the heir, but that, should he predecease the Rajah, then the Committee of Administration must consult with the British Government.[1]

The Centenary Celebrations lasted for a week, from 20 September to 28 September 1941. All the leading chiefs and representatives from all the peoples and communities of the country gathered together at Kuching, bearing gifts for the Rajah. There were many varied festivities. The climax was a ceremony on 26 September, when the Datu Patinggi, Haji Abdillah, solemnly presented the Sword of State to the Rajah, and all the chiefs followed with their gifts; and addresses were read by the heads of the Malay, the Dyak and the Chinese communities. Pledges of loyalty were renewed, in an atmosphere of enthusiastic devotion that was deeply impressive. It was shown beyond doubt that the rule of the Brookes was held in respect and affection by all of their subjects.[2]

But that rule was now no longer absolute. The Constitution had come into force two days before. The document setting forth the Constitution opened by enunciating the nine Cardinal Principles on which the Brooke Rajahs had based their claim. These were:

1. That Sarawak is the heritage of Our Subjects and is held in trust by Ourselves for them.
2. That social and education services shall be developed and improved and the standard of living of the people of Sarawak shall steadily be raised.

3. That never shall any person or persons be granted rights inconsistent with those of the people of this country or be in any way permitted to exploit Our Subjects or those who have sought Our protection and care.

4. That justice shall be easily obtainable and that the Rajah and every public servant shall be freely accessible to the public.

5. That freedom of expression both in speech and writing shall be permitted and encouraged and that everyone shall be entitled to worship as he pleases.

6. That public servants shall ever remember that they are but the servants of the people on whose good-will and co-operation they are entirely dependent.

7. That so far as may be Our Subjects of whatever race or creed shall be freely and impartially admitted to offices in Our Service, the duties of which they may be qualified by their education, ability and integrity duly to discharge.

8. That the goal of self-government shall always be kept in mind, that the people of Sarawak shall be entrusted in due course with the governance of themselves, and that continuous efforts shall be made to hasten the reaching of this goal by educating them in the obligations, the responsibilities, and the privileges of citizenship.

9. That the general policy of Our predecessors and Ourselves whereby the various races of the State have been enabled to live in happiness and harmony together shall be adhered to by Our successors and Our servants and all who may follow after them.

After a clause defining terms the Constitution proceeded to set up a Supreme Council consisting of not less than five members, a majority of whom should be members of the Sarawak civil service, and a majority members of the Council Negri. The Chief Secretary and the Treasurer were to be members *ex officio*; and the members of the already existing Supreme Council should remain members for the rest of their lives. The remaining members would be appointed by name by the Rajah. These appointed members would retire after three years but could be reappointed. Membership automatically ceased if the member retired from the Sarawak service or was absent from Sarawak for more than twelve months. Members could resign at will. Three members were to form a quorum. The advice given by the majority of the members present and active should be construed as the advice of the Council. All powers and prerogatives hitherto possessed by the Rajah passed now to the Rajah-in-Council, except for his power to nominate members of the Council.

Below the Supreme Council was the Council Negri, to be composed of twenty-five members; fourteen were to be drawn from the Sarawak Civil Service, of whom the Chief Secretary, the Treasurer and Residents of the five Divisions, and the Secretaries for Native and for Chinese Affairs, were *ex officio* members and the remaining five to be appointed by the Rajah-in-Council by name. The other eleven were to be un-official members appointed by the Rajah-in-Council to represent as far as possible the various peoples dwelling within the State and their interests. These held their position for three years but could be re-appointed. They could resign at will. At least five members must be natives of Sarawak. In addition any member of the already existing Council Negri who was not appointed under either category was to be a member till he died or resigned, though the number of twenty-five members was thereby exceeded. In the event of the absence or illness or incapacity of any member, the Rajah-in-Council could appoint a deputy to take his place. The Council Negri should meet at least twice a year under the chairmanship of the Chief Secretary. Henceforward no legislation was to be enacted by the Rajah-in-Council except by the advice and consent of the Council Negri, nor was any public money to be spent without its approval, though the Treasurer could with the authority of the Rajah-in-Council order expenditure subject to the subsequent consent of the Council Negri. The Rajah had the right to veto a Bill passed by the Council Negri, but if it were passed at three separate sessions he was obliged to endorse it.

Finally, on the death of the Rajah the person who should have been proclaimed Heir to the Raj should succeed him, subject to the provisions of the 1888 Treaty with Great Britain; and he should be proclaimed Rajah within a calendar month by the Supreme Council, which in the meantime should act as Regent. Should the Rajah have occasion to be absent from the State, the Rajah-in-Council could appoint an officer to administer the government and enjoy all the Rajah's powers and prerogatives. Should the Rajah be a minor or incapacitated, the Supreme Council was to appoint such an officer. Only a British subject or a native of Sarawak was to be competent to become Rajah.

A schedule listed the races now considered to be indigenous to Sarawak. They were: the Malays, the Ibans (Sea Dyaks), the Land Dyaks, the Kayans, the Kenyahs, the Klementans, the Melanaus, the Muruts, and any admixture of them. A second schedule prescribed the oaths to be taken by members of the two Councils. In both cases the member swore to uphold the nine Cardinal Principles.[1]

The Constitution was approved by the British Government; and soon afterward an agreement was made providing for a British Adviser to be appointed to Sarawak to keep closer watch on foreign policy and all other matters concerning the Protecting Power. This was signed in November; but instructions provided its immediate application.[1]

The time had come for administrative reforms. In particular the time had come to integrate more of the indigenous population into responsible posts in the Government. Many people, especially in Britain, felt that a new Constitution was needed and that in the mid-twentieth century it was no longer proper that a British subject should enjoy absolute power over a large tract of territory. The Sarawak Constitution of 1941 had certain merits. It made no attempt to revolutionise forms to which the people had grown accustomed; it promised a continuance of the principles which had made the rule of the Brookes popular. And it meant that the governmental decisions no longer depended on the whims of one individual person. It also promised that members of the various races in the country would play a larger part in the administration. But it represented only a very small step along the path towards self-government. The Rajah had in fact surrendered his absolute power to a bureaucracy which he himself nominated. It was possible to say that the autocracy remained, disguised and rendered less efficient. Though native races and interests were to be represented on the Council Negri, the representatives were to be nominated by the Rajah and his nominees. There was no question of elected representatives; and, indeed, a suitable electoral system would have been difficult as yet to achieve. So far the only experiment in elective self-government had been the institution of village councils, first in 1928 among the Land Dyaks, who had never obeyed an hereditary chieftainship and so were better adapted than the other races for such an experiment, and later among other communities. But the most serious criticism that can be brought against the new Constitution is that none of the peoples of Sarawak seems to have wanted it. Its terms, with the insistence on the nine Cardinal Principles and its use of Councils with familiar names, seem designed to reassure the local public that nothing much was being changed. In fact, one fundamental point was changed. The traditional democracy of the East has nothing to do with elective assemblies. It depends on the right of every citizen high or low, rich or poor, to have direct personal access to the sovereign. If the sovereign is unworthy or incompetent, this right is of little value; but all the Brooke Rajahs had scrupulously maintained this accessibility. Each one of their subjects had been able to bring his problems and his grievances himself to them, for their consideration and judgment. Even if his wishes were not granted he had the satisfaction of feeling that his case had received the direct attention of the supreme authority; and a Rajah-in-Council cannot be accessible in the same personal way as a Rajah. It needs a considerable education in Western political thought to perceive the advantages of a Rajah-in-Council.

Few if any of the citizens of Sarawak had enjoyed such an education; except perhaps among the Chinese, who gained nothing from the Constitution; for they were specifically not considered to be one of the indigenous races. But the various communities accepted the new Constitution with little demur. Not many of them understood its provisions or its implications. But it was the will of their Rajah which must be obeyed.[1]

The Rajah himself gave the impression of being weary of government. He had played his part in the Centenary Celebrations with his habitual dignity, good humour and charm. But it may be that he no longer felt himself strong enough to shoulder the activities and responsibilities of direct rule and that his qualms about his successor, whoever that might be, decided him to entrust the government to a Council, so that he might himself pass towards retirement. He was unmoved by the criticism that he had disregarded his father's will, though to many of the older Malays such unfilial action was almost inconceivable. He had already rid himself of some of his possessions in Kuching, such as the Sylvia Cinema which he had built. A few days after the Centenary had been celebrated, he went with his Private Secretary to Malaya, to a house that he possessed in the Cameron Highlands, and from there a few weeks later to Australia. The administration in Sarawak was left in the hands of the Chief Secretary, Captain Le Gros Clark.[2]

Whether or not the new Constitution would have worked well can never be known. There was time for only one meeting of the new Council Negri, on 17 November, before Sarawak was swept into a tempest that made constitutional problems irrelevant. The danger of the war spreading throughout the Far East had already been realised; but a general feeling of optimism endured till suddenly, on 7 December 1941, news came of the sudden attack of the Japanese on Pearl Harbour and their simultaneous advance against the British and Dutch possessions in Asia.[3]

Within a few days it was clear that Sarawak would be engulfed. The Protecting Power, with desperate obligations all over the world, was powerless to protect. The small garrison of the 2/15th Punjabis, which was all that had been afforded to guard the country, could never hope to defeat the forces that the Japanese were putting into the field; and there were neither ships nor aeroplanes to ward off the invaders. Almost immediately enemy aeroplanes appeared in the sky on reconnaissance flights. Then, after a little preliminary bombing, an invasion force of about 10,000 men arrived off Miri, on 16 December. The Oil Company officials, with the help of the tiny garrison, had time to destroy the installations before leaving in three ships for Kuching. They were attacked from the air on the voyage. On 19 December there was a heavy air-raid on Kuching. Several lives were lost; and a fire broke out in the fuel yard of the Borneo Company, which was with difficulty brought under control. Sibu and other smaller towns were bombed during the next few days. Japanese transports were now sailing down the coast. Some were sunk and others damaged by the gallantry of Netherlands submarines and aeroplanes; but the Japanese losses were small in comparison with their strength. On 24 December the Japanese began to advance up the Sarawak river. By Christmas Day Kuching was in their hands.

The suddenness of the attack, the inadequacy of the British Imperial forces and conflicting orders from the military authorities in Singapore prevented any organised attempt at resistance. The civil authorities had no instructions from outside and little time to decide how to deal with an enemy occupation. The Rajah was in Australia; the Tuan Muda was in London, in charge of the Sarawak Office there, and his son had been recently dismissed from the Sarawak service. At this miserable crisis of her history there was no Brooke in Sarawak. Captain Le Gros Clark, as officer in charge of the Government, decided that he and the administrative officers must stay on in Kuching; the civil population could not be deserted, nor the town abandoned without some official authority. The medical and hospital staffs should remain. Everyone else should escape out of the country as best he could. Most of the European women had been sent away at the very beginning of the emergency. The women attached to the Missions, apart from the Catholic nuns who refused to leave their convent, had been moved, as the Japanese approached, up-country to Simanggang, together with the few wives of officials that remained.

After Government files and Treasury notes had been burnt and installations destroyed, Captain Le Gros Clark and his assistants waited to receive the Japanese with dignity, and were bundled off unceremoniously into an improvised prisoners' camp. Meanwhile there was a flow of refugees along the road to Siniawan and Bau, then up the river Sadong and over the watershed into Netherlands territory. After putting up a rather disorganised resistance and after demolishing the aerodrome, the officers in charge of the Punjabi troops managed to collect them and to retreat in fair order, with no serious loss. They retired south-eastward in two columns, one making for Sambit, on the south coast of Borneo, the other for Pankalang Boen, further to the west. It was a long and terrible march. The first column found its way blocked by the Japanese and rejoined the second. But it was too late; on 8 April the whole force had to surrender to the enemy and was taken off to a prison camp. Some civilians, such as the Judicial Commissioner and the Treasurer, had been ordered to leave on Christmas Eve; others escaped on Christmas Day. They were well received in the villages through which they passed, but the villagers were anxious to move them on. Their route led them to Sanggau, where there were a number of Netherlands officials, who arranged for their transport to Pontianak.

Another Japanese force sailed up the Igan river and occupied Sibu on 27 December. The Europeans working in the lower Rejang districts had time to escape into the Second Division, travelling by rough tracks through Engkilili to Lubok Antu, close to the frontier. There refugees from Simanggang joined them; and they crossed into the upper Kapuas valley, in Netherlands territory, to Samitau and thence, with the aid of the Dutch, to Pontianak. It was a hard journey but everyone survived. Europeans on the upper Rejang had a still harder time. Their only route of escape was over the high watershed. A party including several women and children left Kanowit for Kapit and Pelagus and up the rapids to Belaga. There they turned across the mountains and over the frontier, coming at last to the isolated town of Long Nawang, where there was a small Dutch settlement. No Europeans were left there when they arrived; but the native officers were friendly and efficient; and there was adequate food and housing for the party. Some of the men decided to press on, to reach Long Iram and Samarinda; but it would be a long and arduous journey, and no one knew how far the Japanese had advanced into the intervening country. Five of them had set out and reached Samarinda after eighteen days in the jungle. Some of the other men at Long Nawang who were unwell decided to return to Sarawak, where they were taken into captivity. The remainder of the party remained at Long Nawang. They were eventually handed over to the Japanese, who put them all to death, men, women and children.

Apart from the group at Samarinda, who managed to secure air passages to Java, the refugees from Sarawak waited for some days at Pontianak. The Rajah, who had been in Australia when the war began, made an attempt to return to Sarawak; but by the time that he reached Batavia, it was too late. On his return to Australia he sent one of his officials who chanced to be there, Mr Pitt-Hardacre, to Batavia to arrange for the transport of the refugees from Borneo. Aeroplanes were sent to Pontianak to bring them to Batavia. Some went thence to Britain; most joined the Rajah at Sydney. His Private Secretary also flew to Batavia with a vague scheme for returning to Sarawak to stir up unrest there; but this was held to be impracticable and unwise.[1]

There was some disappointment among the Europeans that the indigenous peoples of Sarawak reacted so passively to the Japanese invasion. In Kuching there had been remarkably little panic, though there was some looting as the Europeans left. In Sibu both the panic and the looting were on a larger scale. But there was no resistance against the enemy. It was not surprising. For a century Sarawak had had complete confidence in its rulers. Even the Chinese rebellion, which had nearly extinguished the Raj, had been speedily suppressed and the rebels severely punished. Now, quite suddenly, the whole structure of the Government had collapsed. The Rajah's officials, even with the power of Britain to back them, had been swiftly and totally overcome; and it would have been a very sanguine prophet who would venture to predict that their rule would ever be restored. Perhaps if the Rajah had been in the country the personal loyalty that he inspired might have roused his subjects to action. But there was little that they could have done. The number who actually co-operated with the invaders was small. On the other hand there were many cases of loyalty and devotion to individual European friends and later of courageous kindness to the inmates of the prison camps. But the general attitude was of stunned apathy and caution. The Malay Datus retired to their houses, so as not to be found working for the Europeans when the Japanese arrived; and their example was followed by many humbler officials. Up-country Dyaks and Kayans waited in their villages to see what would happen. The Chinese communities, which had never felt the same loyalty as the Malays or Dyaks to the old regime, were at first hopeful that the Japanese would wish to conciliate them. They had disliked the Indian soldiers; the Japanese might not be any worse. Had the Japanese been less brutal and more generous and more tactful, there might have been a calm acquiescence in their rule. But, though they arrived with high-sounding promises of freedom for the Asian peoples, they soon showed that their boasted 'Co-Prosperity Sphere' was to be run by the Japanese for the Japanese and that any suggestion of disagreement would lead to savage punishment. It was not long before the people began to sigh wistfully for the return of the Europeans.[1]

For three and a half years Sarawak lay behind a curtain. Little news penetrated to the outside world. There were no agents working there to send reports to the Allied Governments. In spite of the efforts of the Red Cross few letters sent from the prison-camps reached their destination. The civilian prisoners were kept in a compound on the outskirts of Kuching. Their condition was never good and steadily worsened. They were soon joined by civilian prisoners taken in North Borneo, including many women and children. The sexes were segregated; but the women and children fared little better than the men. As time went on food ran very short and medicaments were almost non-existent. There was little that could be done for the sick, and no one could remain healthy. It was a tribute to the fibre and courage of the prisoners that so many survived the long ordeal. Many died of disease. Others were done to death by the Japanese. Among these was Captain Le Gros Clark, who to the last acted as the prisoners' leader and spokesman. Conditions in the military prisoners' camp close by were even worse. The death-roll there was appallingly high.[2]

The Japanese concentrated themselves in the towns and along the coast. Not many of them penetrated far up-country. There the indigenous tribes were left very much to themselves; and it was not long before they were assailed with the temptation to go head-hunting again, with the Japanese as their victims. Japanese officials or soldiers who strayed away on their own were seldom heard of again; and several longhouses received the adornment of a Japanese head or two. One Kayan house can boast of the head of a rash Director of Education, complete with his gold-rimmed spectacles, which are still lovingly polished every day. Before long they had made themselves thoroughly hated. The Malays resented them passively on the whole; but the Chinese began to plot actively against them and to try to make contact with the free world outside. If they were discovered or even suspected they were promptly executed.

As the years went on food became a problem. Sarawak had always imported rice; but now such rice as reached the country was controlled by the Japanese, who allowed very little on to the market. The products of the country were taken over by the Japanese, at their own price. Material life grew more and more difficult and miserable. When the tide of war turned in the East and the Japanese found themselves on the defensive conditions worsened further. Not only did they require all the foodstuffs for themselves, so that the civil population in the towns was close to starvation, but they were also more nervous and suspicious than ever and ready to execute victims on the slightest hint of trouble. All the peoples of the island sighed eagerly for their going.[1]

It was a long wait. Borneo lay slightly off the routes along which the Allied strategists prepared to advance. The British High Command was concentrating on Burma, far to the west, while the Americans aimed at moving straight from New Guinea into the Philippines and on to Japan itself, by-passing Borneo and the other East Indian Islands, which would automatically be liberated when the main objective was reached. It was not till the early months of 1945 that some enterprising enthusiasts who knew Borneo at last received permission to drop behind the Japanese lines in Sarawak and North Borneo. They may not have made much difference to the general strategy of the war; but they helped to disconcert and weaken the morale of the Japanese in Borneo and to raise the spirits of the local peoples. As news of the guerrilla warfare spread through the country the old loyalties revived. It seemed that there would after all be an end to the long nightmare of oppression.[2]

The end came suddenly. News of the victory in Europe had hardly penetrated to Borneo before, on 10 June 1945, Australian soldiers began to land on Labuan and the shores of Brunei Bay. The Japanese fought fiercely at first, but they could receive no help now from outside, and in the interior the guerrillas gained momentum. When Japan sought an armistice on 15 August, all regular resistance ceased; though it was not till nearly a month later, on 11 September, that Australian forces under Major-General Wootten entered Kuching and received the formal surrender of the Japanese army. A few Japanese took to the jungle, and subsisted precariously there for a few more months. Two years passed before they were entirely rounded up.[3]

It had been part of Allied policy to refrain from any premature attack on Kuching or from any bombing of the town for fear of harming or causing reprisals to be inflicted on the prisoners concentrated there. The town had, therefore, suffered little material damage; but the condition of its inhabitants was poor, while that of the released prisoners was appalling. Of the other towns, Sibu was not much damaged, but Miri was in ruins as a result of air-raids. It was a slow business to restore administrative order and the functioning of essential services. For seven months the whole country remained under military control, while its former officials recovered from their experiences in prison-camps or were re-assembled from other parts of the world. The Rajah had spent most of the war in Australia. The seat of his Government in exile was at Sydney, though it moved later to London; while the Sarawak Office in London, under the Tuan Muda, kept up the necessary liaison with the British Government. But there had been little to do, beyond the administration of such of the country's financial assets as were not under enemy control, arrangements for the employment of the Sarawak officials who had managed to escape and the welfare of the prisoners' dependants.[1]

Military rule came to an end on 15 April 1946, when the Supreme Allied Commander, Lord Mountbatten, signed at Kuching a proclamation restoring civil government and handed over the administration to the Rajah. The Rajah and Ranee had arrived a few days previously, amid scenes of touching enthusiasm. To many onlookers it seemed extraordinary that a man who could command such personal devotion should have already decided to abandon his people.[2]

During the later months of the war the British Colonial Office had raised the question of the future relationship between Sarawak and Britain. Some closer integration would probably be advisable. Prosperous though Sarawak had been she had suffered greatly, and her rehabilitation would be costly. She would certainly have to appeal for help to Britain; and the British authorities would require some control over the spending of whatever help they provided. In addition it appeared to many officials in London that the Brooke policy of slowing down economic development in order to prevent exploitation would have to be changed. Sarawak would lag far behind the British Colonial possessions in social welfare and educational advance unless she could pay for them by making fuller use of her economic resources. The Rajah was at first reluctant to discuss any change in the status of

Sarawak at a moment when the peoples of Sarawak were under enemy domination and could not be consulted; but he agreed that there might well be preliminary discussions. He had now forgiven his nephew for his attitude in 1941, and appointed him Rajah Muda once more, making him Officer Administering the Government, at the head of a Provisional Government empowered to negotiate with the Colonial Office. The negotiations went slowly, chiefly because the Provisional Government wished to obtain the best legal advice on the international status of Sarawak, in opposition to the Colonial Office's claim to be able to legislate for Sarawak under the Foreign Jurisdiction Act. Meanwhile Sarawak had been liberated; and the Rajah had changed his mind about the whole business. In October he dismissed the Rajah Muda and the Provisional Government for its intransigence and himself resumed control of the Government. About the same time he informed the British Government that he wished to cede his State to His Majesty the King. He was informed that the cession would be accepted.[1]

James Brooke had for many years hoped that Britain would take over his State. As early as 1843 he had offered to give it to the British Crown. The offer was renewed in definite terms in 1866, in a memorandum in which he only stipulated that the religion and customs of the people be respected. When the British Government under Lord Derby spurned the offer, he seriously considered handing the territory to France or Belgium or the Netherlands. Rajah Vyner was reverting to his great-uncle's plan. Rajah Charles had shown that Sarawak could exist and prosper as an autonomous entity. But his son felt that circumstances had changed.[2]

There were many arguments in favour of his decision. He himself seems largely to have been moved by distrust of his heir, and by his own age and poor health. But he could give more valid reasons. Sarawak would almost certainly need help, technical as well as financial, from Britain; and it might well be that the British public, which had just returned a Labour Government to power, might not wish to provide help to a country ruled by a dynasty of English gentlemen. It was certain that Britain intended also to take over North Borneo from the Company. Could Sarawak stand aside? Might it not cause discontent among its peoples if they found their neighbours enjoying advantages denied to them because the Raj could not afford them? He no doubt felt, as some of his officials seem to have felt, that the British Government could now do more for his subjects than he could ever manage, and that the Raj was an anachronism in the modern world. It would be rash to maintain that his decision was unwise. But it would be idle to maintain that it was judiciously carried out.[1]

Sir Frank Swettenham, in a wise book on British Malaya, says: 'When you take the Malay, Sultan, Haji, Chief or simple village headman, into your confidence, when you consult him on all questions affecting the country, you can carry him with you, secure his keen interest and co-operation, and he will travel quite as fast as is expedient along the path of progress.' The Dyaks and their kindred races are equally responsive to such treatment. Rajah James was well aware of this. If the country was to be transferred he thought that the transfer should be gradually made. At the time when he made his offer of cession in 1863 he wrote to Miss Burdett-Coutts that: 'the development of the country would go hand in hand with developed government and thus with mature knowledge of the state of things, and the wants and wishes of the people, Sarawak would *grow into a British Colony* without risk of sudden change, and all this might be done in a few years—in three or ten, as it suits the interests of England.'[2]

Had such sage words been studied, Sarawak would have been spared much misery. But, once the decision had been made, both the Rajah and the Colonial Office were impatient to implement it. In January, MacBryan, who was once again the Rajah's Private Secretary, was sent to Sarawak with a high Colonial Office official, to prepare the ground. His methods were unfortunate. Malay Datus complained that they had been made to sign papers that they did not understand, in the belief that they were hastening the Rajah's return, and sums of money were bestowed on them. The Datu Patinggi, senior of them all, handed his gift back to the Military Authorities administering the country. He was not accustomed to receive bribes. Nevertheless it was held that the Supreme Council endorsed the Rajah's action. Leaders of the Chinese community seem to have been more genuinely agreeable.[3]

On 6 February a proclamation from the Rajah to his people was issued in Sarawak. For the first time his intentions were made official. Considering that the Rajah's powers had been limited by the Constitution of 1941 and that he had always stressed the need to consult the people, his last paragraph reads strangely. 'It is the case in Sarawak', he wrote, 'that all authority derives from the Rajah. The people trust the Rajah and what the Rajah advises for the people is the will of the people. I am the spokesman of the people's will. No other than myself has right to speak on your behalf. No one of you will question whatever I do in his high interest....'[1]

On the same day the Secretary of State for the Colonies made a statement in reply to a question in the House of Commons on the proposed terms for the cession. He stated that the accumulated reserve funds of Sarawak amounted to approximately £2,750,000, of which £1,000,000 would be set aside as a trust-fund, of which the Rajah, his family and dependants should receive the income, but which would revert eventually to Sarawak. Members of the House wished to be assured that the peoples of Sarawak were being fully consulted. The Secretary of State indicated that that was a matter for the Rajah to arrange.[2]

News of the proposed cession was received with some disquiet in Britain amongst the British who knew the East, and in Sarawak, where only the Chinese showed any pleasure. That the Rajah had once again violated his Accession Oath in not consulting the Tuan Muda was primarily a private matter that only concerned the brothers; but the East does not like the violation of oaths nor disrespect to a dying father's wishes. The Rajah lost prestige and sympathy by so firmly disregarding the will of Rajah Charles. But the people of Sarawak had been accustomed for a century to have confidence in their Rajahs. To many of them if the Rajah wished for cession it must be right; but they were puzzled and unhappy about it.

During a rather acrid debate in the House of Commons on 27 March it was announced that two Members of Parliament, a Labour Member, Mr Rees-Williams, and a Conservative, Mr Gammans, were to visit Sarawak to ascertain whether public opinion there was ripe for cession. Both of them had experience of Malaya and spoke Malay. The Rajah was already about to leave for Kuching. It was asked whether the Tuan Muda and his son the Rajah Muda would be permitted to go too. The Secretary of State replied that it was for the Rajah to decide; but later, no doubt in view of feelings expressed in the House, he secured the Rajah's agreement that the Tuan Muda should be flown out to Kuching to be present at any vital meeting of the State Councils.[3]

The Members of Parliament visited such centres as could be reached by the minesweeper in which they travelled round the country. They reported that there was sufficient feeling in favour of cession for a Bill to go at once before the Council Negri to approve of the Rajah's proposals. It is a little difficult to understand their advice. Mr Gammans on his return to England wrote an article full of understanding of the country. Most of the people that he had met could not comprehend the full meaning of cession. To them it was the issue of being ruled by the Rajah whom they knew, or the King of England, whom they did not know. Would they, they asked, be able to go and see him as they could go and see the Rajah? Would that cost more than the eight dollars that it cost to go to the Astana at Kuching? 'The only people who favoured cession for its own sake', he wrote, 'were the Chinese, who obviously felt that British rule would lead to more trade, and probably, if what has happened recently in Malaya is any criterion, to ultimate political domination.' Some of the more educated Malays and Dyaks, and some local-born Chinese were bitterly opposed to cession. 'But', he added, 'the majority either regretfully but fatalistically accepted the Rajah's proclamation as something which could not be altered, or obviously had so much faith and confidence in him that when he said that it was for their benefit they were prepared to trust him and support him.' So he felt that on balance cession to the British Crown would be the best thing for the people. Yet the need for haste which he and his Parliamentary colleague recommended is less explicable. Presumably they thought that if cession were to take place there should be no interval which might give an atmosphere of hesitation and uncertainty and might allow its opponents to whip up agitation against it.[1]

The vital meetings of the Council Negri took place on 16 and 17 May. Thirty-four members attended the debate on the Second Reading and thirty-five the debate on the Third Reading. Twenty-six were non-Europeans. As Mr Gammans, who was present with Mr Rees-Williams, noted, the arrangements left something to be desired. Nothing was done about translating speeches for the benefit of native members, while the Chairman, Mr Archer, the Chief Secretary, made no attempt to be impartial.

Of those that spoke in the debate, two Malay members supported the proposal. One of them, the Datu Pahlawan, moved its adoption but said that he did so grudgingly. The other supporter represented the Malays and Melanaus of the Third Division. The Datu Patinggi and three other Malays, representing the Limbang, the Baram and the Batang Lupar districts, spoke against it. Of the Sea Dyaks, one, who had at first agreed to second the motion, spoke in opposition, saying that cession flouted the nine Cardinal Principles; the other regretted it but said that if it was the Rajah's will he would support it. The only Chinese to speak was in favour. Of the Europeans, one Resident spoke in opposition. The proposal seemed to him inopportune and premature; the people had had no time to consider it. An impressive speech was made by the Rev. Peter Howes, a missionary with wide experience in the country. The people were not ready, he said; and he asked, if everyone's rights were to be respected, as it had been announced, what about the Tuan Muda's rights? The Tuan Muda, who was present but did not vote, had already intervened with dignity to say that, in his opinion, there had been unnecessary haste to force a decision; he had wanted a new relationship with Britain but more time to arrange it. But he wished to make it clear that the line of succession would submit to the wishes of the people. 'I tell you', he said, 'I would rather see this line of succession come to an end than that any family differences of opinion on this subject should be the cause of quarrelling or ill-feeling among the people of Sarawak.'

The three Europeans who spoke in favour of the proposal stressed the points that Sarawak could not bear the financial burden of rehabilitation and progress alone nor her requirements for technical development. The Chief Secretary, who spoke last, emphasised that the Rajah had reached his decision after long thought, and he must be obeyed. Sarawak could no longer stand alone.

The voting on the Second Reading was eighteen in favour of cession and sixteen against it; but the non-European votes were twelve in favour and thirteen against. The two Chinese members voted in favour, the representative of the Indians against. Nine Malays, Dyaks and kindred tribes voted in favour, twelve against. At the Third Reading the figures were nineteen in favour of and sixteen against cession. One of the official non-Europeans had changed his mind, and another in favour of cession was absent ill; but there seems to have been an additional European member who voted against cession.[1]

When the figures reached London, the British Government hesitated for a moment, then decided that as the Cession Bill had been passed by the Council Negri, there were no grounds for rejecting the cession, especially in view of the report of the two Members of Parliament. The Supreme Council in Sarawak therefore authorised the Rajah to execute the instrument of cession on 20 May, while the British Representatives in Sarawak signed it on behalf of His Majesty.[2]

On 26 July 1946 the Privy Council in London ordered the annexation of Sarawak to the British Crown as from 1 July. On 1 July Sarawak's incorporation as one of His Majesty's colonies was publicly proclaimed. The rule of the White Rajahs was ended.[3]

EPILOGUE

The cession had been hurriedly and clumsily handled. It is a story from which few of the principal characters emerge with enhanced credit. Sarawak was to suffer for it.

It would be pointless for a historian of the White Rajahs to dwell in detail on the aftermath of their rule. What's done cannot be undone. Once cession was effected, nothing short of a successful rebellion could have revoked it. But its opponents in Sarawak, seeing how narrowly the Bill had been passed—and passed only by the votes of European officials—could not believe that it might not be possible to repeal it. Demonstrations would show their sentiments; and there must be constitutional ways of agitating for a revision. The ex-Rajah Muda, to whom they looked for leadership, equally hoped to find some constitutional means for redress. But the Constitution offered little scope. It was roughly that of 1941, with the Governor-in-Council replacing the Rajah-in-Council. It may be that the Rajah Muda underrated the difficulty of finding constitutional means that could be effective. It may be, too, that he underrated the fatalism which made many of the opponents of cession accept it passively now that it had come. But, especially among the Malay communities, there was still bitter resentment. Many Malay officials resigned their posts in protest. It would have been hard for a Brooke not to respond to the appeals of friends whose loyalty to the family was so strong.

It cannot be said that the Government handled the problem wisely. It forbade Anthony Brooke to enter Sarawak; and the ban was maintained even when it was necessary to go there to collect evidence for a libel-suit. Whether it was legally or ethically correct to refuse a British citizen his rights on the ground that he might cause trouble is uncertain; but it was foolish because it showed fear; and a Government that shows fear deserves to be punished. It was foolish, too, because it showed the Malays that nothing would be gained by keeping to constitutional methods and encouraged the wilder amongst them to take direct action.[1]

The climax came in 1949. The first Governor, Sir Charles Arden-Clarke, was transferred late that summer to the Gold Coast. His successor, Mr Duncan Stewart, arrived in Kuching in mid-November.

On 3 December he arrived by launch at Sibu. As he stepped ashore a young Malay came up and stabbed him. He died a week later.[1]

The loss of this able and innocent official was the outcome of the handling of the cession and its aftermath. But the tragedy, pointlessly cruel though it seemed, brought good in its train. To the Malays so brutal an assassination came as an outrage to their sense of decency. With the full approval of Anthony Brooke they began to quieten down their anti-cessionist agitation. Cession Day, which was celebrated—a little tactlessly, one may think—as a public holiday, had hitherto been the day on which the various anti-cessionist societies had staged their biggest demonstrations. Early in 1951 Anthony Brooke telegraphed to them to urge them not to demonstrate ever again; and in a dignified notice to the press he announced that he was asking his friends and supporters in Sarawak to accept His Majesty's Government. It seemed no longer possible that any of the Brookes should ever go back to rule the country that their family had created.[2]

All that is an old story which is ended. It is profitless now to debate whether the events of 1946 were justified or to speculate what the State of Sarawak would be had the rule of the Brookes been maintained. The traveller who visits the country today will see much to cheer and reassure him. There is progress and activity all round. Communications are being improved. Roads are being built, air-strips carved out of the jungle. More and more schools are rising; more and more students are going to Britain for technical training. There is an excellent broadcasting service. Agricultural research is aiding the farmers. Health-services are greatly improved; above all the curse of malaria is practically eliminated. It may be that from being under-governed, Sarawak is now over-governed. Officials proliferate, and taxation rises. It may be that the villagers up-country would be happier without all the regulations and form-filling that invade modern life. But they will have the chance to express their views; for there have been constitutional developments. Local self-government operates, on a multi-racial basis, both in the towns and, now, in the countryside, where first it was planned on a racial basis. There is a new Constitution which has introduced an elective system into the Council Negri.

But it is not the material things that impress the traveller. Indeed, he may sigh at some of the aesthetic outrages committed in the name of progress. The charm of Sarawak lies in its human atmosphere. There is none of the constraint there that is found in so many lands that are or have been colonies. The European can travel round the towns and villages and everywhere be welcomed and judged as a human being. Indeed, the hardest task that will await him is to face up to the exuberance of longhouse entertainment. If he is averse to late nights and if his stomach is unsuited to the unlimited consumption of *borak*, he had better keep to the Kelabit and Murut highlands, where, under the stern, efficient eye of the Borneo Evangelical Mission, such things are no longer permitted.

This atmosphere is a legacy from the days of the White Rajahs, and it has been maintained. Many of the officials of the old Raj stayed on after the cession, to preserve the continuity of governance. The nine Cardinal Principles were embodied in the new Constitution, though their interpretation may have been slightly modified to suit modern conditions. The Colonial Office has chosen with care the officers that it has sent to Sarawak. Above all the country was blessed for many years after 1950 with a Governor well fitted to follow in the Rajahs' steps, dignified if need be, but essentially informal, easily accessible and eager himself to see every corner of the land. In some of the Malay kampongs there are still irreconcilable foes of cession, who sigh for the return of the King over the Water: but they are no more significant than the Jacobites of the eighteenth century.

Of the future no one can foretell. A State that contains peoples of different races, traditions and cultural levels has difficulties to face. As yet the peoples of Sarawak live in harmony, the harmony which the Brookes brought to them. If the various communities are wise the harmony will continue; for each has a role to play, and discord would bring misery to them all. Much depends on the Chinese, who are swiftly becoming the most numerous of the communities. Their industry and enterprise have made a vast contribution to the advance of the country; it is to be hoped that they will remain loyal to its interests. Their path is not easy. Under the Brookes they were never able to feel entirely accepted; while the influence of their great mother-country has always been strong; and today an energetic government there is showing a keen and disruptive interest in Nan Yang. Though the connection between Borneo and China is very ancient, few of the Chinese families now in Sarawak have been there for more than three or four generations. Yet most of them rightly regard themselves as fully integrated citizens. They may well hope for the leadership in political as well as economic life; but leadership only leads to chaos unless it is won by patience and wisdom and consideration for the rights of others. For the Malays, too, have a long tradition of leadership, while the Dyaks and their kindred are quick, when the opportunity comes, to learn the ways of the world and to use their learning. May they all continue to work with one another.

History cannot explain the future for us, but it can help to explain the present. If we look with contentment at Sarawak today we must look back too with gratitude at its creators. The White Rajahs had their faults. They suffered mishaps, they sometimes made mistakes. But their achievement was extraordinary. In an age when colonial methods were not always pretty, when the lust for power or for commercial gain too often dictated policy, they showed how a few Europeans could bring peace and contentment to a fierce and lawless country, with the goodwill and even the love of its peoples. Their weapons were human sympathy, selflessness and a high integrity. As time moved relentlessly on, their material methods may have become outmoded. But matter is transient; only the spirit is eternal. Let us pray that the spirit which guided them will guide in the years to come all those to whom Sarawak entrusts her destiny.

NOTES

PAGE 3

1 Captain Daniel Beekman, *A Voyage to and from the Island of Borneo in the East-Indies*, pp. 34–5. Even Crawfurd, writing in the early nineteenth century, believed Borneo to be larger than New Guinea (J. Crawfurd, *A Descriptive Dictionary of the Indian Islands*, p. 57).

PAGE 4

1 Beekman, *op. cit.* p. 35.

PAGE 5

1 The best description of the Bornean forests can be found in O. Beccari, *Wanderings in the Great Forests of Borneo*, esp. pp. 4–16, 379 ff. See also T. Harrisson, *Bornean Jungle, passim.*

PAGE 6

1 The interesting and important results of the excavations at Niah and elsewhere in Sarawak in recent years have been described by Mr Harrisson, who has been in charge of them, in a number of articles. See in particular *Sarawak Mus. J.* VIII, 12 (new series), pp. 549–666 (a collection of articles by Mr Harrisson and his collaborators). There is a useful summary of the work done to date in *Sarawak Ann. Rep.* (1958), pp. 136–45.

2 The older works on Bornean anthropology, such as Ling Roth, *The Natives of Sarawak and British North Borneo*, and C. Hose, *Natural Man: A Record from Borneo*, are now out of date owing to the progress in anthropological studies. The origins of the Bornean tribes is still controversial; and no authoritative work has yet appeared. I have made use of the most recent census (1947) and subsequent registers of population as published yearly in the *Sarawak Annual Report* and the state of the races as published by the Registrar of Births and Deaths in June 1956. For the individual races there is a useful series of short articles by local experts, first given as wireless talks and subsequently published in the *Sarawak Gaz.* to which I refer. See J. L. Noakes, *A Report on the 1947 Population Census*.

3 I. A. N. Urquhart, 'Nomadic Punans and Pennans', *Sarawak Gaz.* no. 1209 (30 November 1958). See also G. Arnold, *Longhouse and Jungle*, pp. 95–114, and Urquhart, 'Some Notes on Jungle Punans', *Sarawak Mus. J.* v, 3 (new series).

PAGE 7

1 T. Harrisson, 'The Kelabits and Muruts', *Sarawak Gaz.* no. 1208 (31 October 1958). See also T. Harrisson, *World Within*, pp. 3–133, for a vivid description of Kelabit life before the last war.

2   C. H. Southwell, 'The Up-river People—Kayans and Kenyahs', *Sarawak Gaz.* no. 1207 (30 September 1958).

3   R. A. Bewsher, 'The Bisaya Group', *Sarawak Gaz.* no. 1210 (31 December 1958).

PAGE 8

1   J. F. Drake-Brockman, 'The Land Dayak', *Sarawak Gaz.* no. 1206 (31 August 1958). See also W. R. Geddes, *The Land Dayaks of Borneo,* and *Nine Dayak Nights.*

PAGE 9

1   A. J. N. Richards, 'Sea Dayaks—Ibans', *Sarawak Gaz.* no. 1205 (31 July 1958). See also E. H. Gomes, *Seventeen Years among the Sea Dyaks of Borneo,* and J. D. Freeman, *Report on the Iban of Sarawak.* I have used 'Sea Dyak' rather than 'Iban' throughout this book because it is the term used by all the older authorities (cf. Rajah Charles, letter dated 10 November 1892, from which I quote), and is probably still the more familiar to the general reader.

PAGE 10

1   See books cited above, especially the books by Freeman, Geddes, Gomes and Harrisson.

2   For an explanation of head-hunting, see Harrisson, *World Within,* pp. 90–9.

PAGE 11

1   R. G. Aikman, 'Melanaus', *Sarawak Gaz.* no. 1210 (31 December 1958).

PAGE 12

1   For the early history of the Malays, much of which is still controversial, see R. O. Winstedt, 'History of Malaya,' *J. R. Asiat. Soc. Malay Branch,* XIII, 1, pp. 18–31, and F. J. Moorhead, *History of Malaya,* pp. 28–115. The genealogy of the Sultans of Brunei is given in H. Low, 'Sĕlĕsīlah (Book of the Descent) of the Rajas of Brunei', *J. R. Asiat. Soc. Straits Branch,* V, pp. 1 ff. See also W. H. Treacher, 'The Genealogy of the Royal Family of Brunei', *ibid.* XV, pp. 79–81, and H. R. Hughes Hallett, 'A Sketch of the History of Brunei', *J. R. Asiat. Soc. Malay Branch,* XVIII, 2. The genealogy of the senior branch of the Sarawak princely family is given by M. Yusof Shibli, 'The Descent of some Kuching Malays', *Sarawak Mus. J.* V, 2 (new series). I am also indebted to Haji Yusof for other genealogical information.

2   J. C. Moulton, 'A Hindu Image from Sarawak', *J. R. Asiat. Soc. Straits Branch,* LXXXV (1922); *Sarawak Ann. Rep.* (1958), pp. 143–5; S. Baring-Gould and C. A. Bampfylde, *A History of Sarawak,* pp. 38–9. See also T. Harrisson, 'Indian Pioneers in Borneo', *Sarawak Mus. J.* VI, 6 (new series), pp. 511–17.

3   Low, 'Sĕlĕsīlah of the Rajas of Brunei', p. 6. See below, n. 1, to p. 57.

PAGE 13

1 *Sherip* is the Malay form of the Arabic word *sharīf*, applied to descendants of the Prophet. For the baleful influence of these Arab adventurers see Raffles's report to Lord Minto, quoted in Lady Raffles, *Memoir of Sir Thomas Stamford Raffles*, pp. 73–4.

2 Winstedt, *op. cit.* pp. 37–59; Moorhead, *op. cit.* pp. 116–47.

3 W. P. Groeneveldt, *Essays relating to Indo-China*, I, pp. 166 ff.; R. Braddell, 'P'o-li in Borneo', *Sarawak Mus. J.* v, 1 (new series), pp. 5–9; Ju-K'ang T'ien, *The Chinese of Sarawak*, appendix 1 (unpublished), 'The Early History of the Chinese in Sarawak', *passim.*

4 See Harrisson, '"Export wares" found in West Borneo', *Oriental Art*, v, 2 (new series), pp. 3–12; Baring-Gould and Bampfylde, *op. cit.* pp. 36–8. Pigafetta reports that Chinese coins were in circulation at Brunei in 1521. See below, p. 18, note 1.

PAGE 14

1 Groeneveldt, *Essays relating to Indo-China*, I, pp. 166 ff.; Ju-K'ang T'ien, *loc. cit.*

2 • Ju-K'ang T'ien, *op. cit.*, quoting the traveller Wang Ta-Yuan; Harrisson, '"Export wares" found in West Borneo', and 'Humans and Hornbills in Borneo', *Sarawak Mus. J.* v, 3 (new series), pp. 400–1; S. Cammann, 'Chinese Carvings in Hornbill Ivory', *ibid.* pp. 393–9.

3 Ju-K'ang T'ien, *op. cit. passim.*

PAGE 15

1 Low, 'Sĕlĕsīlah of the Rajas of Brunei'; Treacher, 'Genealogy of the Royal Family of Brunei'; Baring-Gould and Bampfylde, *op. cit.* pp. 37–8.

PAGE 17

1 *Travels of Ludovico de Barthema*, pp. 247–8.

2 See J. Crawfurd, *A Descriptive Dictionary of the Indian Islands*, pp. 57–66, for the early history of the Europeans in Borneo.

PAGE 18

1 *The First Voyage Round the world, by Magellan*, ed. Stanley, pp. 17–21 (Genoese pilot's account), 110–18 (Pigafetta's account), 202–5 (Maximilian's account), 227 (Alvo's log-book). Pigafetta's great pagan city cannot be identified, if, indeed, it ever existed.

PAGE 20

1 The name is explained in the sixteenth century by Martin de Rada, who says that 'Burneyes island is not all Burneyan'. Boxer, *South China in the Sixteenth Century*, p. 262 n.

2 Crawfurd, *A Descriptive Dictionary*, pp. 64–5; J. R. Logan, 'Borneo: Notices of European Intercourse with Borneo Proper prior to the Establishment of Singapore', in *J. Indian Archipelago* (1848), pp. 495–9. Gonsavo Pereira, who confirmed the treaty with Brunei in 1530, is the first

writer to mention Sarawak, which he calls 'Cerava'. There is a story of a Portuguese embassy in 1527, which was summarily dismissed for offering the Sultan a tapestry showing the marriage of Henry VIII with Catherine of Aragon. The Sultan thought that the figures depicted on it would steal his kingdom (Low, 'Sĕlĕsīlah of the Rajas of Brunei', p. 30). It is probably fictional. Tomé Pires, writing in about 1512, did not himself visit the island. He says that the Borneo islands are inhabited by heathens and that the Borneans seem to be peaceful men (*Suna Oriental of Tomé Pires*, II, p. 89).

3 Boxer, *op. cit.* pp. lxxvi, lxxx.
4 See V. Harlow, 'Early British Pioneers in Borneo,' *Sarawak Mus. J.* VI, 6 (1955), pp. 444–5.

PAGE 21

1 G. Irwin, *Nineteenth-century Borneo*, p. 7.
2 *Ibid.*; Sir W. Foster, *England's Quest for Eastern Trade*, pp. 248–51; Harlow, 'Early British Pioneers in Borneo', p. 445.

PAGE 22

1 Irwin, *op. cit.* pp. 4–6; Crawfurd, *Descriptive Dictionary*, pp. 65–6.
2 Irwin, *loc. cit.*

PAGE 24

1 Crawfurd, *History of the Indian Archipelago*, III, pp. 211 ff.; Lady Raffles, *Memoir of Sir Stamford Raffles*, pp. 75–8; Hunt's sketch of Borneo or Pulo Kalamantan, in H. Keppel, *Expedition to Borneo of H.M.S. Dido*, pp. 386–8; O. Rutter, *The Pirate Wind*, pp. 25–48.

PAGE 25

1 Daniel Beekman, *op. cit.* See also T. Harrisson, 'The First British Pioneer-Author in Borneo', *Sarawak Mus. J.* VI, 6 (1955), pp. 452–69; Irwin, *op. cit.* pp. 7–8.

PAGE 28

1 C. N. Parkinson, *Trade in the Eastern Seas*, pp. 336–56; Harlow, *The Founding of the Second British Empire*, I, pp. 63–95; Irwin, *op. cit.* pp. 8–10.
2 Irwin, *loc. cit.*; Rutter, *British North Borneo*, pp. 94–6.

PAGE 29

1 Irwin, *op. cit.* pp. 6–7.

PAGE 30

1 *Ibid.* pp. 12–13.

PAGE 31

1 Lady Raffles, *Memoir of Sir Stamford Raffles*, pp. 1–85, esp. pp. 59–64; Irwin, *op. cit.* pp. 12–14.
2 Lady Raffles, *op. cit.* pp. 91–6; Irwin, *op. cit.* pp. 14–16.

PAGE 32

1 Irwin, *op. cit.* pp. 16–17.

PAGE 33

1 *Ibid.* pp. 17–19; C. A. Gibson-Hill, 'John Clunies Ross and Alexander Hare, Merchant', *J. R. Asiat. Soc. Malay Branch*, 1952, parts 4 and 5, pp. 22 ff.

PAGE 34

1 Irwin, *op. cit.* pp. 21–2.

PAGE 35

1 Lady Raffles, *op. cit.* pp. 46–8; Irwin, *op. cit.* pp. 22–8. Spencer St John later met an Illanun pirate who had been present at the action in October 1812 (*Life of Sir James Brooke*, p. 21).

PAGE 36

1 Irwin, *op. cit.* pp. 28–32.

PAGE 37

1 *Ibid.* pp. 32–4.

PAGE 40

1 *Ibid.* pp. 34–49; Gibson-Hill, *art. cit. passim.* It is strange that no one has attempted to write a life of Hare, who does not even feature in the *Dictionary of National Biography*.

PAGE 41

1 Irwin, *op. cit.* pp. 52–67.

PAGE 45

1 Gertrude L. Jacob, *The Rajah of Sarawak*, I, pp. 1–3. Miss Jacob provides the fullest account of James Brooke's young days, as she had access to the family papers and knew personally many of his childhood friends. See also Burke's *Landed Gentry* (1955), article 'Brooke of Sarawak'.

PAGE 47

1 Jacob, *op. cit.* pp. 3–9; S. St John, *Life of Sir James Brooke*, pp. 1–2.

2 Jacob, *op. cit.* pp. 9–11; St John, *Life*, pp. 2–6. Owen Rutter, in the preface to his edition of the letters of James Brooke and Miss Burdett-Coutts (*Rajah Brooke and Baroness Burdett-Coutts*, p. 18), quotes a story told him by John Dill Ross that the wound was in a more intimate part of the body, and that was why James Brooke never married. If this is true, it is difficult to understand why an early nineteenth-century mother should have displayed the bullet so prominently; and it adds a complication to the obscure story of Reuben George Brooke (see below, p. 136). See Emily Hahn, *James Brooke of Sarawak*, p. 16. It is more likely that James Brooke never married because he never wanted sufficiently to do so.

NOTES

PAGE 49

1 Jacob, *op. cit.* pp. 11–32, quoting copiously from James's letters and diaries; St John, *op. cit.* pp. 6–8.

PAGE 50

1 Jacob, *op. cit.* pp. 11–32, esp. pp. 13, 21, 28.
2 *Ibid.* pp. 32–48, again with copious quotations; St John, *op. cit.* pp. 8–10. James and Miss Burdett-Coutts were apparently already acquainted with each other when they met in 1847. As the Burdett family occasionally visited Bath, the first meeting must have taken place about this time.

PAGE 51

1 Jacob, *op. cit.* pp. 48–58.
2 *Ibid.* pp. 58–60; St John, *op. cit.* pp. 10–11.

PAGE 52

1 Jacob, *op. cit.* pp. 60–4. James purchased *Royalist* from the Rev. T. D. Lane, who was already a member of the Royal Yacht Squadron, and who proposed James for election to the club. He was elected on 14 May 1836 (information kindly supplied by the Secretary, Royal Yacht Squadron).
2 *Ibid.* pp. 65–6, 70–89 (giving a very slightly abridged version of the Prospectus). The Prospectus was published in a summarised form in the *J. R. Geogr. Soc.* VII, pt 3 (1838), pp. 443–8, and in the *Athenaeum* of 13 October 1838. It was first published in full in Templer's *Private Letters of Sir James Brooke* (1853), I, pp. 2–33.

PAGE 54

1 For French and Dutch reactions see Irwin, *Nineteenth-century Borneo*, p. 98.
2 Jacob, *op. cit.* pp. 66–9.

PAGE 55

1 H. Keppel, *Expedition to Borneo of H.M.S. Dido*, I, pp. 5–13; R. Mundy, *Narrative of Events in Borneo and Celebes*, I, pp. 5–13. Both Keppel and Mundy compiled their books from James Brooke's journals, but each made their own extracts and at times altered the wording. Mundy was anxious as far as possible to avoid repeating passages already published by Keppel; and his transcription seems more accurate than Keppel's. Templer, *Private Letters of Sir James Brooke*, I, p. 55.

PAGE 57

1 S. Baring-Gould and C. A. Bampfylde, *A History of Sarawak*, pp. 43–54; Mundy, *Borneo and Celebes*, I, pp. 178–90; Templer, *Private Letters of Sir James Brooke*, I, p. 114. See also H. Low, 'Sělěsīlah (Book of the Descent) of the Rajas of Brunei', *J. R. Asiat. Soc. Straits Branch*, V (1880), and H. R. Hughes Hallett, 'A Sketch of the History of Brunei', *ibid. Malay Branch*, XVIII, 2 (1940). The revolt in Sarawak was started by the intrigues of Pangiran Usop with the Sultan of Sambas (Templer, *loc. cit.*). See below, p. 59.

PAGE 58
1 Baring-Gould and Bampfylde, *op. cit.* pp. 55–8; St John, *Life of Sir James Brooke*, pp. 50–3; Jacob, *The Raja of Sarawak*, I, pp. 170–3.

PAGE 59
1 O. Rutter, *The Pirate Wind*, pp. 31–42; Baring-Gould and Bampfylde, *op. cit.* pp. 92–7.
2 Templer, *op. cit.* pp. 55–61; Keppel, *Expedition to Borneo*, I, pp. 13–16.

PAGE 60
1 Keppel, *Expedition to Borneo*, I, pp. 17–28.

PAGE 62
1 Templer, *op. cit.* I, pp. 64–70, 71–8; Keppel, *Expedition to Borneo*, I, pp. 28–93; Mundy, *op. cit.* I, pp. 17–30. Kuching, a name that means 'cat', is so-called from a creek of that name that flows through the town. The town was officially called Sarawak till 1871. See Baring-Gould and Bampfylde, *op. cit.* p. 64, and below, p. 206 n. 6.
2 Templer, *op. cit.* I, pp. 78–81; Jacob, *op. cit.* I, p. 118.
3 Keppel, *Expedition to Borneo*, I, pp. 108–37; Mundy, *op. cit.* I, pp. 30–176.

PAGE 64
1 Keppel, *Expedition to Borneo*, I, pp. 138–89; Mundy, *op. cit.* I, pp. 176–8; Templer, *op. cit.* pp. 91–104; Jacob, *op. cit.* I, pp. 129–44; St John, *Life*, pp. 27–49.
2 Keppel, *Expedition to Borneo*, I, pp. 208–14; Templer, *op. cit.* I, pp. 105–7; Jacob, *op. cit.* I, pp. 148–9.

PAGE 65
1 Keppel, *Expedition to Borneo*, I, pp. 192–200; Mundy, *op. cit.* I, pp. 240–1; Jacob, *op. cit.* I, pp. 145–8.
2 Keppel, *Expedition to Borneo*, I, p. 201; Mundy, *op. cit.* I, pp. 241–5; Jacob, *op. cit.* I, p. 149; St John, *Life*, pp. 53–4.
3 Irwin, *Nineteenth-century Borneo*, pp. 98–100.
4 Keppel, *Expedition to Borneo*, I, pp. 205–7, 215–35; Mundy, *op. cit.* I, pp. 245–73; Templer, *op. cit.* I, pp. 105–7.

PAGE 66
1 Keppel, *Expedition to Borneo*, I, pp. 235–51; Jacob, *op. cit.* I, pp. 156–64.
2 Templer, *op. cit.* I, pp. 97–103.

PAGE 67
1 Keppel, *Expedition to Borneo*, I, pp. 251–2; Mundy, *op. cit.* I, pp. 268–71; St John, *Life*, pp. 55–7.
2 In his first issue of laws James Brooke calls himself 'James Brooke, esquire, governor (rajah) of the country of Sarawak...'.
3 Irwin, *op. cit.* pp. 99–102; Hahn, *James Brooke of Sarawak*, pp. 66–7.

PAGE 68

1 Westermann and Williamson had joined James in Singapore. The former, who, according to St John (*Life of Sir James Brooke*, p. 61), was 'so little interested in the country that he never even learned the language', seems to have left at the end of 1842. A new surgeon, John Treacher, arrived early in 1843. Williamson is described by St John (*loc. cit.*) as 'a coloured interpreter from Malacca, a useful but not a very trustworthy man'. But Keppel (*Expedition to Borneo*, II, p. 16) calls him 'active and intelligent' and 'an excellent prime minister'. He was drowned accidentally early in 1846. Crymble is called by St John (*loc. cit.*—St John does not give names, but they are easily identified) 'a shipwrecked Irishman, formerly a clerk, brave as a lion but otherwise not much use'. Keppel (*loc. cit.* in this note) refers to Douglas and (I, p. 317) to Capt. Elliott's visit. Mackenzie is mentioned in James's letters. For Williamson see also St John, *Life*, pp. 106–7.

2 *A Letter from Borneo, with notices of the country and its inhabitants, addressed to James Gardner, Esq.* By James Brooke, Esq. London, published by L. and G. Seeley, 1842.

PAGE 69

1 Keppel, *Expedition to Borneo*, pp. 267–9.

2 *Ibid*, pp. 253–5, 273–4, 285–90; St John, *op. cit.* pp. 59–60.

PAGE 70

1 Mundy, *Narrative of Events*, I, pp. 285–94; Jacob, *The Raja of Sarawak*, I, pp. 193–6; St John, *Life*, pp. 63–4.

2 Keppel, *Expedition to Borneo*, I, pp. 296–312.

3 *Ibid.* pp. 275–6.

4 *Ibid*, pp. 293–6; Mundy, *op. cit.* I, pp. 308–10.

PAGE 71

1 *Ibid.* pp. 59–60; Keppel, *Expedition to Borneo*, I, pp. 278–90.

2 Templer, *op. cit.* I, pp. 144 ff.; Keppel, *Expedition to Borneo*, I, p. 293; St John, *Life*, pp. 63–4. The 'Brooke Diamond' sent about now by James to his mother turned out to be a white topaz (Templer, *op. cit.* I, p. 88 n.).

PAGE 72

1 Keppel, *Expedition to Borneo*, II, pp. 276–7, 315–16, 318–32.

PAGE 73

1 *Ibid.* pp. 332–3; Mundy, *op. cit.* I, pp. 321–2; St John, *Life*, pp. 67–9.

2 Keppel, *Expedition to Borneo*, esp. pp. 322–3; St John, *Life*, pp. 66–8.

3 Keppel, *Expedition to Borneo*, I, pp. 333–6; Mundy, *op. cit.* I, pp. 323–4; St John, *Life*, pp. 69–71.

4 Keppel, *Expedition to Borneo*, I, pp. 336–7; Mundy, *op. cit.* I, p. 336.

PAGE 74

1 Templer, *op. cit.* I, pp. 191–6; St John, *Life*, p. 73; Hahn, *James Brooke of Sarawak*, pp. 84–5.

2 Keppel, *Expedition to Borneo*, I, pp. 336–8; Mundy, *op. cit.* I, pp. 337–42; Templer, *op. cit.* I, pp. 196–205, 209–16.

3 Templer, *op. cit.* I, pp. 238–41, 246–56; Mundy, *op. cit.* I, pp. 338–9; *Selection of Papers relating to Borneo*, pp. 1–2; E. Belcher, *Narrative of the Voyage of H.M.S. Samarang*, I, p. 18.

PAGE 75

1 Keppel, *Expedition to Borneo*, I, pp. 1–2; Mundy, *op. cit.* pp. 342–3.

2 Templer, *op. cit.* I, pp. 141, 292; Marryat, *Borneo and the East Indian Archipelago*, pp. 97–8; Keppel, *Expedition to Borneo*, II, pp. 15–16 and 305–6 (a memoir of George Steward). Arthur Crookshank, who was to play a large part in Sarawak history, was a nephew of James's brother-in-law, the Rev. Charles Johnson. A steward called Stonehouse (or Stonhouse) arrived in 1844 (*Selection of Papers relating to Borneo*, p. 61).

PAGE 77

1 Keppel, *Expedition to Borneo*, II, pp. 2–73, a full account of the expedition written by Keppel himself; Mundy, *op. cit.* I, pp. 344–7.

PAGE 78

1 Belcher, *op. cit.* I, pp. 55–7; Marryat, *op. cit.* pp. 6–24.

2 Belcher, *op. cit.* I, pp. 170 ff.; Marryat, *op. cit.* pp. 97–8.

PAGE 79

1 Mundy, *op. cit.* pp. 353–6; Belcher, *op. cit.* I, p. 60; Foreign Office MS. 12/2.

2 Templer, *op. cit.* II, pp. 8–12.

3 *Ibid.* I, pp. 273–8.

4 *Ibid.* II, pp. 1–2; Jacob, *op. cit.* I, pp. 260–2.

5 Keppel, *Expedition to Borneo*, II, pp. 72–4; St John, *Life*, pp. 86–9.

PAGE 81

1 Keppel, *Expedition to Borneo*, II, pp. 75–129; Mundy, *op. cit.* I, pp. 375–9; Jacob, *op. cit.* I, pp. 263–4.

2 Belcher, *op. cit.* I, pp. 159–77; Marryat, *op. cit.* pp. 105–18; Mundy, *op. cit.* I, pp. 375–83.

PAGE 82

1 Templer, *op. cit.* II, pp. 24, 41–4; *Selection of Papers relating to Borneo*, pp. 3–4, 11, 26. The memorandum is given in Keppel, *Expedition to Borneo*, II, pp. 143–62.

2 *Selection of Papers relating to Borneo*, pp. 53–71; Keppel, *Expedition to Borneo*, II, pp. 163–6; Mundy, *op. cit.* II, pp. 9–31. Irwin, *Nineteenth-century Borneo*, pp. 78–9, points out with some justice that, owing to Wise's later quarrel with James Brooke, the latter's biographers have not

done justice to the energy and enthusiasm with which at first he worked for Sarawak.

3 Keppel, *Expedition to Borneo*, II, pp. 167–9; Templer, *op. cit.* II, p. 60.

PAGE 83

1 Keppel, *Expedition to Borneo*, II, pp. 169–85; Mundy, *op. cit.* II, pp. 31–40; F.O. MS. 12/3; C.O. MS. 144/1.

PAGE 84

1 Templer, *op. cit.* II, pp. 25–31; Mundy, *op. cit.* II, pp. 41–82; Jacob, *op. cit.* I, pp. 279–81.

2 It seems that there was some hitch about the publication of Keppel's book, owing to a warning from Wise. The first printing never went beyond a proof (of which a copy, marked in Wise's hand, 'Memo. Suppressed 10th Sept, 1845', exists in the British Museum). The second edition was published in 1846, with one or two passages critical of the Dutch omitted. The third edition, published the following year, contained a supplementary chapter written by Walter K. Kelly, on the events of 1846. See Templer, *op. cit.* II, p. 107.

PAGE 87

1 Mundy, *op. cit.* II, pp. 87–94 (James Brooke's narrative of his receipt of the news of the massacre; it ends abruptly in the middle of a sentence) and pp. 96–313 (Captain Mundy's detailed Journal of the events in Brunei and Marudu Bay and of the cession of Labuan); Keppel, *Expedition to Borneo* (3rd edition), II, pp. 238–60; St John, *Life*, pp. 108–17. St John, who spent many years in Brunei before writing this book, was inclined to think that Hasim and his brothers had helped to bring their fate on themselves by their arrogance.

PAGE 88

1 Mundy, *op. cit.* II, pp. 357–67; Jacob, *op. cit.* II, pp. 351–4; St John, *Life*, pp. 118–24.

2 St John, *Life*, pp. 123–4.

PAGE 89

1 Irwin, *op. cit.* pp. 101–8; Jacob, *op. cit.* I, pp. 346–51. The relevant papers can be found in Colonial Office MS. 144/1.

2 Jacob, *op. cit.* II, pp. 355–7.

3 *Ibid.* pp. 357–8.

4 *Ibid.* pp. 361–3.

PAGE 90

1 *Ibid.* pp. 358–61; St John, *Life*, p. 129; *Mr Brooke and Borneo*, pamphlet issued by the Borneo Church Mission Institution; Mrs McDougall, *Sketches of our Life in Sarawak*, pp. 13–14; C. J. Bunyon, *Memoirs of Francis Thomas McDougall and of Harriette his Wife*, pp. 22–5; MS. letter from Spencer St John to S. Baring-Gould, dated 1 May 1907.

PAGE 91

1   St John, *Life*, pp. 124–6, 234–7; Irwin, *op. cit.* pp. 127–30. Jacob, *op. cit.* II, pp. 7–8.

2   Keppel, *Visit to the Indian Archipelago in H.M. Ship Maeander*, I, p. 32.

PAGE 92

1   St John, *Life of Sir James Brooke*, pp. 130–6.

2   Jacob, *The Raja of Sarawak*, I, pp. 362–4; St John, *Life*, pp. 136–42.

PAGE 93

1   Jacob, *op. cit.* I, p. 378; Baring-Gould and Bampfylde, *History of Sarawak*, pp. 158, 163 n.; Mrs McDougall, *Letters from Sarawak*, pp. 101–2.

2   Jacob, *op. cit.* II, pp. 3–4. Irwin, *Nineteenth-century Borneo,* pp. 130–1, giving references to show that the company concerned, Gliddon and Co. of Singapore, themselves lost interest in the mines as they found that they could not be worked economically.

3   Jacob, *op. cit.* I, pp. 5–8; Irwin, *op. cit.* pp. 135–6. James's letter to Wise was dated 28 August 1848. Wise sent a truculent reply in October, refusing to give explanations. For James's loss of money, of which little is known, see *Parliamentary Papers*, no. 357 (1852), pp. 128 ff.

4   St John, *Life*, pp. 142–3; McDougall, *Letters from Sarawak*, pp. 58–9; Jacob, *op. cit.* I, pp. 364–6. The purple cross was soon replaced by a black one, as black dye was easier to obtain.

PAGE 94

1   Keppel, *Visit to the Indian Archipelago*, II, pp. 39–87; St John, *Life*, pp. 144–54; Jacob, *op. cit.* I, pp. 366–71.

2   St John, *Life*, pp. 154–7, 171–2; Jacob, *op. cit.* I, pp. 371–2. A letter from James to Lord Palmerston, dated 21 June 1849, gives details of the treaty with Sulu.

PAGE 96

1   Keppel, *Visit to the Indian Archipelago*, II, pp. 302 ff.; St John, *Life*, pp. 174–90—St John was himself present at the battle; McDougall, *Letters from Sarawak*, pp. 84–8. See also *Parliamentary Papers*, no. 378 (1851), pp. 1–4, and W. J. Roff, 'Mr T. Wallage, Commanding H. C. Str. Nemesis', in *Sarawak Mus. J.* VI, 4, 1954.

2   St John, *Life*, pp. 212–15; Jacob, *op. cit.* I, pp. 377–9.

3   St John, *Life*, pp. 212–15; Bunyon, *Memoirs of Francis Thomas McDougall*, pp. 123–36.

PAGE 98

1   *Parliamentary Papers*, nos. 87, 91 and 357 (1852), giving all the reports on Labuan coal. See Irwin, *op. cit.* pp. 133–6; Hahn, *James Brooke of Sarawak*, pp. 142–4.

2   *Hansard*, House of Commons, 21 August 1848.

3   *Parliamentary Papers*, no. 682 (1851) and 517 (1852), giving full details

on both sides. Keppel, writing to Wise on 2 September 1849, in a vain attempt to soothe everyone's feelings, says that Wise should never have worked to raise 'that misshapen, useless structure, the Labuan government', adding 'My friend Brooke has as much idea of business as a cow has of a clean shirt. Napier is no better.... Scott, the Civil Engineer,... had done the only good that has been done.' Colonial Office MS. 144/6.

PAGE 99

1   *Parliamentary Papers*, no. 1462 (1852), pp. 11 ff.; Jacob, *op. cit.* II, pp. 8–9. Wise opened his campaign by a letter, dated 26 November 1849, to the Prime Minister, Lord John Russell (*ibid.* p. 9), calculated to cause disquietude. Hume was first informed about the wars in Borneo by an article in the *Straits Times* about the Kalaka expedition of March 1849, which was reprinted in the *Daily News* of 25 June. The *Straits Times*, which was consistently hostile to James, no doubt because it represented the Singapore merchants, whom he would not allow into Sarawak, published a particularly virulent account of the Batang Maru battle. Hume's case can be found in full in his *Letter to the Rt. Hon. Earl of Malmesbury*, published in 1853.

PAGE 100

1   *Hansard*, House of Commons, 11 February, 21 March, 23 May and 12 July 1850.

2   St John, *Life*, pp. 217–19.

PAGE 101

1   St John, *Life*, pp. 219–25; Jacob, *op. cit.* II, pp. 32–3. See also W. F. Vella, *Siam under Rama III*, pp. 134–9. I am grateful to H.R.H. Prince Chula Chakrabongse of Thailand for information derived from Siamese sources and traditions. He will be dealing fully with the embassy in a forthcoming book, *Lords of Life*.

PAGE 102

1   St John, *Life*, pp. 231–3; Jacob, *op. cit.* II, pp. 38–9; *Parliamentary Papers*, nos. 339 and 534 (1852), *passim*; Rajah James, letters to Admiral Austen, dated 29 and 30 May and 11 and 16 July 1850. Another letter, to the Governor of the Straits Settlement, dated 31 January 1851, renews his protests against Woods's appointment as Deputy Sheriff, saying as a climax: 'I herewith publicly denounce Mr Woods, the Deputy Sheriff of Singapore, with wilfull malicious and unretracted falsehood.' Another letter, dated 2 February, expresses his surprise at the appointment of an 'immoral person, poluted by vice and shameless in want of truth'. (The spelling is presumably that of his Sarawak copyist.)

2   United States State Department Archives, Sarawak; Foreign Office MS. 12/8; St John, *Life*, pp. 220, 240–1.

PAGE 103

1   *Hansard*, House of Commons, 10 July 1851. Miles's illiterate letter is

given in full in Hahn, *op. cit.* pp. 170–1. St John some time about now provided Gladstone with full answers to two questionnaires about the Batang Maru battle: St John, *Life*, pp. 193–210, giving no date for the correspondence.

2 Jacob, *op. cit.* II, pp. 48–51, giving extracts from Cobden's speech as printed in *The Times* of 29 November 1851.

PAGE 105

1 *Parliamentary Papers*, nos. 1462 and 1536 (1852), giving all the relevant correspondence; Irwin, *op. cit.* pp. 153–5; Hahn, *op. cit.* pp. 164–74; Rajah James, letters dated 28 December 1850 and 7 and 9 January 1851; Keppel, *Visit to the Indian Archipelago*, II, pp. 389–96. For a more sympathetic view of Burns see T. Harrisson, 'Robert Burns: the first Ethnologist and Explorer of Interior Sarawak', in *Sarawak Mus. J.* v, 3, November 1951, which reprints Burns's own article on the Kayans. Mr Harrisson shows that Burns was treated high-handedly by James and his officials, but does not succeed in making him out other than a disreputable figure though a good anthropologist. Burns's case was forcibly put at the time in the *North British Mail* of 7 October 1851.

2 *Hansard*, House of Commons, 18 and 23 March 1852. Miles's real name was Sidd, which Mr Drummond misread as Loyd.

3 St John, *Life*, p. 239.

PAGE 106

1 Jacob, *op. cit.* II, pp. 53–6.

2 St John, *Life*, p. 238; Jacob, *op. cit.* II, p. 58.

3 Jacob, *op. cit.* II, pp. 58–61.

4 St John, *Life*, pp. 239–40; Jacob, *op. cit.* II, pp. 62–3. Hume's pamphlet was addressed to the outgoing Foreign Secretary, Lord Malmesbury. The first anti-Brooke pamphlet was 'A Naval Execution' by 'W.N.', published in 1850, giving a highly coloured account of the battle of Batang Maru. It was followed in 1851 by 'Borneo Facts versus Borneo Fallacies', by L. A. Chamerovzow, secretary of the Peace Society, which is full of inaccuracies and shows complete ignorance of Borneo. In 1853 there came 'Adventures of Sir James Brooke, K.C.B., Rajah of Sarawak', by George Foggo, secretary to the National Monuments Society, which consists largely of bloodthirsty passages extracted out of their context from James's own writings, with a rehash of Hume's misinformation about piracy. The Eastern Archipelago Company issued a rather less sensational defence of its actions in 1853 or 1854, in answer to the pamphlet that James Brooke himself wrote replying to Hume's of that year (*A Vindication of his Character and Proceedings in reply to the Statements Privately Printed and Circulated by Joseph Hume, Esq., M.P.*, by Sir James Brooke, K.C.B., Rajah of Sarawak). James was advised by his lawyer not to prosecute Hume for libel (Jacob, *op. cit.* II, p. 65).

PAGE 107
1 Jacob, *op. cit.* II, pp. 67–73; St John, *Life*, pp. 241–3.
2 Jacob, *op. cit.* pp. 76–7, 89–101, giving the texts of the relevant letters.

PAGE 108
1 St John, *Life*, pp. 244–6; Jacob, *op. cit.* II, p. 86.
2 St John, *Life*, pp. 244–6; McDougall, *Letters from Sarawak*, pp. 136–69.
3 St John, *Life*, p. 246.

PAGE 109
1 *Ibid.* pp. 263–5; Jacob, *op. cit.* II, pp. 75–6; C. Brooke, *Ten Years in Sarawak*, I, pp. 36–41.
2 St John, *Life*, pp. 247–9; Jacob, *op. cit.* II, pp. 77–81, quoting an account of the illness written by Mr Horsburgh.

PAGE 110
1 St John, *op. cit.* pp. 248–52.

PAGE 111
1 C. Brooke, *Ten Years in Sarawak*, I, pp. 82–101.
2 Jacob, *op. cit.* II, p. 101; C. Brooke, *Ten Years in Sarawak*, I, pp. 101–7.

PAGE 112
1 St John, *Life*, pp. 255–60; Jacob, *op. cit.* II, pp. 114–17.
2 C. Brooke, *Ten Years in Sarawak*, I, pp. 106–18.
3 St John, *Life*, pp. 255.

PAGE 113
1 C. Brooke, *Ten Years in Sarawak*, I, pp. 121–8; St John, *Life*, pp. 265–71, wrongly dating the expedition May.

PAGE 117
1 *Parliamentary Papers*, nos. 130 (1859) and 253 (1855), giving full report of the proceedings and the reports of Commissioners; Jacob, *op. cit.* II, pp. 128–73, giving a full summary of the proceedings and the full text of the Rajah's protest; St John, *Life*, pp. 270–3, a brief account, not uncritical of the Rajah's behaviour. A full text of the evidence called *The Borneo Question* was published in Singapore soon afterwards.
2 Jacob, *op. cit.* II, pp. 183–4. Gladstone was to compare the Bulgarian Massacres in 1877 to Brooke's massacre of Dyaks (*Hansard*, 7 May 1877). He amplified the charge in an article in *The Contemporary Review* (1877), pp. 181–98.

PAGE 118
1 Jacob, *op. cit.* II, pp. 180–2, 188–93, 204–10.
2 St John, *Life*, pp. 277–9; Jacob, *op. cit.* II, pp. 210–16.
3 St John, *Life*, pp. 279–80; Jacob, *op. cit.* II, pp. 217–20.

PAGE 120

1 St John, *Life*, pp. 273–6; A. R. Wallace, *The Malay Archipelago*, I, p. 54 and *My Life*, I, pp. 341, 345–7.
2 St John, *Life*, pp. 288–9; Jacob, *The Rajah of Sarawak*, II, pp. 223, 233; McDougall, *Sketches of our Life at Sarawak*, pp. 121–5.

PAGE 121

1 Jacob, *op. cit.* II, pp. 192–4; St John, *Life*, p. 282; C. Brooke, *Ten Years in Sarawak*, I, pp. 149–54.
2 Jacob, *op. cit.* II, pp. 194–9; St John, *Life*, pp. 285–6.

PAGE 122

1 C. Brooke, *Ten Years in Sarawak*, I, pp. 158, 168–98; Jacob, *op. cit.* II, pp. 218–19; Baring-Gould and Bampfylde, *History of Sarawak*, pp. 166–7.
2 St John, *Life*, p. 277.
3 Jacob, *op. cit.* II, pp. 211–17; St John, *Life*, pp. 279–81.

PAGE 123

1 St John, *Life*, pp. 281–2; McDougall, *Our Life in Sarawak*, p. 107; Bunyon, *Memoirs of Francis Thomas McDougall*, pp. 113–15; G. C. Turner, 'Bishop McDougall and his wife Harriette', in *Borneo Chronicle*, centenary no. May 1955, and H. P. Thompson, 'Consecration of Bishop McDougall', *ibid.* McDougall was consecrated Bishop of Labuan on St Luke's Day, 18 October 1855. The Rajah then issued a decree on 1 January 1856, creating the Bishop of Labuan Bishop also of Sarawak.

PAGE 124

1 St John, *Life*, pp. 282–3; Jacob, *op. cit.* II, pp. 213–14, 233; L. V. Helms, *Pioneering in the Far East*, pp. 130–5.
2 Jacob, *op. cit.* II, pp. 236–7.
3 *Sarawak Gazette*, no. 1213, 31 March 1959, article by R. Outram, 'Sarawak Chinese'.

PAGE 125

1 Keppel, *Visit to the Indian Archipelago*, I, pp. 352–3, describes the coming of refugees from Pamangat, after a war between the Dutch and the Chinese at Sambas. He says that they are anti-*kongsi* and that 'the influx of a large body of Chinese promises well for the future'. St John, *Forests of the Far East*, II, p. 332, estimates the refugees as numbering about 3000. He is less enthusiastic about them. *Idem, Life of Sir James Brooke*, pp. 291–3, describes the growth of secret societies. See also Baring-Gould and Bampfylde, *op. cit.* pp. 185–9.

PAGE 126

1 Baring-Gould and Bampfylde, *op. cit.* pp. 187–8.
2 C. Brooke, *Ten Years in Sarawak*, I, pp. 27–30.

PAGE 127

1 St John, *Life*, pp. 286, 292–4; C. Brooke, *Ten Years in Sarawak*, I, pp. 207–14.

2 St John, *Life*, p. 294; Baring-Gould and Bampfylde, *op. cit.* p. 191.

3 St John, *Life*, pp. 294–5.

PAGE 132

1 Jacob, *op. cit.* II, pp. 237–44, quoting from the Rajah's own letters and giving a brief account by his servant Penty; Helms, *op. cit.* pp. 164–92, mainly a long account by his secretary, Tidman; McDougall, *Our Life in Sarawak*, pp. 120–56—Mrs McDougall wrote this account twenty-five years later but presumably based it on letters, etc., as well as on her own and her husband's memories; St John, *Forests of the East*, II, pp. 336–64, and *Life of Sir James Brooke*, pp. 294–315—St John visited Sarawak five months later and made up his account from what he heard then from the Rajah and other participants; C. Brooke, *Ten Years in Sarawak*, I, pp. 214–25. I have attempted to correlate the versions as far as possible.

2 Jacob, *op. cit.* II, pp. 245–6; St John, *Life*, p. 314.

PAGE 133

1 St John, *Forests of the East*, II, p. 364, *Life*, p. 313.

2 St John, *Life*, pp. 315–17; Jacob, *op. cit.* II, pp. 244–5. St John was pleased to find the Rajah cheerful and uncomplaining, but soon noticed a melancholy and lack of buoyancy (*Life*, p. 319). The loss of his library especially affected him. St John dilates upon its excellence.

PAGE 134

1 St John, *Life*, pp. 315, 318; Jacob, *The Raja of Sarawak*, II, pp. 246–7, 251–2.

2 St John, *Life*, pp. 318–19.

3 Jacob, *op. cit.* II, pp. 249–51; C. Brooke, *Ten Years in Sarawak*, I, pp. 253–63. A sudden spate on the river caused the death of a number of the Tuan Muda's men.

4 St John, *Life*, pp. 319–20; Jacob, *op. cit.* II, pp. 259–61.

PAGE 135

1 Jacob, *op. cit.* II, pp. 261–2.

2 St John, *Life*, pp. 321–2; *Rajah Brooke and Baroness Burdett-Coutts*, ed. O. Rutter, pp. 42–3.

3 Jacob, *op. cit.* II, pp. 264–8; St John, *Life*, p. 323; *Rajah Brooke and Baroness Burdett-Coutts*, pp. 44–5.

4 St John, *Life*, pp. 321.

PAGE 136

1 Jacob, *op. cit.* II, pp. 268–300, a full account of the negotiations with Lord Derby; *Rajah Brooke and Baroness Burdett-Coutts*, pp. 45–53.

2 The story of Reuben George is not mentioned at all in the Rajah's earlier biographers but is treated at length by Emily Hahn, *James Brooke of Sarawak*, pp. 223–9, from letters kept by Brooke Brooke's descendants. The existence of this young man certainly added to Brooke Brooke's disquiet, but Irwin, *Nineteenth-century Borneo*, p. 186, n. 594, surely simplifies things in calling it 'the real reason for the falling-out of uncle and nephew'. The doubt felt by some of the Rajah's closest friends is illustrated in a letter from A. A. Knox to the Second Rajah, dated 30 June 1868, just after the First Rajah's death. It says, 'as he did acknowledge that young man George, I suppose it was right to make provision for him. He could scarcely do less without stultifying his former act....'

3 Jacob, *op. cit.* II, pp. 285–7; St John, p. 323; *Rajah Brooke and Baroness Burdett-Coutts*, pp. 47–9.

PAGE 137

1 Jacob, *op. cit.* II, p. 307; St John, *Life*, p. 326; Mrs McDougall, *Our Life in Sarawak*, pp. 167–9; Bunyon, *Memoirs of Francis Thomas McDougall*, pp. 178–80; Hahn, *op. cit.* pp. 234–5.

2 Helms, *Pioneering in the Far East*, pp. 216–31, quoting the letter in full, having presumably been shown it by Brooke. It is dated 19 December 1858.

3 St John, *Life*, pp. 326–7. During the depression of 1931–2 it was suggested to Rajah Vyner that he should advance some money to the Company. He replied that it had done its best to ruin his great-uncle, and he did not therefore see why he should help it now (personal information).

4 St John, *Life*, pp. 326–7; Jacob, *op. cit.* II, pp. 312–13; *Rajah Brooke and Baroness Burdett-Coutts*, pp. 54–9.

PAGE 138

1 Jacob, *op. cit.* II, pp. 312–13; Helms, *loc. cit.*; St John, *Life*, pp. 326–7; *Rajah Brooke and Baroness Burdett-Coutts*, p. 61.

PAGE 139

1 Jacob, *op. cit.* II, pp. 303–5; St John, *Life*, p. 324; Hahn, *op. cit.* pp. 232–3.

2 St John, *Life*, pp. 324–6; C. Brooke, *Ten Years in Sarawak*, I, pp. 269–321; Jacob, *op. cit.* II, p. 318.

3 C. Brooke, *Ten Years in Sarawak*, I, pp. 329–34; St John, *Life*, pp. 328–9.

PAGE 140

1 C. Brooke, *Ten Years in Sarawak*, I, pp. 325–9, 335–58; St John, *Life*, pp. 329–31; Jacob, *op. cit.* II, pp. 318–19; *Rajah Brooke and Baroness Burdett-Coutts*, pp. 65–7.

PAGE 141

1 C. Brooke, *Ten Years in Sarawak*, I, pp. 358–63; St John, *Life*, pp. 331–2. Mrs McDougall, *Our Life in Sarawak*, pp. 174–86; Bunyon, *op. cit.* pp. 195–200.

2 St John, *loc. cit.*; Mrs McDougall, *Our Life in Sarawak*, p. 186.

PAGE 142

1 C. Brooke, *Ten Years in Sarawak*, II, pp. 1–13; Baring-Gould and Bampfylde, *History of Sarawak*, pp. 235–40.

PAGE 143

1 Baring-Gould and Bampfylde, *op. cit.* p. 241.
2 *Rajah Brooke and Baroness Burdett-Coutts*, pp. 66–71; Irwin, *op. cit.* pp. 185–6.
3 *Rajah Brooke and Baroness Burdett-Coutts*, pp. 63–4, 72–3, 78–82; St John, *Life*, pp. 333, 336; Jacob, *op. cit.* II, pp. 3–4, 321–2. Neither St John nor Miss Jacob mentions Miss Burdett-Coutts by name. Presumably she wished her generosity to remain anonymous during her lifetime.

PAGE 144

1 C. Brooke, *Ten Years in Sarawak*, II, pp. 30–59; St John, *Life*, pp. 337–9; *Rajah Brooke and Baroness Burdett-Coutts*, pp. 93–4; Personal information.

PAGE 145

1 St John, *Life*, pp. 340–1; Jacob, *op. cit.* II, p. 326.

PAGE 146

1 St John, *Life*, pp. 341–2; *Rajah Brooke and Baroness Burdett-Coutts*, pp. 98–9, 118–21; Jacob, *op. cit.* II, pp. 327–9.
2 St John, *Life*, pp. 342–5; *Rajah Brooke and Baroness Burdett-Coutts*, pp. 122–4; Jacob, *op. cit.* II, pp. 328–34. Baring-Gould and Bampfylde, *op. cit.* pp. 262–5.

PAGE 147

1 C. Brooke, *Ten Years in Sarawak*, II, pp. 104–53; Jacob, *op. cit.* II, pp. 340–1; *Rajah Brooke and Baroness Burdett-Coutts*, p. 128; Baring-Gould and Bampfylde, *op. cit.* p. 265.
2 St John, *Life*, pp. 387–8. The details of the forming of the corps are obscure. See *Sarawak Gaz.* no. 942, 1 March 1932.
3 St John, *Life*, pp. 347–9; *Rajah Brooke and Baroness Burdett-Coutts*, pp. 124–6; Helms, *op. cit.* p. 219.

PAGE 148

1 St John, *Life*, pp. 350–1; *Rajah Brooke and Baroness Burdett-Coutts*, pp. 85, 141–2, 234; Hahn, *op. cit.* pp. 233–5.
2 St John, *Life*, pp. 351–3; *Rajah Brooke and Baroness Burdett-Coutts*, pp. 174–6; Bunyon, *op. cit.* pp. 240–3. In the Sarawak archives there exists a letter from St John to Baring-Gould, dated 1 May 1907, in which he says that the Rajah wrote the pamphlet, *The Bishop of Labuan, a Vindication*, which was published in St John's name, and gives other details.

3 *Rajah Brooke and Baroness Burdett-Coutts*, pp. 134, 137, 152–3.

4 *Ibid.* pp. 139, 146; St John, *Life*, pp. 353–4.

PAGE 149

1 Helms, *op. cit.* pp. 212–13; Mrs McDougall, *Our Life in Sarawak*, pp. 204–14; Bunyon, *op. cit.* pp. 227–40; Baring-Gould and Bampfylde, *op. cit.* pp. 269–74.

PAGE 150

1 *Rajah Brooke and Baroness Burdett-Coutts*, pp. 147–52; St John, *Life*, pp. 353–5; Jacob, *op. cit.* II, pp. 344–5; Helms, *op. cit.* p. 233; Hahn, *op. cit.* pp. 251–2.

PAGE 151

1 *Rajah Brooke and Baroness Burdett-Coutts*, pp. 154–5, 158.

2 *Ibid.* pp. 155–9.

PAGE 152

1 *Ibid.* pp. 162–9.

2 *Ibid.* pp. 170–91.

PAGE 153

1 C. Brooke, *Ten Years in Sarawak*, II, pp. 230–312; Jacob, *op. cit.* pp. 347–9.

2 *Rajah Brooke and Baroness Burdett-Coutts*, pp. 191–6; St John, *Life*, pp. 356–8; Helms, *op. cit.* pp. 234–9. When Wallace, the naturalist, tried to put in a kind word about Brooke to Miss Burdett-Coutts she never spoke to him again, though the Rajah remained as cordial to him as ever (A. R. Wallace, *My Life*, II, pp. 51–2).

PAGE 154

1 *Rajah Brooke and Baroness Burdett-Coutts*, pp. 203–8, 214–15, 217–19; St John, *Life*, p. 358.

2 *Rajah Brooke and Baroness Burdett-Coutts*, pp. 211–14; Jacob, *op. cit.* II, pp. 350–1.

3 *Rajah Brooke and Baroness Burdett-Coutts*, pp. 212–14; Jacob, *op. cit.* II, pp. 351–3; St John, *Life*, pp. 358–69; Irwin, *op. cit.* pp. 188–9 (pointing out that the commission furnished to the first Consul was so worded as to justify the Foreign Office in saying in 1877 that formal recognition had never been granted. The Consul was to obtain his *exequatur* from 'the local authorities', no specific mention being made of the Rajah). Ricketts was moved to Manila, where he tried in vain to boost Sarawak exports. Several friendly and helpful letters of his to Charles Brooke, written in 1868, are extant.

4 *Rajah Brooke and Baroness Burdett-Coutts*, pp. 226–9, 235, 237–8, 245–7, 257–8. Miss Burdett-Coutts embarrassed the Rajah and the Tuan Muda by wishing to employ no Chinese on the Quop estate. The Rajah managed to override her.

PAGE 155

1 *Ibid.* pp. 220–5, 270–4, 292–5; St John, *Life*, pp. 372–3; Irwin, *op. cit.* pp. 189–90. James wrote to Lord Derby in 1866 definitely offering to cede the country in return for cash. A letter from St John to Charles Brooke, dated 10 March 1868, warns Charles not to trust any of his relatives (meaning Crookshank) should Brooke be well enough to go East to assert his rights.

2 J. C. B. Fisher, 'Sarawak Postal History', *Sarawak Mus. J.* VIII (10 December 1957), pp. 236–8. See also G. E. Hansford and L. A. Noble, *Sarawak and its Stamps.*

3 *Rajah Brooke and Baroness Burdett-Coutts*, pp. 218–20, 230–42, 254–64, 280–1; St John, *Life*, pp. 373–4; Jacob, *op. cit.* II, pp. 356–64. The last quarrel is mentioned in letters to Charles Brooke written by Crookshank (9 February 1868), St John (10 March 1868) and by Knox (30 June 1868, after the Rajah's death). The latter, who was understandably prejudiced against the ladies, says 'Nothing could have equalled the hardship and cruelty of their conduct to him during the last six months of his life, although they are crying and making sorry now that it is too late'. He believed that Mrs Brown was desperately jealous of the Rajah's influence over Miss Burdett-Coutts. Even Crookshank, in a letter dated 3 July 1868, says 'God forgive them for their wickedness'.

PAGE 156

1 *Rajah Brooke and Baroness Burdett-Coutts*, pp. 285–91, 299–306; St John, *Life*, pp. 375–7; Jacob, *op. cit.* II, pp. 364–7. His sister Emma Johnson was with him at the end, to his delight (letter from Crookshank to Charles Brooke, dated 16 June 1868).

PAGE 159

1 Baring-Gould and Bampfylde, *History of Sarawak*, pp. 307–8; *Rajah Brooke and Baroness Burdett-Coutts*, pp. 306–7.

PAGE 160

1 St John, *Life of Sir James Brooke*, pp. 274–5.

2 Charles Brooke, *Ten Years in Sarawak*, with an Introduction by H. H. the Rajah Sir James Brooke. See especially, I, pp. 89, 207.

3 C. Brooke, *Ten Years in Sarawak*, II, pp. 330–9.

PAGE 161

1 *Rajah Brooke and Baroness Burdett-Coutts*, pp. 233–4, 236–7; St John, *Life*, pp. 274–5 and 328. See above, p. 119.

2 Personal information. See also below, p. 218.

3 Baring-Gould and Bampfylde, *op. cit.* p. 310.

PAGE 162

1 *Ibid.* pp. 111–13. See also Alleyn Ireland, *Far Eastern Tropics*, pp. 71–6.

PAGE 163

1 *Sarawak Gaz.* no. 59 (1 March 1873); personal information. A list of the

senior officers in 1868 and their salaries is given in the Rajah's MS. Order Book, I, p. 31. See also *Sarawak Gaz.* no. 1079 (2 February 1948) for prices in the 1870's.

PAGE 164

1 *Sarawak Gaz.* no. 8 (17 December 1870).

2 *Rajah Brooke and Baroness Burdett-Coutts*, pp. 309–10. A series of letters written to Charles Brooke by Crookshank and Knox in 1868 show how involved and extensive the late Rajah's debts were.

3 Baring-Gould and Bampfylde, *op. cit.* p. 426; *Sarawak Gaz.* no. 221 (2 June 1884.)

PAGE 165

1 Baring-Gould and Bampfylde, *op. cit.* pp. 427–38; Alleyn Ireland, *op. cit.* pp. 76–7. The Borneo Company had hoped to make a fortune out of cinnabar. Helms wrote hopefully of this in 1868, in a series of letters to Charles. But the ultimate results were disappointing.

2 Baring-Gould and Bampfylde, *op. cit.* pp. 446–7; Eda Green, *Borneo*, pp. 117–18; Ranee Margaret, *Good Morning and Good Night*, pp. 45, 62–3; Rajah Charles, MS. letter, dated 13 July 1916. As early as 1862 Walter Watson, district officer at Skrang, complains in a letter to Charles (dated 24 March) of the trouble caused to him by a visit to his station of 'Mrs Chambers with her suite of husband, 2 sucking padres and a host of Chinamen'.

PAGE 166

1 Rajah Charles, letter to Sir Thomas Fairbairn, dated 11 August 1880; Order Book, *passim*, esp. pp. 76, 238. A recommendation for a candidate was not to have gone to Eton (letter from Crookshank to Rajah, dated 25 September 1868).

2 On the occasion of the *Sarawak Gazette*'s 1000th number (2 January 1937), Rajah Vyner wrote, with truth, 'The *Sarawak Gazette* is, and I can say quite honestly, always will be, the most accurate and interesting record of Sarawak history as time marches on'.

PAGE 167

1 Baring-Gould and Bampfylde, *op. cit.* pp. 320–2.

2 See above, p. 154.

PAGE 168

1 Ranee Margaret, *Good Morning and Good Night*, pp. 20–34.

PAGE 169

1 The Ranee gives an honest and frank account of her relations with her husband in *Good Morning and Good Night*. For the Rajah's point of view see below, pp. 220–1.

2 Ranee Margaret, *Good Morning and Good Night*, pp. 51–4.

PAGE 170

1 *Ibid.* pp. 73–98, 186–96 and *My Life in Sarawak*, pp. 43–60, 109–34; H. de Windt, *My Restless Life*, pp. 29–60.

2 Ranee Margaret, *Good Morning and Good Night*, pp. 132–3; Baring-Gould and Bampfylde, *op. cit.* pp. 400–1. A monument for the children stands in the Astana grounds, erected in 1874, of Anglesea marble (*Sarawak Gaz.* no. 93, 5 January 1875).

3 Rajah Charles, letter to Hope Brooke, dated 18 October 1879.

4 Baring-Gould and Bampfylde, *op. cit.* pp. 320, 323–4.

PAGE 171

1 *Ibid.* pp. 374–82.

PAGE 172

1 General Council, *Proceedings*, 1883 and 1884, pp. 10–12; Baring-Gould and Bampfylde, *op. cit.* pp. 315–18; Order Book, p. 283.

PAGE 173

1 Baring-Gould and Bampfylde, *op. cit.* pp. 318–19; Rajah Charles, letters to Resident at Pontianak, dated June 1880 and to Commander, West Borneo, dated 12 June 1885; Ranee Margaret, *op. cit.* pp. 114–18.

2 *Sarawak Gaz.* no. 130 (16 April 1877).

PAGE 174

1 Earl of Derby to Charles Brooke, 10 May 1875, F.O. MS. 12/42; Ranee Margaret, *Good Morning and Good Night*, pp. 243–4.

PAGE 175

1 See article, Sir John Pope-Hennessy, in *Dictionary of National Biography*, also Maxwell Hall, *Labuan Story*, pp. 188–91, giving the local traditions about him. He had been acquainted with Rajah James and had even stayed at Burrator.

2 Sarawak General Council, *Proceedings*, pp. 1–2; Pope-Hennessy to Foreign Office, 23 April 1868; C.O. M.S. 144/28. See above, p. 87.

PAGE 176

1 Sultan of Brunei to Pope-Hennessy, 13 April 1868, F.O. MS. 12/34*a*; Pope-Hennessy to Charles Brooke, 23 April 1868 and Charles Brooke to Lord Stanley, 30 April 1868, C.O. MS. 144/28; Foreign Office to Pope-Hennessy, 2 December 1868, F.O. MS. 12/34*a*.

2 See above, pp. 87, 110, 146; Irwin, *Nineteenth-century Borneo*, pp. 193–4.

PAGE 177

1 *Sarawak Gaz.* no. 21 (15 July 1871).

2 Baring-Gould and Bampfylde, *History of Sarawak*, pp. 332–5; Ranee Margaret, *Good Morning and Good Night*, pp. 144–60.

PAGE 178

1 Bulwer to Earl Granville, 18 June 1872, C.O. MS. 144/37; Ussher to Earl of Derby, 15 September 1876, *ibid.* 144/64.

PAGE 179

1 Irwin, *op. cit.* pp. 195–6; Tregonning, *Under Chartered Company Rule,* pp. 5–8.

PAGE 180

1 Irwin, *op. cit.* pp. 196–8; Tregonning, *op. cit.* pp. 8–10.

PAGE 182

1 Irwin, *op. cit.* pp. 198–201; Tregonning, *op. cit.* pp. 10–15.
2 Irwin, *op. cit.* pp. 202–6; Tregonning, *op. cit.* pp. 16, 23.

PAGE 183

1 Charles Brooke to Treacher, 6 April 1878, Overbeck to Treacher, 7 April 1878, Treacher to Earl of Derby, 17 April 1878, C.O. MS. 144/50.
2 Charles Brooke to Earl of Derby, 11 April 1878, and Pauncefote's minute on it, F.O. MS. 12/53; Marquess of Salisbury to Charles Brooke, C.O. MS. 144/51. See Irwin, *op. cit.* pp. 207–8.

PAGE 184

1 Borneo Company, minutes of Board Meetings of 16 June and 14 August 1878; Charles Brooke to Foreign Office, 10 December 1878, Colonial Office to Foreign Office, 9 February 1879, Foreign Office minute, 15 February 1879, F.O. MS. 12/52; Treacher to Marquess of Salisbury, 3 May 1879, Sultan of Brunei to Treacher, 18 May 1879, Marquess of Salisbury to Charles Brooke, 25 August 1879, Charles Brooke to Marquess of Salisbury, 29 August 1879, C.O. MS. 144/52.

PAGE 186

1 Irwin, *op. cit.* pp. 210–12; Tregonning, *op. cit.* pp. 17–30.
2 Leys to Foreign Office, 18 January 1882, Charles Brooke to Leys, 13 June 1882, C.O. MS. 144/56; *Sarawak Gaz.* no. 204, 1 January 1883. The instruments of cession were not signed till 1885. For the texts see *The Laws of Sarawak, 1958,* VI, pp. 15–20.
3 Rajah Charles, letters dated 29 August and 3 December 1883.

PAGE 187

1 *Foreign Office Confidential Papers, Affairs of Borneo and Sulu,* pt. VIII (1885), no. 4, Rajah Brooke to Earl Granville, 4 January 1885, nos. 26–30, Treacher to Foreign Office, 22–28 December, 1884; Rajah Charles, series of letters to Treacher, written daily from 10–24 March 1885 and at irregular intervals till 5 May 1885; *Sarawak Gaz.* nos. 228 and 229 (3 January and 2 February 1885). *Laws of Sarawak, 1958,* VI, pp. 13–14 (text of transfer of Trusan to the Rajah).

2 Colonial Office to Foreign Office, 22 May 1885, C.O. MS. 144/60; *Sarawak Gaȝ.* no. 234 (1 July 1885).
3 Tregonning, *op. cit.* pp. 32–3, 39–40.

PAGE 190

1 Baring-Gould and Bampfylde, *op. cit.* pp. 348–9; Tregonning, *op. cit.* pp. 33–4.
2 *Foreign Office, Affairs of Borneo*, pt. X (1887), no. 1, Leys to Earl of Iddesleigh, 23 November 1886.
3 *Ibid.* pp. 16–23, 34, British North Borneo Company to Foreign Office, 23 February 1887, draft answer to parliamentary question by Admiral Mayne, 28 February 1887; British North Borneo Company to Foreign Office, 9 March 1887, pp. 40–2, 71–2, Leys to Foreign Office, 13 and 22 March 1887, pp. 63–4, British North Borneo Company to Foreign Office, 23 April 1887, and Leys to Foreign Office, 25 April 1887, p. 109.

PAGE 191

1 *Ibid.* pp. 105–17 and X, 2, pp. 1–114, giving the whole correspondence between the Foreign and Colonial Offices, Rajah Charles, the British North Borneo Company, Sir Frederick Weld, Dr Leys and Mr Davies.

PAGE 192

1 *Ibid.* no. 146, p. 90, Rajah Brooke's memorandum on Protectorate, 27 October 1887, X, 3, no. 64, pp. 35–6, Foreign Office draft for Sarawak Protectorate, 3 May 1888, no. 85, pp. 57–8. Agreement as passed by Sarawak Council, 14 June 1888, no. 112, p. 72. Agreement returned counter-signed, 11 September 1888; *Sarawak Gaȝ.* no. 270 (2 July 1888), Rajah Charles, letter (thanking for G.C.M.G.) dated 22 June 1888.
2 Tregonning, *op. cit.* pp. 37–8; Baring-Gould and Bampfylde, *op. cit.* pp. 351–2.
3 *Foreign Office, Affairs of Borneo*, XIII, no. 59, pp. 57–8, Hamilton to Foreign Office, 12 December 1889.

PAGE 193

1 Tregonning, *op. cit.* pp. 39–40; Maxwell Hall, *op. cit.* pp. 236–9; Rajah Charles, letter dated 16 January 1889.

PAGE 194

1 *Foreign Office, Affairs of Borneo*, XI–XIII, no. 133, pp. 79–80, Hamilton to Lord Knutsford, 8 September 1888; Tregonning, *op. cit.* pp. 35–6, 38, 53; Baring-Gould and Bampfylde, *op. cit.* pp. 357–8, 368–70. For the disputes over the administration of the Brooketon area see *Foreign Office: Brunei Confidential Despatches from the Secretary of State*, series of letters and despatches dated 8 June 1906, 6 and 13 November 1906, and 7 and 13 March 1907. The Rajah's right to farm gambling there was upheld by Sir F. Swettenham, *ibid.* 21 September 1907 and 25 March 1914. For the return of the district to Brunei see below, p. 236.

2 *Foreign Office, Affairs of Borneo,* XIV–XVI, 1889–90, no. 1, p. 1, Colonial Office to Trevethen, no. 32, pp. 19–20, Smith to Lord Knutsford (telegram) 4 April 1890, no. 41, p. 23, Rajah Brooke's proclamation, no. 55 pp. 32–46, papers forwarded by Dickson to Foreign Office concerning the whole question, no. 92, Foreign Office to Smith, 11 November 1890, no. 98, p. 86, Sultan of Brunei to Queen Victoria (telegram) 12 December 1890, and no. 102, reply to Sultan, 22 December 1890; Baring-Gould and Bampfylde, *op. cit.* pp. 352–6.

PAGE 195

1 Tregonning, *op. cit.* pp. 41–2, 48.

PAGE 196

1 *Sarawak Gaz.* nos. 336, 338 and 339 (2 January, 3 March and 2 April 1894); Tregonning, *op. cit.* pp. 49–55.

2 Rajah Charles, letters dated 11 April and 18 May 1900, and 17 February 1901; *Sarawak Gaz.* nos. 403 and 427 (1 August 1899 and 1 June 1901).

PAGE 197

1 *Foreign Office, Affairs of Borneo,* XXVIII (1903), Colonial Office to Foreign Office, 14 March 1903; Hewett to Foreign Office, 10 and 11 April, 7 and 25 June 1903, and reporting Rajah's offer, 12 August 1903; McArthur to Foreign Office, 9 August 1904.

2 *Ibid.* British North Borneo Company to Foreign Office, 25 October 1904; Foreign Office to British North Borneo Company, 30 November 1904. *Sarawak Gaz.* no. 469 (2 February 1905); Tregonning, *op. cit.* pp. 43–4. *Laws of Sarawak, 1958,* VI, pp. 23–30 (text of the transfer).

PAGE 198

1 *Foreign Office, Affairs of Borneo,* XXVIII, Conway Belfield to Foreign Office, 1 and 29 May 1905; Rajah Charles, letters dated 13 December 1904, 28 January, 26 February, 23 April, 26 May, 20 June and 25 July 1905. *Laws of Sarawak, 1958,* VI, p. 31. *Tulin* was territorial ownership without sovereignty.

2 *Foreign Office, Affairs of Borneo,* XXVIII, McArthur to Foreign Office, 25 September, 10 and 29 November 1904; Rajah Charles, letter dated 29 November 1904.

3 *Foreign Office: Brunei, Confidential Despatches from Secretary of State,* copies of correspondence to date, 21 February 1906; Lord Elgin to Anderson, 19 October 1906; *Affairs of Borneo,* XXVIII, Swettenham to Colonial Office, 17 January 1905.

PAGE 199

1 *Foreign Office: Brunei,* despatches from Brunei, dated 9 and 10 May and 27 August 1906.

2 *Ibid.*, correspondence between Foreign Office, Colonial Office and Treasury, summarised 5 July 1907, and notification to Sarawak and British North Borneo Company, dated 4 October 1907.

3 *Foreign Office, Affairs of Borneo*, XVII, nos. 36 and 42, Inland Revenue to India Office, Foreign Office to Inland Revenue, 14 and 21 March 1888.

PAGE 200

1 Ranee Margaret, *Good Morning and Good Night*, pp. 272–3, and MS. letter to Bampfylde, dated 11 September 1901: Rajah Charles, letters dated 18 October 1901, 27 January 1902 and 31 December 1911.

PAGE 201

1 N. Denison, 'Journal of a Trip from Sarawak to Miri', *J. R. Asiat. Soc. Straits Series*, no. 10 (1883), entry dated 7 May 1872; see above, p. 57.

2 S. St John, letter quoted in Baring-Gould and Bampfylde, *op. cit.* p. 354, and his own *Rajah Brooke*, p. 216; Helms, letter quoted in Baring-Gould and Bampfylde, *op. cit.* pp. 410–11.

PAGE 202

1 General Council, *Proceedings* (1891), p. 15; Baring-Gould and Bampfylde, *History of Sarawak*, pp. 373–4. The words 'sit in their arm-chairs', recorded by Mr Bampfylde, were omitted in the official summary of the speech.

2 Baring-Gould and Bampfylde, *op. cit.* pp. 381–4. For the revenue and expenditure figures for 1883 see *Sarawak Gaz.* no. 221, 6 June 1884.

PAGE 203

1 Edmond Cotteau, *Quelques notes sur Sarawak, passim.*

2 Personal information.

3 *Sarawak Gaz.* no. 582, 16 June 1911. See also Aikman, *Episodes from Sarawak History* (unpublished), Episode VII. For criticism of the court, a letter from R. S. Douglas, dated 17 July 1911, to Secretariat, complaining that there were still too many cases concerning the Chinese in the ordinary courts.

PAGE 204

1 F. Domingo de Rosario, born 1843, died 1924. As 'Mingo' he features in Ranee Margaret's *My Life in Sarawak*, pp. 215–36.

PAGE 205

1 Report from C. W. Daubeny, Baram Division, dated 2 August 1886.

2 See list of forts given in *Outlines of Sarawak History*, pp. 30–2.

3 Order Book, p. 238. See above, p. 166.

PAGE 206

1 Letter from Gerard Fiennes, dated 10 May 1887.
2 Order Book, *passim*, esp. pp. 36, 40, 74, 254.
3 Order Book, p. 41.
4 Letter from Gerard Fiennes, dated 10 May 1887.
5 *Sarawak Gaz.* nos. 85–92, autumn of 1874, no. 132, 26 June 1877, no. 270, 2 July 1888, no. 437, 1 June 1902. See also Ranee Margaret, *My Life in Sarawak*, pp. 176–83.
6 *Sarawak Gaz.* no. 286, 1 November 1889. Kuching only had become the official name of the town, previously called Sarawak in official documents, in 1872. See *Sarawak Gaz.* no. 1067, 10 October 1942.

PAGE 207

1 Baring-Gould and Bampfylde, *op. cit.* pp. 420–2; *Sarawak Gaz.* no. 1099, 7 October 1949. Datin Isa figures largely in the Ranee Margaret's books.
2 Letter from Gerard Fiennes, dated 16 August 1887.
3 Order dated 12 May 1901.
4 *Rajah Brooke and Baroness Burdett-Coutts*, p. 189. In August 1864 the Rajah reports on a scheme to encourage the Chinese to grow pepper, *ibid.* p. 229.

PAGE 208

1 Helms, *Pioneering in the Far East*, p. 253; Order Book, pp. 85–6, Order dated 1873. Ju K'ang T'ien, *The Chinese of Sarawak*, Appendix 1 (not published), *passim*.

PAGE 209

1 Ju K'ang T'ien, *loc. cit.*; Order Book, p. 236, Order dated 11 November 1880.
2 Agreement Book, agreements dated 9 July 1900 and 5 March 1901; personal information.

PAGE 210

1 See Orders, dated 1871, 1893, and Sarawak Supreme Court Law Reports, 1947, pp. 1–5, 1948, pp. 6–9, 1950, pp. 1–2, 17–22. A secret society called the Orchid was discovered and suppressed in 1906 (*Sarawak Gaz.* no. 486, 2 July 1906).
2 See series of Orders on Indian Immigration, dated 1896.

PAGE 211

1 Rajah Charles, letters dated 2 March 1890, 6 and 9 September 1897. See above, p. 165.
2 Rajah Charles, letters dated 27 December 1899, 10 July 1901, 8 July 1902, 5 December 1904; Sharp, *The Wings of the Morning*, *passim*.
3 Rajah Charles, letters dated 9 October and 20 November 1892, 4 June 1898, and 20 February 1908; Sharp, *loc. cit.*

PAGE 212

1 Rajah Charles, letters dated 6 May 1907, 20 December 1909, 24 January 1910, 1 October 1913.

2 Eda Green, *Borneo*, pp. 123–45; Baring-Gould and Bampfylde, *op. cit.* pp. 446–8.

PAGE 213

1 Rajah Charles, letters dated 13 August 1880, 2 February 1883; St John, *Life in the Forests of the Far East*, II, pp. 365–70 (the history of Fr Cuateron); Baring-Gould and Bampfylde, *op. cit.* pp. 448–9. For the history of earlier Catholic missions in Borneo see P. Aichner, 'Pioneer Priests', *Sarawak Mus. J.* VI, 6 (new series), p. 510.

2 Baring-Gould and Bampfylde, *op. cit.* p. 449. See above, p. 209.

3 Quoted in De Windt, *My Restless Life*, p. 57.

PAGE 214

1 Rajah Charles of Sarawak, *Queries; Past, Present and Future*, p. 4; letter dated 5 August 1909.

2 *Sarawak Gaz.* no. 249 (1 October 1886); Green, *op. cit.* pp. 119–20; Order Book, p. 270; Baring-Gould and Bampfylde, *op. cit.* pp. 441–2.

PAGE 215

1 *Sarawak Gaz.* no. 210 (2 July 1883), no. 442 (1 November 1902); Baring-Gould and Bampfylde, *loc. cit.*

2 Order Book, p. 72; Green, *op. cit.* p. 125; Baring-Gould and Bampfylde, *op. cit.* pp. 399–400; *Sarawak Gaz.* no. 344 (1 September 1894), reporting a scare that the Government intended to bury heads in the foundations of the new reservoir; Rajah Charles, letter dated 14 June 1909; personal information.

3 *Sarawak Gaz.* no. 368 (1 September 1896).

4 *Sarawak Gaz.* no. 414 (2 July 1900). A marine telegraph to Singapore was planned in 1897 (Rajah Charles, letter dated November, 1897). The Baram was connected by telegraph by the beginning of 1908.

PAGE 216

1 Baring-Gould and Bampfylde, *op. cit.* pp. 428–9.

2 The Rajah's correspondence is full of letters to members of his family begging them to spend less money. On 30 May 1896 he wrote to the Ranee saying that if she could not live on a yearly income of £3000, as well as her private income, and pay for their two younger sons, he would really have to resign.

3 Baring-Gould and Bampfylde, *op. cit.* pp. 429–38; Aikman, *Episodes in Sarawak History*, Episode VIII, Economics.

PAGE 217

1 Baring-Gould and Bampfylde, *op. cit.* pp. 426–8; Longhurst, *Borneo Story*, pp. 56–64.

2 Rajah Charles, letters dated 6 May 1891 and 17 April 1897; *Sarawak Gaz.* nos. 561 (1 August 1910), 576 (16 March 1911) and 657 (1 August 1914). See C. Hose, *Fifty Years of Romance and Research*, pp. 232 ff., for the whole early history of the oil fields.

PAGE 218

1 In 1921 Mr J. C. Moulton, then Curator of Raffles Museum, Singapore, and later Chief Secretary of Sarawak, was given access to Rajah Charles's papers in order to write his Life (*Sarawak Gaz.* no. 817, 1 October 1921). Nothing seems to have resulted from it.

PAGE 219

1 Rajah Charles, letters dated 6 August 1880, 13 April 1908, and (about the Band) 28 May 1890, 28 July 1894, 16 December 1896, 22 May 1910. He wrote out rules for the Band in September 1888.
2 Rajah Charles, letters dated 4 February 1893, 8 September 1896, 11 November 1899 (about the Museum, which was opened in 1897), 21 November 1894; *Sarawak Gaz.* no. 676 (16 May 1915); Ranee Sylvia, *Three White Rajahs*, p. 77.
3 Rajah Charles, letters dated 3 March 1898, 14 December 1900, 9 September 1910, 15 June 1911, 18 April 1914. Personal information.

PAGE 220

1 Personal information.
2 Order Book, pp. 65, 97; personal information.
3 Personal information.

PAGE 221

1 See Ranee Margaret, *Good Morning and Good Night, passim.*
2 Rajah Charles, letters dated 18 October 1906, October 1912, 13 March 1913; Gerard Fiennes, letters dated 10 May and 8 July 1887.

PAGE 222

1 A number of Rajah Charles's letters, especially between 1912 and 1914, contain reprimands to his son, e.g. those dated October 1912, cited above, and 10 June 1912 and 5 February 1913. See also Ranee Sylvia, *Sylvia of Sarawak*, pp. 177–82.

PAGE 223

1 Ranee Sylvia, *Three White Rajahs*, pp. 95, 110; Dayang Muda of Sarawak, *Relations and Complications*, p. 123.
2 Harry Keppel Brooke, born 1879, married Dorothy Craig, and died after a long illness in 1926, leaving one son.
3 Rajah Charles, letters dated 2 February 1903, 9 December 1903. The Brooke family subsequently sued Mr Booty, who was eventually sent to prison for ten years. He seems to have been very stupid rather than dishonest; his partner Mr Bailey had been the prop of the firm but had gone mad and been relegated to a lunatic asylum (information supplied by Dame Rebecca West, whose relatives were among Mr Booty's clients).

PAGE 225

1 Baring-Gould and Bampfylde, *History of Sarawak*, pp. 387–90; *Sarawak Gaz.* no. 341 (1 June 1894), no. 438 (1 July 1902), no. 447 (1 April 1903), no. 463 (2 August 1904), no. 497 (5 June 1907); Rajah Charles, letters dated 11 August 1896, 14 August 1897, 3 October 1897, 13 May 1902, 16 June 1904 (giving instructions about the order of march).

2 *Outlines of Sarawak History*, p. 17; *Sarawak Gaz.* no. 517 (10 August 1908) and no. 529 (1 April 1909).

3 Letter book at Simanggang, *passim*.

4 Baring-Gould and Bampfylde, *op. cit.* p. 359; *Sarawak Gaz.* no. 413 (1 June 1900); personal information.

PAGE 226

1 *Sarawak Gaz.* no. 672 (16 March 1915).

2 Rajah Charles, letters dated 18 September and 5 November 1915.

3 *Sarawak Gaz.* no. 706 (2 October 1916). *Ibid.* no. 722 (1 June 1917); Dayang Muda, *Relations and Complications*, pp. 148–9. The Rajah was finally interred in Sheepstor churchyard, next to his uncle James, on 12 June 1919. The inscription on his tomb gives the wrong date for his birth, 1828 instead of 1829.

PAGE 227

1 Rajah Charles, letter dated 12 June 1888. In a letter dated 28 September 1903 he tells a correspondent in England that if he voted at all he would vote Liberal. Gerard Fiennes, letter dated 10 May 1887.

PAGE 228

1 Rajah Charles, *Queries, Past, Present and Future*, pp. 4–7, 12–14; De Windt, *My Restless Life*, pp. 57–8, quoting an interview given by the Rajah; personal information.

2 Dayang Muda, *op. cit.* p. 117.

PAGE 231

1 *Sarawak Gaz.* nos. 722, 727, 746, 750 (1 June, 16 August 1917, 4 June, 1 August 1918). Ranee Sylvia, *Sylvia of Sarawak*, pp. 231–8.

2 *The Facts about Sarawak*, pp. 21–7. This pamphlet, published in 1946, on behalf of the ex-Rajah Muda, Mr Anthony Brooke, while frankly polemical in intent, accurately reproduces a number of relevant documents. The Rajah's accession oath is given *ibid.* pp. 28–9.

PAGE 232

1 Personal information.

2 The Ranee Sylvia published two books about Sarawak, *Sylvia of Sarawak* (1936), and *The Three White Rajahs* (1939).

PAGE 233

1 See the *Sarawak Gaz.* in general for the developments of these years. Also personal information.

2 The relevant figures are given annually in *Whitaker's Almanack*. See also Aikman, *Episodes in Sarawak History*, Episode VIII, *passim*.
3 See the *Sarawak Gaz.* in general.

PAGE 234

1 *Sarawak Gaz.* nos. 893 and 895 (1 February and 2 April 1928).
2 Compton Mackenzie, *Realms of Silver*, pp. 266–7.
3 *Outlines of Sarawak History*, p. 26.
4 'Report on living conditions in Sarawak', submitted to the Colonial Office, 28 April 1928.
5 A number of officers recruited in 1934 were the first to pass an entrance examination. Personal information.

PAGE 235

1 *Sarawak Gaz.* no. 813 (1 March 1921).
2 Ranee Sylvia, *Sylvia of Sarawak*, p. 270.
3 *Sarawak Gaz.* no. 977 (1 February 1935).

PAGE 236

1 E. Mjöberg, *Durch die Insel der Kopfjäger, passim*, esp. chs. 24 and 26. See also R. Nicholl, ' Quis curabit ipsos Curatores' in *Sarawak Museum Gazette*, VIII, 10 (new series), pp. 1–7.
2 Personal information.
3 *Sarawak Gaz.* nos. 744 (2 May 1918), 815 (1 August 1921), 816 (1 September 1921), 859 (1 April 1925).
4 *Ibid.* nos. 853 (1 October 1924), 938 (2 November 1931).
5 *Ibid.* nos. 840 (3 September 1923), 915 (2 December 1929).
6 See Aikman, *Episodes in Sarawak History*, Episode VII, *passim*.

PAGE 237

1 *Sarawak Gaz.* nos. 839 and 879 (1 August 1923 and 1 December 1926), no. 672 (3 March 1915); *Outlines of Sarawak History*, pp. 23, 25–6.
2 *Sarawak Gaz.* no. 800 (1 September 1920); *Outlines of Sarawak History*, p. 24.

PAGE 239

1 *Sarawak Gazette*, nos. 854 and 855 (3 November and 1 December 1924); *Outlines of Sarawak History*, pp. 24–5.
2 *Sarawak Gaz.* no. 1185 (30 November 1956). He made two tape-recordings of his memories a few months before his death.

PAGE 240

1 *Ibid.* no. 746 (1 February 1932); *Outlines of Sarawak History*, p. 26. At the end of 1933 Asun was allowed to move to Kuching, but was relegated to the left bank of the river.
2 *Sarawak Gaz.* no. 977 (1 February 1935); *Outlines of Sarawak History*, pp. 27–8.
3 *Sarawak Gaz.* no. 942 (3 March 1932).

PAGE 241

1 *Ibid.* no. 901 (1 October 1928).
2 *Ibid.* nos. 936 and 942 (1 September 1931 and 3 March 1932).
3 *Ibid.* no. 999 (1 December 1936).
4 *Ibid.* no. 1002 (1 March 1937).
5 *Ibid.* nos. 1004 and 1012 (1 May 1937 and 3 January 1938).

PAGE 242

1 The steady economic advance of Brunei can be studied in the statistics published yearly in *Whitaker's Almanack*. The sudden rise in the production and export of oil dates from the middle 1930's.

PAGE 244

1 Anthony Brooke was born on 10 December 1912. The proper spelling of his name is Anthoni, which is the traditional spelling in the Brooke family, but it was abandoned for the more usual form. For Rajah Charles's prejudice in favour of his second son's family see Dayang Muda, *Relations and Complications*, p. 134.
2 *Sarawak Gaz.* nos. 1027 and 1028 (1 April and 1 May 1939).
3 Private letters; personal information. See also *Sarawak Gaz.* nos. 1030 and 1031 (1 July and 1 August 1939).

PAGE 245

1 Proclamation dated 17 January 1940. Personal information.

PAGE 247

1 Personal information. See O. Rutter, *Triumphant Pilgrimage*.
2 *Sarawak Gaz.* nos. 1042, 1043, 1049 and 1050 (1 July and 1 August 1940, 1 February and 7 March 1941). By 1 August 1940 Sarawak had given $1,848,619, and another $1,000,000 was given early in 1941.
3 The financial agreement is printed in *The Facts about Sarawak* (see above, p. 231 n. 2).

PAGE 248

1 Private letters. *Sarawak Gaz.* no. 1051 (1 April 1941).
2 The Jubilee programme is given in full in *Sarawak Gaz.* no. 1057 (15 September 1941). A colour film of the celebrations survived the Japanese occupation, with the loss of only one reel.

PAGE 250

1 The Constitution was enacted and published on 24 September 1941.

PAGE 251

1 The Agreement (reproduced in *The Facts about Sarawak*, pp. 42–3) between His Majesty's Government and the Rajah in Council was signed at Singapore on 22 November 1941, the Governor of the Straits Settlements signing on behalf of H.M. Government as Commissioner for the Malay States. See Aikman, *Episodes in Sarawak History*, Episode x.

PAGE 252

1　See *ibid.* Episode IX.
2　*Sarawak Gaz.* no. 1059 (1 November 1941). Personal information.
3　*Sarawak Gaz.* no. 1061 (1 December 1941).

PAGE 255

1　Personal information, including reports from participants. For a summary see A. E. Percival, *The War in Malaya*, pp. 165–75.

PAGE 256

1　Personal information.
2　The *Sarawak Gaz.* no. 1109 (10 August 1950) contains a long factual article about the history of the prison camps and conditions there. For a doubtfully reliable but well written account of life in the women's camp see Agnes Keith, *Three Came Home.* Personal information.

PAGE 257

1　Personal information. See also T. Harrisson, 'The Chinese in Borneo 1942–5', *International Affairs* (July 1950).
2　See Tom Harrisson, *World Within*, a full and lively account of the guerrilla warfare in which the author was one of the leading figures.
3　*Ibid.* pp. 305 ff., for a very personal account of the end of hostilities. Personal information.

PAGE 258

1　For the financial arrangements about war damage see *Sarawak Gaz.* no. 1095 (7 June 1949), giving some account of the extent of the damage. For the government in exile see *The Facts about Sarawak*, pp. 4–6.
2　Personal information.

PAGE 259

1　See *Hansard*, House of Commons, 6 February 1946. A number of relevant letters are printed in *The Facts about Sarawak*, pp. 65–76.
2　See above, pp. 74, 155 and note 1.

PAGE 260

1　These arguments appear in the course of the discussions and debates on the cession.
2　F. Swettenham, *British Malaya*, pp. 344–5; *Rajah Brooke and Baroness Burdett-Coutts*, p. 185.
3　See *The Facts about Sarawak*, pp. 10–11, 77–8.

PAGE 261

1　*Ibid.* pp. 78–9, for the text of the Rajah's Message, dated 6 February 1946.
2　*Hansard*, House of Commons, *loc. cit.*
3　*Hansard*, House of Commons, 27 March 1946. See *The Facts about Sarawak*, pp. 55–6.

PAGE 262

1 *Hansard,* 15 May 1936; Mr Gammans's article was published in the *Sunday Times* of 2 June 1946.

PAGE 263

1 A full report of the speeches and voting at the debates of the Council Negri on cession is given in the *Sarawak Gaz.* no. 1062 (2 September 1946). Those in favour of the Second Reading were seven Europeans, one Eurasian, two Chinese and nine Malays, Dyaks, etc. (the 'native races' under the Constitution). Those against were three Europeans, one Indian and twelve Malays, Dyaks, etc. See also *Hansard,* House of Commons, 22 May 1946, and a letter by Mr F. H. Pollard to *The Times,* 2 July 1946.

2 *Hansard,* House of Commons, 26 June 1946.

3 Order in Council, 26 June 1946. By this Order Sarawak was 'annexed' not ceded to His Majesty's dominions.

PAGE 264

1 *Hansard,* House of Commons, 18 December 1946.

PAGE 265

1 *Sarawak Gaz.* nos. 1101 and 1102 (7 December 1949 and 1 January 1950).

2 *Ibid.* nos. 1115, 1116 and 1119 (10 February, 10 March and 12 June 1951). The Malay and Dyak Associations replied to Anthony Brooke that they would not abandon their aim to restore Brooke rule, but that they would make no further demonstrations.

BIBLIOGRAPHY

I. OFFICIAL SOURCES

Public Record Office:

Colonial Office Records, 144–6, 352, 404, 434, 487 (Labuan).

Foreign Office Records, 12/1–86; 37/421, 450, 487–8; 93/16; 97/249, 251, 253–4.

Foreign Office Confidential Papers:

Affairs of Borneo and Sulu, 1885–90.

Affairs of Borneo, 1903–5.

Brunei: Confidential Dispatches from Secretary of State 1906–14.

Despatches from Brunei, 1906.

Report on Living Conditions in Sarawak, submitted to the Colonial Office, Secretary of State, 1928.

Hansard, *British Parliamentary Debates.*

British Parliamentary Papers, XXX (1842), XLII (1847–8), XXII and LVI (1849), X, XXIII, XXXIII and LV (1850), XXXIII, XXXVI and LVI (1851), XXXI (1852), LXI (1852–3), XLII (1854), XXIX (1854–5), XLII (1872), LXXVII (1878–9), LXXXI (1882), LII (1887), LXXIII (1888), XCV (1892).

A Selection from Papers relating to Borneo, printed for the use of the Government Offices, London, 1846 (compiled by H. Wise).

Government of Sarawak:

General Council, Minutes, 1867–1927.

Supreme Court Reports, 1928–51.

Rajah James, Letter-book, 1845–51 (MS.) (incomplete).

Rajah Charles, Letter-book, 1880–1915 (MS.).

Letter-books from out-stations, miscellaneous (MS.).

Order books and various letters and documents lodged in Sarawak Museum.

The Laws of Sarawak, 1958, VI, Kuching, 1958.

Borneo Company Minutes.

II. OTHER PRINTED SOURCES

Aichner, P. 'Pioneer Priests, A.D. 1688', *Sarawak Mus. J.* VI, 6 (new series), 1955.

Aikman, R. G. *Episodes in Sarawak History.* Broadcast talks issued in typescript by the British Council, Kuching.

—— 'Melanaus', *Sarawak Gaz.* no. 1210 (31 December 1958).

Allison, A. *How the Church Mission People are treated in the East,* Singapore, 1898.

—— *The Real Pirates of Borneo,* Singapore, 1898.

Arnold, G. *Longhouse and Jungle,* London, 1959.

Banks, E. 'Ancient Times in Borneo', *J. R. Asiat. Soc. Malay Branch,* XX, 2, 1947.

—— 'The Natives of Sarawak', *J. R. Asiat. Soc. Malay Branch,* XVIII, 2, 1940.

Baring-Gould, S. and C. A. Bampfylde, *A History of Sarawak under its Two White Rajahs,* London, 1909.

Barthema, Ludovico de, *The Travels of Ludovico de Barthema*, trans. Jones and Badger, Hakluyt Society, London, 1863.

Bastin, J. 'Raffles and British Policy in the Indian Archipelago', *J. R. Asiat. Soc. Malay Branch*, May 1954.

Beccari, O. *Wanderings in the Great Forests of Borneo*, trans. E. H. Giglioli, London, 1904.

Beekman, D. *A Voyage to and from the Island of Borneo in the East-Indies*, London, 1718.

Belcher, E. *Narrative of the Voyage of H.M.S. Samarang, During the Years 1843–46*, 2 vols., London, 1851.

Bewsher, R. A. 'The Bisaya Group', *Sarawak Gaz.* no. 1210 (31 December 1958).

The Borneo Question, compiled from the *Singapore Free Press* and other sources, Singapore, 1854.

Boxer, C. R. *South China in the Sixteenth Century*, Hakluyt Society, 2nd series, cvi, London, 1953.

Boyle, F. *Adventures among the Dyaks of Borneo*, London, 1865.

Braddell, R. 'P'o-li in Borneo', *Sarawak Mus. J.* v, 1 (new series), Kuching, 1949.

Brooke, C. (Rajah of Sarawak). *Queries, Past, Present and Future*, London, 1907.

—— *Ten Years in Sarawak*, 2 vols., London, 1866.

Brooke, G. *see* Sarawak, Dayang Muda of.

Brooke, J. (Rajah of Sarawak). 'Expedition to Borneo', *J. R. Geogr. Soc.* 1838.

—— *A Letter from Borneo, with Notices of the Country and its Inhabitants*, London, 1842.

—— *Statement relative to Sarawak*, London, 1863.

—— *A Vindication of his Character and Proceedings*, London, 1853.

Also see Keppel, Mundy, Templer and Rutter.

Brooke, J. Brooke, *A Statement regarding Sarawak*, London, 1863.

Brooke, M. *See* Sarawak, Ranee Margaret of.

Brooke, S. *See* Sarawak, Ranee Sylvia of.

Bunyon, C. J. *Memoirs of Francis Thomas McDougall and Harriette his Wife*, London, 1889.

Burns, R. 'The Kayans of the North-West of Borneo', *J. Indian Archipelago*, 1849.

Callaghan, J. M. *American Relations in the Pacific and the Far East, 1784–1900*, Baltimore, 1901.

Cammann, S. 'Chinese Carvings in Hornbill Ivory', *Sarawak Mus. J.* v, 3 (new series), 1951.

Chamerovzow, L. A. *Borneo Facts versus Borneo Fallacies*, London, 1851.

Chiang Liu, 'Chinese Pioneers, A.D. 1900', *Sarawak Mus. J.* vi, 6 (new series), 1955.

Collingwood, C. *Rambles of a Naturalist*, London, 1868.

Cook, O. *Borneo, the Stealer of Hearts*, London, 1924.

Cotteau, E. *Quelques Notes sur Sarawak (Bornéo)*, Paris, 1886.

Crawfurd, J. *A Descriptive Dictionary of the Indian Islands and Adjacent Countries*, London, 1856.

—— *History of the Indian Archipelago*, 3 vols., London, 1820.

Dalton, C. *Men of Malaya*, London, 1942.

Denison, N. *Jottings made during a Tour amongst the Land Dyaks of Sarawak*, Singapore, 1879.

—— 'Journal of a Trip from Sarawak to Meri', *J. R. Asiat. Soc. Malay Branch*, no. 10, 1883.

De Windt, H. *My Restless Life*, London, 1909.

Drake Brockman, J. F. 'The Land Dayak', *Sarawak Gaz*. no. 1206 (31 August 1958).

Earl, G. W. *The Eastern Seas*, London, 1837.

Everett, A. H. 'Notes on the Distribution of the useful Minerals in Sarawak', *J. R. Asiat. Soc. Straits Branch*, I, 1878.

Fisher, J. C. B. 'Sarawak Postal History', *Sarawak Mus. J.* VIII, 10 (new series), 1957.

Foggo, G. *Adventures of Sir James Brooke, K.C.B., Rajah of Sarawak*, London, 1853.

Forrest, T. *Account of North Borneo*, London, 1776.

Foster, W. *England's Quest of Eastern Trade*, London, 1933.

Freeman, J. D. *Iban Agriculture*, London, 1955.

—— *Report on the Iban of Sarawak*, Kuching, 1955.

Geddes, W. R. *Nine Dayak Nights*, Melbourne/Oxford, 1957.

—— *The Land Dayaks of Sarawak*, London, 1954.

Gibson-Hill, C. A. 'John Clunies Ross and Alexander Hare, Merchant', *J. R. Asiat. Soc. Malay Branch*, XXV, 4 and 5, 1952.

Gladstone, W. E. 'Piracy in Borneo and the Operations of July, 1849', *Contemporary Rev.* 1877.

Gomes, E. H. *Seventeen Years among the Sea Dyaks of Borneo*, London, 1911.

Green, E. *Borneo, the Land of River and Palm*, Westminster, 1912.

Grey, Earl, *The Colonial Policy of Lord John Russell's Administration*, 2 vols., London, 1853.

Groenveldt, W. P. *Essays relating to Indo-China*, 2nd series, 2 vols., London, 1887.

—— *Notes on the Malay Archipelago and Malacca compiled from Chinese Sources*, Batavia/The Hague, 1876.

Gueritz, E. P. 'British Borneo', *Proc. Royal Colonial Institute*, XXIX, 1897–8.

Haddon, A. C. *Head-hunters, Black, White and Brown*, London, 1901.

Hahn, E. *James Brooke of Sarawak*, London, 1953.

Hall, J. Maxwell, *Labuan Story*, Jesselton, 1958.

—— *Makan Siap: Table tales of North Borneo*, Singapore, 1950.

Hansford, G. E. and Noble, L. A. *Sarawak and her Stamps*, London, 1935.

Harlow, V. T. 'Early British Pioneers in Borneo', *Sarawak Mus. J.* VI, 6 (new series), 1955.

—— *The Founding of the Second British Empire*, vol. I, London, 1952.

Harrisson, T. *Borneo Jungle*, London, 1938.

—— '"Export Wares" found in West Borneo', *Oriental Art*, V, 2 (new series), 1959.

—— 'Indian Pioneers in Borneo: *c.* 500 A.D. on,' *Sarawak Mus. J.* VI, 6 (new series), 1955.

—— 'Robert Burns: the First Ethnologist and Explorer of Interior Sarawak', *Sarawak Mus. J.* V, 3 (new series), 1951.

Harrisson, T. 'The Caves of Niah: A History of Prehistory', *Sarawak Mus. J.* VIII, 12 (new series), 1958.

—— 'The Chinese in Borneo, 1942–5', *International Affairs*, July 1950.

—— 'The First British Pioneer-Author in Borneo', *Sarawak Mus. J.* VI, 6, 1955.

—— 'The Great Cave of Niah', *Man*, LVII, 1957.

—— 'The Kelabits and Muruts', *Sarawak Gaz.* no. 1208 (31 October 1958).

—— *World Within*, London, 1959.

Helms, L. V. *Pioneering in the Far East*, London, 1882.

Hornaday, W. T. *Two Years in the Jungle*, London, 1885.

Hose, C. *Fifty Years of Romance and Research*, London, 1928.

—— *Natural Man: A Record from Borneo*, London, 1926.

—— *The Field-Book of a jungle Wallah*, London, 1929.

Hughes-Hallett, H. R. 'A Sketch of the History of Brunei', *J. R. Asiat. Soc. Malay Branch*, XVIII, 2, 1940.

Hume, J. *A Letter to the Right Honourable the Earl of Malmesbury, relative to the Proceedings of Sir James Brooke, K.C.B., etc., in Borneo*, London, 1853.

Hunt, J. 'Sketch of Borneo, or Pulo Kalamantan', *Malayan Miscellanies*, I, 8, Bencoolen, 1820, reprinted in Keppel, *Expedition to Borneo* (see below).

Ireland, A. *The Far Eastern Tropics*, London, 1905.

Irwin, G. *Nineteenth-century Borneo: A Study in Diplomatic Rivalry*, The Hague, 1955.

Jacob, G. L. *The Raja of Sarawak*, 2 vols., London, 1876.

Ju-K'ang T'ien, *The Chinese of Sarawak*, London School of Economics Monographs on Social Anthropology, no. 12, London, 1953 (with an unpublished appendix on the early history of the Chinese in Sarawak).

Keith, A. *Three Came Home*, London, 1948.

Keppel, H. *A Sailor's Life under Four Sovereigns*, 3 vols., London, 1899.

—— *A Visit to the Indian Archipelago in H.M. Ship Maeander, with Portions of the Private Journal of Sir James Brooke, K.C.B.*, 2 vols., London, 1853.

—— *The Expedition to Borneo of H.M.S. Dido for the Suppression of Piracy: with Extracts from the Journal of James Brooke, Esq.*, 2 vols., London, 1846.

Lawrence, A. E. 'Stories of the First Brunei conquests on the Sarawak Coast', *Sarawak Mus. J.* I, 1 (new series), 1911.

Lindsay, H. H. *The Eastern Archipelago Company and Sir James Brooke*, London, n.d. (1854?).

Ling Roth, H. *The Natives of Sarawak and British North Borneo*, 2 vols., London, 1896.

Lobscheid, W. *The Religion of the Dyaks*, Hong Kong, 1866.

Logan, J. R. *Journal of the Indian Archipelago*, 2 vols., Singapore, 1848.

Longhurst, H. C. *The Borneo Story*, London, 1957.

Low, H. *Sarawak*, London, 1848.

—— 'Sĕlĕsilah (Book of the Descent) of the Rajas of Brunei', *J. R. Asiat. Soc. Straits Branch*, V, 1880.

MacDonald, M. *Borneo People*, London, 1956.

McDougall, Mrs (H.). *Letters from Sarawak, addressed to a Child*, London, 1854.

—— *Sketches of our Life at Sarawak*, London, n.d. (1882?).

Mackenzie, C. *Realms of Silver*, London, 1953.

Magellan, *The First Voyage round the World, by Magellan*, ed. Lord Stanley of Alderley, Hakluyt Society, London, 1874 (including accounts by Anonymous Portuguese, Pigafetta, Maximilian the Treasurer and Francisco Alvo).

Marryat, F. S. *Borneo and the Indian Archipelago*, London, 1848.

Maxwell W. G. and Gibson, W. S. *Treaties and Engagements affecting the Malay States and Borneo*, London, 1924.

Mjöberg, E. *Durch die Insel der Kopfjäger: Abenteuer im Innern von Borneo*, Brockhaus/Leipzig, 1929.

Moorhead, F. J. *History of Malaya*, London, 1957.

Morrison, H. *Sarawak*, London, 1957.

Moulton, J. C. 'A Hindu Image from Sarawak', *J. R. Asiat. Soc. Malay Branch*, LXXXV, 1922.

'Mr Brooke and Borneo', *Colonial Church Chronicle and Missionary Journal*, November 1847.

Mundy, R. *Narrative of Events in Borneo and Celebes, down to the Occupation of Labuan: from the Journals of James Brooke, Esq., Rajah of Sarāwak, and Governor of Labuan*, 2 vols., London, 1848.

Nicholl, R. 'Quis Curabit Ipsos Curatores?', *Sarawak Mus. J.* VIII, 10 (new series), 1957.

Noakes, J. L. *A Report on the 1947 Population Census*, Kuching/London, 1950.

Noble, J. *Notes sur Bornéo*, Coulommières, 1921.

North, M. *Recollections of a Happy Life*, London, 1892.

Outlines of Sarawak History under the Brooke Rajahs, 1839–1946, compiled by A. B. Ward and D. C. White, Kuching, n.d.

Outram, R. 'Sarawak Chinese', *Sarawak Gaʒ.* no. 1213 (31 March 1959).

Parkinson, C. N. *Trade in the Eastern Seas (1793–1813)*, Cambridge, 1937.

Percival, A. E. *The War in Malaya*, London, 1949.

Pfeiffer, I. *A Lady's Second Journey round the World*, London, 1855.

Pires, *The Suma Oriental of Tomé Pires*, ed. A. Cortesão, Hakluyt Society, London, 1944.

Posewitz, T. *Borneo*, Berlin, 1889.

Raffles, Lady, *Memoir of the Life and Public Services of Sir Thomas Stamford Raffles, F.R.S.*, London, 1830.

Rajah Brooke and Baroness Burdett-Coutts, Letters, ed. O. Rutter, London, 1935.

Rajah Brooke and Borneo, London, 1850.

Rajahate of Sarawak, Brighton, 1875.

Richards, A. J. N. 'Sea Dayaks—Ibans', *Sarawak Gaʒ.* no. 1205 (31 July 1958).

Roff, W. J. 'Mr T. Wallage, Commanding H. S. Str. *Nemesis*', *Sarawak Mus. J.* VI, 4 (new series), 1954.

Ross, J. D. *Sixty Years: Life and Adventures in the Far East*, 2 vols., London, 1911.

Rutter, O. *British North Borneo*, London, 1922.

—— *The Pirate Wind*, London, 1930.

—— *Triumphant Pilgrimage*, London, 1937.

St John, S. *The Malay Archipelago: its History and Present*, London, 1853.

St John, S. *Life in the Forests of the Far East*, 2 vols., London 1863.
—— *Life of Sir James Brooke, Rajah of Sarawak*, Edinburgh, 1879.
—— *Rajah Brooke: An Englishman as Ruler of an Eastern State*, London, 1899.
Sandin, B. 'Iban Movements: From the Deluge', and 'The Sea Dayak Migration to Niah River', *Sarawak Mus. J.* VIII, 10 (new series), 1957.
Sarawak, Dayang Muda of (G. Brooke), *Relations and Complications*, London, 1929.
The Sarawak Gazette, 1870–1941, 1946–
Sarawak, Ranee Margaret of (M. Brooke), *Good Morning and Good Night*, London, 1934.
—— *My Life in Sarawak*, London, 1913.
Sarawak, Ranee Sylvia of (S. Brooke), *Sylvia of Sarawak: An Autobiography*, London, 1936.
—— *The Three White Rajahs*, London, 1939.
'Scrutator', *Borneo Revelations*, Singapore, n.d.
Sharp, A. F. *The Wings of the Morning*, London, 1954.
Shelford, R. W. C. *A Naturalist in Borneo*, London, 1916.
Smythies, B. E. 'Dr A. W. Nieuwenhuis—"A Borneo Livingstone"', *Sarawak Mus. J.* VI, 6 (new series).
Southwell, C. H. 'The Up-river People—Kayans and Kenyahs', *Sarawak Gaz.* no. 1207 (30 September 1958).
Swettenham, F. *British Malaya*, London, 1906.
Templer J. C. (ed.), *The Private Letters of Sir James Brooke, K.C.B., Rajah of Sarawak*, 3 vols., London, 1853.
The Facts about Borneo, London, 1946.
Treacher, W. H. 'British Borneo: Sketches of Brunei, Sarawak, Labuan and North Borneo', *J. R. Asiat. Soc. Straits Branch*, XX and XXI, 1889–90.
—— 'The Genealogy of the Royal Family of Brunei', *J. R. Asiat. Soc. Straits Branch*, XV, 1885.
Tregonning, K. G. *Under Chartered Company Rule (North Borneo 1881–1946)*, Singapore, 1958.
Turner, G. C. 'Bishop McDougall and his wife Harriette: Some personal Records', *Borneo Chronicle*, Centenary number, May 1955.
Urquhart, I. A. N. 'Nomadic Punans and Pennans', *Sarawak Gaz.* no. 1209 (30 November 1958).
Varthema, Ludovico de, *see* Barthema.
Vella, W. F. *Siam under Rama III, 1824–1851*, Locust Valley, New York, 1957.
Wallace, A. R. *My Life*, 2 vols., London, 1905.
—— *The Malay Archipelago*, London, 1869.
Winstedt, R. D. 'History of Malaya', *J. R. Asiat. Soc. Malay Branch*, XIII, 1, 1935.
'W. N.' *Borneo: Remarks on a Recent 'Naval Execution'*, London, 1850.
Yusof Shibli, M. 'The Descent of some Kuching Malays', *Sarawak Mus. J.* V, 2 (new series), 1950.

GLOSSARY OF TERMS AND TITLES

Note on transliteration. There is no standard system for the transliteration of Malay names and titles. In particular the vowel-sounds are very variously reproduced. When dealing with place-names in the former Netherlands territories I have used the Dutch form. For other names I have used the form that appears to be most generally familiar.

Abang: courtesy title given to the male descendants of Datus (Malay). See below.

Awang: courtesy title given to the sons of Pangirans (Malay). See below.

Bandahara: 'treasurer' (Sanskrit). The Pangiran Bandahara of Brunei was officially the State Treasurer.

Bandar: 'port' or 'harbour' (Persian). The Datu Bandar was in origin the official in charge of the port. He became later one of the three chief local officials who administered Sarawak under the Sultan of Brunei. The title was not hereditary, but was reserved for a member of the former ruling family of Sarawak.

Batang: river (Malay).

Bongsu: youngest son (Malay). The title of Tuan Bongsu was given to a ruler's youngest son.

Bukit: hill (Malay).

Dang: abbreviated form of Dayang. See below.

Datin: wife of a Datu.

Datu: literally 'Grandfather' (Malay). In Sarawak the highest title except for Rajah. In Brunei the title next in rank below Pangiran.

Dayang: courtesy title given to the female descendants of Rajahs or Datus.

Di Gadong: meaning unknown. The Pangiran Di Gadong was one of the two highest officials in Brunei. According to Spencer St John he was the Minister of Finance.

Haji: title given to anyone who has performed the pilgrimage to Mecca (Arabic).

Imam: official in charge of a mosque (Arabic). The Datu Imam was the chief Muslim religious authority in Sarawak.

Kampong: Malay village.

Kongsi: self-governing Chinese colony engaged in mining or trade.

Laksamana: Admiral (Sanskrit).

Muda: young man. The Sultan Muda was the heir-apparent of Brunei. In Brunei the heir-presumptive was usually called the Rajah Muda; in Sarawak the Rajah Muda was the Rajah's heir-apparent.

Pamancha: meaning unknown. The Pangiran Pamancha was one of the two highest officials in Brunei. According to Spencer St John he was minister of the Interior.

Pangiran: title given to the princes of the Royal house of Brunei (Javanese).

Panglima: commander. Malay title sometimes given to Dyak chieftains.

Patinggi: high (Malay). The Datu Patinggi was the highest official in Sarawak.

Pengulu: headman (Malay). Title given to Dyak tribal chiefs.

Rajah: king (Sanskrit). Title formerly borne by rulers of Brunei and later given to princes closely related to the Sultan. When given to the ruler of Sarawak it suggested dependence on the Sultan.

Ranee: wife of Rajah.

Serah: Malay system by which subjects were forced to sell their produce to their lord.

Sultan: a supreme Muslim ruler. Title adopted by the rulers of Brunei to show overlordship over other rulers. The Sultan of Brunei's official title was *Iang di Pertuan*, 'he who rules' (Malay).

Tanjong: cape, headland (Malay).

Temanggong: commander-in-chief. The Pangiran Temanggong of Brunei was the official commander of the Brunei army. The Datu Temanggong was the third of the Sarawak high officials.

Tuan: Lord (Malay). Tuan Besar, 'High Lord', and Tuan Muda 'Young Lord' were titles given to princes of the Rajah's family.

INDEX

Note. The names Borneo and Sarawak, with the names of the chief races, Malay, Dyak and Chinese which occur continuously in the text, are not listed in the index.

1755778R0022

Printed in Great Britain
by Amazon.co.uk, Ltd.,
Marston Gate.